Published in Canada by Inanna Publications and Education Inc.
212 Founders College, York University
4700 Keele Street, Toronto, Ontario M3J 1P3
Telephone: (416) 736-5356 Fax (416) 736-5765
Email: cwscf@yorku.ca Web site: www.yorku.ca/cwscf

Published in the rest of the world by Zed Books Ltd., 7 Cynthia Street, London N1 9JF and Room 400, 175 Fifth Avenue, New York, NY 10010, USA in 2005.

www.zedbooks.co.uk

Distributed in the USA exclusively by Palgrave Macmillan, a division of St Martin's Press, LLC, 175 Fifth Avenue, New York, NY 10010.

A catalogue record for this book is available from the British Library.
US CIP data is available from the Library of Congress
ISBN 1 84277 350 X hb
ISBN 1 84277 351 8 pb

Printed and Bound in Canada.

Cover Design: Val Fullard

Library and Archives Canada Cataloguing in Publication:
Feminist politics, activism and vision : local and global challenges / edited by Luciana Ricciutelli, Angela Miles and Margaret H. McFadden.

(Women, power and justice ; 1) Includes index.
ISBN 0-96812 90-8-0

1. Women in politics. 2. Feminism—International cooperation.
I. Ricciutelli, Luciana, 1958- II. McFadden, Margaret H. III. Miles, Angela Rose IV. Series

HQ1236.F39 2004   305.42   C2004-905330-2

FEMINIST POLITICS, ACTIVISM AND VISION

LOCAL AND GLOBAL CHALLENGES

EDITED BY LUCIANA RICCIUTELLI, ANGELA MILES
AND MARGARET H. McFADDEN

A PROJECT OF THE FEMINIST JOURNALS NETWORK

INANNA PUBLICATIONS AND EDUCATION INC.
TORONTO, CANADA

ZED BOOKS LTD.
LONDON AND NEW YORK

CONTENTS

V. Conclusion

ACKNOWLEDGEMENTS

The editors would like to express our appreciation for the support of the tireless coordinator of the Feminist Journals Network, Marilyn Porter, and all the Network members: *The Ahfad Journal: Women and Change* (Sudan); *Alam-e-Niswan: Pakistan Journal of Women's Studies* (Pakistan); *Asian Journal of Women's Studies* (Korea); *Atlantis: A Women's Studies Journal* (Canada); *Australian Feminist Studies* (Australia); *Babiker Badri Scientific Association for Women's Studies* (Sudan); *Canadian Woman Studies/les cahiers de la femme* (Canada); *European Journal of Women's Studies* (Belgium); *Feminist Studies* (US); *Gender, Technology and Development* (India); *International Feminist Journal of Politics* (UK); *Journal of Women's Studies* (Vietnam); *Jurnal Perempuan* (Indonesia); *Kvinneforskning: Norwegian Journal for Women's Research* (Norway); *Lola* (Uruguay); *Manushi: A Journal About Women and Society* (India); *National Women's Studies Association Journal* (US); *Nordic Journal of Women's Studies* (*NORA*) (Denmark); *Rainbo* (UK); *Recherches Féministes* (Canada); *Review of Women's Studies* (Philippines); *Revista Estudos Feministas* (Brazil); *Travesias: Teuras del Delate Feminista* (Argentina); *Women: A Cultural Review* (UK); *Women's World* (Uganda). A special thank you to Lise Isaksen (*Kvinneforskning: Norwegian Journal for Women's Research*), Anna Nsubuga (*Rainbo*), Jindy Pettman (*International Feminist Journal of Politics*), Jae Kyung Lee (*Asian Journal of Women's Studies*), Bente Meyer (*NORA*) and Ahmed Abdel Magied (*The Ahfad Journal: Women and Change*) who made very helpful comments on the early outlines of this book.

While we have benefited enormously from the invaluable input of many, and have been inspired by the spirit of the Network, the editors cannot claim the Network's endorsement for the book's main argument and must accept responsibility for any limitations.

PREFACE

PEGGY ANTROBUS

The stories of local struggles recounted in this book provide the kind of inspiration needed at a time when so many of our gains are jeopardized by the spread of neo-liberal globalization and religious fundamentalisms; solidarity among women challenged by resurgent racism; and our very lives endangered by militaristic responses to the 'war on terrorism' and the AIDS pandemic. And yet at this time, when local concerns—from livelihoods to water, from health care to citizenship—are so strongly influenced by global trends, one of the greatest challenges to women's movements is clarifying the links between the local and the global. At the same time, the structure of the book and many of the contributors show that much feminist organizing today is grounded in awareness of these local/global links.

This is not as simple as it may seem. Having worked at all these levels, I have learned that there are important differences in what can be done and achieved at various levels, and that some activists attempting to link local to global (and vice versa) use inappropriate strategies, or have unrealistic expectations of outcomes from their efforts. Moreover, these different spaces are often placed in contradiction to each other, and yet effective strategy requires them to be complementary. The strength of this volume is its inclusion of articles addressing each and all these levels of practice, many of which speak eloquently to the importance and fragility of local/global connections.

We all need to pay more attention to the differences between levels in terms of cultural sensitivities, resources, the kinds of action taken and the strategies pursued. It is the same with 'insider-outsider' strategies: both spaces are important for effective action. What is important is that they are seen as complementary rather than contradictory.

The resolution of these problems and choices of effective organizing at the different levels depends on leadership. Strategic choices do not happen in a vacuum. Leadership is key! Where does the leadership exhibited in these stories come from? From where does their power come? What values do they reflect? Not knowing many of the women, one can only speculate.

I recall a workshop with a group of grassroots women in the Caribbean. We were talking of sources of empowerment. Two themes stood out from the many discussed: spirituality and sexuality. But the women made it clear that they were not speaking of religion ("religion is disempowering for a lot of women") or sexual activity ("that can be oppression too!"). One of the facilitators, a strong feminist from a background of leftist struggles and a woman greatly admired for her leadership in this region, turned to me and said: 'Do you realize that these women are talking about things that never get discussed in this field of "women and development"'?

It was a moment of truth: if the most important sources of power never get discussed, how relevant is all this talk of empowerment? In a recent issue of the online journal, *Feminist Africa*, Patricia McFadden (2003) addresses the issue of sexuality, echoing Audre Lorde's (1979) reference to the erotic as power; and, in another volume published by Zed Books Ltd., Alda Facio (2004) (one of the contributors to this book), speaks of 'feminist political spirituality as a strategy for action'.

Is it possible that the silence surrounding these parts of us is due to the fact that they are private, intimate, so easily misunderstood that we feel we have to protect ourselves? If so, this is exactly why it is essential that we reclaim and re-affirm the early feminist recognition that they are important parts of who we are as human beings, part of the power and passion that makes our work possible—and make space for talking about them in our movement-building.

Then there are the values of those in leadership positions. What are these? Do we have leaders who are truly committed to values that reinforce equity, democracy, solidarity with women, cooperation, compassion and respect for women, children and the elderly; truly committed to respecting and celebrating diversity and difference; leaders with humility, tolerance and openness to learning from others, and from their own mistakes, who accept the need for multiple strategies? Do feminist leaders manifest this by ensuring that everyone has a voice, especially—for those among us who are privileged—women from groups and communities marginalized by class, race and ethnicity, religion, age and different physical and mental abilities? Indeed, recognizing the incredible leadership emerging from these groups and making space for them?

That much misrepresented community named 'Third World women' had to insist on recognition from their sisters from the 'North'; but in this community too there are differences of race/ethnicity, class, education, religion, location, age and physical ability that create categories of exclusion.

Do our feminist leaders live their feminism by demonstrating their con-sciousness of all the sources that oppress women, their commitment to change things in solidarity with women? Not all feminists are activists; not all feminists identify with women from different classes, races and cultures.

I believe that much more needs to be done to incorporate an understanding of differences, especially those of race/ethnicity, class and culture into our analyses of the political economy, religious fundamentalism, violence, militarism and environmental degradation. The articles in this volume are exemplary in meeting this challenge as they affirm the possibilities of solidarity and of liberating change for all.

In fact, I think that no progress can be made toward a more peaceful and humane world without attention to our differences *and* our connections. Together, these are the strength of our movement.

Peggy Antrobus is from the Caribbean. In 1975, she established the Jamaican Women's Bureau and was a founding member of Development Alternatives with Women for a New Era (DAWN) in 1985. She participated in all the conferences of the United Nations Decade for Women and in the global conferences of the 1990s. Her book, The Global Women's Movement, *was published by Zed Books in the Fall of 2004.*

References

Lorde, A. (1979) 'The uses of the erotic: the erotic as power', in A. Lorde, *Sister Outsider: Essays and Speeches*, Trumansberg, NY: Crossing Press.

Facio, A. (2004) Feminist political spirituality as a strategy for action', in J. Kerr, E. Sprenger and A. Symington (eds.), *The Future of Women's Rights: Global Visions and Strategies*, London: Zed Press.

McFadden, P. (2003) 'Sexual Pleasure as Feminist Choice'", *Feminist Africa*, 2. Online: http://www.feministafrica.org/2level.html.

INTRODUCTION

ANGELA MILES

On the morning of September 11, 2001, a group of feminist Journal editors and activists from around the world were in Halifax, Nova Scotia talking about the ways in which we could work together to build and share feminist knowledge internationally. It was the last day of a week-long workshop. We had already established the Feminist Journals Network with 25 journals from 17 countries on four continents. We were excited by the idea of publishing a series of edited collections, including 'ovular' articles from member journals, to make important feminist writing more widely available. We had just begun to plan this first volume when one of our number burst into the room to tell us that the twin towers of the World Trade Centre in New York had been 'bombed'.

The silence was deafening. About twenty of us were stranded in Halifax for days where we comforted each other as we worried about our families and took in the enormity of what had happened. We grieved immediately for those who had died. When we learned that the perpetrators were not crazed American militiamen but 'Muslim extremists' we feared for what the future would bring, especially to regions of the world already subject to overwhelming US power and already all too familiar with US 'retaliation' and casual disregard for foreign lives; and to civil liberties everywhere.

The changed circumstances at once vividly highlighted the urgency of the work our Network was planning to do. During subsequent days of enforced and anxious idleness we came to understand even more fully than we had, the huge potential of the international links we were forging for feminist knowledge creation. In that moment of crisis we feminists from Argentina, Australia, Belgium, Canada, Denmark, India, Indonesia, Norway, Pakistan, Philippines, South Korea, Sudan, Uganda, the UK, Uruguay and the USA, brought an unparalleled richness of experience, history, knowledge and perspective to our sharing of personal and political angers, fears, suspicions, anxieties and expectations. Without aiming to, and without benefit of the additional revelations that time would bring, each of us developed a deeper feminist understanding of the roots and consequences of this event than any of us could have developed alone. We marveled at the broadening of our individual consciousnesses and at the rich analysis we developed together over those few days. This experience affirmed the central importance of feminist principles and feminist movement in our theorizing. For we had shared a classic feminist personal and political process informed by experiential and academic knowledge, fueled by activist values and visions. We were profoundly confirmed in our commitment to bridge these and other divides in our organizing as journals and in our publishing, as we have done in this, our first edited collection.

The diverse articles collected here raise crucial historical, organizational, ethical, conceptual, strategic and practical issues facing feminists today. How can the political power and spirit of feminism be sustained as women gain some institutional access and 'gender' gains the attention of governments and NGOs? What value basis can best ground feminist visions and feminist movement? What are the powers arrayed against feminist change? What can and should be the relationship of local feminisms to global feminisms? of theory to practice? of feminists to women's movement? to each other? to governments? to the academy? to NGOs? to United Nations processes and agencies? to the planet? All these questions (and more) are asked and answers are offered here in the interest of understanding how decades of impressive grassroots victories at the local level and creative new forms of communication and organizing at the global level can best be parlayed into sufficient power to successfully resist economic and religious fundamentalisms and transform the world.

These questions are raised by authors with direct experience of the issues in practice and a shared understanding that autonomous women's movement is the most significant source of feminist theory, power and vision. The authors gathered here know that it is not sufficient to simply name the deep differences of power and immediate interests among women. These differences must be resisted. However, when possible, differences must be used to enrich our collective strategies and shared politics. We must find ways to use differences which 'divide and conquer ... [to instead] define and empower' (Lorde 1984: 112).

The personal accounts, political speeches, creative writing, scholarly and policy-oriented analyses in this collection reveal diverse but clearly connected issues being addressed at local, national, regional and global levels in generative ways which both honour local specificities and enrich global movement. Each author addresses the specifics of a particular context and struggle in ways that contribute significantly to our general understanding of the challenges and opportunities facing feminists in our common struggle. A portrait emerges of a vibrant multi-centered transnational movement struggling not just for women's equality in existing structures but to redefine wealth, work, peace, democracy, leadership, sexuality, family, human rights, development, community and citizenship for a future world that welcomes diversity and honours and supports all life.

I: Neo-Liberal Context

Articles by Vandana Shiva and Arlie Hochschild in the opening section of this volume present formative feminist analyses of the economic context of current global and local activism. Shiva's analysis of rural subsistence, 'Women: The Custodians,' and Hochschild's of urban care-giving labour, 'Love and Gold', address different but connected processes of global exploitation whose effects women and feminists are resisting and attempting to shape in their families, communities, national government policies and in international agreements. While their approaches are not identical, both authors affirm the non-market value of life against neo-liberal processes of commodification (of women, seeds, and care/love) which impact particularly harshly on women and on the economic South, and in which women's work is central and remains invisible. It is clear from these articles that feminism must be about far more than seeking equal participation for women and that only feminisms committed to transforming patriarchal, capitalist and colonial relations can sustain the global cross-class and cross-race alliances necessary for radical change.

II: Feminist Organizing/National, Regional and Global Frames

In this section, academics and activists address major strategic questions facing feminists today as we struggle to find ways to build on earlier success while resisting increasingly aggressive and sophisticated opposition locally and globally.

Jan Jindy Pettman, in her article, 'Global Politics and Transnational Feminisms,' sets the stage with her broad analysis of the new opportunities and constraints facing transnational feminist politics. She documents a 'vital yet beseiged' movement with decades of remarkably successful organizing experience confronting a new period of neo-liberal globalization, international mobilization of reactionary, often religious-based politics which are deeply anti-woman, intensified by the post 9/11 'war on terror' and newly militarized global politics which prioritizes 'border protection and hard masculinity'.

In her article, 'Feminist Networks, People's Movements and Alliances: Learning from the Ground,' Devaki Jain draws on decades of influential personal involvement in transnational feminist dialogue, theorizing and organizing in her analysis of this crucial moment. She addresses head-on the painful truth that 'none of the considerable successes of women's [regional and global] networks have reduced the misery or redressed the exclusions and oppression endured by women.' She warns that feminists must find a way to 'move out of the conventional grip of the arrival hall' where merely 'being the subject of governments' consideration is an achievement and ... lobbying for a conference document becomes the consuming energy.' In the face of devastating current conditions, she argues for a political mobilization of women grounded in grassroots women's struggles, united even if temporarily by their sex and allied with newly powerful people's movements around specific strategically selected issues.

Charlotte Bunch in 'Feminism, Peace, Human Rights and Human Security,' also writing from extensive personal involvement, provides an authoritative description of just such global feminist political debate and mobilization around crucial issues. While honouring women's differences and the varying contexts of their local struggles, feminists share a common goal of universal peace that goes far deeper than the absence of war; and they usefully generalize about women's vulnerability to violence and war and the particular ways women contribute to peace-building. So feminist peace activists who wish to work toward 'a positive peace with human rights and human security at its core' must grapple continuously with the tensions between the local and the global and the universality and specificity of their work and vision.

Bisi Adeleye-Fayemi, in 'Creating and Sustaining Feminist Space in Africa: Local and Global Challenges in the Twenty-First Century,' describes the current economic and political conditions facing all African women and describes the many forms their practice takes. However, drawing on decades of activist leadership she focuses mainly on the specific principles, achievements and challenges of her own radical strand of feminism in Africa. She uses the term 'African feminist' to refer to those who are African and feminist and to identify real issues linking feminist identities to African realities. But she is leery of the way the term can be used as a qualifier and can mean buying into a watered down agenda. For she 'believe(s) in a definition of feminism which is dynamic enough to articulate the interconnectedness and specificities of women's experiences, identities and struggles all over the world and which does not have to be qualified'.

Writing in the same radical activist spirit, Nighat Said Khan in 'Up Against the State: The Women's Movement in Pakistan and its Implications for the Global Women's Movement,' addresses the main political challenges facing this strand of feminism. She notes the dangers of 'NGOization' and 'genderization' and the way attempts to redefine the movement by including development activities and projects have 'depleted much of ... [its] dynamism, energy and flexibility.' Reflecting on her own many years of experience in Pakistan and South Asia she poses a question of concern to feminists globally when she asks: 'How do we get out of this stagnation and out of the apathy that funding and postmodernism or the non-existence of ideology inculcates, or where do we go from here?'

Sonia Alvarez's article, 'Advocating Feminism: The Latin American NGO "Boom"', usefully analyzes in some detail the varied and contested Latin

American experiences of the 'NGOization' that is recognized as a political concern by many authors in this volume: 'The 1990s witnessed a veritable "boom" in NGOs specializing in gender policy assessment, project execution, and social services delivery, propelling them into newfound public prominence while increasingly pushing many away from earlier, more movement-oriented activities.' Alvarez advocates collective strategies that would enable NGOs to 'serve as more genuine intermediaries for larger civil society constituencies' and calls urgently 'for more regularized public spaces in which feminists ... demand accountability from NGOs regarding their state-contracted and donor-funded projects, and perhaps even (re)invent more transgressive public interventions that would move beyond the policy realm and thereby help revitalize the movement face of NGOs'.

In her article 'Organizing for Domestic Worker Rights in Singapore: The Limits of Transnationalism' Lenore Lyons shows that despite the creative efforts of women in Singapore and the fact that feminists from many countries are cooperating around the feminization of migrant labour, the Singapore national government has been able to limit the empowering potential of global feminist alliances in that country. She cautions that 'this embeddedness of the national within transnationalism is often overlooked in romanticized accounts of global civil society' and concludes 'we must stop to remind ourselves that transnationalism does not transcend difference but is embedded within it. For transnational activism to be successful, feminists must consciously delineate the boundaries of their engagement, paying close attention to the different situations "on the ground" in those places where they seek to forge alliances'.

III: Women's Local Struggles and Feminist Politics

This section explores the implicit and explicit feminist and global meanings of women's radical grassroots activism in communities around the world. These very different articles illuminate: 1) the amazing collective power of women united in autonomous women-defined struggles for a world which values life and honours and supports women and their work in sustaining it, 2) the need for effective global feminist networks to remain grounded in women's local power, often drawn from traditional sources, and 3) the importance of transregional and transnational feminist connections to women struggling locally, not least in resisting male 'allies' persistent attempts to control and limit their feminist aims and visions.

Terisa Turner and Leigh Brownhill's 'The Curse of Nakedness: Nigerian Women in the Oil War' analyses peasant women's militant and effective resistance to oil companies' ecological, economic and social destruction in the Niger Delta. They argue that links forged in these struggles, between production and consumption, the waged and unwaged, and the local and global, are necessary and vital elements of a possible alternative future. If the women can avoid containment within largely male-defined union struggles limited to the terms of labour commodification, their struggles hold the promise of 'global gendered class alliances ... [for] the defence and re-invention of the commons and the subsistence political economy, North and South'.

Annelise Orleck's 'We Are That Mythical Thing Called The Public: Militant Housewives in the US During The Great Depression' presents women's activism in defence of sustenance in a very different time and place. Working class urban housewives' nationwide multi-ethnic rebellion in the US in the 1930s 'was not simply a reaction to the economic crisis gripping the nation. It was a conscious attempt on the part of many housewives to change the system that they blamed for the Depression.' Housewives' militant direct action and sustained lobbying forced the government to play a regulatory role in food and housing costs, investigate profiteering on staple goods and the structure of the meat industry, pass rent-controls, and increase the provision of schools and parks and federally funded public housing.

Rekha Pande's article 'Solidarity, Patriarchy and Empowerment: Women's Struggles Against Arrack in India' tells the story of rural Indian women's successful mobilization against the widespread sale of arrack (a locally produced spirit) in communities in Andhra Pradesh. The movement began in 1991 when women in a literacy class were inspired to take direct action to close down the arrack shop in their village. Women in villages across the state followed their radical example and rapidly built a state-wide movement that successfully took on the powerful and violent liquor contractors, a state government financially dependent on revenue from the trade, local vendors, brutal husbands and opportunistic political parties to temporarily achieve a prohibition of the sale of arrack. Although this prohibition has not lasted, there have been significant long-term gains for women: 'Women became aware of their strengths and their ability to effect change in their villages and in society as a whole.... Their struggles against arrack brought the issue of violence against women to the public platform'.

In 'Coming to Terms with the Past in Bangladesh: Naming Women's Truths' Bina D'Costa reports the difficulties feminists have faced in bringing women's experiences centrally into Bangladesh's official historical narrative of the 1971 war for independence from Pakistan. Some 200,000 Bengali women were raped by soldiers during this war. D'Costa calls for strong South Asian regional support, 'especially from Indian and Pakistani women's groups with expertise in charting women's experiences of partition ... to design, and gain support for a fact-finding project to document and produce a report comprising the narratives of women's experiences in 1971. This project could be an important step on the path of reconstructing history and addressing multiple truths in order to clear the way for justice'.

Line Nyhagen Predelli's article 'Missionary Women and Feminism in Norway, 1906-1910' raises the crucial relationship between women's activism and feminism in another light. In 1908 missionary women sought membership for their organizations in the Norwegian branch of the feminist International Council of Women (ICW). Unlike the earlier cases in this Section, the priorities of their associations were not defined autonomously by the women members. Norwegian National Council of Women members were torn between the desire to connect with and influence the largest and most diverse mobilization of Norwegian women of the time and the fear that their inclusion would jeopardize ICW's feminist principles. In their initial response to the eventually successful application, the NNCW leadership declared that the ICW 'does not adhere to any faith and rests on a pillar of tolerance. At the international meetings [of the ICW] representatives of different religious societies—both Jewish and heathen [sic]—have been present—and at this very moment one is seeking to establish national councils among Chinese, Japanese and Turkish women'.

IV: Feminist Challenges in Practice and Vision

From very different locations and varied perspectives the authors of the articles in this section grapple with central political and strategic questions related to the sources of and challenges to feminism's transformative power.

Sally Roesch Wagner in 'The Indigenous Roots of United States Feminism' asks 'How did the early radical suffragists come to their vision, a vision not of band-aid reform but of a reconstituted world completely transformed'? She finds her answer in the early suffragists' knowledge of the respect and authority women enjoyed among the Haudenosaunee, the six nations of the Iroquois Confederacy where women controlled their own personal property, wife battering was not known, any man whose wife wished it must withdraw from her home to his own clan, agriculture was publicly honoured, decisions were made by consensus and required the approval of both men and women, women selected (and demoted) the male rulers and decided whether a nation should go to war. Indian women's violence-free egalitarian life inspired suffrage theorists to think 'far beyond equal rights for women [to] a different paradigm, an egalitarian one of human harmony' and gave them a 'sure knowledge that they too could create a social structure of equality'.

In 'Women Human Rights Activists as Political Theorists' Brooke Ackerly finds cutting-edge theory building happening in the exchanges among activists participating in two online international working groups—End-of-Violence and CEDAW-in-Action—sponsored by UNIFEM between October 1998 and January 2000. Contrary to the unappetizing choice between homogenizing universalism or immobilizing relativism that continues to define much academic theoretical debate around human rights, she argues that in their practice feminists are developing a unique model of human rights theory. This theory makes it possible to reinforce norms of international customary human rights law and critically assess claims of legitimate cultural deviance from those norms without disrespecting differences across *and* within cultures: 'In *practice* we must treat one another as human beings. In *practice* we must adjudicate between competing claims without denying either claim. In *practice* we can attribute responsibility even where formal institutions and organizational charts cannot. In *practice* we reconcile universal human rights with cultural difference without abandoning the inviolability of some rights and the problematic nature of some social practices. In *theory* we can do likewise (imperfectly)'.

Sylvia Tamale in 'Alternative Leadership in Africa: Some Critical Feminist Reflections,' also draws on new thinking emerging in feminist practice in conceptualizing the alternative forms of leadership she argues are needed in Africa today: 'Not only are we looking to transformational styles of leadership, but leadership that also has economic, political and social transformation as its goal'. This leadership is a process and not a tenured position and serves both women and men, poor and rich, and the powerless and powerful. It is inclusive, participatory, and horizontal and is centrally informed by feminist values such as participation and collaboration, diversity and pluralism, inclusiveness and consensus-oriented policy making.

R. Amy Elman's detailed study of the limits of citizenship for women and other marginalized groups in the European Union, in 'Testing the Limits of European Citizenship: Ethnic Hatred and Male Violence', provides eloquent testimony that the transformative change Tamale calls for is needed every-where. Feminism's relationship to citizenship must be ambivalent, for it entails both privilege and exclusion, affording benefits to those who possess it and legitimizing discrimination (and worse) against those without it. Focusing on women residing on the periphery—third country nationals and battered wives—Elman shows that racism, poverty and male violence pose crucial obstacles to women's participation in and benefit from the project of EU integration: 'Considering women's pervasive ethnic, economic and physically brutal subordination, it is extraordinary that the EU is still considered a peaceful and affluent region'. However, women's subordination is not considrered to be an unacceptable failing of democracy.

Writing just before the Asian financial crash in 1997, Cho Haejoang, in 'Feminist Intervention in the Rise of "Asian" Discourse', shows that the promise of economic growth and prosperity also poses problems for feminist mobilizing and solidarity. She is critical of the term 'Asian feminism' as implying a non-existent homogeneity of the region and failing to confront the patriarchal agendas of anti-western nationalists who want to overcome their dependence on the western world, and transnational capitalists who think that endorsing Asian solidarity will help open up new markets. However, she welcomes 'Asian feminist alliances': 'We will start a comprehensive discussion beyond the dimensions of narrow rationalism and individualism presumed by western modernity ... [and] open up a new ... politics of ordinary life.....' She advocates local feminisms cognizant of the differences between the experiences of men and women and between classes and generations, focused on developing sisterhood and cultural alternatives to pervasive, immobilizing "colonial postmodern" individualism, alienation and greed'.

In 'Back to Womanhood: Feminism in Globalized Israel' Erella Shadmi argues from her own decades of activist experience that the loss of the women-identification that grounded Women in Black and the Lesbian Feminist Community in an earlier period has weakened the Israeli women's movement. She sees signs that in facing the challenges of working across differences of class, race and sexualities to resist the brutality of neo-liberal globalization, women in Israel are beginning to rediscover the women's identitification necessary to sustain this solidarity. She argues that 'a woman-centered grounding' and 'a return to womanhood' is needed to put the Israeli feminist movement in the forefront of anti-globalization and peace-directed politics.

V: Conclusion

Alda Facio's whimsical yet powerful concluding article, 'The Empire Strikes Back But Finds Feminism Invincible,' is an account of the ways feminists met their political challenges in the centuries of struggle before they finally triumphed, as recounted by a history professor hundreds of years after the feminist revolution. Facio highlights the importance of theoretical clarity and basic feminist principles of solidarity in the face of sophisticated mechanisms dividing women from each other and their potential allies and mystifying post-9/11 militarized, colonial, patriarchal and capitalist exploitation. She shows us that feminist change in every period has been won by women who imagined the impossible, and that now, more than ever, the only practical strategies are visionary ones: 'Feminists needed to ... remember what they had discovered many times, that feminism was not about getting for women what men already had ... or making proposals that could fit neatly into the patriarchal mode..... [It] was about women valuing and seeking the power that lies in friendship and solidarity in an environment that encouraged ... distrust or even hate.... [W]omen belonged to all walks of life, sectors of society, all races, classes, ages, abilities, sexualities, etc. and if they could unite, they would be invincible.... To create this new way of being in reality, feminists had to convince all those opposing the Empire's strategy of globalization, that the caring and nurturing of human beings had to be at the center of all utopias.... So it came to pass that feminists began to lose their fear of being labelled essentialists or inefficient idealists. They allowed themselves once more to be rebels, transgressors and subversives. More importantly, they became dreamers and builders of other realities'.

Facio's article nicely encapsulates many of the themes of this volume. The spirit of the articles collected here recalls us to 'women' as the necessary subjects of feminism. The authors present radical strategic political and cultural understandings of feminisms which are: 1) committed to the central project of women's solidarity enriched by deepening understandings of the challenges and rewards of working with and through our differences; 2) opposed to colonial, class and race as well as patriarchal oppression; 3) sustaining and sustained by women's militant and creative commitment to survival and resistance in communities around the world; 4) increasingly aware of both the possibilities and limits of engagement with the state, the United Nations and multi-lateral agencies; and 5) conscious of the dangerous inadequacy of looking to economic growth and western 'modernization' to liberate women. The rigorous critical analyses and practical strategies for change these authors present are informed by hard-headed realism and strategic 'utopianism'. These are necessary partners enabling feminisms capable of transforming the world.

References

Lorde, A. (1984) *Sister Outsider: Essays and Speeches by Audre Lorde*, Trumansberg, N.Y: Crossing Press

I.
NEO-LIBERAL CONTEXT

WOMEN

THE CUSTODIANS

VANDANA SHIVA

Women are the leading experts in, and custodians of, biodiversity. They have been society's seed keepers, food processors and healers. And biodiversity itself has been venerated in female form. The indigenous communities of the Andes see corn, potato, coca and quinoa as goddesses. The ancient Rig Veda hymn worships healing plants as mothers.

Mothers, you have a hundred forms
and a thousand revelations.
You who have a hundred ways of working,
make this man whole for me.
Be joyful, you plants that bear flowers
and you that bear fruit.
Like mares that win the race together,
the growing plants will carry us to the other side.
You mothers called plants, I say
to you who are goddesses,
let me win a horse, a cow, a robe – and
your very life, O man.
When I take these plants in my hand,
yearning for the victory prize,
the life of the disease vanishes as if before
a hunter holding onto life itself.
From him through whom you plants creep
limb by limb, joint by joint,
you banish disease like a giant
coming between fighters.

Fly away, disease, along with the
blue jay and the jay;
disappear with the howling of the wind,
and with the rain storm.
Let one help the other;
let one stand by the other.
All of you working together, hear
this prayer of the soul.

The rise of industrial medicine and industrial agriculture was based on a war against biodiversity and women. The witch hunts of Europe were an attack on women as experts.

The myth that the scientific revolution was a universal process of intellectual progress is constantly undermined by feminist studies and the history of the science of non-western cultures. These link the rise of reductionism to the subordination and destruction of women's knowledge in the west, and the knowledge of non-western cultures (Shiva 1989). The witch hunts of Europe were largely a process of undermining the authority, and destroying the expertise, of European women. In 1511, the English Parliament passed an act directed against 'common artificers, as smythes, weavers and women who attempt great cures and things of great difficulties: in the witch they partly use sorcerye and witch-craft' (Shiva 1989). By the sixteenth century, women in Europe were totally excluded from the practice of medicine and healing because 'wise women' ran the risk of being declared witches.

A deeper, more violent form of exclusion of women's knowledge and expertise, and of the knowledge of tribal and peasant cultures, is now under way with the spread of the male-centered paradigm of science. This marginalizes women and destroys biodiversity. It is pushing millions of people to starvation and millions of species to extinction.

Who Feeds the World?

My answer is very different to that given by most people. It is women and small farmers working with biodiversity who are the primary food providers in the Third World. Contrary to the popular assumption, their biodiversity-based small farm systems are more productive than industrial single crop systems.

Diversity and sustainable systems of food production have been destroyed in the name of increasing food production. However, the destruction of diversity is accompanied by the disappearance of important sources of nutrition. When measured in terms of nutrition per acre and biodiversity, the so-called 'high yields' of industrial agriculture do not imply more production of food and better nutrition. 'Yield' usually refers to production per unit area of a single crop. 'Production' refers to the total harvest of several different crops. Planting only one crop in the entire field as a monoculture will of course increase its yield. Planting multiple crops in a mixture will entail low yields of individual crops but a high total production of food. Yields have been defined in such a way as to eclipse food production on small farms by small farmers. This obscures the production by millions of women farmers in the Third World, farmers like those in my native Himalayas who fought against logging in the Chipko movement, who in their terraced fields grow amaranth and various kinds of soybean, millet, beans and peas. From the point of view of biodiversity, biodiversity-based productivity is superior to single-crop productivity. I call this blindness to the high productivity of diversity a 'monoculture of the mind,' which creates single crops in our fields.

The Mayan peasants in Chiapas are called unproductive because they produce only two tons of corn per acre. However, the overall food output is twenty tons per acre when the variety of beans, squashes, vegetables and fruit trees is taken into account. In Java, small farmers cultivate 607 species in their home gardens, with an overall species diversity comparable to a deciduous tropical forest. In sub-Saharan Africa, women cultivate as many as 120 different plants in the spaces left among the cash crops. A single home garden in Thailand has more than 230 species, and African home gardens have more than 60 species of trees. Rural families in the Congo eat leaves from more than 50 different species of trees. A study in eastern Nigeria found that home gardens occupying only two per cent of a household's farmland accounted for half of the farm's total output. Similarly, home gardens in Indonesia are estimated to provide more than 20 per cent of household income and 40 per cent of domestic food supplies (FAO 1998).

Research done by the United Nation's Food and Agriculture Organization has shown that small biodiverse farms can produce thousands of times more food than large, industrial monocultures (Shiva 2001b). Diversity is the best strategy for preventing drought and desertification. What the world needs to feed a growing population sustainably is more intense biodiversity, not the increasing use of chemicals or genetic engineering. Although women and small peasants feed the world through biodiversity, we are repeatedly told that without genetic engineering and the globalization of agriculture the world will starve. In spite of all empirical evidence showing that genetic engineering does not produce more food and in fact often leads to a net decline in yields, it is constantly promoted as the only option to feed the hungry (Shiva 2001b).

This deliberate blindness to diversity, the blindness to nature's production, production by women, and production by Third World farmers, allows destruction and appropriation to be projected as creation. Take the case of the much derided 'golden rice,' or genetically-engineered vitamin A rice as a cure for blindness. It is assumed that without genetic engineering, we cannot eliminate vitamin A deficiency. However, nature gives us many plentiful sources of vitamin A. If rice was not polished, rice itself would provide vitamin A. If herbicides were not sprayed on our wheat fields, we would have bathua, amaranth, mustard leaves as delicious and nutritious greens. Women in Bengal use more than 150 plants as greens. Here are a few: hinche sak (*Enhydra fluctuans*), palang sak (*Spinacea oleracea*), tak palang (*Rumex vesicarius*), lal sak (*Amaranthus gangeticus*), champa note (*Amaranthus tristis*), gobra note (*Amaranthus lividus*), ghenti note (*Amaranthus tennifolius*), banspata note (*Amaranthus lanceolatus*), ban note (*Amaranthus viridis*), sada note (*Amaranthus blitum*), kanta note (*Amaranthus spinosus*), bethua sale (*Chenopodium album*), brahmi sak (*Bacopa monrieri*) and sushin sak (*Marulea quadrifolio*), to name but a few. But the myth of creation presents biotechnologists as the creators of vitamin A, denying nature's many gifts and women's knowledge of how to use this diversity to feed their children and families.

Capitalist Patriarchs

The most efficient means of bringing about the destruction of nature, local economies, and small autonomous producers is to render their production invisible. Women are considered by their families and communities to be 'nonproductive' and 'economically inactive.' The devaluation of women's work, and of work done in sustainable economies, is the natural outcome of a system constructed by a capitalist patriarchy. This is how globalization destroys local economies; the destruction itself is counted as growth. Women themselves are devalued. Because much of their work in rural and indigenous communities is undertaken in collaboration with nature, and is often in conflict with the do-minant market-driven development and trade policies, and because work that satisfies needs and ensures sustenance is devalued in general, there is less attention given to life and life support systems. The devaluation and invisibility of sus-tainable, regenerative production is most glaring in the area of food. While a patriarchal division of labour has assigned women the role of feeding their families and communities, patriarchal economies and patriarchal views of science and technology magically make women's work in providing food disappear. 'Feeding the world' becomes disassociated from the women who actually do it and is projected as dependent on global agribusiness and biotechnology corporations. However, industrialization, the genetic engineering of food, and the globalization of trade in agriculture are recipes for creating hunger, not for feeding the poor.

Everywhere, food production is becoming a loss-creating economy, with farmers spending more buying costly inputs for industrial production than the price they receive for their produce. The consequence is rising debts and suicides in both rich and poor countries. Economic globalization is leading to concentra-tion in the seed industry, the increased use of pesticides and, finally, increased debt. Capital-intensive, corporate-controlled agriculture is spreading into regions where peasants are poor but had been, until now, self-sufficient in food. In the regions where industrial agriculture has been introduced through globalization, higher costs are making it virtually impossible for small farmers to survive. The globali-zation of non-sustainable industrial agriculture is decimating the incomes of Third World farmers with a combination of currency devaluation, increases in produc-tion costs and the collapse of commodity prices (Shiva, Jafri and Jalees 2003).

Farmers everywhere are being paid a fraction of what they received for the same commodity a decade ago. In the US, wheat prices at the farm dropped from

US$5.75 a bushel to US$2.43; soybean prices dropped from US$8.40 to US$4.29; and corn prices fell from US$4.43 to US$1.72 (Institute for Agriculture and Trade Policy 2003). In India from 1999 to 2000, prices for coffee dropped from R 60 to R 18 per kilogram while prices of oil seeds declined by more than 30 per cent. In a report to the Senate Standing Committee on Agriculture and Forestry, the National Farmers Union (2000) in Canada put it like this :

> While farmers growing cereals—wheat, oats, corn—earn negative returns and are pushed into bankruptcy, the companies that make breakfast cereals reap huge profits. In 1998, cereal companies Kellogg's, Quaker Oats, and General Mills enjoyed return on equity rates of 56, 165 and 222 per cent, respectively. While a bushel of corn sold for less than US$4.00, a bushel of cornflakes cost US$133. In 1998, the cereal companies were 186 to 740 times more profitable than the farms. Farmers may be making too little because others are taking too much.

The World Bank has admitted that behind the polarization of domestic consumer prices and world prices are large trading companies in international commodity markets (Shiva et al. 2000). If farmers earn less, consumers, especially in poor countries, pay more. In India, food prices doubled from 1999 to 2000 and consumption of food cereals dropped by twelve per cent in rural areas, increasing the food deprivation of the already undernourished and pushing up mortality rates. Economic growth through global commerce is based on pseudosurpluses. More food is being traded while the poor are consuming less. When growth increases poverty, when real production becomes a negative economy, and speculators are called wealth creators, something has gone wrong with the concepts and categories of wealth and wealth creation. Pushing the real production by nature and people into a negative economy implies that production of real goods and services is declining, creating deeper poverty for the millions who are not part of the dotcom route to instant wealth.

Women, as I have said, are the world's primary food producers and processors. However, their work in production and processing has now become invisible. According to the updated Food and Agriculture Integrated Development Action report, released by the Confederation of Indian Industry (CII) and McKinsey and Co. (*CII-McKinsey FAIDA Report 2003*), American food giants recognize that Indian agribusiness has lots of room to grow, especially in food processing. India processes a minuscule one per cent of the food it grows, compared with 70 per cent for the US, Brazil and the Philippines. It is not that we Indians eat our food raw. Global consultants simply fail to see the 99 per cent food processing done by women at household level, or by small cottage industries, because they are not controlled by global agribusiness. Ninety-nine per cent of India's agriprocessing has been deliberately kept at household level. Now, under the pressure of globalization, things are changing. Pseudohygiene laws, which shut down the food economy based on local small scale processing under community control, are part of the arsenal of global agribusiness to establish market monopolies by force and coercion, not competition. In August 1998, small-scale local processing of edible oil was banned in India by a packaging order, which made sale of unpackaged oil illegal, requiring all oil to be packed in plastic or aluminum (Shiva 1998). This shut down the tiny *ghanis*, or cold press mills. It destroyed the market for our various oilseeds: mustard, linseed, sesame, groundnut and coconut. This coup by the edible oil industry has affected ten million livelihoods. The substitution *atta,* or flour, for packaged and branded flour will influence one-hundred million people. These millions are being pushed into a new poverty. Moreover, compulsory packaging will produce an environmental burden of millions of tons of plastic and aluminum.

The globalization of the food system is destroying the diversity of local food cultures and local food economies. A global monoculture is being forced on people by classifying everything that is fresh, local and handmade as a health hazard. Human hands are being defined as the worst contaminants, and work for human hands is being outlawed, to be replaced by machines and chemicals bought from global corporations. These are not recipes for feeding the world, but ways of stealing livelihoods from the poor to create markets for the powerful.

Biopiracy

Women farmers in the Third World are mainly small-scale. They provide the basis of food security, and they provide food security in partnership with other species. The partnership between women and biodiversity has kept the world fed throughout history, feeds it at present, and will do so in the future. It is this partnership that needs to be preserved and promoted to ensure food security. Agriculture based on diversity, decentralization, and improving small farm productivity by ecological methods is a female-centered, nature-friendly agriculture. In this women-centered agriculture, knowledge is shared, other species and plants are kin, not property, and sustainability is based on renewal of the earth's fertility, the regeneration of biodiversity, and the richness of species on farms to provide farm-grown inputs. In our paradigms, there is no place for monocultures of genetically engineered crops and monopolies of intellectual property rights (IPR) to seeds.

Monocultures and monopolies are emblematic of the male-dominated focus in agriculture. The war mentality underpinning armed forces and industry is evident from the names given to herbicides that destroy the economic basis of the survival of the poorest women in the rural areas of the Third World. Monsanto's herbicides are called 'Roundup', 'Machete' and 'Lasso.' American Home Products, which has merged with Monsanto, calls its herbicides 'Pentagon', 'Prowl', 'Scepter', 'Squadron', 'Cadre', 'Lightening', 'Assert' and 'Avenge.' This is the language of war, not sustainability. Sustainability is based on peace with the earth. The violence intrinsic to methods and metaphors used by global agribusiness and biotechnology corporations is a violence against nature's biodiversity and women's expertise and productivity. The violence intrinsic to the destruction of diversity through monocultures and the destruction of the freedom to save and exchange seeds through IPR monopolies is inconsistent with women's various nonviolent ways of interacting with nature and providing food security. This diversity of knowledge systems and production systems is the way forward to ensure that Third World women continue to play a central role as depositories of knowledge, producers and providers of food.

One of the varieties we conserve and grow at the Navdanya farm in Doon Valley is the famous Basmati rice. This rice, which women farmers like Bija Devi, have been growing in my valley for centuries, is today being claimed as the recent invention of a novel type of rice by a US Corporation called RiceTec (patent no. 5,663,454). The *neem* that our forebears used for centuries as a pesticide and fungicide has been patented for these uses by WR Grace, another US corporation (Shiva 2001a). We have challenged Grace's patent at the European Patent Office, with the European Parliament Greens.

Biopiracy, by which western corporations steal centuries of collective knowledge and innovation carried out by Third World women, is now reaching epidemic proportions. It is now being justified by Monsanto in the guise of a 'partnership' between agribusiness and Third World women. For us, theft cannot be the basis of partnership. Partnership implies equality and mutual respect. This means that there is no room for biopiracy: those who have engaged in such piracy should apologize to those they have stolen from and whose intellectual and natural creativity they want to undermine through IPR monopolies. Partnership with Third World women requires changes to the World Trade Organization-Trade Related International Property Rights (WTO-TRIPs) agreement that protects the pirates and punishes the original innovators, as in the case of the US-India TRIPs dispute. It will also involve changes in the *US Patent Act*, which allows the blatant theft of our biodiversity-related knowledge. These changes are essential to ensure that collective knowledge and innovation is protected and women are recognized and respected as depositaries of knowledge and biodiversity experts.

Women farmers have been the seed keepers and seed growers for millennia. Basmati is just one of 100,000 varieties of rice developed by Indian farmers. Diversity and perpetuity are the main features of our seed culture. In Central India, which is the Vavilov center for rice diversity, at the beginning of the agricultural season, farmers gather before the village deity, offer their varieties of rice and then share the seeds. This annual festival of Akti reaffirms the duty of saving and sharing seed among farming communities. It establishes partnership among farmers and with the earth.

IPRs on seeds are however criminalizing this duty to the earth and to each other by making seed saving and seed exchange illegal. The attempt to prevent farmers from saving seed is not just being made through the new genetic engineering technologies. Delta and Pine Land, now owned by Monsanto, and the US Department of Agriculture (USDA) have established new partnership through a jointly held patent (No. 5,723,785) for seed which has been genetically engineered to ensure that it does not germinate on harvest, thus forcing farmers to buy seed at each planting season. Termination of germination is a means for capital accumulation and market expansion. However, abundance in nature and for farmers shrinks as markets grow for Monsanto. When we sow seed, we pray, 'May this seed be inexhaustible.' Monsanto and the USDA on the other hand are saying, 'Let this seed be terminated so that our profits and monopoly are inexhaustible.' There can be no partnership between the terminator logic that destroys nature's renewability and the commitment to continuity of life held by women farmers of the Third World. The two worldviews do not merely clash. They are mutually exclusive. There can be no partnership between the logic of death on which Monsanto bases its expanding empire and the logic of life on which women farmers in the Third World base their partnership with the earth to provide food security for their families and communities.

Genetic engineering and IPRs will rob Third World women and impoverish their creativity, innovation and decision-making power in agriculture. Instead of women deciding what is grown in fields and served in kitchens, agriculture based on globalization, genetic engineering and corporate monopolies on seeds will establish a food system and worldview in which the men in charge of global corporations control what is grown in our fields and what we eat. Corporate executives investing capital in theft and biopiracy will pose as the givers and owners of life. We will not be partners in this violent usurpation of the creativity of nature and Third World women by global biotechnology corporations. Calling themselves life sciences industry, they push millions of species and millions of small farmers closer to extinction.

And it is not just other species, but the females of the human species that are being pushed to extinction. The violence unleashed by the Green Revolution and new agricultural technologies is also evident in the emergence and growth of female feticide in Punjab, the home of the Green Revolution. I first noted this connection in *Staying Alive* (1989). The prosperous northwestern states have only 17 per cent of India's population but account for 80 per cent of its female feticides. The juvenile sex ratio has dropped to 927 girls for every 1,000 boys, indicating that 250,000 female feticides take place every year. I wrote in *Staying Alive* that women were becoming the disposable sex in a world where cash is the only measure of worth—of women, as of everything else.

The future of biodiversity and the future of food security rests on bringing women and small farmers back to the centre of food systems. Women live by the culture of conservation and sharing. The world can be fed only by nourishing all the world's creatures. By giving food to other creatures and other species, we maintain conditions for our own food security. By feeding the earthworms, we feed ourselves. By feeding cows, we feed the soil and in providing food for the soil, we provide food for humans. This worldview of abundance is based on sharing and on a deep awareness of humans as members of the earth's great family; awareness that, in impoverishing other beings, we impoverish ourselves, and in nourishing other beings, we nourish ourselves. That is the basis of sustainability. It was to defend biodiversity and protect women's creativity and knowledge that I set up

Navdanya in India. We have also initiated a global movement, Diverse Women for Diversity, for the safeguarding of biological and cultural diversity. Without diversity there can be no peace, no sustainability and no justice.

Vandana Shiva has contributed in fundamental ways to changing the practices and paradigms of agriculture and food. Her books, The Violence of Green Revolution *and* Monocultures of the Mind *have become basic challenges to the dominant paradigm of non-sustainable, reductionist Green Revolution Agriculture. Her book* Biopiracy, Stolen Harvest, Water Wars, *made visible the social, economic and ecological costs of corporate-led globalization. In 1998, she founded 'Diverse Women for Diversity', an international movement of women working on issues of food, agriculture, patents and biotechnology. More recently, in 2004, she started Bija Vidyapeeth, an international college for sustainable living in collaboration with Schumacher College, UK. Dr. Shiva has been a visiting professor and lectured at the Universities of Oslo, Norway; Schumacher College, UK; Mt. Holyoke College, US; York University and University of Victoria, Canada; University of Lulea, Sweden; as well as numerous organizations and institutions around the world. She has also served as an adviser to governments in India and abroad as well as NGOs such as the International Forum on Globalization, Women's Environment and Development Organization and Third World Network. She is Chair of the International Commission on the Future of Food.*

References

CII-McKinsey FAIDA Report 2003 (2003) New Delhi: CII and McKinsey and Co.

Food and Agriculture Organization (FAO) (1998) 'Women's contribution to food security', Bangkok, 16 October.

Institute for Agriculture and Trade Policy (2003) *United States Dumping on World Agricultural Markets,* Minneapolis: Insitute for Agriculture and Trade Policy.

National Farmers Union (2000) *The Farm Crisis, EU Subsidies and Agribusiness Market Power,* Ottawa: National Farmers Union. Online: http://www.nfu.ca/feb17-brief.htm.

Shiva, V. (1989) *Staying Alive,* London: Zed Books.

Shiva, V. (1998) 'Mustard and soya', *Navdanya,* October.

Shiva, V. (2001a) *Patents, Myths and Reality,* New Delhi: Penguin India.

Shiva, V. (2001b) *Yoked to Death,* New Delhi: Research Foundation for Science, Technology and Ecology.

Shiva, V., A. Jafri, A. Emani, S. Bhutani and U. Prasad (2000) *Licence to Kill: How the Unholy Trinity, the International Monetary Fund and the World Trade Organization, are Killing Livelihoods, Environment and Democracy in India,* New Delhi: Research Foundation for Science, Technology and Ecology.

Shiva, V., A. Jafri, and K. Jalees (2003) *The Mirage of Market Access,* New Delhi: Research Foundation for Science, Technology and Ecology.

LOVE AND GOLD

ARLIE RUSSELL HOCHSCHILD

Vicky Diaz, a 34-year-old mother of five, was a college-educated schoolteacher and travel agent in the Philippines before migrating to the United States to work as a housekeeper for a wealthy Beverly Hills family and as a nanny for their two-year-old son. As Vicky explained in an interview with Rhacel Parreñas,

> My children ... were saddened by my departure. Even until now my children are trying to convince me to go home. The children were not angry when I left because they were still very young when I left them. My husband could not get angry either because he knew that was the only way I could seriously help him raise our children, so that our children could be sent to school. (qtd. in Parreñas 2001: 87)

In her book *Servants of Globalization*, Parreñas (2001) tells a disquieting story of what she calls the 'globalization of mothering'. The Beverly Hills family pays 'Vicky' (which is the pseudonym Parreñas gave her) $400 a week, and Vicky, in turn, pays her own family's live-in domestic worker back in the Philippines $40 a week. Living like this is not easy on Vicky and her family.

> Even though it's paid well, you are sinking in the amount of your work. Even while you are ironing the clothes, they can still call you to the kitchen to wash the plates. It ... [is] also very depressing. The only thing you can do is give all your love to [the two-year-old American child]. In my absence from my children, the most I could do with my situation is give all my love to that child. (qtd. in Parrenas 2001: 87)[1]

Vicky is part of a global care chain: a series of personal links between people

LOVE AND GOLD |

across the globe based on the paid or unpaid work of caring. A typical global care chain might work something like this: an older daughter from a poor family in a Third World country cares for her siblings (the first link in the chain) while her mother works as a nanny caring for the children of a nanny migrating to a First World country (the second link) who, in turn, cares for the child of a family in a rich country (the final link). Each kind of chain expresses an invisible ecology of care, one care worker depending on another and so on. A global care chain might start in a poor country and end in a rich one, or it might link rural and urban areas within the same poor country. More complex versions start in one poor country and extend to another slightly less poor country and then link to a rich country.

Such global care chains are now on the rise. For some time now, promising and highly trained professionals have been moving from ill-equipped hospitals, impoverished schools, antiquated banks, and other beleaguered workplaces of the Third World to better opportunities and higher pay in the First World. As rich nations become richer and poor nations become poorer, this one-way flow of talent and training continuously widens the gap between the two. This is the brain drain. But now in addition a parallel, more hidden and wrenching trend is growing, as women who normally care for the young, the old and the sick in their own poor countries move to care for the young, the old and the sick in rich countries, whether as maids and nannies or as day-care and nursing-home aides. This is a care drain.

The movement of female care workers from South to North is not altogether new. The causes of this increase in scope and speed are many. One is the growing split between the global rich and poor. Since the 1940s, the gap between North and South has widened. In 1960, for example, the nations of the North were twenty times richer than those of the South. By 1980, that gap had more than doubled, and the North was 46 times richer than the South. In fact, according to a United Nations Development Program study, 60 countries are—in absolute terms—worse off in 1999 than they were in 1980 (*New York Times* 2001). Multinational corporations are the 'muscle and brains' of the new global system. As William Greider (1997) points out, the 500 largest such corporations (168 in Europe, 157 in the United States, and 119 in Japan) have increased their sales sevenfold in the last twenty years. Though multinationals create some jobs in poor countries, through the small enterprises and farms they put out of business, they are one engine of this growing inequality.

As a result of this polarization, the middle class of the Third World now earns less than the poor of the First World. Before the domestic workers Rhacel Parreñas (1999: 123) interviewed in the 1990s migrated from the Philippines to the United States and Italy, they had averaged $176 a month, often as teachers, nurses, and administrative and clerical workers. But by doing less skilled—though no less difficult—work as nannies, maids, and care-service workers, they can earn $200 a month in Singapore, $410 a month in Hong Kong, $700 a month in Italy, or $1,400 a month in Los Angeles. To take another example from an extraordinary documentary, 'When Mother Comes Home for Christmas', as a fifth-grade dropout in Colombo, Sri Lanka, Josephine Perera could earn $30 a month plus room and board as a housemaid, or she could earn $30 a month as a salesgirl in a shop, without food or lodging. But as a nanny in Athens she could earn $500 a month, plus room and board. In the absence of a *public* and structural solution to the gap between the rich North and the poor South, women like Vicky Diaz and Josephine Perera close the gap *privately*, by moving from South to North—at great emotional cost.

Even as the gap between the globe's rich and poor grows wider, the globe itself—its capital, its cultural images, its consumer tastes, and peoples—have become more integrated. Thanks to the spread of western, and especially American, movies and television programs, the people of the poor South now know a great deal more about the rich North than the rich North know about them. But what they learn is what the rich North *has*. Indeed, in front of the global TV, the South is daily exposed to a material striptease.

Rising inequality and the lure of northern prosperity have contributed to what Stephen Castles and Mark Miller call a 'globalization of migration' (1998: 8; see also Zlotnik 1999). For men and women alike, migration has become a private solution to a public problem. Since 1945 and especially since the mid-1980s, a small but growing proportion of the world's population is migrating. They come from and go to more different countries. While migration is by no means an inexorable process, Castles and Miller observe that, 'migrations are growing in volume in all major regions at the present time' (1998: 5). The International Organization for Migration estimates that 120 million people moved from one country to another, legally or illegally, in 1994 (Castles and Miller 1998). Of this group, about two per cent of the world's population, 15 to 23 million are refugees and asylum seekers. Of the rest, some move to join family members who have previously migrated. But most move to find work.

In addition, half of all the world's migrants today are women. In Sri Lanka, one out of every ten adults—a majority of them women—works abroad. (That figure excludes returnees.) As Castles and Miller explain:

> Women play an increasing role in all regions and all types of migration. In the past, most labour migrations and many refugee movements were male dominated, and women were often dealt with under the category of family reunion. Since the 1960s, women have played a major role in labour migration. Today women workers form the majority in movements as diverse as those of Cape Verdians to Italy, Filipinos to the Middle East and Thais to Japan. (1998: 9)[2]

Many such female workers migrate to fill domestic jobs. Demand for domestic servants has risen both in developed countries, where it had nearly vanished, and in fast-growing economies such as Hong Kong and Singapore, where, write Castles and Miller, 'immigrant servants—from the Philippines, Indonesia, Thailand,

Korea and Sri Lanka—allow women in the richer economies to take up new employment opportunities' (1998: xi).

Vastly more middle-class women in the First World do paid work now than in the past. In the United States in 1950, for example, 15 per cent of mothers of children aged six and under did paid work while 65 per cent of such women do today. Seventy-two per cent of all American women now work. Most also work longer hours for more months a year and for more years, and hence badly need help caring for the family (Hochschild 1997). The grandmothers and sisters who 30 years ago might have stayed home to care for the children of working relatives are now out working themselves. Just as Third World grandmothers may be doing paid care work abroad, so too more grandmothers of the rich North are working—another reason First World families are looking outside the family for good care.

Women who want to succeed in a professional or managerial job in the First World also face strong pressures at work. Most careers are still based on a well known, male pattern: doing professional work, competing with fellow professionals, getting credit for work, building a reputation, doing it while you are young, hoarding scarce time, and minimizing family work by finding someone else to do it. In the past, the professional was a man; the 'someone else' was his wife. The wife oversaw the family, itself a flexible, preindustrial institution concerned with human experiences which the workforce excluded: birth, child rearing, sickness, death. Today, a growing 'care industry' has stepped into the traditional wife's role, creating a very real demand for migrant women.

But if First World middle-class women are building careers that are molded according to the old male model, by putting in long hours at demanding jobs, their nannies and other domestic workers suffer a greatly exaggerated version of the same thing. Two women working for pay is not a bad idea. But two working mothers giving their all to work is a good idea gone haywire. In the end, both First and Third World women are small players in a larger economic game whose rules they have not written.

The impact of these global rules extends to many who have no voice. For many, if not most, women migrants have children. The average age of women migrants into the United States is 29, and most come from countries, such as Mexico, where female identity centers on motherhood, and where the birth rate is high. Often migrants, especially the undocumented ones, cannot bring their children with them. So most mothers try to leave their children in the care of grandmothers, aunts and fathers, in roughly that order. An orphanage is a last resort. A number of nannies working in rich countries hire nannies to care for their own children back home either as solo caretakers or as aides to the female relatives left in charge back home. Carmen Ronquillo, for example, migrated from the Philippines to Rome to work as a maid for an architect and single mother of two. She left behind her husband, two teenagers—and a maid (Parreñas 1999).

Whatever arrangements these mothers make for their children, most feel the separation acutely, expressing guilt and remorse to the researchers who interview them. Says one migrant mother who left her two-month-old baby in the care of a relative, 'The first two years I felt like I was going crazy. You have to believe me when I say that it was like I was having intense psychological problems. I would catch myself gazing at nothing, thinking about my child' (Parreñas 1999: 123). Recounted another migrant nanny through tears, 'When I saw my children again, I thought, "Oh children do grow up even without their mother". I left my youngest when she was only five years old. She was already nine when I saw her again, but she still wanted me to carry her' (Parreñas 1999: 154).

Surprisingly, more women than men migrant workers stay in the North. In staying, these mothers remain separated from their children, a choice freighted, for many, with terrible sadness. But as much as these mothers suffer, their children suffer more. And there are a lot of them. An estimated 30 per cent of Filipino children—some eight million—live in households where at least one parent has gone overseas. These children have counterparts in Africa, India, Sri Lanka, Latin America and the former Soviet Union.

How are these children doing? Not very well, according to a survey which the Scalabrini Migration Center in Manila conducted with more than seven hundred children in 1996. Compared to their classmates, the children of migrant workers more frequently fell ill; they were more likely to express anger, confusion and apathy; and they performed more poorly in school. Other studies of this population show a rise in delinquency and child suicide (Frank 2001). When such children were asked whether they would also migrate when they grew up, leaving their own children in the care of others, they all said no.

Faced with these facts, one senses some sort of injustice at work, linking the emotional deprivation of these children with the surfeit of affection their First World counterparts enjoy. In her study of native-born women of colour who do domestic work, Sau-Ling Wong (1994) argues that the time and energy these workers devote to the children of their employers is diverted from their own children.

But is it only time and energy that are 'drained' or is it love itself? In a sense time and energy are resources like minerals extracted from the earth. The nanny cannot be in two places at once. Her day has only so many hours. The more time and energy she gives the children she is paid to love, the less time and energy she can give her own children. But is love itself also a resource? And if it is a resource, can children have a 'right' to it? In its wisdom, the United Nations Convention on the Rights of the Child (1989) implies that love, too, is like a resource. It asserts all children's right to an 'atmosphere of happiness, love, and understanding'.

But if love is a resource, it is a renewable resource. For the more we love and are loved, the more deeply we can love. Thus, love is not fixed in the same way that most material resources are fixed. It creates more of itself. We are talking, then, of a global heart transplant, and one which will bear on the lives of many people for years to come.

But how are we to understand the 'extraction' of love from the South and its import to the North? We get some help at this juncture from Freud, according to

LOVE AND GOLD |

whom we don't 'withdraw' and 'invest' feeling but rather displace or redirect it. The process is an unconscious one, whereby we don't actually give up a feeling of, say, love or hate, so much as we find a new object for it—in the case of sexual feeling, a more appropriate object than the original one, whom Freud presumed to be our opposite-sex parent. While Freud applied the idea of displacement mainly to relationships within the nuclear family, it seems only a small stretch to apply it to relationships like that of nanny and the employer's child.

The way some employers describe it, a nanny's love of her employer's child is a natural product of her more loving Third World culture, with its warm family ties, strong community life, and long tradition of patient maternal love of children. In hiring a nanny, many such employers implicitly hope to import a poor country's 'native culture', thereby replenishing their own, rich country's depleted culture of care. They import the benefits of Third World 'family values'. Says the director of a co-op nursery I interviewed in the San Francisco Bay Area,

> This may be odd to say, but the teacher's aides we hire from Mexico and Guatemala know how to love a child better than the middle-class white parents. They are more relaxed, patient, and joyful. They enjoy the kids more. These professional parents are pressured for time and anxious to develop their kids' talents. I tell the parents that they can really learn how to love from the Latinas and the Filipinas.

When asked why Anglo mothers should relate to children so differently than do Filipina teacher's aides, the nursery director speculated, 'The Filipinas are brought up in a more relaxed, loving environment. They aren't as rich as we are, but they aren't so pressured for time, so materialistic, so anxious. They have a more loving, family-oriented culture'. One mother, an American lawyer, expressed a similar view:

> Carmen just enjoys my son. She doesn't worry whether … he's learning his letters, or whether he'll get into a good preschool. She just enjoys him. And actually, with anxious busy parents like us, that's really what Thomas needs. I love my son more than anyone in this world. But at this stage Carmen is better for him.

Filipina nannies I have interviewed in California paint a very different picture of the love they share with their First World charges. Theirs is not an import of happy peasant mothering but a love that partly develops on American shores, informed by an American ideology of mother-child bonding and fostered by intense loneliness and longing for their own children. If love is a precious resource, it is not one simply extracted from the Third World and implanted in the First; rather, it owes its very existence to a peculiar cultural alchemy that occurs in the land to which it is imported.

For María Gutierrez, who cares for the eight-month-old baby of two hardworking professionals (a lawyer and a doctor, born in the Philippines but now living in San Jose, California), loneliness and long work hours feed a love for her employers' child. As María told me:

> I love Ana more than my own two children. Yes, more! It's strange, I know. But I have time to be with her. I'm paid. I am lonely here. I work ten hours a day, with one day off. I don't know any neighbors on the block. And so this child gives me what I need.

Not only that, but she is able to provide her employer's child with a different sort of attention and nurturance than she could deliver to her own children. 'I'm more patient', she explains, 'more relaxed. I put the child first. My kids, I treated them the way my mother treated me'.

I asked her how her mother had treated her and she replied:

> My mother grew up in a farming family. It was a hard life. My mother wasn't warm to me. She didn't touch me or say 'I love you'. She didn't think she should do that. Before I was born she had lost four babies—two in miscarriage and two died as babies. I think she was afraid to love me as a baby because she thought I might die too. Then she put me to work as a 'little mother' caring for my four younger brothers and sisters. I didn't have time to play.

Fortunately, an older woman who lived next door took an affectionate interest in María, often feeding her and even taking her in overnight when she was sick. María felt closer to this woman and her relatives than she did to her biological aunts and cousins. She had been, in some measure, informally adopted—a practice she describes as common in the Philippine countryside and even in some towns during the 1960s and 1970s.

In a sense, María experienced a pre-modern childhood, marked by high infant mortality, child labour, and an absence of sentimentality, set within a culture of strong family commitment and community support. Reminiscent of fifteenth-century France, as Philippe Ariès describes it in *Centuries of Childhood* (1962), this was a childhood before the romanticization of the child and before the modern middle-class ideology of intensive mothering (Hays 1996). Sentiment wasn't the point; commitment was.

María's commitment to her own children, aged twelve and thirteen when she left to work abroad, bears the mark of that upbringing. Through all of their anger and tears, María sends remittances and calls, come hell or high water. The commitment is there. The sentiment, she has to work at. When she calls home now, María says,

> I tell my daughter 'I love you'. At first it sounded fake. But after a while it

became natural. And now she says it back. It's strange, but I think I learned that it was okay to say that from being in the United States.

María's story points to a paradox. On the one hand, the First World extracts love from the Third World. But what is being extracted is partly produced and 'assembled' here: the leisure, the money, the ideology of the child, the intense loneliness and yearning for one's own children. In María's case, a premodern childhood in the Philippines, a postmodern ideology of mothering and childhood in the United States, and the loneliness of migration blend to produce the love she gives to her employers' child. That love is also a product of the nanny's freedom from the time pressure and school anxiety parents feel in a culture that lacks much of a social safety net. In that sense, the love María gives as a nanny does not suffer from the disabling effects of the American version of late capitalism.

If all this is true—if, in fact, the nanny's love is something at least partially produced by the conditions under which it is given—is María's love of a First World child really being extracted from her own Third World children? Yes, because her daily presence has been removed, and with it the daily expression of her love. Even though the nanny herself does the extracting, both she and her children suffer a great loss. As one young woman from the Dominican Republic who was left behind from the age of twelve to fourteen reflected, 'I kept feeling, "couldn't we do this together?" And now I'm 33 and I think those were two years we can never re-live. They are lost'. Such separations are, indeed, globalization's pound of flesh.

But curiously, the employers in the North know very little about it. A Mexican nanny's love for her American employer's child is a thing in itself. It is unique, private—we could even say 'fetishized'. Marx talked about the fetishization of things, not of feelings. He might note how these days we make a fetish of an SUV, for example—we see the thing independent of its context. We disregard the men who harvested the rubber latex, the assembly-line workers who bolted on the tires, and so on. But just as we mentally isolate our idea of an object from the human scene within which it was made, so, too, we unwittingly separate the love between nanny and child from the global capitalist order of love to which it very much belongs.

The notion of extracting resources from the Third World harks back to imperialism in its most literal form: the nineteenth-century North's extraction of gold, ivory and rubber from the South. That openly coercive, male-centered imperialism—which persists today—was always paralleled by a quieter imperialism in which women were more central. Today, as love and care become the 'new gold', the female part of the story has grown in prominence. In both cases, whether through the death or displacement of their parents, Third World children pay the price.

In the classic nineteenth-century form of imperialism, the North plundered the natural resources of the South. Its main protagonists were virtually all men: explorers, kings, missionaries, soldiers, and the local men who were forced at gunpoint to do things such as harvest wild rubber latex and the like. European states lent their legitimacy to these endeavours, and an ideology emerged to support them: 'the white man's burden' in Britain and *la mission civilisatrice* in France. Both, of course, stressed the great benefits of colonization for the colonized, and enlisted some of the colonized to actively cooperate with, and even administer colonial rule.

Nineteenth-century imperialism was more physically brutal than the imperialism of today, but it was also far more obvious. Today the North does not extract love from the South by force: there are no colonial officers in tan helmets, no invading armies, no ships bearing arms sailing off to the colonies. Instead, we see a benign scene of Third World women pushing baby carriages, elder care workers patiently walking, arms linked, with elderly clients on streets or sitting beside them in First World parks.

Today, coercion operates differently. While the sex trade and some domestic service is brutally enforced, the new emotional imperialism does not, for the most part, issue from the barrel of a gun. Women choose to migrate for domestic work. But they choose it because economic pressures all but coerce them to. The yawning gap between rich and poor countries is itself a form of coercion, pushing Third World mothers to seek work in the First for lack of options closer to home. But given the prevailing free market ideology, migration is viewed as a 'personal choice'. The problems it causes we see as 'personal' problems. But a global social logic lies behind them, and they are, in this sense, not simply 'personal'.

Through this social logic, migration creates not a white man's burden, but a dark child's burden. We need much more careful research on the children left behind if we are to find out how such children are really doing. We need to know further, how these children grow up and what happens to them when they too become adults and have children. For anecdotal evidence suggests that the young daughters of women who leave children behind to migrate for work—when they themselves are grown and have children—also leave their children behind to migrate for work.

How then are we to respond to all this? I can think of three possible approaches. First, we might say that all women everywhere should stay home and take care of their own families. The problem with Vicky is not that she migrates, but that she neglects her traditional role as mother. A second approach might be to deny that a problem exists: the care drain is an inevitable outcome of globalization, which is itself good for the world. The supply of labour has met a demand for it. The market is working and the market is always right. If the first approach condemns global migration, the second celebrates it.

According to a third approach—the one I take—loving, paid childcare with reasonable hours is a very good thing. And globalization brings with it new opportunities, such as a nanny's access to good pay. But it also introduces painful new emotional realities for Third World children. We need to embrace the needs of Third World societies, including their children. We need to develop a global sense of ethics to match emerging global economic realities. If we go out to buy a pair of Nike shoes, we want to know how low the wage and how long the hours were for the Third World worker who made them. Likewise, if Vicky is taking care of a two-year-old six thousand miles from her home, we should want to know what is happening to her own children.

If we take this third approach, what should we or others in the First World do? One obvious course would be to develop the Philippine and other Third World economies to such a degree that their citizens can earn as much money inside their countries as outside them. We would then change the social logic that underlies the care drain. Then the Vickys of the world could support their children in jobs they'd find at home. While such an obvious solution would seem ideal—if not easily achieved—Douglas Massey (1998), a specialist in migration, points to some unexpected problems, at least in the short run. In Massey's view, it is not underdevelopment that sends migrants like Vicky off to the First World but development itself. The higher the percentage of women working in local manufacturing, he finds, the greater the chance that any one woman will leave on a first, undocumented trip abroad. Perhaps these women's horizons broaden. Perhaps they meet others who have gone abroad. Perhaps they come to want better jobs and more goods. Whatever the original motive, the more people in one's community migrate, the more likely one is to migrate too.

If development creates migration, and if we favour some form of development, we need to find more humane responses to the migration such development is likely to cause. For those women who migrate in order to flee abusive husbands, one part of the answer would be to create solutions to that problem closer to home—domestic-violence shelters in these women's home countries, for instance. Another might be to find ways to make it easier for migrating nannies to bring their children with them. Or as a last resort employers could be required to finance a nanny's regular visits home.

A more basic solution, of course, is to raise the value of caring work itself, so that whoever does it gets more rewards for it. Care, in this case, would no longer be such a 'pass-on' job. And now here's the rub: the value of the labour of raising a child—always low relative to the value of other kinds of labour—has, under the impact of globalization, sunk lower still. Children matter to their parents immeasurably, of course, but the labour of raising them does not earn much credit in the eyes of the world. When middle-class housewives raised children as an unpaid, full-time role, the work was dignified by its aura of middle-classness. That was the one upside to the otherwise confining cult of middle-class, nineteenth- and early-twentieth-century American womanhood. But when the unpaid work of raising a child became the paid work of child-care workers, its low market value revealed the abidingly low value of caring work generally—and further lowered it.

The low value placed on caring work results neither from an absence of a need for it nor from the simplicity or ease of doing it. Rather, the declining value of childcare results from a cultural politics of inequality. It can be compared with the declining value of basic food crops relative to manufactured goods on the international market. Though clearly more necessary to life, crops such as wheat and rice fetch low and declining prices, while manufactured goods are more highly valued. Just as the market price of primary produce keeps the Third World low in the community of nations, so the low market value of care keeps the status of the women who do it—and, ultimately, all women—low.

One excellent way to raise the value of care is to involve fathers in it. If men shared the care of family members worldwide, care would spread laterally instead of being passed down a social class ladder. In Norway, for example, all employed men are eligible for a year's paternity leave at 90 per cent pay. Some 80 per cent of Norwegian men now take over a month of parental leave. In this way, Norway is a model to the world. For indeed it is men who have for the most part stepped aside from caring work, and it is with them that the 'care drain' truly begins.

In all developed societies, women work at paid jobs. According to the International Labour Organization, half of the world's women between ages 15 and 64 do paid work. Between 1960 and 1980, 69 out of 88 countries surveyed showed a growing proportion of women in paid work. Since 1950, the rate of increase has skyrocketed in the United States, while remaining high in Scandinavia and the United Kingdom and moderate in France and Germany. If we want developed societies with women doctors, political leaders, teachers, bus drivers, and computer programmers, we will need qualified people to give loving care to their children. And there is no reason why every society should not enjoy such loving paid childcare. It may even be true that Vicky Diaz is the person to provide it—so long as her own children come with her or otherwise receive all the care they need. In the end, we need to look to Article 9 of the United Nations Convention on the Rights of the Child (1989)—which notes that a child 'should grow up in a family environment, in an atmosphere of happiness, love and understanding', and 'not be separated from his or her parents against their will...' Article 9 sets out an important goal for the world order, for the United States, and for feminism. It says we need to value care as our most precious resource, to notice where it comes from and to care where it ends up. For, these days, the personal is global.

Arlie Hochschild is a professor of Sociology at the University of California at Berkeley. She is the author of seven books including The Managed Heart, The Second Shift, The Time Bind *and* The Commercialization of Intimate Life. *She has edited, with Barbara Ehrenreich,* Global Woman: Nannies, Maids and Sex Workers in the New Economy.

Notes

[1]   In 1997, I lived for six months in Trivandrum, in the state of Kerala, India, as a

Fulbright Scholar, a state in which many men and women worked abroad, especially in the Arabian Gulf. But it was not until I read Parreñas' dissertation on careworkers that I was moved to reflect on love as a form of gold, interview Philippina and Thai nannies living in Redwood City and San Jose, California and reflect on this form of psychological colonialism. I was also very moved by the film 'When Mother Comes Home for Christmas', directed by Nilita Vachani. On the whole, until very recently there has been little focus on a 'care drain', even among academics who focus on gender issues. Much writing on globalization focuses on money, markets and male labour. Much research on women and development, on the other hand, has focused on the impact of 'structural adjustments' (World Bank loan requirements that call for austerity measures) and deprivation. Meanwhile, most research on working women in the United States and Europe focuses on the picture of a detached, two-person balancing act or the lone 'supermom', omitting child-care workers from the picture. Fortunately, in recent years, scholars such as Evelyn Nakano Glenn (1986,1991, 1994), Janet Henshall Momsen (1999), Mary Romero (1992, 1997), Grace Chang (2000) and Pierrette Hondagneu-Sotelo (1992, 1997, 2001) have produced important research on which this article builds (see Arlie Hochschild 2000; Ehrenreich and Hochschild 2003). Many thanks for research assistance to Bonnie Kwan.

[2] Also see the Technical Symposium on International Migration and Development, the United Nations General Assembly, Special Session on the International Conference on Population and Development, The Hague, The Netherlands, June 29–July 2, 1998, Executive Summary, p. 2. See also *Migrant News*, 2 , (November 1998), p.2.

References

Ariès, P. (1962) *Centuries of Childhood: A Social History of Family Life*, New York: Vintage Books.

Castles, S. and M. J. Miller (1998) *The Age of Migration: International Population Movements in the Modern World*, New York and London: The Guilford Press.

Chang, G. (2000) *Disposable Domestics: Immigrant Women Workers in the Global Economy*, Cambridge, MA: South End Press.

Ehrenreich, B. and A. Hochschild (eds.) (2003) *Global Woman: Nannies, Maids and Sex Workers in the New Economy*, New York: Metropolitan Press.

Frank, R. (2001) 'High-paying nanny positions puncture fabric of family life in developing nations', *Wall Street Journal*, December 18.

Glenn, E. N. (1986) *Issei, Nisei, War Bride: Three Generations of Japanese American Women in Domestic Service*, Philadelphia: Temple University Press.

Glenn, E. N. (1991) 'From servitude to service work: historical continuities in the racial division of paid reproductive labor', *Signs: Journal of Women in Culture and Society*, 18, 1, 1-43.

Glenn, E. N., G. Chang and L. Forcey (eds.) (1994) *Mothering: Ideology, Experience, and Agency*, New York: Routledge.

Grieder, W. (1997) *One World, Ready or Not: The Manic Logic of Global Capitalism*, New York: Simon and Schuster.

Hays, S. (1996) *The Cultural Contradictions of Motherhood*, New Haven: Yale University Press.

Hochschild, A. (1997) *The Time Bind: When Work Becomes Home and Home Becomes Work*, New York: Metropolitan Books.

Hochschild, A. (2000) 'The nanny chain', *American Prospect,* January 3.

New York Times (2001) September 1: A8.

Hondagneu-Sotelo, P. (1994) *Gendered Transitions: Mexican Experiences of Immigration,* Berkeley: University of California Press.

Hondagneu-Sotelo, P. (2001) *Doméstica: Immigrant Workers Cleaning and Caring in the Shadow of Affluence,* Berkeley: University of California Press.

Hondagneu-Sotelo, P. and E. Avila (1997) 'I'm here, but I'm there: the meanings of Latina transnational motherhood', *Gender and Society,* 11, 5, 548-571.

Massey, D. (1998) 'March of folly: U.S. immigration policy after NAFTA', *The American Prospect, 37,* 22-33.

Momsen, J. H. (1999) *Gender, Migration and Domestic Service,* London: Routledge.

Parreñas, R. S. (1999) 'The global servants: (im)migrant Filipina domestic workers in Rome and Los Angeles', Ph.D. dissertation, Department of Ethnic Studies, University of California, Berkeley.

Parreñas, R. S. (2001) *Servants of Globalization: Women, Migration, and Domestic Work,* Stanford, CA: Stanford University Press.

Romero, M. (1997) 'Life as the maid's daughter: an exploration of the everyday boundaries of race, class, and gender', in M. Romero, P. Hondagneu-Sotelo and V. Ortiz (eds.), *Challenging Fronteras: Structuring Latina and Latino Lives in the U.S.,* New York: Routledge, 195-209.

Romero, M. (1992) *Maid in the U.S.A.,* New York: Routledge.

Wong, S. C. (1994) 'Diverted mothering: representation of caregivers of color in the age of "multiculturalism"', in E. Nakano Glenn, G. Chang, and L. R. Forcey (eds.), *Mothering: Ideology, Experience and Agency,* New York: Routledge, 67-91.

Zlotnik, H. (1999) 'Trends of international migration since 1965: what existing data reveal', *International Migration,* 37, 1, 22–61.

United Nations Convention on the Rights of the Child (1989) Annex GA Res. 44/25 Doc. A/Res/4425. Adopted 20 November. Online: http://www.unhchr.ch/html/menu3/b/ k2crc.htm.

II.

FEMINIST ORGANIZING:

NATIONAL, REGIONAL AND GLOBAL FRAMES

GLOBAL POLITICS
AND TRANSNATIONAL FEMINISMS

JAN JINDY PETTMAN

Transnational feminist politics is both a response to and a part of contemporary global politics. This article focuses on the changing international context, opportunities, and constraints for transnational[1] feminist politics. It begins with the moment of opportunity provided by the end of the Cold War, and a review of these politics through the remarkable series of international conferences—beginning with the 1985 World Conference on Women in Nairobi and culminating in the ten-year follow-up conference in Beijing in 1995—which provided impetus and fora for developing transnational feminisms. Ironically, by the time of the Beijing conference, these transnational feminisms were already under threat, both from intensifying globalization/neo-liberalism, and from rising exclusivist, often religious or identity-based, politics. The combined effects of these threats led some feminists to caution against holding a fifth international women's conference, lest the tentative gains of the decade from Nairobi to Beijing be lost. The events of 9/11 and the consequent 'war on terror' precipitated another dramatic change in international politics, re-staging global militarism, border protection and hard masculinity. These threats further undermined the possibilities for transnational feminist politics—even as they made such politics all the more urgent. The article concludes by asking how best can we theorize, and practice, transnational feminist politics in the face of these contemporary forces.

Here I focus on a particular site of transnational feminist politics, the international conferences and networks that developed around them in the two decades from the mid-1970s, facilitated in part by the particular configuration of international politics and economy.[2] I argue that the conditions that were benign or even conducive through the first years of the 1990s were already deteriorating by the mid-90s, and have deteriorated further since 9/11. These changed international politics severely test feminists and other progressive forces. However, the growth of transnational women's movements and particular campaigns and politics against the forces of globalization, exclusivist identity politics and global militarism offer valuable lessons, resources and strategies for continuing to build transnational feminist politics. Some of those lessons are included here.

Building Transnational Feminisms and Women's Politics

Transnational women's organizing has a long history including, for example, in opposition to war and in support of women's suffrage. From the mid-1970s especially, second-wave women's movements and anti-colonial struggles generated international networks and claims, in particular through a series of women's international conferences and the related Women-in-Development (WID)/Gender in Development (GAD) movement. The 1985 Nairobi conference is noted for the emergence of strong southern networks and voices, among them the launch of Development Alternatives with Women for a New Era (DAWN), a southern feminist network dedicated to analysis and advocacy for gender and economic justice (Sen and Grown 1987). It marked the emergence of an international women's movement, with rapidly gathering momentum, experiences, contacts, language and know-how in international politics. It encouraged the development of 'women's machinery' in government and some international agencies. It made visible (though usually still marginal) attention to women, or less likely to gender relations, in development and other policy issues and political campaigns. While the texture and shape of women's movements, and of explicitly feminist politics, varied across place and sector, 'women' became increasingly active players in international, especially United Nations (UN) related, politics. They were accorded a (limited) place as a constituency, or more often added as a problem or victim group that needed (selective) attention.

In the process, many women organized, and women's international NGOs and networks flourished. The politics around WID became emblematic of the gains, and dangers, of engaging in international politics, in the international politics of development and aid. The WID field revealed very different understandings of women's lives, gender justice and social change, only some of them feminist (Moser 1992). There was radical potential within a focus on inequality, and more particularly on empowerment of women. However, other approaches, including treating women as problems or victims to be dealt with or saved, reproduced existing gender relations. Strategic arguments that women were a valuable resource for development were easily appropriated into national and international agency developmentalist objectives. However, Sarah White (1999) warns us against too easy a classification and characterization of these different strands. An NGO in the South 'might represent the same program as welfare to its national government, as efficiency to multilateral donors, and as empowerment to a more radical northern NGO' (124).

Kate Young (1997) usefully distinguishes the potentially transformative move from WID to GAD. GAD in its more radical form enabled a focus on gender relations, as social constructions, and struggled over. It saw women as agents, with knowledge of their own lives. It offered a holistic view, contextualizing gender along with other power relations. It problematized development and questioned who gains, who pays, and what kinds of development might be good for women (which women?). A variety of approaches could be utilized, including to make spaces, or win funding, within the ultimate goal of transformation. It meant moving away from easy, piecemeal solutions to recognize the market-dominated nature of contemporary economics and power relations. This move pushed GAD politics beyond those specifically marked women or gender issues to macroeconomics and international politics more broadly. It warned, too, that even once elaborated, tested and circulated, any new language was subject to appropriation by others, including anti-feminists. To be transformative, then, necessitated robust feminist theory and politics. Furthermore, it required a thoroughgoing recognition that institutions, including the market, are gendered, that they produce gender, and have their own gender interests (Goetz 1997).

'Empowerment' is another key contest that is struggled over between feminists (Kabeer 1999; Parpart, Rai and Staudt 2002). It, too, is regularly appropriated by others to blunt its feminist and political edge and to displace responsibility onto those less powerful. Such concepts, like the shift to GAD and its multiple political uses, exemplified crucial issues in transnational feminist politics. Keys include: the struggle for a new and more effective conceptual and political language, identifying what the problem is, and whose problem it is; devising strategies and identifying targets; opening spaces for action and alliance-building; and guarding against the appropriation and domestication of such language that marks resistance to gender justice (or to social or administrative change more generally). Along the way, many conversations, networks, workshops, reports, friendships, conflicts and solidarities helped build alternative, feminist imaginings for the future. They also marked the emergence of what Maila Stivens (2000) would later call a global feminist public.[3]

Post Cold War Transnational Politics

The abrupt and largely unanticipated (by international relations and international politicians) end of the Cold War ushered in a brief moment of opportunity in the fluidity and confusion of the changing global scape. In this moment, the UN initiated a series of international conferences to map that scape and its role within it. This moment offered, at the most optimistic reading, a more felicitous environment for those seeking new ways of being in the world. The 1991 Gulf War and the break up of the former Yugoslavia—initially seen as a throwback to old wars, but in hindsight a harbinger of the new wars of the '90s and the new millennium—provided deadly reminders that militarism and its gendered dangers were still with us. However, much international attention and activism in the mid-1990s focused on new social movement, including women's, advocacy. Transnational feminist politics gained momentum, and mobilized around women's body rights and wrongs, in particular violence against women, reproductive rights, and sexuality (Pettman 1997). Here, UN sponsored international conferences of the early to mid-1990s were catalytic in building transnational feminisms. There were however deep divisions and different feminist 'takes' on these and other issues, including around sex tourism and international trafficking in women (Kempadoo and Doezema 1998; Pettman 2003a), and indeed on the desirability of devoting feminist energy to international fora and governments at all.

The International Conference on Environment and Development held in Rio de Janeiro in 1992 marked the emergence of visible women's caucuses and concerns in a 'mainstream' international conference. It generated new international non-governmental organizations (INGOs) and networks that facilitated growing feminist engagement in the prepcoms and politics of later UN conferences. The World Conference on Human Rights in Vienna in 1993 saw the spectacular staging of the Vienna Tribunal and became the site of sustained and effective feminist intervention. It named violence against women as the most common crime globally, even though experienced in different forms and given different meanings in particular locales. That conference was also crucial in the assertion that women's rights are human rights, joining feminist politics to existing internationalist doctrines and understandings.

Jutta Joachim examined the outcomes of Vienna in terms of the 'political opportunity structure in which international women's organizations were embedded' (1999: 143), which provided a window for placing issues to do with gender violence on the international agenda. She identified crucial resources and strategies in transnational feminist politics around such violence. Building on previous international conferences and their networks, transnational feminists could draw on accumulating documentation. For example, ISIS International was formed in 1974, to create opportunities for women's voices to be heard, strengthen feminist analyses through information exchange, promote solidarity and support feminist movements across the globe. By the early 1990s, transnational feminists were more experienced in dealing with UN and state officials and modes. They worked to legitimize the issues as international responsibilities, and urged particular understandings that underscored a gender analysis and also provided linkages with UN discourse. They developed 'mobilizing structures' including the use of organizational entrepreneurs and gender experts (Joachim 2003). They worked to develop an international constituency around these issues, making allies, and publicizing their positions. They were helped by the contemporary international political climate, including recent groundbreaking attention to war rape in the former Yugoslavia, and the adoption of gender reports and focus by other international advocacy groups like Amnesty International.

These transnational learnings and networks facilitated a major impact on the 1994 International Conference on Population and Development in Cairo. As always, there were deep divisions amongst feminists on the problems, the language, and the necessary strategies to tackle sexuality and reproductive issues internationally. But feminist politics at Cairo shifted the international language from population debate and unmet needs, to reproductive rights, sexuality rights, and empowerment. Sonia Correa and Rosalind Petchesky (1994) provide an illustration of transnational feminist intervention in the lead-up to Cairo. They sketch the development of a language that is women-centred, moving beyond population, family, national and ethnic forms, and insist on a gender analysis that identifies which women can make what kinds of reproductive choices. They 'define the terrain of reproductive and sexual rights in terms of power and resources' (1994: 222), bringing in an international political economy approach that assesses enabling conditions for reproductive choice. They make connections between sexuality, human rights and development, against government and agency-feigned reluctance to involve themselves with 'family' matters (while recognizing that states and other patriarchal institutions take a great interest in sexuality and reproduction). They challenge the devastating effects of globalization, neoliberalisms and structural adjustment programs (SAPs) that further reduce women's opportunities and resources. They recognize differences amongst and between women too. At the same time they refuse the patriarchal 'cultural alibi'.

It is important to distinguish between the feminist principle of respect for difference and the tendency of male-dominated governments and fundamentalist religious groups of all kinds to use 'diversity' and 'autonomy of local cultures' as reasons to deny the universal validity of women's human rights. (Correa and Petchesky 1994: 118)

They cite cases of good practice, where 'women's assertion of their particular needs and values, rather than denying the universal application of rights, clarifies what those rights mean in specific settings' (Correa and Petchesky 1994: 118).[4]

Campaigns around violence and reproduction, in which international conferences figured strategically, reveal the accumulated learnings of and offer models for transnational feminists. Many of these are familiar to feminists engaged in national and local struggles, though adapted to the complicated political, diplomatic and administrative arenas of the international. They include challenging the public/ private divide, which in international politics is doubly removed through the barrier of sovereignty and states' rights; resisting trivializing and rationalizing while expanding definitions of politics and political responsibility in international fora; respecting women's own experiences and developing ways to voice those experiences in the removed and reified international meeting places; respecting cultural diversity and (as) politics, locating issues, claims and strategies within social context, whilst refusing to give women over to cultural/national uses.

Especially in the decade 1985-95, the UN-sponsored international conferences functioned as crucial sites for feminist networking, lobbying, knowledge-making, and for building solidarities. DAWN describes them as 'a niche' for their transnational analysis and advocacy, and for alliance building (Slatter 2001). We could debate whether these gatherings and their attendant webs and flows amount to an international women's movement. And they do prompt questions concerning who participates, who is heard, and whose understandings are authorized. These conferences and the politics around their staging can also overshadow the myriad organizing and struggles at more local levels, including in dire and dangerous circumstances. In feminist politics around international conferences, questions of representation and voice are especially pertinent. So too are the ways that 'difference' is perceived and practiced, erased or denied. Clearly women's experiences of violence or reproduction or sexuality, for example, depend in part on their nationality, location, class, race/ethnicity, age and other factors, mediated in complex ways through surrounding cultural politics and government and other institutional practices. Transnational feminisms are themselves part of the struggle over the theoretical and political complexities of balancing difference with the need to develop specific women's and gendered politics internationally (Grewal and Caplan 1994; Mackie 2001).

North-South divides were central in early international women's conferences, but by the mid-1990s Bina Agarwal could argue that 'among women's groups there is growing recognition of the importance of forging strategic links. One could say "romantic sisterhood" is giving way to strategic sisterhood for confronting the global crisis of economy and polity' (1995: 9).

While issues of difference, diversity and power relations are always present amongst transnational feminists too, shared politics and global connections were significantly replacing romantic (and imperialistic) sisterhood.[5] While this shift represented hard learnings, in theory and practice, around difference, it also reflected changed international circumstances. For as transnational feminists politicked, the international politics that was their milieu was already changing. The Cairo conference signals a new moment, for there for the first time a substantial anti-feminist coalition mobilized against the gains of the preceding years and ongoing feminist struggles (Otto 1996; Joachim 2003). By the 1995 Beijing conference these reactive forces were powerfully placed, and much feminist effort was required to hold the line rather than consolidate and extend outcomes. By the 2000 Beijing+5 Review, the momentum had fallen away. Feminist activists were poorly represented, and the Review was marked by exclusions and back-downs. Intensifying globalization and identity-based exclusivist international politics confronted women everywhere, and put a premium on making common cause against shared opponents and costs.

Caught in the Crunch: Between Globalization and Fragmentation

Transnational feminist politics is significantly shaped by changing international political economy, the context within which these politics are pursued, and the cause, often, for their organizing. The early '90s were relatively open internationally, and different social movements, including transnational feminists, seized the opportunities (often inadvertently) offered. By the mid-1990s however, feminist politics were confronting a devastating pincer movement that threatened to cut the ground from beneath them (Pettman 2004). In Cairo and Beijing there was increasing recognition of the damaging, and gendered, effects of globalization, especially in its neo-liberal and SAP forms. And around both conferences reactionary political forces mobilized with the explicit aim of defeating feminist and women's rights goals and organizations internationally.

The post Cold War period was widely characterized as 'new times' in which the market dominated. The global victory of the West/democracy/liberal capitalism appeared to remove viable alternatives for organizing society and economy. Globalization especially in its neo-liberal manifestation in formerly designated first world, in 'transition' or ex-second world economies and through SAPs in third world states, followed similar patterns.[6] These included opening up the economy through trade liberalization, deregulation of financial and economic policies, priority to the market, competition and profit, and cutting back on 'unproductive' expenditure including welfare and state support for social reproduction (Scholte 2000; Peterson 2002). These dramatic changes represented a shift from public to private, from often inadequate but hard-won social responsibility and funding, and generated a crisis in reproduction that fell most heavily on women. They also reduced the political space and available language for rights and justice claims (Brodie 1994). 'The state' was often seen as rolling back, giving up on its more social mandates, and acting more as an agent or subcontractor for global capital. It became increasingly unclear where power did reside, and what therefore were appropriate targets and strategies for action. However, with power and wealth increasingly globalized, a global response from progressive forces, including transnational feminisms, became imperative.

Feminist critique revealed globalization as having gendered impacts; further, as being itself a gendered process, and affecting gender relations, including family forms and notions of work (Marchand and Runyan 2000; Peterson 2002; Pettman 2003a; Rai 2002). Women were already positioned differently in terms of work, in a sexual division of labour within and beyond the household. In addition to their primary domestic and care responsibilities, many women made complicated negotiations to cross the public/private boundaries, and compensated for the reduced social and welfare expenditure. Feminized employment in these sectors was also often cut. Meanwhile the changing global division of labour led to growing demand for casualized, poorly paid and often vulnerable labour on the global assembly line and in an increasingly transnational provision of sexual and domestic services (Pettman 2003b). These often involved labour migration, which in turn affected family form and gender relations. These 'gender realignments' led to reactionary gender politics, including new masculinisms and familialist asser-tions, mostly secular in, for example, former East Europe, but increasingly religiously fused in some Middle East states and the US

Globalization both stimulated and facilitated global feminisms, including those organizing specifically against the gendered and antisocial impacts of neo-liberalism/SAPS. Once again, feminists were confronted with complex and contested theoretical and political terrain. Women were often presented as victims, exploited by capital, states and patriarchal families and employers. Their further incorporation into the emerging global political economy was urged upon governments, donors and employers, by international financial institutions who now saw women as resources to be harnessed, a logical extension of the 'efficiency' approach to WID. Feminists struggled with issues around exploitation and liberation. Some women opted for factory employment as more congenial than domestic service, and others opted for migration as domestic workers, including in some cases to escape oppressive or violent families, and/or with a sense of adventure or possibility that confused more dour academic and NGO campaign tellings (Pettman 2003b). Some women gained from the exploitation of other women; highly educated and English-speaking women enjoyed a mobility and remuneration denied to their poorer sisters (though those marked by non-dominant race/ethnicity still faced difficulties beyond those of gender alone).

In these challenging and increasingly global times, transnational feminists struggled to make sense of the macroeconomics and power politics behind globalization, whilst also paying close attention to their manifestations in particular places and relations (Slatter 2001; Sen and Madunago 2001). Reviewing her ground-breaking 'Under Western Eyes' (1986) Chandra Mohanty remarks:

> I now see the politics and economics of capitalism as a far more urgent locus of struggle... global economic and political processes have become more brutal, exacerbating economic, racial, and gender inequalities, and thus they need to be demystified, re-examined, and theorized. (2003: 509)

Now she is pursuing 'an anticapitalist transnational feminist practice' (2003: 509), seeing 'antiglobalization as a key factor for feminist theorizing and struggle' (2003: 517). Increasingly, others too are responding to these 'new new times'. They are organizing, developing their own transnational practice through links across borders, and borrowing from and contributing to documenting women's own experiences. Increasingly, global technologies, especially email and the web, facilitated these knowledges and connections. Global technologies stimulated new kinds of transnational feminist solidarity, 'weaving the web' and 'building interconnections of meshworks and glocalities among women's groups' (Harcourt, Rabinovich and Alloo 2002: 42; see also Harcourt 1999).[7]

The anti-globalization movement, though often masculinist or disregarding of gender, questioned the inevitability, and the desirability, of market economics and restructuring/SAPs. Meanwhile, globalization's impact and anti-globalist reactions extended well beyond feminist and other democratic and progressive movements. State legitimacy in some regions was further undermined by the loss of Cold War alliance props and by the worsening living circumstances of poorer people and women and children in particular.[8] Globalization and western capitalist dominance also stimulated anti-modern movements that focused on women and family as emblematic of the struggle for good, or god, or identity. Rising coercive national, ethnic or religious-based politics trapped women in familiar roles, as reproducers of the community, as markers of cultural identity, as weak links in border defences (Yuval-Davis 1998). Women were largely, and often forcibly, constrained within roles as victim or those for whom men must fight, igniting the dangerous burden of protection.

The 'new wars' (Kaldor 1999) frequently fought to coincide territory and identity. They were fuelled by transnational linkages, through exiles, grievances, arms trade and 'foreign' fighters, aid and instructors. They utilized new technologies and techniques in dirty wars, where the distinction between combatants and others were even less clear, and where the everyday, and women's bodies, were part of the war zone. These politics made all dissent, and links outside the community, suspect or dangerous. They reduced the political spaces to examine and challenge gender relations, and enforced (supposedly) traditional gender roles.

In the new wars and identity exclusivities, women were not only victims. Some women were agents in the new causes, including against other women. Others struggled against the new mobilizations and exclusions (Moghadam 1994; Eisenstein 1996). Some linked into transnational feminist action for peace, and drew on international networks and understandings of gendered violence, the gendered impact of war and gendered agency. As with earlier moves towards a robust GAD, feminist interventions named the gendered division of labour in peace and war, and insisted on the politics of both gender inequality and violence, refusing conservative naturalizations that cast both as inevitable. They contributed theoretical insights and political mobilization to re-vision international identity and conflict politics. One outcome was the 2000 UN Security Council Resolution that urged involving women and gender mainstreaming in all stages and aspects of peace negotiations and resolution.[9]

In these dangerous times, squeezed between global capital, patriarchal states and exclusivist identity politics, the momentum and possibilities of international conferences and transnational networks appeared to be faltering. Transnational feminism seemed both vital, and besieged. In these circumstances, some transnational feminists caution against organizing another international women's conference. For example, DAWN is

> acutely aware of how global conferences can be used to erode earlier agreements.... The current global environment is not at all conducive to advancing gains for women through a new round of inter-governmental negotiations. In DAWN's assessment, the risks of seeing gains made seriously eroded, or, worse, reversed are simply too high. (Slatter 2001: 4)

Transnational Feminisms in the Wake of 9/11 and the War on Terror

Into this already hostile international environment came 9/11, with its devastating violence and loss—though other states and people had experienced horrific and large-scale terror, and wars and political violence haunted many. But 9/11 rapidly became both symbolic and catalytic, globalizing terror and militarized response. Thus, 9/11 and the consequent 'war on terror' marked another dramatic change in global politics, which now confronts transnational feminisms with new challenges (Pettman 2004).

Despite ongoing violence and wars in many states, and ongoing western implication in them, including through the global arms trade and substantial US foreign military bases, western commentators on globalization before 9/11 usually stressed either its economic and/or its culture/communicative dimensions. The world appeared clearly (though deceptively) divided between zones of peace and zones of turmoil. Such representations are at odds with much globalization rhetoric, and distracted from the continuing priority western states gave to 'defence' and security defined in military terms. September 11th and the war on terror foregrounded global militarization, the continued and perhaps increasing significance of the prerogative state, and sovereignty in the sense of border protection. The state had not disappeared, or been emasculated. Rather it had been refashioned as a market-security state, where supposedly open economies were intertwined with government surveillance and intervention within and between states. 'Hard' masculinity was privileged, based on force and power over/dominance relations. States were constructed as bounded, masculine actors, though some were feminized through defeat, occupation or humiliation: gender as always marking and representing power relations more generally (Cohn 1993). International politics were increasingly militarized, masculinized, exclusivist, and violence-based. President Bush's declaration—'either you are with us or you are with the terrorists'—totally denied the politics of ambiguity or multiplicity, intrinsic to transnational feminisms (Charlesworth and Chinkin 2002; Tickner 2002; *IFJP* 2002; Joseph and Sharma 2003. See also Cockburn 2000).

In the short-term, these militarist/patriotic/patriarchal declarations almost erased feminist responses to 9/11 and the 'war on terror'. They spread exclusivist identity demands and compulsory patriotism/loyalty more obviously and powerfully in western states too. The resurgence of the 'clash of civilizations' approach to international politics further obscured divisions within states and faiths, and denied or made suspect links across the borderlines. Deeply anti-democratic and militarized states and anti-state movements dominate the global terrain, and assault the gains and hopes of transnational feminists, among others. Though once again, reactionary forces generate resistances, too.

Feminists have learnt much through the long struggles against violence of all kinds, and for peace. Transnational feminists are well placed to theorize and strategize, to mobilize and lobby to resist these constructions and compulsions, and to imagine more peaceful futures. Over the decade before 9/11 especially, feminists had worked in and documented war zones, taking account of women's experiences and of the gendered politics of war and peace (Nordstrom 1997; Mertus 2001; Waller and Rycenga 2000; Moser and Clarke 2001). They had traced the ways in which international politics and militarism produce, as well as utilize, particular kinds of masculinity, though these are differently raced and classed, and also contested (Enloe, 2000; Zalweski and Parpart 1998; Carver 1998). They had scrutinized and resisted the uses of 'women' for anti-feminist purposes, and now decried the sudden expressions of concern for Afghan women in the wake of 9/11 as 'rights of convenience' (Enloe 2002: 13). They contested American exceptionalism and supposed victimization, seeking to internationalize political attention and to recognize international complicity with, or disregard of, gendered violence in other locations. Once again, they critiqued notions of security that privileged the military option, and legitimized violence. They called for situated and contextualized—and gendered—readings. They utilized and nurtured the networks and circulating knowledges of women, and proposed other strategies and other ways of being in the world (Pettman 2004).[10]

A Future for Transnational Feminisms?

DAWN names the evils which hurt women most and which obstruct the realization of the kind of world we envision as: globalized greed, militarism and patriarchal fundamentalism, in all its diverse but related forms. (Slatter 2001: 5)

Similarly, Mohanty describes the new scape in terms of the rise of transnational financial and other institutions like the World Trade Organization (WTO), the rise of religious fundamentalisms, the profoundly unequal 'informational high-way' and increasing militarization and masculinization of the globe. She believes 'these political shifts to the right, accompanied by global capitalist hegemony, privatization, and increased religious, ethnic, and racial hatreds, pose very concrete challenges for feminists' (2003: 508). This particular concurrence of global politics—global market, and exclusivist, patriarchal and militarized state and anti-state forces—requires the kinds of rigorous, critical, inclusive scrutiny and re-vision that transnational feminisms offer at their best.

Already, economic globalization has unintentionally brought many North, South and former East feminists closer together to critique and resist gendered globalization. Rising fundamentalisms and exclusivist identity politics joined right-wing movements against women's rights and transnational feminisms, and were met in turn with feminist counter-challenge. So too global militarism both confronts and is confronted by feminists organizing for non-violent international, state and social relations. The 'triad' of contemporary global politics—capital, exclusivist identities and militarism—presents a powerful, anti-feminist, scape. While feminists have accumulated considerable knowledge, networks and strate-gies relevant to resisting each of these domains of dominance, so too are other critiques and resistances becoming more visible. Part of the challenge to transnational feminists, then, is to grapple with analysis, develop practice and connections that enable inclusive, transversal feminist politics (Yuval-Davis 1999). The odds are daunting, but the very severity of the times compels the closest feminist attention, energy, commitment and solidarity.

Jindy Pettman is Convenor of Women's Studies and Professor in International Relations at the Australian National University. She was founding co-editor of the International Feminist Journal of Politics. *Her publications include* Worlding Women: A Feminist International Politics *(Routledge, 1996). Her current research interests include gender and globalization in Asia, and gender in the 'war on terror'.*

Notes

1 I use transnational in preference to international, reserving the latter for state-to-state or interstate relations. 'Transnational' here indicates the range of connections which over-flow states, or pass between different groups and people in different states. These connections are often both a response to globalization and changes in states' mandates, and also utilize new global technologies and identities. See, for e.g., Grewal and Kaplan (1994); Eschle (2001); Bysteydzienski (2001); Mackie (2001); Pettman (2003a).

2 My focus here is not on debates amongst feminists and others on the relative strengths and shortcomings of individual conferences, though some of these debates are briefly noted in terms of my interest in the transnational politics around, and of, these conferences.

3 Vera Mackie utilizes notions including transnational publics and counter-public, and then adapts Ben Anderson's 'imagined communities' to describe trans-national feminism's affiliations (cited in Mackie 2001). Chandra Mohanty explores difference within notions of cross-cultural feminist work that presume a common feminist political project. She declares her commitment 'to building a noncolonizing feminist solidarity across borders' (2003: 503).

4 See Brooke Ackerly's article in this collection for an elaboration of these learnings; the special issue of *Development* (2002) revisiting body/place, and how globalization plays out in particular localities; and Alldred (2002) as another example of place-based critique.

5 Hopefully moving towards what Nira Yuval-Davis calls transversal feminism (1999). See also Mohanty's 'complication/solidarity' model (2003: 520)

6 Indeed, the disruption of the (already inadequate) characterization of the Cold War world as three worlds—first or welfare/liberal capitalism, second or state-socialist, and third or development states—is one way of figuring globalization. In this sense, the world is now 'post-development'. What that makes of GAD, and how formerly separate development studies (focusing on the 'third world') and international political economy (centering on the first) is another issue. See, for e.g., Pettman 2003a.

7 Though the web itself is fused with global and national inequalities. See, for e.g., Jain, in this collection.

8 There is always a danger of subsuming 'children' under 'women', and not gendering the category 'children', either (Nordstrom 1997). Note lately increasing use of the expression and focus 'women and girls'.

9 Unevenly played out on the ground, as the current near-invisibility of women, beyond the victim/boundary marker, in Afghanistan and Iraq; some way in East Timor and more again in Kosova for example (Charlesworth and Wood 2001; Mertus 2001; Pettman 2004).

10 There are now many feminist responses to 9/11 and the war on terror available in print

or on the web. These include the *International Feminist Journal of Politics* 2002; Tickner 2002; Charlesworth and Chinkin 2002; Joseph and Sharma 2003.

References

Ackerly, B. (2001) 'Women human rights activists as cross-cultural theorists', *International Feminist Journal of Politics* 3, 3, 311-346. [Reprinted here pages 285-312]

Agarwal, B. (1998) 'Environmental management, equity and ecofeminism: debating India's experience', *Journal of Peasant Studies*, 25, 4, 55-95.

Agarwal, B. (1995) 'Beijing women's conference: from Mexico '75 to Beijing '95', *Mainstream*, 49, 9-10.

Alldred, P. (2002) 'Thinking globally, acting locally: women activists' accounts', *Feminist Review*, 70, 149-163.

Brodie, J. (1994) 'Shifting the boundaries: gender and the politics of restructuring', in I. Bakker (ed.), *The Strategic Silence: Gender and Economic Policy*, London: Zed Books, 46-60.

Bysteydzienski, J. (ed.) (2001) *Forging Radical Alliances Across Difference: Coalition Politics for the New Millenium*, London: Rowman and Littlefield.

Carver, T. (1998) 'Gendering international relations', *Millennium*, 27, 23, 43-51.

Charlesworth, H. and M. Wood (2001) 'Mainstreaming gender in international peace and security: the case of East Timor', *Yale Journal of International Law*, 26, 313-317.

Charlesworth, H. and C. Chinkin (2002) 'Sex, gender and September 11', *The American Journal of International Law*, 96, 600-605.

Cohn, C. (1993) 'War, wimps and women: talking gender and thinking war', in M. Cooke and A. Wallacott (eds.), *Gendering War Talk*, Princeton: Princeton University Press, 227-246.

Cockburn, C. (2000) 'Women in Black: being able to say neither/nor', *Canadian Women's Studies/les cahiers de la femme*, 19, 4, 7-10.

Correa, S. and R. Petchesky (1994) 'Reproductive and sexual rights: a feminist perspective', in G. Sen, A. Germaine and L. C. Chan (eds.), *Population Policies Reconsidered*, Harvard: Harvard University Press, 108-123.

Development (2002) Special issue: Place, Politics and Justice: Women Negotiating Globalization, 45, 1.

Eisenstein, Z. (1996) *Hatreds: Racialized and Sexualized Conflicts in the 21st Century*, New York: Routledge.

Enloe, C. (2000) *Maneuvers: the International Politics of Militarizing Women's Lives*, Berkeley and Los Angeles: Univeristy of California Press.

Enloe, C. (2002) 'Forum: the events of 11 September 2001 and beyond', *International Feminist Journal of Politics*, 4, 1, 103.

Eschle, C. (2001) *Global Democracy, Social Movements and Feminism*, Boulder, CO: Westview Press.

Feminist Review (2002) Special issue on Globalization, 70.

Goetz, A. M. (1997) *Getting Institutions Right for Women in Development*, London: Zed Books.

Grewal, I. and C. Kaplan (eds.) (1994) *Scattered Hegemonies: Postmodernity and Transnational Feminist Practices*, Minneapolis: Minnesota University Press.

Harcourt, W. (ed.) (1999) *Women@Internet: Creating New Cultures in Cyberspace*, London: Zed Books.

Harcourt, W., L. Rabinovich and F. Alloo (2002) 'Women's networking and alliance building: the politics of organizing in and around place', *Development,* 45, 1, 42-47.

International Feminist Journal of Politics (IFJP) (2002) 'Forum: the events of 11 September 2001 and beyond', 4, 1, 95-115.

ISIS International. Online: www.isiswomen.org.

Joachim, J. (2003) 'Framing issues and seizing opportunities: the UN, NGOs and women's rights', *International Studies Quarterly,* 47, 247-274.

Joachim, J. (1999) 'Shaping the human rights agenda: the case against violence against women', in M. Meyer and E. Prugl (eds.), *Gender Politics and Global Governance,* New York: Rowan and Littlefield, 142-160.

Joseph, A. and K. Sharma (eds.) (2003) *Terror, Counter Terror Women Speak Out,* London: Zed Books.

Kabeer, N. (1999) 'Resources, agency, achievements: reflections on the measurement of women's empowerment', *Development and Change,* 30, 2, 435-363.

Kaldor, M. (1999) *New Wars and Old: Organized Violence in a Global Era.* Stanford, CA: Stanford University Press.

Kempadoo, K. and J. Doezema (eds.) (1998) *Global Sex Workers: Rights, Resistance, and Redefinition,* New York: Routledge.

Mackie, V. (2001) 'The language of globalization, transnationality and feminism', *International Feminist Journal of Politics,* 3, 2, 180-206.

Marchand, M. and A. S. Runyan (eds.) (2000) *Gender and Global Restructuring,* London: Routledge.

Mertus, J. (2001) 'Grounds for cautious optimism', *International Feminist Journal of Politics,* 3, 1, 93-103.

Moghadam, V. (ed.) (1994) *Identity Politics and Women: Cultural Reassertions and Feminisms in International Perspective,* Boulder, CO: Westview Press.

Mohanty, C. T. (2003) "Under western eyes' revisited: feminist solidarity through anticapitalist struggles', *Signs,* 28, 2, 499-537.

Moser, C. (1992) 'Gender planning in the third world: meeting practical and strategic needs', in R. Grant and K. Newland (eds.), *Gender and International Relations,* Milton Keynes: Open University Press, 83-121.

Moser, C. and F. Clarke (2001) (eds.) *Victims, Perpetrators or Actors? Gender, Armed Conflict and Political Violence,* London: Zed Books.

Nordstrom, C. (1997) *A Different Kind of War Story,* Philadelphia: Philadelphia University Press.

Otto, D. (1996) 'Holding up half the sky … the Fourth World Conference on Women', *Australian Feminist Law Journal,* 6, 7-28.

Parpart, J., S. Rai and K. Staudt (eds.) (2002) *Rethinking Empowerment in a Global/Local World,* London: Routledge.

Peterson, V. S. (2002) 'Rewriting (global) political economy as reproductive, productive and virtual (Foucauldian) economies', *International Feminist Journal of Politics,* 4, 1, 1-30.

Pettman, J. J. (2004) 'Feminist international relations after 9/11', *Brown Journal of World Politics,* 10, 2, 85-96.

Pettman, J. J. (2003a) 'Gendering globalization in Asia through miracle and crisis', *Gender, Technology and Development,* 7, 2, 171-187.

Pettman, J. J. (2003b) 'International sex and service', in E. Kofman and G. Youngs (eds.), *Globalization: Theory and Practice,* London: Continuum, 157-173.

Pettman, J. J. (1997) 'Body politics: international sex tourism', *Third World Quarterly,* 18, 1, 93-108.

Rai, S. (2002) *Gender and the Political Economy of Development,* Cambridge: Polity Press.

Scholte, J. A. (2000) *Globalization: A Critical Introduction*, London: Macmillan.

Sen, G. and C. Grown (1987) *Development, Crises and Alternative Visions: Third World Women's Perspectives*, New York: Monthly Review Press.

Sen, G. and B. Madunago (2001) 'Between globalization and fundamentalism: gender justice in the Cairo+5 and Beijing +5 Reviews', *DAWN Informs*, November, 1-8.

Slatter, C. (2001) 'Tensions in activism: navigating the global spaces at the intersections of state/civil society and gender/economic justice', paper presented to the Gender and Globalization in Asia and the Pacific: Feminist Revisions of the International Workshop. Canberra: Australian National University, 22 November.

Stivens, M. (2000) 'Introduction: gender politics and the re-imagining of human rights in the Asia Pacific', in A. Hilsdon, V. Mackie and M. Stivens (eds.), *Gender Politics and Human Rights in Asia and the Pacific*, London: Routledge, 1-36.

Tickner, J. A. (2002) 'Feminist perspectives on 9/11', *International Studies Perspectives*, 3, 4, 333-350.

Waller, M. and J. Rycenga (eds.) (2000) *Frontline Feminisms: Women, War and Resistance*, New York: Garland Publishing.

White, S. (1999) 'Gender and development: working with difference', in V. Jabri and E. O' Gorman (eds.), *Women, Culture and International Relations*, Boulder, CO: Lynne Reinner, 117-135.

Young, K. (1997) 'Planning from a gender perspective: making a world of difference' in N. Visvanathan (Co-ordinator), L. Duggan, L. Nisonoff and N. Wiegersma (eds.), *The Women, Gender and Development Reader*, London: Zed Books, 51-54.

Yuval-Davis, N. (1998) *Gender and Nation*, London: Sage.

Yuval-Davis, N. (1999) 'The "multi-layered citizen": citizenship in the age of "glocalization"', *International Feminist Review of Politics*, 1, 1, 119-137.

Zalweski, M. and J. Parpart (eds.) (1998) *The 'Man' Question in International Relations*, Boulder, CO: Westview Press.

FEMINIST NETWORKS, PEOPLE'S MOVEMENTS AND ALLIANCES

LEARNING FROM THE GROUND

DEVAKI JAIN

Networking has been a special feature of the feminist movement and reflects in many ways the ideals of the feminist method—flexible and non-hierarchical arrangements to bring collective perspectives to issues and to give collective voice. However, networks and newsletters, alliances and coalitions seem to have reached a stage, to use corporate language, of flooding the market.

Given the flood of these 'informal' connectivities, and given that there is a deep concern about the unipolarity of the current political landscape and about the march of the new 'empire' (Jain 2003; Roy 2004) across the globe, there is need for these networks and coalitions to hammer out some philosophical, if not ideological basis, some minimal purpose, to respond to the current environment.

Women's networks need to mobilize at the global level around a few issues which legitimise 'women' and 'women's identity' and simultaneously call attention to women's influence as a lobby. They need to identify one or two poles around which to politicize the women's movement so that their power as a global force is asserted significantly. There are many local struggles such as the powerful 'sit-ins' of women in Nigeria against oil pipelines and in Colombia against narcotic mafia to mention only a very few. These appear on the global screen, are applauded by vibrant networks but they cannot be sustained or enlarged in space to overpower the empire. It is necessary to build an ideological solidarity and institutional mechanisms to be able to support such local efforts more effectively; to sustain and enlarge the space women have occupied in many 'local' places, so that they encompass the public and political sphere to the full.

Networks are thus a necessary but not a sufficient condition by themselves of bringing women's collective strength together to bear on society and on the state. They need a political premise and purpose, even a mass base to be able to effectively transform.

Between 1975 and 1990 many feminist networks were born which enabled women to build international alliances as well as develop a deeper knowledge base for their struggle for rights.[1] However this is not enough. As knowledge becomes broad-based and diverse due to the increasing availability of internet technology around the world, there is a fragmentation of the space earlier used by the networks for their advocacy work. This seems to have diluted their actions and weakened their impact compared to earlier decades when they were first formed.

This paper touches on some significant achievements involving women's networks while pointing to the slow melt-down of the early participatory and solidarity-building movements. It suggests that the central role of these networks is being lost to people's movements that, nevertheless, need the support of the networks to mobilize at the global level.

Network Values

Networking as a conscious form of organizing has emerged for many reasons, both pragmatic and value-based. The pragmatic considerations have been a recognition that the global problems of today have to be countered on an international scale and that networking improves the effect, visibility and efficacy of the people involved in advancing a cause.

Networks are powerful instruments for working for social change. Their strength lies in their exceptional ability to enhance and deepen critical thinking and creativity through dialogue and exchange; to address global problems by joining forces to take global action; to transcend isolation and strengthen local action; to link local organizing efforts and structures to international ones, to facilitate participation; and to be flexible and respond quickly to new and changing situations.

Feminist networks are based on and validate the belief that coming together and sharing experience, knowledge and information, is by itself useful. They tend to avoid the traditional pyramidal structures that do not allow expression of those who are 'lower' down; they strive to be inclusive and bring people together for common causes while respecting diversity. Networks also imply a reciprocity. They are a coming together of allies; an achieving of 'social synergy'.

They have managed to sustain processes which allow space for evolution, for accommodating difference, for converging and dispersing, for engaging in dialogue and collective decision-making. Platforms are built on issues that cut across differences and on viewpoints or quests that seem to echo widespread anxiety or inspiration. Sally Baden and Anne Marie Goetz (1998), in their assessment of the 1995 Fourth World Conference on Women in Beijing state:

> The creation of coalitions between groups with very different interests certainly seemed to be taking place in Beijing, with for example a broad alliance on reproductive rights between north and south women, which allowed for rather different interpretations of these rights.

Women's Networks

In the last 25 years, hundreds of women's networks have mushroomed: some on specific issues such as health, for example, the International Women's Health Coalition (IWHC); some region-based such as the Association of African Women for Research and Development (AAWORD); some inter-regional on gender and development like Development Alternatives for Women in a New Era (DAWN); some based on class or occupation such as Peasant Women's Groups and Home-workers Network (HOMENET); and some on religion (Islamic Women's Association), on race (Black women's groups), etc. There are networks for law, for economy, for women studies, for peace. And these are on the ground, formulating policies and doing advocacy at regional and international levels.

There are international networks to protect the rights of people who live along the banks of rivers, there are committees to protect rivers from the assault of development. These networks not only mutually reinforce each other, but have been able to hold back some of the most powerful world agencies. For example, during the three-year process (1997-2000) of the World Commission on Dams (2001) it was the international networks of river peoples, indigenous people, natural resources rights groups that 'encircled' the Commission and ensured that the end product was just, and grounded in principles of human development. Other examples include ISIS's campaign on baby food products, which finally led to the placement of a 'warning' label on all baby food products that 'breast milk is best' for the health of an infant (Cabrera-Balleza 1998) and the mobilization by the International Women's Tribune Center, to gather signatures to present to the Chinese government protesting against the selective issue of visas for the 1995 Fourth World Conference on Women in Beijing.

In India, for example, in different parts of the country, women's organizations network at the local and national level taking up a variety of activities and campaigns. They also collaborate with women in the community and the elected women in the *panchayats* (local councils of self-government). For example, two groups of women in a district in Kerala managed by 'networking' to link their production with demand in the district, thus overcoming the problem local women's groups usually have of finding customers for their products (Jain 2002a).

Challenges

What needs to be recognized though is that none of these considerable successes of women's networks have reduced the misery, or redressed the exclusions and oppressions endured by women. In fact, data worldwide show that there is an increase in domestic violence against women (Jain 1998). In India, for example, there are higher and more virulent dowry demands and of course higher incidences of sex-selective abortions (Bhan 2001; Census of India 2001). The improvements in women's lives referred to in *The World's Women 2000* publication are segmented and highly sectional and minimal. Masses of girls, women and female children, worldwide, are under assault. A number of studies and surveys—by United Nations' organizations, as well as other sources emerging at the end of the millennium—reveal this downslide.

Rural women are primary victims of hunger and poverty despite their being crucial partners in combating these problems and achieving global food security, says a Food and Agriculture Organization (FAO) (1995) review:

The most disadvantaged population in the world today comprises rural women in developing countries, who have been the last to benefit—or negatively affected—by prevailing economic growth and development processes. Gender bias and blindness persist; farmers are still generally perceived as 'male' by policy-makers, development planners and agricultural service deliverers.

UNESCO's *World Culture Report 2000*, also emphasizes inequality, in this case the impact of inequality of access to resources, political power, information and the media, on people's capacity to make choices, which in turn is the true capability to exercise rights. The report underscores the fact that women often experience this unequal access due to inhibitors linked or attributed to cultural practices.

The World Health Organization's A-Z of ailments, the *International Classification of Diseases,* gives a code to 'extreme poverty' and calls it the world's most ruthless killer. The 'world's most ruthless killer' is coded as Z59.5. It has meant 'widening gaps between rich and poor, between one population group and another, between age groups and *between the sexes*' [emphasis mine] (van der Gaag 1995: 1; WHO 1995).

It has caused more suffering to more people than anything else on earth. And it has got worse over the last ten years. Despite improvements in education and health, for hundreds of millions of women, Z59.5 has meant lives lived closer to the edge than before. Beneath the rhetoric of 'post-feminism' and 'equality between the sexes' lies another, more sinister, phenomenon.

In a study carried out over twenty years up to 1990, 'the number of rural women in poverty has increased by 50 per cent, reaching an awesome 565 million, while that of men has grown by 30 per cent to about 400 million' (Jazairy qtd. in van der Gaag 1995). The poverty problem is not confined to the Majority World. In the United States, almost half of all poor families are supported by women with no spouse present, and their average income is 23 per cent below the official poverty line (van der Gaag 1995).

There are 110 women per 100 men in households in the poorest expenditure/income quintile. Difference decreases as income increases. These results indicate that in general there are more women than men in poor households. In half of the data sets from Africa and two-thirds of the data sets from southern and southeastern Asia, women are over represented among the poor. Data from 41 countries which account for 84 per cent of the total rural population in developing countries indicate both growing numbers and proportions of women among the rural poor since the mid-1960s (Jazairy, Alamgir and Panuccio 1992; Buvinic 1995).

Women's networks may examine the best practices and the mechanisms that allow networking and learn from and support each other; they may exercise their brilliant minds and develop even deeper analyses. But Rome is burning. The solidarity really has to speak to a larger world that is on the border of ruination due not only to economic and social degradation and environmental abuse, but also to the revival of bigoted attitudes of the Dark Ages including anti-woman venom (Jain 2002b). These views are a total negation of feminism which is built on pluralism and multiple identities, not the divisive 'categorizing of the population of the world into those belonging to the Islamic world, the Christian world, the Hindu World' (Sen 2001) noted by many including Amartya Sen (2001) and Arundhati Roy (2001).

The understanding of women's networks as 'enabling' women has to shift to an emphasis on their role as mobilizing, generating and consolidating women's opinions on national and global issues such that women's struggle toward macro-transformation will ultimately protect them at the micro-level. In the twenty-first century, there is a need to build up women as an opinion lobby with some transactional power either through numbers via votes or through ideas, money or moral power. Networking to keep in touch, by itself, is not enough. Opinion-building and translating this into a political force is beginning to emerge as one of the most critical elements of informing and generating change. But the challenge is to build up greater solidarity politically. The need, therefore, is to turn the networks into transnational political actors with sustained input into the political process and the ability to keep cross-national interests alive.

The very flexibility which is so much a factor in women's networking success can also be a weakness in achieving focused action. As Catherine Hoskyns has noted with respect to the European Women's Lobby's ability to influence the European Lobby,

> On one hand the women's lobby has provided focus and articulate spokes-women, and good sources of information; on the other it has experienced difficult problems with internal democracy, representation and efficiency. The danger is that fluidity and diversity are traded for structure and coherence. (Hoskyns and Newman 2000)

Another challenge for feminists is that it has often been strategic combinations of women that have opened the spaces for women. For example women in government delegations, together with women officials within the Secretariat, and women in the non-governmental organizations (NGOs), can collude, to engineer a desirable outcome. This has been called the *velvet triangle,* a metaphor to capture the three major actors/groups typically involved in gender/women's politics: first, *femocrats* and *feminist politicians*; second, *academics* and *experts;* and third, *non-governmental organizations.* However the same three partners can also be the cause for failure. Women who are officials on delegations often do what their governments want and so can become impediments (Woodword 2000).

Some argue that the greater diffusion of information across national and state boundaries produced by information technology, actually makes the state visibly accountable, especially in international forums, for growing and persisting inequalities (Keck and Sikkink 1998). Feminist arguments have gone further to analyze the role of the state as an actor in the enforcement of human rights and to question early attempts to use male standards to define violations of human rights (Sullivan 1994, 1995; Facio 1996). However, feminists have faced contradictory pulls. For example, governments and institutions in the North are, on the one hand, criticized as intrusive and manipulative when they stipulate that aid to the poorer states of the South be granted on conditions of harsh financial reform which often negatively impacts women much more than men. On the other hand, these same governments and institutions in the North are urged to interfere in the policies of aid-recipient states to ensure that women have equal access with men to the benefits of their loans, and to enact sweeping legal reforms to regulate people's activities in the 'private sphere', within families or households as fully as activities in the public sphere. This is to ensure that women have rights as individuals related to the universalization of rights.

Shortcomings

One of the shortcomings of the current global women's movement is that it has often begun to function in a conventional mode. It has become a 'response' to governments and intergovernmental institutions. Government is seen as the main player in transformation and in drawing up national and international initiatives for changes; the women's movement becomes a monitor, a reporter of progress. This is a conventional relationship—it also diminishes responsibility.

It is often said that there is no women's movement, no united social flow toward a purpose, only a large, scattered, diverse set of women-focused organizations. Far from the earlier 1970s when national initiatives for women were in the hands of women, as at the first United Nations Conference on Women in Mexico City (1975) where the broad based women's movement gave birth to itself, today national initiatives are in the hands of government. This is a major backslide.

Strong alliances between mass-based struggles for justice and the women's agenda are not easily seen. In India, for example, mass-based struggles, like that against arrack (native alcohol) in Andhra Pradesh ('Reworking Gender Relations, Redefining Politics' 1993) have not always been adopted by what can be called a national women's movement.

Today economic reform programs, as the structural adjustment policies are euphemistically called, are attacking the worker movements worldwide. In India the trade union movement was and is one of the strong institutions of democracy. However full of warts and patriarchy, it is one of the bulwarks against state and corporate-sector domination. Yet the national or worldwide women's movements do not appear to be taking a global stand against the deconstruction of this institution. There are many examples of such isolation from mass-based struggles, often led by women but dealing with natural resources. For example, Medha Patkar spearheads the movement against big dams and for the conservation of natural resources (D'Souza 2002). Aruna Roy spearheads the right to information movement in India, for political transparency (cited in Srivastava, Dey and Mishra 2001); Ela Bhatt for rights of home-based workers to legal protection (Jhabvala 2001); Vandana Shiva (2001) for rights over the seed. Yet the visible feminist movement neither collaborates nor voices these demands.

The struggle against racism has much to teach us, as we have to teach those struggling against racism (Jain 2000). The myths are in the mind and the politics is to sustain those myths. A highly political feminist movement, very broad-based, with alliances with other oppressed classes is necessary for the revolution that is needed to stop the careless crimes against women.

Changing the condition of women—the hardships they face whether through poverty or basic discrimination—requires monumental change in the social perceptions of woman, across caste, class, ethnicity and other differences. Studies are showing that owning assets, bringing in income, being educated, even women being equal to men according to social indicators like the Gender Development Index (GDI) or Gender Empowerment Measure as in Kerala in India (*National Human Development Report 2001*), does not reduce rates of violence against women or dowry death nor the basic disregard which makes an adult or adolescent male rape a girl child even if she is a relative or a neighbour.

For this long march to begin what is needed is political mobilization of women, united, even if temporarily, by their sex. We then have to move out of the conventional grip of the 'arrival hall'. Most movements when they gain self-confidence and shape think that being the subject of governments' consideration is an achievement, and the arrival hall, and lobbying for a conference document becomes the consuming energy.

Opportunities

Yesterday's workers' movements and their collective voice are today's people's movements. Workers' movements have had to take a back seat, as much because in economies like India, trade unionized labour represents less than ten per cent of the labour force, as the changing structure of production and trade systems worldwide have blurred, as well as dampened, working-class culture. As trade unions and cooperatives are weakened as a source of strength and voice for the larger masses of the less privileged, people's movements must be seen as the institutional vehicles for carrying the voices of the masses into public debate and policymaking. The left movements have also been marginalized by world events, as well as being weakened by injustice within, criticized by women, the blacks and coloured, the *dalits* and minorities.

The space for the voices of the oppressed once occupied by the left and the unions is then available, and in the last decade or two is being filled by people's movements all over the world, North and South. But people's movements by definition do not have the institutional structure that political parties and trade unions have. They do not have a space in states' institutional framework nor do they come under any legal framework. They are fluid and this enables them to be inclusive as well as broad-based and massive in numbers. But it also demands from them unity of purpose which in turn requires shared knowledge and clarity—attributes of efficiency. These movements need to be taken seriously by agencies of the state and society as the most vital safeguards to democracy and the best means for sustaining democratic spaces outside of the often suffocating conventional structures.

It is only extensive ideological-driven networking—a collaboration with people's movements and more importantly, the coalescing of diverse and dispersed efforts that can channel the flow of resources toward the marginalized, the masses, the poor.

The institutional frameworks that develop at intermediary levels will be the ultimate test of the networking and advocacy skills. Success at this level will determine whether the dispersed initiatives can come together over a period of time to coalesce into structural transformation, or die in the wilderness.

For the Future

Experience reveals and teaches that poverty is a political issue (Jain 1997b; Malloch Brown 2002). Poverty eradication cannot take place unless political institutions are built that represent the voices of the poor, and those institutions become vote banks that, in turn, transform the political leadership to be representative of the poor. The women's movement is the most effective, possibly the least tarnished, and the most united across divides of political and social forces in the world today. Hence, it is the ideal vehicle to spearhead transformation and poverty eradication. Not surprisingly, women today lead the many mass-based significant social and economic rights movements in India. For women, democratic spaces are even more crucial, as their resistance to oppression from family, culture and patriarchy requires open spaces with firmly embedded laws that safeguard individual rights (Jain 1997a). At the state and national levels women are engaged in drafting modifications to the *People's Representation Act* (Kishwar 2003) and other details of electoral reform. Electoral politics has found vibrant support in India, as evidenced by the million-strong force of local women politicians, historically subordinated castes, and minorities. The populace has benefited from the freedoms and inbuilt checks of democracy.

Treatises have been written, by Nobel laureate Amartya Kumar Sen (1999), among others, showing that unless the voices and strength of collective public action are included as a shaping element in our economic models, there is no way of generating equity with development. This is the political element in economics—the space for negotiation in making the choices at the macro level.

Thus, it is time to move beyond the report card approach which focuses on measuring government performance, such as following up the Platform for Action (PFA) adopted at the United Nations Fourth World Conference on Women in Beijing or the Millenium Development Goals (MDG) decided on in Geneva in 2004. Instead, a platform of ideas and practices emerging from large-scale women's actions in the world can be built which would teach and move the UN and the Bretton Woods Institutions (BWI's) toward a revised, reconstructed agenda.

It would be useful to identify one or at most two issues especially affecting poor women around the world that the global women's movement could rally behind. The idea is to move from mobilizing as a negotiating agency, to mobilizing as a social force that commands attention by its very presence and ethics. Unified action always has a better chance of winning than twenty scattered activities. A one-point program of full employment, using that lens to critique everything under the sun, might make a dent. Networks need a goal, a single-minded purpose, that they can use at all levels.

When Gandhiji picked up a fistful of salt from the beaches of Gujarat (Desai 1995), he was not trying to give free salt to the people of India. It was a symbol, an idiom of political assertion, but in a language, a vocabulary that represented the masses of people, not the elites. When President Mandela said in his inaugural speech, we want bread, water and salt it was not that he wanted to limit the lifestyle of his people to bread with salt and water—it was to signal the aspirations of the masses and to use a vocabulary which was representative of both political assertion and identification with the deprived. Imagine if these actions and words had been interpreted in their literal sense? That Gandhiji wanted to literally give free salt or that Mandela only wanted bread with salt and water for his people? How absurd it would have been! Imagine if Gandhiji's salt, *satyagraha*, had not fired the imagination of Indians and opened the flood gates of the movement for freedom. What a loss to the grammar and method of politics and most of all to democratic processes which attempt to move the state toward justice.

What the international NGO movement needs is a fistful of salt, a symbolic unifying gesture to roll back the overwhelming force of the current paradigm of development, not through essays and articles but through international solidarity on one public action.

Devaki Jain is a development economist. Graduating from Oxford, she taught Social Accounting, Public Finance and Statistics in Delhi University (1958). She held Fellowships at the Universities of Harvard, Boston, Sussex and the Scandinavian Institute of Asian Studies, Copenhagen. She received an Honorary Doctorate from University of Westville, Durban. In recognition of her efforts toward promoting the advancement of women and gender equality, she received the United Nations Development ment Programme's Bradford Morse Memorial Award at the United Nations World Conference on Women held in Beijing in 1995.

Notes

[1]   These networks include the African Women's Development and Communication Network (FEMNET); Asia Pacific Women Law and Development (APWLD); Asian Women's Human Rights Centre (AWHRC); Association of African Women for Research and Development (AAWORD); Center for Women's Global Leadership: (CWGL); CLADEM (Latin American Committee for the Defence of Women's Rights); Development Alternatives with Women for a New Era (DAWN); Gender and Science and Technology Association (GASAT); Global Campaign for Women's Human Rights; International Women's Health Coalition (IWHC); International Women's Rights Action Watch (IWRAW); International Women's Tribune Centre (IWTC); ISIS International; KARAT Coalition (regional network) Central and Eastern European Countries; TWAEMAE; Women in Law and Development in Africa (WiLDAF); Women Living Under Muslim Laws (WLUML); Women's Environment and Development Organisations (WEDO); Women's Global Network for Reproductive Rights.

References

Baden, S. and A. M. Goetz (1998) 'Who needs [sex] when you can have [gender]? conflicting discourses on gender at Beijing', in C. Jackson and R. Pearson (eds.), *Feminist Visions of Development: Gender Analysis and Policy,* New York: Routledge, 19-38.

Bhan, G. (2001) *India Gender Profile,* Report commissioned for Sida, Report No. 62, BRIDGE, Brighton, Institute of Development Studies.

Buvinic, M. (1995) 'The feminization of poverty? Research and policy needs', in J. B. Figueiredo and Z. Shaheed (eds.), *New Approaches to Poverty Analysis and Policy II: Reducing Poverty Through Labour Market Policies,* Geneva: International Labour Organization.

Cabrera-Balleza, M. (1998) 'Clarifying the issues: stories developed from WABA's breastfeeding women and work seminar in Manila', *Women in Action,* 3. Online: http://www.isiswomen.org/wia/wia398/eco00005.html.

Census of India (2001) Online: http://www.censusindia.net.

Development Alternatives for Women in a New Era (DAWN). Online: http://www.dawn.org.fj.

Desai, N. (1995) *The Fire and the Rose,* Ahmedabad: Navjivan Publishing House.

D'Souza, D. (2002) *The Narmada Dammed: An Inquiry Into the Politics of Development,* New Delhi: Penguin.

Facio, A. (1996) 'What will you do? women's human rights', excerpts, statement by Center for Women's Global Leadership, 13 September 1995, *Women's Studies Quarterly,* 1 & 2, 66-68

Food and Agriculture Organization (FAO) (1995) *FAO Plan of Action for Women in Development: Cultural Diversity, Conflict and Pluralism,* Twenty-eighth Session 20 October-2 November. Online: http://www.fao.org/docrep/x5585E/x5585e00.htm

Hoskyns, C. and M. Newman (eds.) (2000) *Democratizing the European Union: Issues for the Twenty-first Century,* Manchester: Manchester University Press.

Jain, D. (2003) 'The empire strikes back: a report on the Asian Social Forum', in J. Sen, A, Anand and P. Waterman (eds.), *World Social Forum: Challenging Empires,* New Delhi: The Viveka Foundation, 289-292

Jain, D. (2002a) 'Negotiating feminist space', paper presented at the conference 'Globalism and Localism', Ferrara University and Modena University, 20-22 May.

Jain, D. (2002b) 'The value of particular to the general', paper presented at the conference 'South Asia and the United Nations', United Nations University, Tokyo, 26 May.

Jain, D. (2000) 'Gender inequity as racism', *The Hindu*, 23 September.

Jain, D. (1998) 'Need of the hour: political response to violence against women–perspective from India', paper presented at the Southern African Development Community (SADC) conference on 'Violence Against Women', Durban, 5 March.

Jain, D. (1997a) *For Women to Lead ... Ideas and Experience from Asia*, New York: United Nations Development Programme (UNDP).

Jain, D. (1997b) 'The poverty thing (or this thing called "poverty")', paper presented at a special event of United Nations Development Programme), New York, May 20.

Jazairy, I., M. Alamgir and T. Panuccio (1992) *The State of World Rural Poverty: An Inquiry Into its Causes and Consequences.* New York: IFAD.

Jhabvala, R. (2001) 'Sewa and home-based workers in India: their struggle and emerging role', paper presented at the technical workshop on Indigenizing Human Rights Education in Indian Universities, Karnataka Women's Information and Resource Centre, Bangalore, December.

Keck, M. W. and K. Sikkink (1998) *Activists Beyond Border: Advocacy Networks in International Politics.* Ithaca, NY: Cornell University.

Kishwar, M. (2003) 'An alternative women's reservation Bill', *The Indian Express*, March 18. Online: http://www.freeindiamedia.com/women/31_march_women.htm.

Malloch Brown, M. (2002) 'Foreword', *Human Development Report 2002*, New York: United Nations Development Programme (UNDP).

National Human Development Report 2001 (2002) New Delhi: Planning Commission, Government of India.

'Reworking gender relations, redefining politics: Nellore village women against arrack.' (1993) *Economic and Political Weekly*, Jan. 16-23.

Roy, A. (2004) 'The new American century', *The Nation*, 9 February. Online: http://www.thenation.com/doc.mhtml?i=20040209&s=roy.

Roy, A. (2001) *The Algebra of Inifinite Justice,* New Delhi: Viking.

Sen, A. (2001) 'Exclusion and inclusion,' paper presented at the inaugural conference on 'Including the Excluded,' arranged by South Asians for Human Rights, New Delhi, 12 November.

Sen, A. (1999) *Development As Freedom*, New York: Anchor Books.

Shiva, V. (2001) 'Globalization and environment', paper presented at an international Conference organized by Navadanya, New Delhi India International Centre, New Delhi; 29 September to 1 October.

Srivastava, K., N. Dey and N. Mishra (2001) 'Taking democracy forward: the right to information movement in Rajasthan', paper presented at the technical workshop on Indigenizing Human Rights Education in Indian Universities, Karnataka Women's Information and Resource Centre, Bangalore, December.

Sullivan, D. J. (1995) 'The public/private distinction in international human rights law', in J. Peters and A. Wolper (eds.), *Women's Rights, Human Rights: International Feminist Perspectives*, New York: Routledge. Online: www.rdg.ac.uk/law/femlegalnet/international.htm.

Sullivan, D. J. (1994) 'Women's human rights and the 1993 World Conference on Human Rights', *The American Journal of International Law*, 88, 152-67.

The World's Women 2000: Trends and Statistics (2000) New York: United Nations.

Woodward, A. (2000) 'Building velvet triangles: gender in EU policy making', paper in revision from European Consortium for Political Research 28th Joint Sessions Copenhagen, April.

World Commission on Dams (2001) *Dams and Development: A New Framework for Decision-Making*, London: Earthscan Publications Ltd. Online: http://www.dams.org.

World Culture Report 2000 (2000) UNESCO Publishing, Online: www.upo.unesco.org/books.asp.

World Health Organization (WHO) (1995) *World Health Report 1995: Bridging the Gaps*, Geneva: World Health Organization. Online: http://www.iwhc.org.

van der Gaag, N. (1995) 'Women: still something to shout about', *New Internationalist*, 270, Online: http://www.newint.org/issue 270/270keynote.html.

FEMINISM, PEACE, HUMAN RIGHTS AND HUMAN SECURITY

CHARLOTTE BUNCH

Generalizations about women and peace are difficult, especially for a white US American who has not experienced war first-hand, but whose government has conducted countless military operations around the globe. What I do hope to do here is to raise some questions that come from struggling from that location to be simultaneously a feminist, human rights and anti-war/anti-imperialist activist.

Acknowledging when and where we enter is a central tenet of feminist inquiry. Questions of women and war/peace are very particular, having to do with the specificity of each conflict—of time, place, race, ethnicity, class, religion and other discrete circumstances—as well as related to various social constructions of gender, of masculinity and femininity. In that sense peace and the relation of women to war is a very local issue. And yet, women and war/peace is also a very universal subject discussed in a variety of ways for centuries. Throughout the twentieth century, and especially with the intensification of globalization and the rise of religious and ethnic fundamentalisms, feminists have found it useful to make cross-cultural comparisons, to share analysis and strategies, as well as to build international solidarities for peace. There is a dynamic tension between the universality of this subject and the need for global action by feminists on the one hand, and the necessity of being grounded in the particulars of each situation and not overlooking real differences among women on the other.

Peace, Human Rights and Gender

First, what do we mean by or expect when we talk about peace? Most women's peace activism springs up around particular conflicts and does not begin with a plan for world peace. But we must ask what are the conditions necessary for a permanent peace to be achieved. We should look at the existing regional and international structures for peace-making and peace-keeping, like the United Nations (UN), and at the assumptions of the men who created them to see if those assumptions—like the emphasis on national sovereignty—are a sound basis for peace. We must ask what it will take to en-gender these structures and transform them into more effective vehicles in the quest for peace, security and human rights for all. Otherwise, women will always be re-acting to patriarchal wars.

We face these questions today in a difficult context, made more complex by the events of September 11th in the US and their aftermath. We have seen the most extensive development of nuclear, biological and other weapons of mass destruction in the last half century that would seem to serve as a sufficient argument for why global structures to ensure peace are now a necessity for human survival rather than just a desirable vision. But rather than being more peaceful, we entered the twenty-first century with many unresolved civil and ethnic conflicts and an increasingly militarized daily life where the lines between civilians and combatants seem ever murkier. We have sophisticated local and global terrorisms, a rise in the political use of religious extremism, an expanding arms trade led by the world's one remaining super-power, and the structural violence of the widening economic gap between haves and have-nots.

Indeed, one compelling argument for women playing a greater role in peace building and governance today is the perception that women could hardly make a bigger mess of the world than male leadership has done over the past centuries.

In this turbulent time, what then do women make of peace? The first aspect of peace is an end to violent/armed conflict—the absence of war—or what is called 'Negative Peace'. But this is not enough to ensure that armed conflict will not arise again nor does it address questions of what is needed to end all forms of violence—militarization, the structural violence of racial and economic injustice, or the ongoing violence against women in daily life.

'Positive Peace', on the other hand, is a term used to describe an 'alternative vision' that leads to the reduction of all forms of violence in society and moves toward the 'ideal of how society should be' ('Women Building Peace Campaign of International Alert' cited in Pankhurst and Anderlini 2000). It is also concerned with justice and the larger dynamic of domination or power over 'the other' as a mode of human interaction.

Indicators of the conditions of justice and equity that comprise positive peace are spelled out in the UN Universal Declaration of Human Rights (UDHR), whose framers in 1948 saw the promotion and protection of human rights as critical to preventing genocide and war in the future. The UDHR spells out broad principles of both political/civil rights and socio-economic human rights that constitute a considerable commitment to justice, development and equality as the basis for positive peace. While we know these rights are not the world reality and their pursuit has been misused, nevertheless, movements seeking justice around the globe have continued to utilize the concept of human rights and the vision embodied in the UDHR as standards that their governments and the international community should uphold.

Feminist perspectives of positive peace build on the expanding world of human rights concepts and practice. Demanding the protection and promotion of the human rights of all as a central tenet of peace-building helps to ensure that inequities must be addressed and that peace should not be purchased at the price of simply allowing the prevailing military powers to have their way. Human rights principles also demand that the pursuit of justice not allow for the impunity of war criminals after a peace accord is reached.

Central to feminist conceptualizations of peace and human rights is the recognition of a continuum of violence against women, in which all forms of violence are seen as interrelated. The institutionalization of male dominance is maintained by violence and the threat of violence and leads us to question whether the term 'peacetime' provides an accurate description of the lives of most women. As two South Asian feminists noted when responding to the question of whether feminism disrupts 'peaceful' homes, 'one person's peace can be another's poison' (Bhasin and Khan 1986).

War and armed conflict bring additional violation to women's lives, but these are linked to the gender-based violence and abuse of women in 'normal' life. Thus, violence against women in war brings together the subordination of females with their membership in other targeted groups, expresses women's status as the property of the men in their community, and reflects social acceptance of violations of women more generally.

Further, when violence is tolerated in an everyday way in the family at the core of society, children come to see violence as an inevitable part of conflict and a natural way to deal with differences in all areas of the social order. Thus ending the violence of militarism, war and racism is tied to ending violence in the home. These are mutually reinforcing forms of violence that must be challenged simultaneously.

While it is primarily women activists and feminist theorists from all regions of the world who have pioneered work on the gendered nature of war and conflict (e.g. Boulding 1995; Cock 1991; Enloe 2000; Matsui 1999; Menon 1998; Reardon 1993; Sharoni 1995), one 'scientific' study by a male political scientist is of interest here. Joshua Goldstein has sought to show why there is so much cross-cultural consistency in gendered war roles, even when there is great diversity of cultural forms of both war and of gender roles when considered separately. He concludes what many feminists have contended that gender and war are inextricably linked: 'Gender roles adapt individuals for war roles, and war roles provide the context within which individuals are socialized into gender roles. For the war system to change fundamentally, or for war to end, might require profound changes in gender relations. But the transformation of gender roles may depend on deep changes in the war system' (Goldstein 2001: 6-11).

Human Security vs. National Security

The term 'human security' has come into greater use recently as a way to describe an integrated vision of positive peace, human rights, and development. The United Nations Development Program (1994) *Human Development Report,* as well as United Nations Secretary General Kofi Annan in his *Millenium Report* (2000), speak of security less as defending territory, more in terms of protecting people. Non-govermental organizations (NGOs) have called for redefining security in terms of human and ecological needs instead of national sovereignty and borders. This requires a new social order that ensures the equal participation of marginalized groups, including women and indigenous people, restricts the use of military force, and moves toward collective global security (*Hague Agenda for Peace and Justice in the 21st Century* cited in Hill and Ranson 2001).

Rita Manchanda notes: 'the human security discourse has come up from below, from peoples and groups excluded from the national security debate, defined and articulated by civil society groups, social movements and marginal groups, especially women' (2001: 1). This term has emerged as an alternative to the state centered concept of 'national security', rooted in the military security-defense domain and academically lodged with 'realists' in the field of international relations.

Feminists challenge the military paradigm by asking questions about whose security does 'national security' defend? For example, in looking at East Asia, some have concluded:

> The security treaties ... that provide for US bases, military operations, and port visits in South Korea, Japan, and the Philippines also compromise the security of local people. Negative social effects of the US military presence on host communities include military prostitution, the abuse of local women, and the dire situation of mixed-race children fathered by US military men. (Kirk and Francis 2000: 229)

Wider acceptance of the paradigm of human security holds promise for women, but we know how easily feminist perspectives can become marginalized as a concept becomes more mainstream. For example, a Joint Proposal to Create a Human Security Report from Harvard University and the UN University presented in May of 2001 outlined an ambitious plan to create a report that would map key systemic causes of armed conflict and violent crime as well as a human insecurity index. Yet, while no group lives in greater insecurity than females around the globe, the proposal *never* once mentions women, gender, masculinity, rape, violence against women or any other concept that has emerged out of several decades of feminist work. A similar absence was reflected in a call from *Human Rights Dialogue* for essays on 'Human Rights and Public Security'. Much of the feminist discourse on these issues has never been read by men in the field and can still be overlooked unless women are vigilant about ensuring that the evolution of this concept fully encompasses the female half of humanity.

Efforts to advance peace and the concept of human security were set back by the events of September 11th and the ensuing resurgence of the masculine dominated discourse on defense. Media response to this crisis proved a rude reminder that when it comes to issues of terrorism, war and national security, feminism is not on the map. There was rich discussion about these events among women on the internet, but public commentary in the western media was dominated by male 'authority' figures. Even the UN High Commissioner for Human Rights, Mary Robinson, one of the first to frame a response to 9/11 from the perspective of international law by suggesting justice for this act of terrorism be pursued internationally as crimes against humanity, rather than as a call to war, was quickly side-lined by the US and the UN.

It is women who have been targeted by fundamentalist terrorism in many places from Algeria to the US, and it is mostly feminists from all parts of the world who have led the critique of this growing problem globally. Nevertheless, only when it became convenient for military purposes to discuss the rights of Afghan women did the issues of women and fundamentalism surface in the mainstream media. However, this discussion has not been extended to the rights of women in other conflicts, and non-Islamic fundamentalist attacks on women like those happening in Gujarat, India are not being highlighted. Thus, what could have led to an examination of threats to women's human rights posed by political fundamentalism, terrorism, and armed conflict in many guises was used instead by the US and other western powers to demonize the 'Islamic other' and to justify more militarization of society.

The justification of fighting against 'terrorism' has been used to curtail human rights both in the US and elsewhere. It has also led to an increase in defense budgets in many countries over the past year from the US and Israel to Colombia and the Philippines. Meanwhile the donor countries' pledges at the recent UN Financing for Development World Conference (March 2002) fell far short of what is needed to even begin to fulfill the millennium goals for advancing human security. Thus, human security as a guiding global principle is far from being embraced as a replacement for the nationalist security paradigm.

Since September 11th, governments in all parts of the world have used terrorism as an excuse to jettison commitment to some human rights in the name of fighting terrorism or providing for national or public 'security'. Thus, the newly gained recognition of women's rights as human rights, including rape as a war crime, which is not yet deeply entrenched, is jeopardized by the current rise in militaristic national security discourse and the accompanying eclipse in commitment to human rights. The need for articulating an approach to global security that ensures human rights and human security for all is more urgent than ever in the post-September 11th world.

Women's Role in Peace-Building

One of the areas in which there is the greatest agreement among feminists is about the gendered character of war, militarism and armed conflict and the harm it causes women. Even where there is considerable diversity in the construction of sex roles, what is remarkable is the way in which war still operates in very specific gendered ways, and military forces use and rely on women as critical parts of the war process even as they privilege masculinity. In short, gender matters to war makers and what happens to women is not just an accidental by-product of war or biology. Nowhere is this clearer than in the violence that women experience in war and conflict.

Since militarism is clearly gendered and women are victimized by war, does this mean that women are more peaceful or that peace is feminine? Images of women advocating for peace as those who are more nurturing and non-violent abound from the early twentieth century to the Madres of Plaza de Mayo in Argentina or the Russian Mother's movement. While such images may serve a useful purpose for women in a particular time or place—particularly when these are the only roles in which society gives them legitimacy, they pose a number of problems for feminists claiming equality and agency. Since the human species has experienced so many centuries of social construction of roles based on gender, especially in relation to war, it is probably not possible to determine conclusively whether such traits are inherently biological or not. Therefore, rather than trying to prove or disprove a biological argument, it is more useful to look at the issue of what women bring to peace-building in other ways.

Women play many roles in armed conflict—not only as peacemakers or victims but also as perpetrators and supporters of war. There is a growing body of work addressing the complexity of women's relationships to war and militarism (e.g., Enloe 2000; Moser and Clark 2001; Turshen and Twagiramariya 1998). Too many women commit acts of violence and support men who do so, whether in war or in the family, to say that women as a group are innately non-violent. However, it is also true that men commit the vast majority of acts of violence in the world, both against other men and against women and children—as armed forces, agents of the state and in the private sphere. Therefore it would also be absurd to claim that women and men are equally violent, or that women as a group do not have any proclivities toward resolution of conflicts non-violently—at least within the constraints of a patriarchal world where gender roles equate 'manhood' with toughness under fire and female violence is generally discouraged.

While not all men are violent nor all women peaceful, a world structured by gender has produced real differences in how most men and most women experience war and violence—both as victims and as perpetrators. These gender differences are further complicated by the particularities of each culture and community, making universal generalizations about them difficult, but this does not make 'women' as a political category useless.

As Cynthia Enloe observes:

> To avoid seeing all women as natural allies simply because they are women, then, is crucial for building reliable causal analyses and for crafting effective strategies. However, arriving at this conclusion does not require a person to lose all confidence in the belief that 'women' is an authentic political category

useful in making sense of the causes and consequences of militarization. (2000: 297)

Women peace activists have made creative use of women as a constituency to have significant impact on ending armed conflicts and have courageously intervened between groups of warring men, from Ethiopia and Somalia to South Asia. Having different life experiences than men means that women bring different issues to the table and bring awareness of different needs and different possible solutions to the process. A number of studies have begun to document the specific ways in which women generally have a more cooperative and less hierarchical approach to solving problems and are more inclusive in bringing others into the process, which can lead to giving more people a stake in the peace agreements and compromises reached (Anderlini 2000; Boulding 1995; Cockburn 1998; Moser and Clark 2001).

While women should be part of all aspects of peace processes because of the specific life experiences and perspectives they bring to the table, we must be aware that women are not all the same. Since women's lives are affected by their race, ethnicity, class, sexual orientation, religion, history and culture and other factors, as well as gender, it is important to ensure that women are more than a token presence and that those involved represent diversity in background. From the research that has been done, having more women involved in decision-making does usually matter in the results that will be achieved especially if a critical mass of at least about 30-35 per cent is reached. However, it also matters where those women come from, what their commitment is to women's rights, and what are their overall politics.

The need for women to be part of all aspects of the peace-building process should be self-evident and does not rest on claims to their being innately more peaceful. This is a right that rests on the simple but profound principles of justice and democracy. As half or more of humanity, women have the right to be part of the decision-making on all critical activities that deeply affect their lives. Gender balance, as a democratic principle, should apply to the full range of peace-building activities.

Women's Peace Activism

Women's activism around peace takes many forms, often depending on a group's politics as well its values and life circumstances. In looking at examples of such activism, a variety of dilemmas and questions that feminists concerned with peace face are raised: Are feminists pacifists or do we believe in just wars and liberation struggles? Does holding military forces accountable to the rules of war and integrating women into military forces only strengthen them and reinforce social acceptance of military solutions? Do mothers' movements necessarily reinforce gender stereotypes? What actions can feminists take when society is polarized around male defined or nationalistic options none of which we want to support?

How do feminists who usually create non-formal and often marginal ways of working for peace get taken seriously in the formal peace-making processes?

One of the most significant forms of feminist peace organizing in the last two decades is embodied in efforts by women to cross national and ethnic lines and reach out to women of the 'other' side, as well as to critique their own government or community's position. The issues of nationalism or communalism can be difficult for feminists. Some may feel that their own community oppresses women, but they may still be torn by loyalties to that community in the face of its domination by other forces or simply by virtue of being part of it. The nationalist/communitarian forces will certainly pressure or even try to force women to be loyal, often as symbols of the culture. In some cases, women feel that being a fighter for their group can be a way to prove themselves as political actors with agency. However, for women to play a significant role in ending conflict usually requires standing aside and being critical of nationalism, or at least of how the warring parties are manipulating it. There are a number of examples of women's peace initiatives that have taken this step—in Northern Ireland, Cyprus, Mali, the former Yugoslavia, the Middle East, and across the India-Pakistan border—to name a few. Central to such efforts is women's rejection of the nationalist project of dividing groups along racial/ethnic, religious, and/or cultural lines and dehumanizing 'the other'. In refusing this logic, activists often face violence, repression, or rejection from members of their own communities for being traitors.

Let me end with a few comments about women's global networking for peace. International solidarity has played an important role in sustaining many feminist peace activists, especially when they challenge the dominant nationalist or communalist discourse. Women have supported each other through keeping lines of communication open and accurate information flowing, with money and care packets, with counseling and hand holding, with assistance in escaping difficult situations and finding asylum, with petitions to governments, the UN, and other bodies. Global networking has also achieved a number of important gains in relation to war and armed conflict at the international level.

In the past decade, women's efforts at the UN have led to more attention to women and armed conflict, which became a full chapter of the Beijing *Platform for Action* (UN 1996) and received considerable attention at the Beijing+5 Review in 2000. Women raised the profile of sexual violence in war in the Ad Hoc Tribunals on the former Yugoslavia and Rwanda and made certain that issues of gender-based violence and persecution were incorporated into the Statute of the International Criminal Court. Another major breakthrough was the passage of UN Security Council Resolution 1325 on Women, Peace and Security in October of 2000, which mandates the inclusion of women in all of the peace processes as well as gender mainstreaming into all these activities. The dilemma posed by global networking at the UN is how to ensure that such gains are not simply rhetorical, and that they are implemented effectively in a gender and culture specific way at all levels.

This leads back to the importance of making sure that *women's peace activism is both local and global,* and that the dynamic tension between the universality and specificity of this work is recognized and grappled with continuously. Only through such a process can women's peace activism not only respond to the needs of each situation but also impact the larger global structures creating many of these conflicts so that we can move toward a pro-active vision of positive peace with human rights and human security at its core, rather than continue to be called upon to clean up after the endless succession of male determined armed conflicts.

This article is adapted from a paper written for the 'Women and Peace Panel' at the 'Women, Peace Building and Constitution-Making International Conference', 2-5 May, 2002, Colombo, Sri Lanka.

Reprinted with permission from Canadian Woman Studies/les cahiers de la femme, *22 (2) (Fall 2002/Winter 2003): 6-11.*

Charlotte Bunch, Founder and Executive Director of the Center for Women's Global Leadership at Douglass College, Rutgers, the State University of New Jersey, has been an activist, author and organizer in the women's, civil, and human rights movements for over three decades. Previously Bunch was a Fellow at the Institute for Policy Studies and a founder of Washington D. C. Women's Liberation and of Quest: A Feminist Quarterly. *She is the author of numerous essays and has edited or co-edited nine anthologies including the Center's reports on the Beijing+5 process in 2000 and the World Conference on Racism in 2001. Her books also include two classics*: Passionate Politics: Feminist Theory in Action *and* Demanding Accountability: The Global Campaign and Vienna Tribunal for Women's Human Rights. *Bunch is a Distinguished Professor in the Women's and Gender Studies Department at Rutgers University.*

References

Anderlini, S. (2000) *Women at the Peace Table: Making a Difference,* New York: United Nations Development Fund for Women.

Bhasin, K. and N. Khan (1986) *Feminism and its Relevance in South Asia,* New Delhi: Kali for Women.

Boulding, E. (1995) 'Feminist interventions in the art of peacemaking: a century overview', *Peace and Change,* 20, 4.

Cock, J. (1991) *Colonels and Cadres: War and Gender in South Africa,* Oxford: Oxford University Press.

Cockburn, C. (1998) *The Space Between Us: Negotiating Gender and National Identities in Conflict.* London: Zed Books.

Enloe, C. (2000) *Maneuvers: The International Politics of Militarizing Women's Lives,* Berkeley: University of California Press.

Goldstein, J. S. (2001) *War and Gender,* London: Cambridge University Press.

Hill, F. and P. Ranson (2001) *Building a women's peace agenda: based on discussions at the*

May 1999 Hague Agenda for Peace and Justice in the 21st Century Conference, New York: New York Gender Focus Group of the Hague Appeal for Peace.

Kirk, G. and C. Bowen Francis (2000) 'Redefining security: women challenge US military policy and practice in East Asia', *Berkeley Women's Law Journal,* 15, 229-271.

Manchanda, R. (2001) 'Redefining and feminizing security', unpublished manuscript.

Matsui, Y. (1999) *Women in the New Asia,* London: Zed Books.

Menon, R. (1998) 'Borders and bodies: recovering women in the national interest', in I. Sajor (ed.) *Common Grounds: Violence Against Women in War and Armed Conflict Situations,* Quezon City: Asian Centre for Women's Human Rights, pp.301-338.

Moser, C. O. N. and F. C. Clark (eds.) (2001) *Victims, Perpetrators or Actors? Gender, Armed Conflict and Political Violence,* London: Zed Books.

Pankhurst, D. and S. Anderlini (2000) *Mainstreaming Gender in Peacebuilding: A Framework for Action,* London: International Alert.

Reardon, B. (1993) *Women and Peace: Feminist Visions of Global Security,* Albany: State University of New York Press.

Sharoni, S. (1995) *Gender and the Israeli-Palestinian Conflict: The Politics of Women's Resistance,* Syracuse: Syracuse University Press.

Turshen, M. and C. Twagiramariya (eds.) (1998) *What Women Do in Wartime: Gender and Conflict in Africa,* London: Zed Books.

United Nations (UN) (2000) *We the Peoples: The Role of the United Nations in the 21st Century,* Report of the UN Secretary General Kofi Annan to the Millennium Summit, New York: United Nations.

United Nations (1996) *The Beijing Declaration and The Platform for Action: Fourth World Conference on Women, Beijing, China, 1995,* New York: United Nations Department of Public Information.

United Nations Development Program (UNDP) (1994) *Human Development Report 1994,* New York: Oxford University Press.

UP AGAINST THE STATE

THE WOMEN'S MOVEMENT IN PAKISTAN AND ITS IMPLICATIONS FOR THE GLOBAL WOMEN'S MOVEMENT

NIGHAT SAID KHAN

The government will never allow these modern, westernised women to create a free society.[1]

While the Pakistani women's movement has definite implications for the Asian women's movement and perhaps Africa, Latin America, Europe and women of the diaspora, some may conclude that much of what I say here might not be relevant for North America both academically and in terms of the women's movement. Yet, to a large extent, the onus of a global movement, including a global women's movement, lies with the North since even the combined struggle of the South will not, and cannot, be successful in bringing about global change in what is called the new world order, since this ordering is determined by a handful of countries and significantly by the United States. We in the South can do our best but until the women's movement and feminist academics in the North are also against their respective states and the international world order, we will never see a global women's movement.

To struggle for a global restructuring, for global political, economic and social transformation, for a just and equitable world, we have to reclaim global ideologies that appear to have been discarded. I refer here to Marxism, socialism and feminism—reformulated in the light of the imperatives of the present—but still forming the core of an ideology and a struggle to challenge global capitalism, the supposedly 'free' market, political, social and racial hegemony and of course, patriarchy.

I carry within me the accumulated fatigue of a country trying to find its bearings for the last 52 years since Independence. I carry my own fatigue of fighting, as a student activist, the Martial Law of General Ayub Khan from 1958 to 1969, and of trying to mobilize against the Martial Law of General Yahya Khan from 1969 to 1971 when the army was unleashed against the people of East Pakistan and rape was part of military strategy. I found myself in opposition to the civilian dictatorship of Prime Minister Z. A. Bhutto, and fought against the military regime of General Zia-ul-Haq from 1977 to 1988. From 1988 to 1999, eleven years of four elected governments and three interim ones, many of us were once again on the battle lines, particularly during the two regimes of Prime Minister Nawaz Sharif, with 1999 bringing the confrontation to literally a life and death situation.

For the Institute of Women's Studies, Lahore (IWSL), that I represent, and myself personally, 1999 was a particularly difficult year with the Nawaz Sharif government initiating a vicious campaign against us. The Institute, and myself by name, were continuously accused (through the press and television) among other things of being anti-state, anti-government, anti-Islam, of leading women astray, of immorality, debauchery and of being pro-Hindu and pro-Jewish (*The Nation* 1998). At least four different police and intelligence agencies including the military intelligence, and the Inter-Services Intelligence, were assigned to 'monitor' our activities and for two months (May and June 1999) we had six army trucks and jeeps stationed outside our building!

A minister of the provincial government also made repeated calls through the press for the public to burn our building down (and our homes) and to literally skin us alive. We received threats and were followed by right-wing militants.

Women's groups, non-governmental organizations (NGOs) and the press, to a large extent, came out in support of the Institute. All the leading English dailies wrote supportive editorials and the monthly news magazines denigrated the government. The government had not expected this support. Its tactic, in fact, was to single out one organization, isolate it and force it to close down, with the intent that others would simply get scared and back off from similar political activities. Since that was not forthcoming and the Institute stood firm on its position and its stand, which it stated publicly through the press, another women's organization, Aurat Foundation, was attacked for anti-government activities. NGOs, particularly women's organizations, and the press were perceived as the last bastions of opposition, a position that far outweighed their size or their ability to destabilize a government. But to the extent that they voiced opposition and tried to alert the public, and further since they confronted the government on the streets, in the press and even in court, this opposition was perceived as a threat.

Intelligence agencies continued to harass women's groups and NGOs, and Islamic fundamentalists and militant organizations continued to threaten and intimidate these groups. In May 1999 the government again started its verbal campaign and harassment, this time also on television, and attacked Dastak, a women's refuge (*Nawa-e-Waqt* 1999); Shirkat Gah, a women's resource centre; Ajoka, a women's theatre group; the Human Rights Commission of Pakistan; AGHS, a women's law firm (*The News* 1999a); Aurat, a woman's publication and information service (*The News* 1999b); and ASR²/IWSL (*Dawn* 1999)—all of these women's organizations or led by women. The accusations and language used was again emotive: pro-west, pro-Indian, anti-Islam, against Islamic values, foreign agents, national integrity, immorality, etc.

In April, a young woman was murdered by her parents in the office of her lawyers Hina Jilani and Asthma Jahangir, because she had approached the lawyers to assist her in getting a divorce. Since she was a Pathan and came from the North West Frontier Province, the supposedly secular opposition party there supported the murder as being part of its tradition of honour killings. The murderers have not been arrested and in a strange twist of justice, arrest warrants were issued on the lawyers whom Samia, the young woman, had approached for assistance.

While the government's incitement to violence by the public abated under pressure from other NGOs, the press, international agencies and donor countries, the government with the assistance of an organization of American lawyers started drawing up a law that would allow them to disband organizations such as ours. I have been somewhat preoccupied with this. Also, I have been looking for funds since donors committed to supporting the IWSL decided not to fund Pakistan, ironically because of its lack of good governance and its curtailment of human and women's rights. Over the summer of 1999, I was able to get some donor agencies to reconsider their positions, but we subsequently got caught in the range of sanctions imposed as a result of the coup.

This experience, however, needs to be contextualized, as indeed Pakistan itself needs to be, since whatever is now, or may have happened in Pakistan, has not occurred unrelated to regional and global imperatives. I am not suggesting that all expressions of nationality, religion, race, identity and culture are part of a global conspiracy. Yet, Islamic fundamentalism, which most concerns me today, was created and encouraged by global capitalism, particularly by the United States, for its own ideological, political and economic purposes. For the people of those countries where Islamic fundamentalist regimes were imposed and supported, this meant two things: one that a monolithic and one dimensional Islam was forced upon them, and secondly, that this imposition of a repressive and narrowly defined Islam led to intense divisions within these countries because of the various sects, and multiple interpretations that exist within Islam. Pakistan was one of the countries where an Islamic fundamentalist regime was forced upon the people in 1977 and which was supported militarily and economically by the United States to fight communism in Afghanistan. Perhaps it is in order, at this point, to state that despite the present position of the Pakistani state, Pakistan was not intended to be an 'Islamic' Republic and further that its identity as an Islamic Republic has been and continues to be contested.

Indeed the first constitution of Pakistan, passed in 1956, while declaring Pakistan to be an Islamic Republic, separated religion from the state by emphasizing that, the 'Almighty Allah' has given temporal authority to the people as a sacred trust. Affirmative action for women was recognized in this constitution by giving women two votes, one for the general constituency and one for seats reserved for women. The constitution was never put in place. The army took over in 1958 and sought to 'modernize' and liberalize Pakistan by opening the doors to capitalist development. General Ayub Khan made changes in the Islamic Personal Law by promulgating a Muslim Family Laws Ordinance, which gave rights to women within a liberal interpretation of Islam. Pakistan still has one of the more liberal personal laws in the Muslim world. The position of women was further strengthened under Prime Minister Z. A. Bhutto who was liberal and progressive in terms of women's rights. All services and professions, with the exception of the armed services, were opened to women. In 1975, at the United Nations World Conference on Women in Mexico, Bhutto declared that the Peoples' Government of Pakistan was fully committed to the complete equality, emancipation and integration of women in the development process. Bhutto also set up a Women's Rights Commission, which recommended fundamental changes in legal rights, personal laws, inheritance, political participation and affirmative action an all levels. Bhutto was deposed in 1977.

The year 1977 was a turning point for Pakistan. General Zia-ul-Haq declared martial law, and justified his takeover by saying that he had to Islamize Pakistan. Apart from the support of the United States, other western countries and the military, he was supported by Islamic fundamentalist parties, and the Jamat-e-Islami joined this government. At one level, it meant no more than military repression using the language of religion. Yet, Pakistan today borders on being a theocratic state, not because the clergy is supported by the people but, because the state, in giving a voice to the clergy, has created its own nemesis.

While not being able to 'convert' the nation, or to bring about any fundamental changes in its capitalist economy, Zia-ul-Haq concentrated on issues such as Islamic punishments, on legal changes, and on refining the definition of Islam and what it means to be a Muslim. Fasting in Ramadan, saying one's prayers, being forced to give charity in the exact percentage determined by Islam became the parameters of being a Muslim, while the larger morality got lost in the ritual. In separating the wheat from the chaff, non-Muslims were completely marginalized and now are only nominal citizens.

However, the lynchpin of this process of Islamization was women. In his first address to the nation Zia-ul-Haq vowed to uphold 'the sanctity of *chadder* and *chardivari*' (the veil and the four walls). The state moved to take over the lives of women, to control their bodies, their space, to decide what they should wear, how they should conduct themselves, the jobs they could take, the sports they could play, and took it upon itself to define and regulate women's morality. This was done through a series of legislative changes such as the Zina and Hudood Ordinances (Islamic punishments), and the Islamic Law of Evidence; through directives such as the dress code, and women not being allowed to participate in spectator sports; but mainly through a persistent ideology that women were not equal to men and that they must be regulated.

Women have been fighting back, especially since 1981. The Hudood Ordinance which specifies Islamic punishments was passed in 1979. It requires the evidence of four Muslim males of good repute for maximum punishment, and makes no distinction between rape, adultery or fornication. The enormity of its implications became evident in 1981 when a woman and a man were arrested for adultery and sentenced to a hundred lashes each and stoning to death. This galvanized women into coming together and forming the Women's Action Forum, which was then an alliance of several women's groups and individuals. Since then women's organizations have fought every anti-women measure, and the first demonstration against martial law and Islamization was a women's demonstration in 1983 against the proposed Law of Evidence which stipulated that the evidence of two women would be equal to that of one man. Despite state repression and state violence, the women's movement grew in size with several other groups and organizations being formed.

Indeed, the women's movement did not confine itself to so-called women's issues. Women were not only in the forefront of the Movement for the Restoration of Democracy but also emerged as leaders of the peace movement (particularly peace between India and Pakistan); the environment movement; within the trade unions; were the first to challenge injustice through public interest litigation (for example on bonded labour); by forming NGOs; and many women played a key role as journalists and editors of major newspapers and journals. While admittedly these were mainly middle class professional women, one of the largest organizations then was the Sindhiani Tehreeq or Sindhi Women's Movement, which had an active membership of over 15,000 mainly peasant women. What is of importance, nevertheless, was the role that women played, as opposed to their male counterparts. I would suggest that this reinforces the argument that not only did women bear the brunt of Islamization, but that men were not only not threatened by it, but since patriarchy and masculinity were reinforced by the state, many men even collaborated—at the very least by their silence. This is not to suggest that men were not fighting against Martial Law—only to say that women were fighting both Martial Law and Islamization; and have continued to fight on several fronts.

General Zia-ul-Haq was killed on Aug 17, 1988 and a woman Prime Minister, Benazir Bhutto, elected in November of that year. Between then and 1999, Pakistan has had four elected governments and three interim ones, a total of seven in eleven years, with the military coup as the eighth! Given the history of direct military rule and a clause inserted by Zia-ul-Haq in the constitution which until recently allowed a President to dismiss a government, the parliamentary system or other form of civilian government has never been allowed to take root in Pakistan. This does not suggest that the governments were not corrupt, inefficient and self-seeking, only that the electoral system has not been allowed to take its own course.

As far as women are concerned there was a difference in Benazir Bhutto's two tenures and that of Nawaz Sharif's. Benazir Bhutto never had a two thirds majority in Parliament to overturn the anti-women legislations passed by Zia-ul-Haq, but instinctively she allowed a greater space and a freedom to express women's concerns. Nawaz Sharif on the other hand passed another Islamic Amendment in 1991, in his first tenure, and was in the process of passing the Fifteenth Amendment to the Constitution which, in effect, would have made the Prime Minister of the Federation the Supreme interpreter of the Quran and Sunnah

(Injunctions in Islam)—literally the Commander of the Faithful. This would have led to a process where the Pakistani state would be very akin to Saudi Arabia with all religious and temporal authority concentrated in a single person. Women's organizations, NGOs and the English-language press vociferously opposed these measures and indeed it was perhaps the movements' success in not letting it become law, and in raising awareness and mobilizing the public against the nuclear tests and nuclear proliferation, that also triggered the massive attack on women's groups.

This 22-year period of Pakistan's history falls into two neat phases, eleven years of Zia's Martial Law and eleven years of parliamentary democracy. The women's movement can also be seen in two distinct phases, partly because the lifting of Martial Law broadened the focus and the strategies of the movement, and also because after the 1985 United Nations World Conference on Women in Nairobi there was a global trend toward 'mainstreaming'. The '80s also gave rise to debates among feminists on the 'end of ideology'; reform versus revolution; the 'difference' debates; the concept of 'religious specificity'; 'gender', etc. While feminist academics and the women's movement in Pakistan were not, by and large, aware of these debates, the positions came through in diluted and often distorted forms, through the donor community (World Bank, the United Nations and bilateral assistance); dependence on funding and on the agendas of the funding agencies, and indeed the scale of funding, changed the nature of the women's movement in Pakistan and elsewhere. In Pakistan for example, the dynamic, spontaneous, non-funded, politically-oriented and feminist organizations such as Women's Action Forum and Sindhiani Tehreeq gave way to non-ideological women's rights groups. While militant and feminists groups still exist, even we in ASR and the IWSL are under pressure to either change our orientation and our politics, or simply to cease to exist for lack of funds—or because we are considered 'passé'.

In other words, while women in Pakistan have fought a brave and courageous struggle and that is today acknowledged by the United Nations, by governments and other institutions, the negative aspect of this support has been that the women's movement itself has lost its political edge and, in some cases, its commitment. This trend has led to some more powerful groups becoming not only part of the establishment but has led to these groups taking on the very male norms that they were earlier challenging.

What is even more unfortunate is that the women's movement has begun to be defined only by a few women-centred groups, mainly in the urban areas. This has tended to exclude and to overlook the efforts that women have been making all over Pakistan, in their own areas of work or expression, and this in turn has meant that the media, the government, the international agencies and even these urban women's organizations, believe that it is only they who give legitimacy to the movement.

There is, however, little validity in the assumption that the interest, issues, understanding, and in some cases, sophistication of urban/professional groups are different from those women not considered part of the movement. If anything,

experience shows that women from different class, ethnic, religious and professional backgrounds are much more able and willing to understand and grapple
with issues of their own subordination. For example, it is often said by urban/
professional women or women's rights groups that the women's movement
cannot be very political, or confrontational, or secular, or conceptual, or feminist,
because the 'average' woman is not yet ready for any of these. Yet we have often
found that these women are much more willing and able to understand and
identify with these notions than the middle-class urban women, and that these
women (and some men) are more willing to travel long distances, put up with
uncomfortable situations, take leave from their jobs, stay away from their families,
and even take enormous personal risks, to be a part of something that they believe
in. To them, the issues of class contradictions in society, the patriarchy inherent
in all religions; militarization; poverty; unemployment, suppression of creativity,
etc. are not only concepts or objective realities, but also what they deal with on a
daily basis. They are, therefore, much more interested in why this happens and
how it may be resolved.

Recently, there have been attempts at redefining the movement by including
development activities and projects. In many cases however, projects, programs
and action plans have subsumed and/or negated the very activism and the
commitment that the movement is premised on. These initiatives have in a
concrete sense depleted much of the dynamism, energy, and flexibility of the
movement. For instance, in most cases these activities are financially supported
which invariably brings with it the constraints of paper work, proposals, reports,
accounts etc., quite apart from the fact that often activities also get defined by the
agendas and the constraints of the funding agencies. This also leads to professionalism, since management and efficiency become important, and to a competition
for resources and financial support. In the case of funded activities, and the
responsibility of 'keeping the office operational', continuity of the issue and the
activity become a further problem since the group must end the program once the
project period is over, and it goes into another program without seeing the first one
to its logical and necessary conclusion.

Paid political and social activism, whether on the part of the academia, the
NGOs, the press, or other institutions that supposedly work in the public interest, also gives a false sense of commitment and fulfilment. If for example, one
is spending several hours a day doing 'good works' there is a tendency to switch
off when one is 'free'. Activism in this sense has increasingly become a job or a
task, and the issues and actions not necessarily internalized. This not only leads
to a further fragmentation of the self and to a false consciousness, but, by
reinforcing the separation of the public and the private, it negates what the
women's movement is trying to struggle for.

The women's movement has moved from being a movement, to becoming
institutionalized, and becoming a part of the establishment. The antithesis has,
therefore, been through the synthesis and is increasingly becoming the thesis.
Women's groups are now institutions, feminists are members of the establish-

ment, women's studies is rapidly being incorporated in many universities, women's lists are carried by mainstream publishers, women's issues are being addressed by governments, and key women are being included in decision making in state structures. If one has a dialectical understanding of history, this thesis or establishment will produce a new antithesis to challenge it. This is a global as well as a national phenomenon, and the movement everywhere is not necessarily responding to the challenge within it, with an openness and a flexibility that would allow it to move to a higher stage of development and a higher stage of politics. The question is, how do we get out of this stagnation and out of the apathy that funding and the non-existence of ideology inculcates?

What has often been identified as the second wave of feminism started in the 1960s. For two decades, until perhaps Nairobi, it was a vibrant political movement that sought to challenge not only patriarchy at all levels but the existing socio-political/economic structures, from the family to the state and to international institutions. Indeed, its most profound critique was of patriarchy and of the state and international structures. It was extremely dynamic, in that it accepted nothing as the norm and opened up new territories, spaces, choices and alternatives.

Those of you active then will recall that women went to Nairobi as a coming together of women in an international women's movement, seeking an understanding, political alliances and common struggles among themselves. Most of us were oblivious to the UN conference and in any case were critiquing not only our Nation States but also the United Nations.

Nairobi should have been a watershed for a stronger women's movement and had it been, we today may not have been saying (in despair) as we are in Asia, that not much has changed since Beijing. History is made by people's movements— people propel history forward by confronting the status quo. History is never made by 'collaborating' (a derogatory term at best) or by being in 'partnership' with the oppressor, or by 'lobbying'. The term and process of lobbying incidentally is very disturbing. It comes out of the American political system where people get paid by interest groups to hang out in the lobbies of power, to further their interests. It is most unfortunate that this very base aspect of the American political system has been taken on by social activists—often to the exclusion of all other forms of political activity.

In any case it seems ironic to me that if we identify the state, the global institutions (including the UN) and patriarchal forces as the oppressors, that is if we identify them as the problem, we then expect them also to be the solution. The question is whether we have this critique any longer—of patriarchy, the state or the UN, or whether we are only interested now in being included in the system. Certainly we are part of the system, as academics, NGOs, as paid social activists, dependent on resources from these very institutions and nation states, following agendas already decided, within spaces already determined.

Apart from the critique of patriarchy and the state, we in Asia no longer critique the family and seem to have totally discarded the feminist critique of marriage. Sexuality and the institution of marriage are the seat of women's oppression. By moving away from discussions, debates, positions, and encouraging alternative ways of relating we not only reinforce patriarchy and the heterosexual family (which with single-headed households is no longer even the norm) but reinforce the dichotomy of the public and the private. The issue of sexuality is also important since the religious right and 'conservatives' are preoccupied with the female body and female sexuality. By shying away from discussing and positioning ourselves on this crucial aspect of women's oppression, we strengthen patriarchy by our silence and also internalize the 'shame' that we are meant to feel regarding our own bodies and our sexuality. Not addressing these issues also leads to the extreme homophobia in the Asian women's movement, where lesbians will at best be encouraged to be silent, or will be marginalized if they are not.

Religious identity and religious conservatism, or worse the strategic use of religion, also dogs the women's movement in the South. Speaking of secularism is discouraged and being able to declare oneself an atheist is anathema. This has stifled debate on a crucial issue, not only because it has defined religion as the only parameter, but also has led to a reinforcement of religious identity which is liable to be tapped by the State or religious forces. Indeed women's groups trying to understand or use religion strategically have been no more successful in mobilizing women than secular groups. Instead, they may well have played into the hands of the religious right by not opposing more directly the use of religion.

Perhaps the most conservative aspect of this movement in the last sixteen years has been the shift from feminism to gender. Feminism very simply is the recognition of patriarchy as a system of male oppression and domination that has a material (that is economic) base. Feminists, therefore, seek a more holistic and structural transformation of society, and a transformation of all relationships including the personal. The women's rights movement is a necessary stage towards this transformation, just as a democratic, liberal stage may be necessary for a greater social and economic structural transformation in general, but as far as feminism is concerned equal rights within the existing system is not an end in itself. This requires an autonomous feminist movement that challenges patriarchy—by first providing a space for women to articulate their own oppression—from and by men.

Under the influence of the donor community and the imperatives of funding, but also to avoid vulnerability and/or marginalization, a large number of feminists and women activists have begun to use the word 'gender' in place of 'women' when discussing the issues of equality and rights. Women's equality has given way to gender equality, women's consciousness has become gender consciousness and awareness of women's issues has become gender awareness. Feminist thought has gone from being alternative and oppositional to mainstream and establishment, and development agencies, like the World Bank and the International Monetary Fund, have appropriated the language of feminism and co-opted it into their own discourse.

The problem with the notion of 'gender' is that it can mean *both* men and women or *either* man or woman. The specificity of women's oppression disappears. In development jargon 'gender' implies that both men and women are equally oppressed by the strict sexual division of labour and that emancipation for both is necessary for society to be free. While it is true that men are also locked in strict masculine/feminine divisions, the important fact is that they are the ones who stand to gain from this division. The impression of equality or equal oppression created by this highly neutralized term obfuscates the fact that women are oppressed and subjugated by men. Men gain from patriarchy, women lose. It is recognized by most feminists that patriarchy cuts across the barriers of class, race, region, ethnicity and religion and is universal. The notion of gender denies patriarchy and, in doing so, denies its structure. In any patriarchal structure, women occupy the lower and subordinate positions and men are powerful.

By denying the structure of power, the 'neutral' word 'gender' depoliticizes the issue of women's subservience. This notion has been derived from liberal philosophy in which all ideas have equal validity and all groups, regardless of their social position, are accorded a morally equal status. For example, in moral terms, workers cannot be equated with capitalists since workers are *exploited* and capitalists are *exploiters* who gain from the relationship. In this structure, one party rules over the other and uses it for its own ends. Patriarchy is a similar structure but the word 'gender' implies that men and women are two equal entities facing each other in a non-confrontational position. In fact, men and women stand in a relationship of mutual conflict, as their interests are not the same. In simple terms men are not equally oppressed. In the structure of social relation, they are positioned differently from women.

Notions of gender training and gender sensitization fail to take into account the vastly different positions from which men and women come. Such activities operate on the assumption that 'gender' oppression is the result of social attitudes, beliefs, religious ideology and cultural values, an assumption supported by the liberal disciplines like social psychology. The material basis of patriarchy, the fact that men control and own most of the world's resources including those produced by women, is denied in this discourse. As long as men control economic and survival resources, no amount of awareness and sensitization is going to make a difference in relations between men and women. The one who owns will inevitably control and use the one who doesn't. Without challenging the material basis of patriarchal relations, gender sensitization and awareness will not change power relations in society. Assuming that they will, is equivalent to saying that by making capitalists and workers aware of and sensitive to the exploitation involved in their relationship, they will both realize what is happening and decide to change things. Economic, political and material struggles are necessary since no groups ever renounce power and control willingly.

As Sunila Abeysekera, a Sri Lankan friend says: one needs to be wary that the process of engendering does not lead to women being endangered as a species! As one who is despairing of the way the world has turned over the last decade or so and as one who strongly believes that a socialist feminist ideological position and struggle is essential to fight capitalist and fundamentalist ideologies, I conclude with four questions which are applicable to all of us: (1) Will the women's movement or feminist academia continue if funds are no longer available? (2) Will 'collaboration', 'partnership', 'lobbying' and hand-outs from the state bring about the changes that we seek—in reality and on the ground—without a simultane-ously active feminist, socialist and anti-racist movement to challenge and confront the global class, patriarchy and hegemonic structures? (3) If we do not have an ideological position and a larger dream will we ever get the energy, the commit-ment and the resistance needed to fight patriarchy, bring about the structural change that we seek? And (4) when academics and NGOs really begin to challenge the status quo—or are perceived to be doing so—will the state or the UN allow them to continue? The political space is being restricted in many countries and in Pakistan we have seen a full-scale attack on women-centered NGOs and feminist academics. What will the institutions do in this case? Backtrack? Compromise? Negotiate a space? Or continue with their confrontation, regardless?

I strongly believe it is time to take stock and to re-examine what we are doing and why. I believe we need to get back and re-look at the critiques and the principles of feminism and Marxism and the feminist and socialist movements. I have faith that fundamentalism, conservatism and patriarchy can be challenged by a counter ideology and by a continuing struggle on all fronts. I believe we need a new all-encompassing dream. I still cling to mine, for as Langston Hughes, a Black American poet said 'Hold fast to dreams for when dreams die life is a broken winged bird that cannot fly'.

Postscript

'Up Against the State' was written at the end of August 1999 when Nawaz Sharif was in power and Islamists were making headway in Pakistan. Soon after, on the 12 of October of that year, the military took over with General Pervez Musharaf as Commander-in-Chief and Chief Executive.

A meeting of the Joint Action Committee for Peace and Democracy (JAC) (an alliance of about 36 organizations and political parties in Lahore) was called. I assumed we would be deciding the wording of our immediate resolution and working out our strategy. The reaction by a majority of the organizations was stunning. They supported the military take-over. This was despite the fact that the JAC was pro-democracy, and that most of its members were familiar with the history of the military as an institution and its role in politics in Pakistan. Only five organizations clearly condemned the military take-over in spite of whatever the Nawaz Sharif government may have been guilty of. These were the Simorgh Women's Resource and Publication Collective, the Human Rights Commission of Pakistan, AGHS, the Labour Party and the ASR Resource Centre. On the insistence of these five organizations and individuals from others, however, a resolution was passed but the arguments were more intense at a meeting a few days later. It became impossible to explain that General Musharaf represented an institution and that it did not matter how personally liberal he may be. As a military man and a politician, he would *have* to compromise to stay in power. Further, he would *want* to stay in power.

However, this view remained a minority position. Stranger still was that many in the press held similar views and even more in literary and cultural circles. Some individuals from non-governmental organizations (NGOs) joined the Musharaf government as Ministers, others were appointed to task forces, others became advisors or consultants. General Musharaf's government had so many NGO persons in it or around it that it was often called the NGO government, much to the embarrassment to those of us who wanted to maintain a distance.

But the government did not perform very well and Pakistan remained isolated from the world until the 11th of September 2001, when Pakistan became a front-line state in the 'war against terrorism'. Some of the alliances formed with NGOs changed when the issue became whether to support, or not, the war in Afghanistan. Most NGOs did not support the war or the blanket bombing of Afghanistan. They argued that the fall-out of the war on Afghanistan would have a direct impact on Pakistan in terms of increased terrorism within Pakistan and in terms of refugees. The instability in Afghanistan continues and indeed the fallout in Pakistan is intense, not least of which is that the Taliban are now in the border areas of Pakistan, and, for the first time in the history of Pakistan, in the October 2002 General Election, an alliance of Islamic political parties, the Mutahidda Majlis e Amal (MMA), won a majority in the North West Frontier Province (NWFP) and enough seats in Baluchistan to influence the government there.

During this very period the Family Laws Ordinance was challenged in the Supreme Court, and other than the same few women who had been fighting it for decades, no one protested, or cared. When it came to power, the NWFP government passed the Shariat Bill and the MMA intends to try to do the same in Baluchistan. Women outside these two provinces seem not to have initiated a larger campaign, nor are they concerned that this may be a harbinger of things to come. Yet, the National Commission on the Status of Women, formed by the Musharaf government, recommended that the Hudood Laws be repealed,[3] a move applauded by women's organizations.

But on January 1, 2004, General Pervez Musharaf asked for and got a 'trust vote' from Parliament to remain as the President of Pakistan while he also remains an in-service member of the Military Corp. This would be unprecedented under most 'democratic' systems, but General Musharaf claims that he is being true to Parliamentary Democracy. This strange twist took place through the passing of the 17th Amendment to the Constitution, in which the President is 'elected for a five-year term from the time of the General Elections in 2002'; granting him the authority to decide for himself when he will shed his uniform and become a 'civilian'; and who and which political party is bona fide to stand for elections in the future. The devolution plan is also to be decided by him and he retains the power to dismiss the government and appoint the military chiefs (with the consent of the Prime Minister, a mere formality).

This is martial law no matter how it is billed. The negotiations to pass this

Amendment took place between the military and the MMA, supported not so behind the scenes by the USA. Up until December 29, 2003, the MMA had been in negotiations with the government over the Legal Framework Order[4] which General Musharaf wanted to automically enshrine in the constitution. The MMA (and other parties) wanted the points to be debated in Parliament and passed by Parliament as an Amendment. This is the 17th Amendment.

On December 29, 2003, when the resolution for the 17th Amendment was tabled for discussion, the Pakistan Muslim League President (*Quaid e Azam*[5]), Chaudhry Shujat Hussain, assured the House that the Hudood Ordinance Laws and other Islamic Provisions in the Constitution would not be scrapped or changed. This then was the deal. Women and religious minorities and their rights could and had been bartered! The deal was struck behind closed doors, a deal between the military and the Mullah,[6] and between them, the United States.

There was not even a whimper from women parliamentarians, women's organizations, or individual women, or the press. It went unnoticed, unrecorded, unheard. *Silence.*

In Pakistan history has repeated itself. Yet again we have the military/Mullah/capitalist/United States alliance. Within Pakistan things have changed. The Islamic forces are more organized and more dangerous. Progressive and liberal Pakistanis have also changed. So have the women from this class and their circumstances. Many women from the upper and middle classes, and the professions, supported the military take-over and some work on task forces or act as advisors or consultants for the Musharaf government. Those who can simply leave the country. For others there are new, well-paid jobs in the banking and finance sector, in the information technology sector; for a certain class there are boutiques, discos and balls; there are cable television and DVDs, international travel, private hospitals for a few, private education for others, universities abroad. It is possible to live in a cocoon. For the few.

Women in the lower, and poor classes are, however, still fighting for their rights. The Hudood Ordinance still exists and Musharaf has promised the MMA that it will not be touched. Honour killings continue, forced marriages are the norm, very few women get even the inheritance determined in the Quran, the educational system, the laws, religion and fundamentalism imposed on women are interpreted by whomever she 'belongs' to; and she is the victim of all forms of violence from within the home to that meted out by the state.

Where is the resistance? A strong, autonomous, cross-class, women's movement is badly needed in Pakistan. Women are *still* 'up against the state'. As women in their late 20s and 30s in the professional middle class are making use of the spaces made for them by their mothers, we can only look to the new generation for hope. They have a responsibility to those less fortunate. They must fulfil it. The onus is on them to make the future.   —January 15, 2004

This article is adapted from the Third Annual Dame Nita Barrow Lecture sponsored by the Centre for Women's Studies in Eduation at the Ontario Institute for Studies in

Education at the University of Toronto in November 1999. Online: http://www1.
oise.utoronto.ca/cwse/lectext.htm.

Nighat Said Khan is the Executive Director of the ASR Resource Centre and Dean of
Studies of the Institute of Women's Studies, Lahore. She is also a founder of the Women's
Action Forum, and several other networks, and has been involved both in academics
and in the movements for women, human, minority, peasants' and workers' rights. She
has also been very active in the peace movement since 1979.

Notes

1   This comment was made by a Minister of the Punjab government at a press conference
     on NGOs on December 27, 1998 and reported two days later in Lahore's daily, *Jang.*
2   ASR stands for *Aser an Urdu*, which means 'impact'. ASR is a resource centre for
     women, minorities, workers and peasants, and for peace activism.
3   The Family Laws Ordinance was passed by General Ayub Khan in 1960. It interprets
     Islamic law somewhat liberally and not only gives some rights to women in terms of
     personal law, but also deems marriage and divorce a matter of law. This is meant to
     prevent men from divorcing women on a whim and also prevents men from marrying
     more than once without the consent of an existing wife. The Shariat Bill is a law which
     requires all laws to be within an Islamic framework. The Hudood Laws, passed by
     General Zia-ul-Haq in 1979, are laws which mete out Islamic punishments for crimes
     that Islam has specifically addressed. These are enforced with the Zina Ordinance
     which is an Islamic law on adultery, rape and fornication.
4   The Legal Framework Order was an order passed by General Musharaf when he came
     into power. It not only entitles him to remain the President of Pakistan but gives this
     office power over and above the Prime Minister and Parliament. It also establishes a
     National Security Council in which the military plays an important role and legally
     becomes a part of the government.
5   This government is formed mainly by the Muslim League *Quaid e Azam* (M. A.
     Jinnah, the founder of the nation, was called *Quaid e Azam* or 'leader of the nation').
     The members are made up of those whom the government was able to break away from
     other parties, mainly the Muslim League of the previous Prime Minister Nawaz Sharif.
     It is widely said that the Inter Services Intelligence (ISI) (a military intelligence cell)
     was responsible for this and that the ISI played a role in getting these members elected.
6   A Mullah is a religious leader, generally one versed in the Quran. He is self-proclaimed
     and tends to have a very narrow interpretation of Islam. The Islamic groups in Pakistan
     tend to be headed by Mullahs.

References

Dawn (1999) Thursday Review, Karachi, 27 May.
Jang (1998) Lahore, 30 December.
Nawa-e-Waqt (1999) Lahore, 24 May.
The Nation (1998) Lahore, 27 December.
The News (1999a) Lahore, 15 May.
The News (1999b) Lahore, 24 May.

CREATING AND SUSTAINING FEMINIST SPACE IN AFRICA

LOCAL AND GLOBAL CHALLENGES IN THE TWENTY-FIRST CENTURY

BISI ADELEYE-FAYEMI

Do you remember,
When we all walked tall and proud
When we were the salt of the earth
When we sang with voices loud and clear
And put the most vain of birds to shame
When we ran free of chains both visible and invisible
Long before the lies, the deception, the myths
Before the gradual destruction of our bodies, our spirits and our minds
Do you remember
When God was a woman?

The year 2000 review of the impact of the United Nations Fourth World Conference on Women (Beijing 1995), commonly referred to as Beijing+5, revealed that whilst there have been some significant gains for women in various parts of the world, there are still considerable obstacles in the way of achieving worldwide equality for women. Over the past 25 years, consciousness has been raised on issues affecting women all over the world, on a macro and micro level. In spite of this, the material conditions of women have not necessarily improved. Lifestyles in most of the 'developing' world have continued to deteriorate for both men and women. Global phenomena such as the debt crises, structural adjustment policies (SAPs), increased militarization and communal violence, have continued to widen the gap between most western nations and developing regions.

The African region has fared particularly badly over the past two decades. If there is a crisis, women are affected in different ways from men, and in most cases, they suffer most. This affects all spheres of development—economic, political, technological and social. Therefore women in Africa have borne the brunt of the continent's misfortunes.

This article examines local and global issues of concern to women in Africa, and the implications of these issues for community transformation. I will begin by looking at some contemporary issues facing Africa, and how these issues impact on African women. I will discuss some features of African feminist theory and practice and how these have impacted on African women's thinking and activism. I will briefly describe some of the strategies used to engage in various levels of discourse, contestation and organizing. Finally, I will look at future directions for the transformation of structures that still impede the empowerment of women in Africa and in many other parts of the world.

Africa and Globalization

My definition of Africa for the purposes of this article is a pan-Africanist, geographical one, i.e., from Cape Town to Cairo. Africa, being a massive continent with 54 countries of varying degrees of economic development and industrialization, historical differences and connectivities, deep race and ethnicity divides, religious differences and specificities, is very difficult to tackle analytically, especially if one is trying to avoid dangerous generalizations. Having said that, it is even trickier to go down the slippery slopes of 'black Africa' or 'sub-Saharan' Africa because these terms have deep political meanings and significance, and their uses can only be justified within carefully prescribed contexts.

Africa as a continent has been weakened by the adverse consequences of globalization. Whilst globalization presents many opportunities, it is a bane to poorer, vulnerable societies and economies. Globalization favours the deregulation of markets, free trade and privatization. It involves movement of finance and capital at the speed of light, and the formation of quasi-governments in the form of multinational, financial institutions such as the World Bank and the International Monetary Fund (IMF). The heavy indebtedness of many countries in the global South, the fracturing of societies due to violent conflicts and rising inequities, and the lack of access to resources keeps plunging the majority of the world's countries into new depths of poverty and disintegration. The use of information technology as humanity's lynch pin further isolates a majority of the countries in the world—computers, for example, cost more than a year's worth of food, shelter and clothing.

As parts of the world grow fantastically rich and most of the other parts grow desperately poorer, we need to ask questions about the real meaning of globalization. Does it mean we exist in a global village where only a few have all the comforts and riches on the basis of their geographical location and race, while the rest literally clean their toilets? Or does it mean seizing opportunities to ensure equal access to terms of trade, fairness, equity and justice?

As the President of Nigeria, Olusegun Obasanjo, remarked at the UN Millennium Summit (2000),

The new millennium is shaped by forces of globalization that are turning our world into a village. Thus, the new millennium will demand of us, more than ever before, to live and work together as members of one human family. But up to now globalization has meant prosperity only for the chosen few of the industrialized countries. For us in the developing world, globalization will continue to ring hollow.... In short, globalization has to be seen to mean the eradication of poverty.

The Current Status of Women in Africa

According to the recent Beijing+5 review process, progress on implementing the Beijing Platform for Action in the Africa region has been slow. A combination of factors such as economic decline, political instability, conflict, lack of adequate communication systems, inadequate institutional mechanisms for mainstreaming gender, and the devastating impact of the HIV/AIDS pandemic have marred the process.[1] Based on the available documentation which emerged from the governmental, non-governmental and United Nations agencies during the Beijing+5 review, as well as from my own experience of participating in the process, I will attempt to provide a summary of the current status of women in Africa.[2]

Economic Status

Approximately 44 per cent of Africa's population, the majority of whom are women, are currently living below the poverty line of US$39 (per capita) per month (United Nations Economic Commission for Africa 1999a). Women continue to lack access to resources such as land, capital, technology, water and adequate food. Macro and micro-economic policies, programs, and development strategies rarely take into account their impact on women and girl-children, especially those living in poverty. The majority of women in Africa, in rural and most urban areas, continue to live in conditions of economic underdevelopment and social marginalization. According to African women's organizations,

> The level of poverty has increased in the last five years and has impacted more negatively on women. Poverty levels have increased as a result of mounting and constant misuse and misappropriation of resources. Governments have undertaken people-blind economic reforms without proper cushioning measures in place to protect vulnerable groups in their countries. This has contributed to the increased impoverishment and disempowerment of women. (*African Regional NGO Report on the NGO Consultations* 1999)

The implementation of economic policies such as SAPs in most of sub-Saharan Africa has compounded the feminization of poverty by contributing to the loss of livelihoods, unemployment, an increase in the number of commercial sex workers and trafficking in women, street children and a total rupturing of the social fabric which binds communities together. This in turn has made more women and girls vulnerable to sexual exploitation and at risk of contracting HIV/AIDS.

Further, over the past six years, at least two million Africans have lost their lives in wars and genocide. Many more have become refugees. These conflicts have placed tremendous burdens on women who suffer displacement, loss of families and livelihoods, various forms of intense, gender-based violence, and the responsibility of sustaining entire communities. Twenty-one out of 54 African countries are affected by conflict. Women and children from countries such as Liberia, Rwanda, Sudan, Sierra Leone, Democratic Republic of Congo, Burundi and Somalia have spent the last decade living under unbelievably difficult circumstances.

Political Status

The official United Nations Platform for Action endorsed by governments in Beijing at the Fourth World Women's Conference (Beijing Declaration and Platform for Action 1995) raised concerns about the continued under-representation of women in most levels of government. The United Nations Economic and Social Council (ECOSOC) set a target of 30 per cent for the inclusion of women in positions of power and decision-making. This target has not been met worldwide. African governments did make specific commitments on this issue. Several countries and political parties created quota systems and affirmative action programs which led to the reservation of between 25 to 50 per cent of elective seats at national and local levels (as well as other appointive positions) for women. As a result some countries such as South Africa (29.3 per cent), Mozambique (25.2 per cent), Seychelles (23.5 per cent) Uganda (21 per cent) and Namibia (22.2 per cent) have significantly higher levels of women's representation in national assemblies and other positions of power and decision-making (United Nations Economic Commission for Africa 1999b). Yet,

> On the whole, the political empowerment of women in the Africa region has been very slow: Africa's regional average representation of women in national legislative assemblies stands at eleven per cent reflecting little progress in achieving the 30 per cent target of women in decision-making positions set by the UN Economic and Social Council. (ECA/Africa Centre for Women 1999)

Access to mainstream decision-making and political power for African women is a long-haul process. Millions of women are illiterate. Those who are literate have to contend with the difficult process of seeking the support of husbands, family and friends and acceptance from party colleagues. They have to mobilize the necessary campaign finances and endure the harsh realities of political campaigns in Africa that can break the toughest of women. The few who do survive the difficulties of running for public office find it extremely difficult to work within structures that are still hostile to the empowerment and equality of women.

Getting women into decision-making structures is one thing. Ensuring that they make an impact is another. There are four key issues involved here. The first is the issue of access for women to political spaces. This they can get through quotas, voter education, public support and awareness, affirmative action, party support, etc. The second level is the issue of participation—representation of women in decision-making structures of say, parliament, their level of political engagement, etc. Third is the issue of transformation on an internal basis—what are the meeting times at parliament? What are the childcare arrangements, if any? What about a women friendly environment and women friendly language? The fourth level is external transformation: how are gender considerations integrated into legislation? (See SADC Gender Unit [1999].)

The implications of women being excluded from decision-making are serious. If women do not have a voice where key decisions affecting their lives are made their capacity for full development and equality is severely limited. Women's involvement in decision-making contributes to redefining political priorities—placing new issues on the political agenda that reflect and address women's gender-specific concerns, values and experiences and provides new perspectives on mainstream political issues. Without the active participation of women and the inclusion of their perspectives at all levels of decision-making, the lofty goals of equality, development and peace cannot be achieved (ECA/Africa Centre for Women 1999).

Social Status

Africa has the lowest literacy rate in the world at only 50 per cent. The majority of the illiterate are women living in rural areas with limited access to clean water, good transportation, adequate food, land, credit facilities and accessible health care.

Women's health in most parts of the continent has been affected by bias in gender policies and programs and socio-cultural practices. Decreased health spending and privatization of health care systems in many countries that do not guarantee universal access to health care have also had a negative impact on the health of women and girls. The continent has one of the highest maternal and infant mortality rates in the world.

The HIV/AIDS pandemic has exacerbated the already vulnerable status of women's health. Africa has the highest number of HIV/AIDS infected people in the world. Women are more vulnerable to infection due to biological, social and economic reasons and they have less negotiating power with partners. Women also spend a great deal of their time and resources caring for other family members who are sick.

Many African countries have ratified the Convention on the Elimination of All Forms of Discrimination Against Women (CEDAW). There are several regional and international agreements guaranteeing the human rights, equality and integrity of women and girls throughout the life cycle.[3] However African women still face discrimination in all spheres of public and private life. Violence against women is still a major problem, religious and cultural fundamentalisms are on the increase, discriminatory laws still control women's lives and bodies and harmful traditional practices still persist. Negative stereotypes and attitudes prevent many women from realizing their full potential and making the contributions towards their communities that they wish to. Women in many parts of the continent are suffering from a backlash and a rollback of gains already made.

Though the majority of women living in Africa are facing many of the challenges I have highlighted, Africa remains a vibrant continent of hopes, dreams and visions of a better tomorrow. Most of the continent's rich history has been rewritten and devalued. Its immense wealth of human, material and natural resources has been plundered and laundered by outsiders and their local collaborators. Yet, slowly but surely, African states are beginning the long and hard journey toward restoring their systems and institutions. This journey cannot happen without the full involvement of civil society institutions and the constituencies they represent. And it certainly cannot happen without the full and equal participation of women.

The African Women's Movement: Contestations

Against this backdrop, I turn to the African women's movement today and its responses to the current situation of African women. Trying to define what a women's movement is in Africa is still a work in progress.

When we think of a movement we are talking about entities which emerge out of political and social crisis and which foster cohesiveness, work towards a common objective, work in solidarity, have continuity, have the capacity to engage in mass mobilization and clarity of purpose. When we apply these conventional criteria to the African women's movement, some might conclude that there is no movement. On closer analysis, however, the contestation which is vital to any movement's success is present within this movement even though it tends to be fragmented and uncoordinated (Oduol and Kabira 1995; Butegwa 1997).

African women have contributed immensely towards the development of the continent in all spheres. They have done this through the formation of organizations, coalitions, associations, unions, faith-based networks, local, national and regional networks, rural and urban-based organizations, and through mixed/mainstream institutions. With activities ranging from income-generation, establishment of co-operatives, consciousness-raising and advocacy campaigns to research and analysis, these organizations and networks have contributed to building this movement—a movement for social justice, equality and empowerment for the society in general, and for women in particular. This movement is politically and ideologically diverse, often to the point of very hot contestations. There are serious divisions which reflect Africa's complexities—ethnicity, language, ideology, colonial legacies, race, age, marital status, class, religion, literacy levels, geopolitical and geographical differences and along various other lines. Considering the sheer size of the African continent and the deep complexities of the issues that the continent faces region by region, how easy is it to speak of an African women's movement? How reasonable is it to assume there can be common interests and agendas forged across these major divides, not to mention being able to work out a platform broad enough to accommodate these shared interests and agendas for mutual action?

It is not easy but it has been possible. While the divisive issues still remain unresolved, there is an African women's movement in so far as there has been a collective, if somewhat pocketed, response to the needs of women in the region. There is usually consensus on issues that are considered to be priorities and that affect the lives of all African women such as poverty, illiteracy, health and reproductive rights, political participation and peace. However, there are differences of opinion and strategy as to how reforms can be achieved. We can therefore talk about different strands within the movement.

A large number of actors and organizations which constitute the African women's movement are mainly concerned with reforming the status quo and pushing for reforms which will ameliorate the conditions under which the majority of African women live. These individuals and organizations accept that these systems are skewed against women. They however fall short of coming up with effective strategies that challenge these systems conclusively. This is because many of them do not want to 'rock the boat'. Most of these individuals and organizations tend to bring a welfarist perspective to the movement, and rather than engage the state to meet its responsibilities, such as provision of basic needs, they opt to take over these responsibilities themselves.

There is another strand within the movement that believes women can achieve their goals by being an integral part of state programs, ostensibly set up for the benefit of women, but which in reality are merely vehicles to use women to mobilize to sustain the interests of the state. For example, in several African countries programs for women have been co-ordinated by First Ladies. These programs, usually well funded by the state, have been used to stifle autonomous organizing in those countries. This was the case in Nigeria during the regimes of Generals Babangida and Abacha (1984-1998 between them) when their wives fronted mass-mobilization programs which swallowed millions of dollars to minimize and marginalize the efforts of autonomously organized women (Amadiume 2000; Abdullah 1995).

Within the women's movement there are also feminist leaders, thinkers and activists[4] who challenge the legitimacy and the fundamental basis of patriarchal institutions, norms and values. As far as this strand of the movement is concerned, any movement to free African women from oppression must be feminist, anti-imperialist and anti-racist, it must have a holistic agenda and the tools to transform African communities and the lives of women within those communities. I will now look briefly into how this strand of the movement manages to create and sustain space for itself within the broader context of the women's movement.

Feminism in Africa

When talking about feminism in an African context, I use the terms 'African feminism' and 'African feminist' with caution. This is for a number of theoretical and political reasons. Being an African woman who is a feminist might not be the same as calling oneself an 'African feminist'. I believe in a definition of feminism which is dynamic enough to articulate the interconnectedness and specificities of women's experiences, identities and struggles all over the world and which does not have to be qualified. I sense a danger in such qualifications because they obfuscate the real issues around difference and diversity, and substitute these understandings with false notions of hierarchy and importance. For example, it moves the discourse away from 'my analysis might be different from yours because of my experiences and realities', to 'my feminism is better than yours' or 'yours is not relevant to mine'. Also, within the context of Africa in particular, where the word feminist can be quite problematic, using the term 'African feminist' as a qualifier could mean buying in to a watered down agenda as opposed to identifying with real issues of linking feminist identities to African realities. Therefore, in this article, I use the term African feminists to refer to those who happen to be both African and feminist.

Establishing the Space and Acquiring the Faith

The feminist movement, for all feminists, is a political and ideological home. This space is made up of the many organizations, associations and entities that constitute the feminist movement. It is a space for feminists to use and to claim for themselves. This space is made up of our friendships, networks, our bonds, organizations and our individual and collective feminist energies. This is the space we use to mobilize around our feminist principles, where we hone our analytical skills and where we seek (and sometimes find) answers to our many questions. What makes the space work is faith, the belief that this space is needed to make our lives better and easier. This is manifested in our processes of self-discovery, our hopes, our dreams, our aspirations, our yearning for more knowledge and revelations. Space and faith are interdependent and cannot survive in and of themselves. We need our space as feminists to walk the road together, and we need faith to keep us together in good and in bad times (AMwA 2000).

So what does having feminist space mean in Africa? There are key features of feminist theory and practice in Africa (Davies and Graves 1986) that are vital to our understanding of how these shape the analysis and activism of African women.

First, feminism in Africa is located in the continent's historical realities of marginalization, oppression and domination brought about by slavery, colonialism, racism, neo-colonialism and globalization. It places the interconnectedness of gender, women's oppression, race, ethnicity, poverty and class at the centre of the discourse. It is impractical to talk about a feminist theory in Africa without an understanding of how these issues have shaped African women's lives and worldview in historical terms. African feminist thought, by implication, is anti-imperialist, socialist-oriented and keenly aware of the implications of social injustices for society as a whole. It is also anti-racist because it challenges the institutionalized racism of global and regional structures that exploit the continent and undermine its progress. This also enables African feminists to add their voices to the work of other feminists from the global South, who critique the eurocentrism of white western feminists.

Second, feminism did not 'arrive' in Africa via western feminism. Many serious African feminist thinkers consider this notion presumption to be an insult. Africa has one of the oldest civilizations and therefore one of the oldest patriarchies.[5] Women living in those communities did have some access to power and leadership though this access varied from one part of the region to another. Based on all the available literature, African women have always lived in deeply patriarchal societies and have always found ways and means of resisting patriarchy using various strategies such as the institution of motherhood, access to political power, religious authority, autonomous institutions, etc. (Amadiume 1988). Colonialism and settler-colonialism merely emphasized existing inequitable structures.

Our female ancestors might not have called it feminism but there was definitely some form of patriarchal resistance. Where I come from we see this in the institution of witchcraft. I am Yoruba, from Southwest Nigeria. We have a strong tradition of women as political, religious and cultural leaders. We also have a strong tradition of witchcraft. All Yoruba women have the potential to become witches. Witches, where I come from, are usually older women. They are wealthy, knowledgeable, opinionated and very assertive (in androcentric terms this trans-lates as aggressive). Many are widowed or divorced. Yoruba women, at a certain age, feel they have paid their dues to their patriarchal communities. Therefore, they no longer feel bound by conventions of obedience or deference to male authority nor are they afraid of sanctions because again, at their age, they have earned respite from certain obligations. For the first time in their lives, these women, called 'witches', are enjoying their freedom in the real sense of the word.

From my point of view, witchcraft is an example of an institution through which women traditionally resisted patriarchy. It undermines the argument that femi-nism was imported into Africa, falsely implying that for centuries African women have crossed their arms and accepted being battered and depersonalized by patriarchy.

Third, we are all familiar with the terms 'African culture' and 'African identity'. What is African culture and what constitutes an African identity? These terms are used by African scholars, practitioners and politicians in discussions aimed at reviving or sustaining vital elements of our humanity which were lost in the many years of brutalization and dislocation. However, these concepts mean different things in the day-to-day lives of African women. Within the context of an African culture as defined by men, a woman is a second-class citizen, her labour is unremunerated, available and disposable, her rights are subject to validation, and her daughters will share her fate. She is socialized into sustaining the very structures that will oppress her throughout her lifecycle. There will be some rewards that come with compliance and punishment for rebellion. This, in essence, is her identity. African feminists point out that definitions of African-ness cannot be constructed outside of the personhood of African women.

Following from this, African feminists question the validity of African institutions that are of no value to the society. Motherhood, as an example, has always been seen as a vital power base for women in almost all African communities. It guarantees women companionship and protection which, unlike their western sisters, they definitely do not expect from their husbands (Ogundipe-Leslie 1985). Yoruba women often say '*omo mi loko mi*' ('my child is my husband'). A feminist analysis of motherhood rejects the devaluing of women who are non-biological mothers and the higher premiums placed on giving birth to boys over girls. There are several other cultural and social institutions that no longer add value to the lives of women, but rather, devalue them, and are therefore no longer acceptable. African women are trying to create new identities for themselves. Identities based on nationality, ethnicity, sexuality, religion and a primordial understanding of African cultures do not serve us well as African women. This is because these identities were crafted outside of our own realities and experiences as women and serve to locate us in spaces that make us invisible, vulnerable, dispensable, transferable and disposable.

Fourth, another site of contestation for African feminists, is the notion of narratives and history. We question the writing and compilation of histories that do not include the lives of women. Where we have heard of some women, it has been mainly through their affiliations with powerful men as fathers, husbands and sons, i.e., the legendary Queen Mothers and Queens. Where are ordinary women in the history of our communities?

Fifth, a significant feature in the lives of African women is the need for self-reliance and economic independence. African women in almost all communities that we know of have always worked. They have worked within and outside the home. They have always made significant contributions to the economies of their communities through provision of free and low-waged labour, and endless reproduction. We are all familiar with the famous statistic, 'African women produce 80 per cent of the continent's food'. African women are always featured in photographs and works of art carrying babies on our backs, water on our heads and firewood in our arms. These images are presented all over the world as representations of the typical, unspoilt, natural African woman who knows the true essence of womanhood. The self-reliance and economic independence of African women is vital to their well-being and integrity, but this is not the same thing as condoning the exploitation and overburdening of women. A feminist perspective allows us to question the unfair use of women's unremunerated labour in the private and public sphere.

Sixth, another arena in which an African feminist theory has emerged is in relation to the experiences of African women with the state. Women's experiences in liberation struggles provided an entry point into political and social activism in several African countries and have resulted in critical lessons in terms of women's relationship with the state, women's citizenship and their democratic rights. For many years now women have contributed to nation-building through active participation in liberation movements in Namibia, Zimbabwe, Eritrea, Kenya,

South Africa, Mozambique, Uganda, Guinea-Bissau, and many other countries around the continent. Yet, the constitutions that emerged from the struggles they fought effectively wrote women out of existence as citizens. Many African constitutions do not recognize women as citizens because in these constitutions women do not have the right to transfer citizenship to another national. Nigerian men have the power and the legal capacity to transfer citizenship to whomever they marry. Nigerian women cannot. Thus, their status as a full citizens is questionable. Millions of African women are therefore not bona fide citizens of the very countries that they fought for and risked their lives to build. Many African constitutions are now being questioned, and re-negotiated where possible, as a result of feminist activism.

Seventh, African feminism, born out of the experience of women at the grassroots level, is interconnected with a global feminism which has worked hard for gains for women around the world. International instruments such as the Convention on the Elimination of all forms of Discrimination Against Women (CEDAW), the 1993 Universal Declaration on Human Rights (which declared that the women's rights are an integral and indivisible part of human rights), and the Beijing Platform for Action are the result of many hard years of feminist struggles all over the world. The voices of African women have been a part of that movement.

How then do these theoretical frameworks inform the activism of African women scholars, thinkers and practitioners and what challenges do they face? It is very difficult to create and sustain feminist space in many African countries for several reasons. Feminism is still very unpopular and threatening. The word still conjures up bogeys of wild, naked white women burning their bras, imperialism, domination, an undermining of African culture, etc. Feminists are subjected to ridicule and insults. They are called 'frustrated', 'miserable spinsters', 'castrators' and 'home wreckers'. In some cases, their lives are threatened.

The public/private divide is a real challenge. A feminist ideology tries to expose the artificial distinctions and points out the consequences for women. For African women, the public/private divide means that women's lives in the public have to be lived out as a reflection of their designated roles in private, as nurturers, caregivers and second-class citizens. Women in the public sphere advocating for rights and challenging the status quo do so at great risk. In private, many articulate women's rights advocates have to deal with the challenges of indifferent or unsupportive partners and, when they chose to leave an abusive relationship, there is a public backlash against them. Hence, society uses the public/private to serve its own interests.

For women living in rural areas, the private sphere means being confined by poverty, lack of electricity, of clean water, of safe health facilities, etc. A popular strategy used to silence feminists is to continually use rural women as a weapon over articulate, mainly urban based middle-class women. Anytime middle-class women open their mouths to raise an issue of concern they are asked 'what about the women in the village?' This is a code for saying 'the women in the village have nothing and they are not complaining, so why are you turning them against us?' This strategy erodes the self-esteem of feminists, dissipates their energies and makes them continuously apologetic for their education and whatever privileges they may have.

Most states are hostile to women's rights issues. While the laws and the constitutions of the countries say one thing, the politicians and opinion leaders are saying other things to discredit 'those lost, polluted women [i.e., feminists] who want to cause trouble with our women who are happy where they are'. The very important and serious work of trying to lobby for legal reforms and constitutional amendments that could raise the status of women is usually undermined with such frivolous statements from government officials. Most African feminists do not work in enabling environments. The media, political parties, trade unions, etc., do not genuinely understand why there has to be a feminist movement. Male colleagues in civil society organizations, who we assume ought to know better, do not always provide the support and solidarity that feminists need. There are also some women who are in leadership positions in government structures and other strategic institutions who lack either the consciousness or clout to push a progressive agenda for women and sometimes become a liability to the feminist movement as a result of their conservative, reactionary positions.

Many women's organizations lack the institutional capacity to sustain long-term activities to improve the lives of women. They run on shoestring budgets, are heavily donor-dependent and donor-driven and do not have the necessary mechanisms for sustained institutional growth and development. Whilst some might argue that so-called professionalism ruins social movements because it adds a dollar price to people's commitment, we need to also be realistic and accept that for movements to survive they need to grow and evolve. Some national and regional women's organizations in Africa that have been around for up to 25 years, have now reached the stage where they either grow stronger and survive or wither and die. An organization needs adequate financial, human and material resources to make its work relevant and sustainable in the long term. Commitment, good will and volunteerism are vital, but they are no longer enough to sustain women's organizations and the work they do.

Also, factors such as ideological differences, donor involvement and poor employment opportunities have contributed to the proliferation of civil society organizations. Many of these organizations are part of an overall developmental strategy that does not necessarily improve the lives of African women, or men. As such, these organizations are often not respected and their work is met with cynicism and suspicion by communities in which they are located, by potential beneficiaries and donors, and this provides governments with an opportunity to discredit all kinds of organizations.

Non-governmental organizations with the appropriate capacity have the ability to provide the necessary conceptual, analytical and practical tools for emerging leaders. Women's organizations in particular have the potential to produce well-grounded leaders through their many awareness raising, self-esteem, inter-generational and capacity-building programs. We have learned as a women's movement in Africa that if the organizations and institutions which constitute the movement are weak, it will ultimately have a negative impact on our strategic agenda (see *Report of the Conference on Governance and Management of African Women's NGOs* 1998).

Another key challenge facing African feminists is a lack of conceptual clarity within the movement itself. Granted, not all women in the progressive strand of the movement call themselves feminists, even though they do work on a day-to-day basis which is clearly feminist. Of concern is the depoliticization of feminism as a result of gender and development language. At a conference in 1998, a woman stood up proudly to announce, 'I have moved beyond feminism to gender'. As Nighat Said Khan states in this volume,

> ... a large number of feminists and women activists have begun to use the word 'gender' in place of 'women' when discussing the issues of equality and rights.... The problem with the notion of 'gender' is that it can mean *both* men and women or either man or woman. The specificity of women's oppression disappears. (94-95)

It is precisely because gender means both men and women that many African women activists describe themselves as 'gender activists' and not 'feminist activists'. Gender is safe. Feminism is threatening. Gender can be accommodated and tolerated by the status quo. Feminism challenges the status quo. As a result, the feminist spaces we have tried to create for ourselves are in danger of being 'genderized'. After years of gender mainstreaming many share the sentiment that men have been 'left behind' and now need to be 'carried along'.

Working with men, building personal and professional partnerships with them and seeking them out as allies is something we all have to do as feminist activists. However, does 'carrying men along' also include employing them to run women's organizations, to edit women's magazines, speak on behalf of women, counsel women suffering from abuse and tolerating the company of men who philander, batter their partners physically and emotionally in private and seek to be our allies in public? Are these men we are 'carrying along' prepared to give up the powers and privileges which patriarchy confers on them?

Many women in the movement say: 'What does it matter what we call ourselves? As long as we are all fighting for women's rights, isn't that what matters?' That is not good enough. The work of fighting for women's rights is deeply political and the process of naming is a political one too. Choosing to name oneself a feminist places one in a clear ideological position. If we do not have an adequate theory of the oppression of women we will lack the analytical tools that might enable us to come up with the appropriate strategies. As a result we end up working on symptoms and not root causes. By naming ourselves as feminists we politicize the struggle for women's rights, we question the legitimacy of the structures that keep women subjugated and we can develop tools for transformatory analysis and action. By 'genderizing' the debate, we collude with the process of accommodating ourselves within oppressive structures.

Opportunities for Creating Space

In spite of its many curses, globalization does bring with it some key opportunities which the global South can take advantage of. An example is the increased demand for democratization processes, and a broadening of the spectrum of rights for women and men. This can strengthen civil society movements and women's movements in particular in the following ways. It opens up the possibilities of universal guarantees that go much further than those given by individual nation states. For example, it raises the possibility of two parallel citizenships, a national citizenship and a global one. A global citizenship is guaranteed through adherence to universally agreed and accepted principles of social justice and human rights. A national citizenship can be enriched through the co-existence of a global one, through the provision of recourse to regional and international mechanisms and legal instruments.

Organizations such as the Federation of Women Lawyers in Kenya, The Federation of Women Lawyers in Uganda, and the Ethiopian Women Lawyers have actively promoted issues affecting women's human rights in those countries and have gained a lot of respect as outspoken and undeterred voices for women. In Nigeria, BAOBAB is an example of a women's organization committed to challenging the use of religion, culture and tradition to undermine women's rights. In the Gambia, GAMCOTRAP has similar objectives, and in Senegal, Mali, Cameroon and other French-speaking parts of Africa, there are national networks and grassroots organizations committed to the same issues. Other examples are Forum for Women in Democracy (FOWODE) in Uganda and Gender and Development Action in Nigeria. All these organizations work on mobilization and awareness-raising around women's rights and issues such as violence against women and harmful traditional practices. They work with women in very poor communities in rural and urban areas, and they work on changing structures, beliefs and attitudes. This is the process of recreating identities and redefining a personhood for African women. Their work is clearly transformatory and feminist.

The South African and Ugandan constitutions make explicit provisions for the protection and promotion of the rights of women. These provisions include quotas and affirmative action for women. These are gains won by the women's movements in those countries through advocacy, analysis, research and institution-building. Many African women now believe that most of their work will be of little effect if they continue to remain on the margins of power-sharing and leadership. There is a deliberate shift toward not only dealing with the issue of access to decision-making, but also to strengthening women's leadership within hostile, patriarchal structures. A good example is the Women's Budget Initiative spearheaded by women in the South African parliament.

There are opportunities for participation in shaping policies and development agendas for reconstruction of war-torn societies and countries in democratic transition. This is characterized by a shift in power relations and a refocus on how, where and by whom power is defined—new actors such as women's organizations, trade unions, human rights organizations and new political power bases. Over the past ten years at least, civil society organizations have kept countries running after they had virtually collapsed, as in Sierra Leone, Liberia and Somalia. Women in particular formed broad-based peace movements in these countries. With this comes a call for new values for defining communal relationships and state/civil society relations. Such values include calls for accountability, transparency, anti-corruption and inclusiveness as crucial frameworks for good governance. Central to the call for these values is the role and participation of women. No society can rejuvenate or reclaim itself without the active involvement and participation of women.

There are possibilities of engagements with the state as new demands for accountability and representation emerge, for example through decentralization programs, affirmative action, and calls for legal and constitutional reform. These are sites where African women have been actively advocating and fighting for political space, legal reforms, representation, affirmative action and gender mainstreaming policies. The Zambian Women's Lobby Group, for example, has carried out research on political participation and raised funds in support of female candidates. FOWODE in Uganda and Gender and Development Action in Nigeria are also active in this arena.

There are the possibilities too, of increased alliances and networking across regions and continents, to sustain gains made at the major UN conferences in the 1990s. While the significance of UN 'jamborees' to the lives of the majority of African people at the grassroots can be debated heatedly, the fact still remains that these meetings provide healthy opportunities for South-South/North-South sharing of information and expertise, and formulation of new strategies. At a regional level, there are many women's organizations working toward building a strategic, pan-African agenda for the empowerment of African women.

For example, Women in Law and Development in Africa (WILDAF) is a leading network of individuals and organizations in over 40 African countries dedicated to using the law as a tool for African women's empowerment. This network has provided a voice for African women at a regional and international level and led most of the contributions of the African women's movement to the UN World Conference on Women's Human Rights in June 1993. They also spearheaded the additional protocol on women's rights to the African Charter on Human and People's Rights.

African Women's Communication and Development Network (FEMNET) is one of the oldest regional networks in Africa. Its main contribution has been in the areas of networking, policy and communications.

Akina Mama wa Afrika (AMwA) is an international NGO for African women with a head office in the UK and an Africa regional office in Kampala, Uganda. In 1996, AMwA established an African Women's Leadership Institute (AWLI).

This project has helped train over 500 African women in regional, sub-regional and national leadership development programs. AMwA's focus is on building transformatory leadership in Africa, and ensuring that women are at the forefront of the process. A particular focus has been bringing younger women into the movement.

Abantu for Development is another regional organization that works in the areas of capacity-building and influencing policies from a gender perspective. Through their Gender, Advocacy and Poverty network, Abantu makes the case for understanding how micro and macro development policies impact on women and can lead to their impoverishment.

The Association for African Women in Research and Development (AAWORD), established in 1976, grew out of a commitment of African women scholars and practitioners who wanted to respond to how African women's experiences were being appropriated at the level of the academy and in development practice.

A regular feature of the work of these national and regional organizations has been linking global and local concerns through their participation in regional and international events. Connected to all these possibilities is the global consensus on the centrality of women's empowerment for the attainment of sustainable development. Even the most reactionary of states would admit this though they do little to put it into practice.[6]

Strategic Directions for the African Women's Movement

The areas important to building and sustaining the women's movement globally have been identified as the following (see *Report of the Conference on Global Feminist Leadership* 1997).

Confronting public structures and institutions: The feminist movement world-wide is now concentrating on confronting state structures to change the systems. This has had mixed results but it is a necessary strategy if we are to see lasting changes in the lives of women, especially the majority of women who live in the world's poorer countries. To do this we need women as public advocates who can work at a policy level in governmental or quasi-governmental institutions, as legal advocates, politicians and lawmakers.

The capacity to develop new knowledge: Feminism has thrived in the academies in the North because feminists in those countries have been able to acquire the spaces and resources. Unfortunately this has led to intellectual hegemonies—the sisters in the North are the ones with the money, technology and access to international publishing, all crucial sites for the production of knowledge. They thus appropriate the knowledge bases of women in the South. Within the global women's movement we have a dichotomy whereby the women from the North are regarded as the thinkers and scholars and the women from the South are the practitioners, with more value and respect given to the former. How many feminist writers on Africa refer to the works of African women? How many books on 'international feminism' include contributions from African feminist scholars and activists? There has been a very effective silencing of African women's voices and experiences. Within the African women's movement we are now challenging ourselves to devote time and energies to writing our own stories, narratives and to theorizing. We have to scale up our contributions to the rich debates on feminist theory and practice worldwide. Only when all voices have been heard, will we be able to talk of a truly global feminism.[7]

Building and sustaining feminist institutions is what has kept the feminist movement alive. Feminist organizations today are somewhat different from what they where when they first started. We need feminist spaces that can consciously move from one phase of development to another. Feminist organizational development is another area calling for more research and attention and it might take a while for us to be able to assess the implications. I believe that the nature and structure of feminist organizing will have to change. Feminist organizations have usually been premised on principles of non-hierarchy, collective work and collective responsibility. The work has also been characterized by its dependence on volunteers.

For feminist spaces to survive, we need a reconceptualization of power and leadership within organizations. As organizations grow more complex and try to cope with the demands of various projects, funding, servicing various stakeholders and retaining relevance, we need effective feminist leaders to engage in this process. Feminist organizations also need to start thinking of acquiring their own resources in order to consolidate and sustain their legacies. We cannot afford to have a political movement which is at the mercy of donor funding.[8]

There is also the issue of racism within the global women's movement. It still there, it hasn't gone away. As an African woman who has lived and worked in Europe for many years, and been a part of many feminist initiatives in the North, I never cease to wonder at this blind spot within the international women's movement. We have spoken about the issues many times. Black women writers have also raised the issues over and over again, but sometimes we still don't seem to have moved forward. For example, it would never occur to an African woman to tell an American or British woman 'your accent is cute', or 'you look so smart', or 'your costume is lovely'. References to people's accents are about race, ethnicity, class and ultimately power. Why would I want to comment on the accent of an American, when I know she is an American. How else would I expect her to speak? How do we expect an African woman professional to dress? And since when did African boubous and bubas become 'costumes?' Costumes are worn by stage performers or at the circus. We do not refer to ball gowns or tuxedos as 'costumes'. This is usually a subtle process of 'othering'. Thus, as Patricia McFadden states,

We must re-define the ways in which we enter as participants in the global women's movement and challenge the exoticisation and objectification of African women.... We have to challenge racial privilege in the Global Women's Movement; just because we are women fighting for the same goal does not make racial privilege go away. (1997)

As African women we are learning to re-define ways in which we engage with the global women's movement in order to sustain our 'glocal' spaces. In many instances, it can be painful and frustrating.

In order to achieve the task of sustaining feminist spaces through these strategic directions, I suggest we focus our energies and interventions on three cross-cutting issues.

Investing in the personal growth of women: This is a priority for the African women's movement. The growing backlash against the women's movement manifested in hostile state responses, media harassment and cultural and religious fundamentalisms makes the task of sustaining individual women's energies difficult. We need to go back to old-fashioned feminist strategies of raising awareness and developing self-esteem.

One of the most important things for African women feminists and activists is space for personal growth and self-discovery. This area is equally as important (and in some instances even more important) as all the capacity-building, strategic planning, management and gender training that we and other organizations provide in Africa. Therefore, the fact that the African Women's Leadership Institute provides a feminist leadership framework at an analytical level, and translates this into practice, is something we are proud to declare as a significant contribution to the African women's movement. Over the past three years, AWLI has provided leadership development opportunities for women's rights activists through regional, sub-regional and national programs. These women are in turn passing their skills on to others in their communities (see AMwA 1997, 1998, 1999, 2000).

Replenishing our ranks: We need more young women in the movement and we need to develop institutional cultures of inter-generational organizing. This is usually a sticky area in the African women's movement. Younger women note the conservatism, matronizing, often selfish behaviour of older women. Older women on the other hand point to the lack of commitment of younger women, who are less willing to challenge gender relations because of where they are in their life cycle.

This is a complex relationship. It is usually older women, free from the challenges of looking after young children, who have the time and space to concentrate on their activism. Younger activists, especially those who are planning to marry or are new in the institution are still testing the waters of their relationships and might be reticent in their commitment to the feminist move-ment. On the other hand, we have seen many young activists challenge the conservative, accommodating politics of older women, calling for newer, more radical approaches.

In the North, the feminist movement has become a victim of its own successes. Young, middle-class women, armed with their university degrees, the right to control their bodies, their credit cards and a marked improvement in the quality of their lives compared with that of their mothers, are saying that we are now in a 'post-feminist era'. There is no such thing as post-feminism until there is a post-patriarchy. As Barbara Ehrenreich remarks,

> ... young, middle-class feminists are not as involved in collective action as we were, but instead see feminism as an individual program for self-improvement. That's fine if you are fortunate and privileged, but what about the women who aren't? How do we make up for that? We need a collective movement. Patriarchy is an old way of organizing human societies—twelve thousand years old. That's quite a thing to overthrow. We still need a revolution.

Through the work AMwA has done at the AWLI, we try to provide platforms for these discussions to take place and develop strategies which take on board the positive contributions and insights of all generations.

I would like to conclude by calling for more discussions and dialogue on the various aspects of globalization and its impact on the world's communities, especially women. As a global women's movement, we need to be cautious, brave and vigilant so that gains we have made are not lost. We need to keep sustaining our feminist spaces in whatever way we can. Our feminist spaces are not the same, and they don't have to be. Some are academic, some are activist-oriented, some are policy-inclined, and some are local, national, or international in focus. They are all differentiated by our varied realities, locations and identities. To sustain these spaces we need commitment, solidarity, critical dialogues, effective leadership, power and money.

As Angela Miles (1996) suggests in her book, *Integrative Feminisms*, we need a diverse, inter-related, interconnected, multi- and inter-disciplinary feminism, which is local, global and collective and links theory with practice. We will not survive without it. It is about choices, hopes, dreams and justice. But much more than all that, the lives of millions of women all over the world depend on it. So, let us keep these spaces, and the faith.

This article is adapted from the Fourth Annual Dame Nita Barrow Lecture sponsored by the Centre for Women's Studies in Eduation at the Ontario Institute for Studies in Education at the University of Toronto in November 2000. Online: http:// www1.oise.utoronto.ca/cwse/lectext.htm.

Bisi Adeleye-Fayemi is co-founder and Executive Director of the African Women's Development Fund. (AWDF, Nigeria/UK). AWDF is a fundraising and grantmaking organization launched in 2001 that supports African women's organizations committed to advancing women's human rights and their political and economic empowerment. Prior to her work with AWDF, Adeleye-Fayemi was Director of Akina Mama wa Afrika (AMwA), an international pan-African NGO that coordinates programs for the development of women's leadership skills and supports women's grassroots organizing. As director of AMwA she initiated the African Women's Leadership Institute, a leadership training program for women's groups in Africa and Europe. She is President of the Association of Women's Rights in Development (AWID) Board of Directors, co-founder and Board member of the Black and Migrant Women in Europe Network, and Board member of ALLAVIDA (UK) and the Partnership for Transparency Fund. She holds an MA in History from the University of Ife, Nigeria and an MA in Gender Studies from Middlesex University, UK. She has experience as a writer, lecturer, trainer, fund-raiser, and as an organizational development specialist.

Notes

1   For a comprehensive review of governmental and non-governmental responses from the African Region to the Beijing+5 review process see the *Synthesis of National Reports on the Progress Made in the Implementation of the Dakar/Beijing Platform for Action* and the *African Regional NGO Report on the NGO* (1999).

2   My organization, Akina Mama wa Africa (AMwA), was one of the eight regional African women's NGOs which had been invited to be a part of the UN/ECA Regional Preparatory Task Force to prepare for the Sixth African Regional Conference, the preparatory meeting (PREPCOM) for the Beijing+5 Review.

3   Examples include the 1989 Convention on the Rights of the Child; the Africa Charter on Human and People's Rights; the UN Conference on the Environments, Rio 1992; UN Vienna Declaration from the World Conference on Human Rights, 1993; the UN Conference on Population and Development 1994; the UN Declaration on Violence Against Women; the UN Social Summit 1995; and the 1995 Beijing Platform for Action.

4   Some key African feminist thinkers and activists include Awa Thiam, Nawal el Sadawi, Patricia McFadden, Amina Mama, Molara Ogundipe-Leslie, Ayesha Imam, Marie-Angeliqe Savane, Sara Longwe, Filomena Chioma Steady, Fatima Mernissi, Abena Busia, Ifi Amadiume.

5   Ifi Amadiume (2000) argues that we had matriarchies. While Awa Thiam (1986), Patricia McFadden (1997) and myself do not necessarily agree with the notion of an African matriarchy as Amadiume describes it, we do accept the historical facts that some African women in certain communities had a revered status.

6   In 1997, at a conference on leadership in Africa which was held in Mozambique, a senior government official from Botswana, in response to a flippant statement that had been made by another male colleague of his about 'this gender business' said, 'I cannot sit here hundreds of miles away from my constituency and say that women do not count. They are the ones who vote for us. Not only that, we African governments promised to do so many things at Beijing, I ask you, what have we done for the women?' I was so pleased to hear this!

7   Some of us have recently set up an African Feminist Initiative which is a collective for analysis, writing and feminist education. Our first publication, *African Feminist Perspectives*, is currently in production.

8   It is for these reasons that an African Women's Development Fund (AWDF) was recently established. The founders of the Fund are African women who have been active in the women's movement for many years: Joanna Foster, former Regional Coordinator, WILDAF; Hilda Tadria, a gender specialist who is currently a Senior Gender Adviser at the UN/ECA; and Bisi Adeleye-Fayemi, Director of AMwA. AWDF will raise money and provide grants for African women's organizations.

References

Abdullah, H. (1995) 'Wifeism and activism: the Nigerian women's movement', in Amrita Basu (ed.), *The Challenge of Local Feminisms: Women's Movements in Global Perspectives,* Boulder: Westview Press.

African Regional NGO Report on the NGO Consultations (1999) held at the Sixth African Regional Conference on Women, Addis Ababa, compiled by the regional NGO task force.

Akina Mama wa Afrika (AMwA) (2000). *Keeping Feminist Space and Faith: Report of the African Women's Leadership Institute Reunion Conference,* Kampala: AMwA.

Akina Mama wa Afrika (AMwA) (1999) *Feminist Leadership in Africa: Report of the Third African Women's Leadership Institute,* Kampala: AMwA.

Akina Mama wa Afrika (AMwA) (1998) *Moving from Accommodation to Transformation, Report of the Second African Women's Leadership Institute,* Kampala: AMwA.

Akina Mama wa Afrika (AMwA) (1997) *Taking the African Women's Movement into the 21st Century, Report of the First African Women's Leadership Institute,* Kampala: AMwA.

Amadiume, I. (2000) *Daughters of the Goddess, Daughters of Imperialism: African Women, Culture, Power and Democracy,* London: Zed Books.

Amadiume, I. (1988). *Male Daughters, Female Husbands,* London: Zed Press.

Beijing+5 United Nations General Assembly Special Session, June 2000, New York.

Beijing Declaration and Platform for Action (1995) Fourth World Conference on Women, 15 September, A/CONF.177/20 (1995) and A/CONF.177/20/Add.1 (1995). Online: http://www1.umn.edu/humanrts/instree/e5dplw.htm

Butegwa, F. (1997) *The Women's Movement in Africa,* Kampala: AMwA.

Davies, C. B. and A. A. Graves (eds.) (1986) *Ngambika: Studies of Women in African Literature,* Trenton, NJ: Africa World Press.

ECA/Africa Centre for Women (1999) *Achieving Good Governance: The Essential Participation of Women,* Report of Fortieth Anniversary Conference on the Economic Empowerment of African Women, Addis Ababa, April.

Khan, N. S. (1999) 'Up against the state: the women's movement in Pakistan-Implications for the global women's movement', Third Annual Dame Nita Barrow Lecture, Ontario Institute for Studies in Education of the University of Toronto, November. [Reprinted here pages 86-99]

McFadden, P. (1997) 'Challenges and opportunities facing the African women's movement into the 21st century', in B. Adeleye-Fayemi and A. Akwo-Ogojo (eds.), *Taking the African Women's Movement into the 21st Century: Report of the First African Women's Leadership Institute (AWLI),* Kampala: Akina Mama wa Africa.

Miles, A. (1996) *Integrative Feminisms: Building Global Visions, 1960s-1990s,* New York: Routledge.

Obasanjo, O. (2000) Speech presented at the UN Millennium Summit, September 6th-8th, 2000

Oduol, W. and W. Kabira (1995) 'The mother of warriors and her daughters: the women's movement in Kenya', in Amrita Basu (ed.), *The Challenge of Local Feminisms, Women's Movements in Global Perspective,* Boulder: Westview Press.

Ogundipe-Leslie, M. (1985) 'Women in Nigeria', in *Women in Nigeria Today/Women in Nigeria,* London: Zed Press.

Report of the Conference on Governance and Management of African Women's NGOs (1998) convened by AMwA, FEMNET and WILDAF, in Nyaga, Zimbabwe, November.

Report of Conference on Global Feminist Leadership (1997) organized by Novib in Cape

Town, South Africa, 22-26 September.

Synthesis of National Reports on the Progress Made in the Implementation of the Dakar/Beijing Platform for Action (1999) Sixth African Regional Conference on Women, 22-26 November, Addis Ababa.

Southern African Development Community (SADC) Gender Unit (1999) *Women in Politics and Decision-Making in SADC: Beyond 30 Percent in 2005.* Report of the proceedings of the conference held in Gaborone, Botswana, 28 March-1 April.

Thiam, A. (1986) *Speak Out, Black Sisters: Feminism and Oppression in Black Africa,* trans. by D. S. Blair, London: Pluto Press.

United Nations Economic Commission for Africa. (1999a). *Report of the Sixth African Regional Conference on Women,* 22-26 November, E/ECA/ACW/RC.V1/99/12

United Nations Economic Commission for Africa. (1999b) *The Political Empowerment of Women: Summary of Progress made by African Governments.* Sixth African Regional Conference on Women, 22-26 November.

ADVOCATING FEMINISM

THE LATIN AMERICAN FEMINIST NGO 'BOOM'

SONIA E. ALVAREZ

Neoliberal social and economic adjustment policies, state downsizing and changing international regimes have dramatically altered the conditions under which
feminist and other struggles for social justice are unfolding in Latin America today.
The restructured terrain on which feminists must now wage their cultural-political
battles, in turn, has triggered a significant reconfiguration of what I will refer to
as the Latin American feminist movement field—favouring particular actors and
types of activities while actually or potentially marginalizing others.

This article focuses on the most visible, and increasingly controversial, actors in
this reshaped movement field: feminist non-governmental organizations (NGOs).
NGOs are hardly new to Latin American feminisms. From the beginnings of
feminisms' second wave in the 1970s, professionalized and institutionalized[1]
movement organizations were established alongside more informal feminist
collectives or associations in many countries and both types of groups typically
centered their energies on popular education, political mobilization and poor and
working-class women's empowerment. However, the 1990s witnessed a veritable
'boom' in NGOs specializing in gender policy assessment, project execution, and
social services delivery, propelling them into newfound public prominence while
increasingly pushing many away from earlier, more movement-oriented activities.

In the 1980s, the professionalization or 'NGOization' of significant sectors of
Latin American feminist movements represented a strategic response to the return
of electoral politics and fragile and uneven processes of democratization in much
of the region. When feminists' former allies in the opposition to the national
security states assumed the reins of government in the mid-to-late 1980s and
1990s, many feminist groups began honing their applied research, lobbying and
rights advocacy skills in the hopes of translating the feminist project of cultural-
political transformation into concrete gender policy proposals.[2] Most newly

professionalized feminist groups fashioned hybrid political strategies and identities—developing expertise in gender policy advocacy while retaining a commitment to movement-oriented activities aimed at fostering women's empowerment and transforming prevailing gender power arrangements.[3] In collaboration with the 'global feminist lobby', local NGOs succeeded in pressuring many Latin American governments to enact a number of feminist-inspired reforms—such as electoral quotas to enhance women's political representation and legislation to combat domestic violence.

In recent years, however, Latin American states' embrace of what has been dubbed the 'New Policy Agenda' —'driven by beliefs organized around the twin poles of neoliberal economics and liberal democratic theory' (Hulme and Edwards 1997a: 5)—has inspired in a less self-evidently progressive set of gender-focused policies, centered on incorporating the poorest of poor women into the market and promoting 'self-help', civil society-led strategies to address the most egregious effects of structural adjustment. As states are downsized, NGOs in general 'have come to be regarded as the vehicle of choice—the Magic Bullet—for fostering [these] currently fashionable development strategies' (Gruhn 1997: 325). And local governments and inter-governmental organizations (IGOs) increasingly have turned to feminist NGOs in particular to evaluate gender-focused policies and administer the targeted self-help, social service and training (*capacitación*) programs for poor and working-class women currently in vogue throughout the region. The technical-professional side of feminist NGOs hybrid identity consequently has been foregrounded and critical feminist advocacy potentially compromised, while NGOs' empowerment goals and a wide range of movement-oriented activities are increasingly pushed onto the backburner. These developments, I shall argue, threaten to de-hybridize feminist NGO strategies and identities.

I begin by situating feminist NGOs within the increasingly heterogeneous Latin American feminist field, describing their varied activities, underscoring their specificity as compared to other types of feminist groups and other (non-feminist) NGOs, and mapping intra-regional differences in the pace and degree of NGOization. Whereas some critics have argued that NGOs as such have a depoliticizing and deradicalizing effect on movement politics (see especially Petras 1997; Lang 1997; Pisano 1996), I will argue that feminist NGOs' political hybridity enabled them to play a critical role in 'advocating feminism' by advancing a progressive gender policy agenda while simultaneously articulating vital political linkages among larger women's movement and civil society constituencies.

I then turn to three recent developments that potentially undermine NGOs' ability to advocate effectively for feminist-inspired public policies and social change. First, I will suggest that states and IGOs increasingly have turned to feminist NGOs as 'gender experts' rather than as citizens' groups advocating on behalf of women's rights. This trend threatens to reduce feminist NGOs' cultural-political interventions in the public debate about gender equity and women's citizenship to largely technical ones. A second and related trend is the growing tendency of neoliberal states and IGOs to view NGOs as surrogates for civil society. Feminist NGOs are now often selectively consulted on gender policy matters on the assumption that they serve as 'intermediaries' to larger societal constituencies. While many NGOs retain important linkages to such constituencies, however, other actors in the expansive Latin American women's movement field—particularly popular women's groups and feminist organizations that are publicly critical of the New [Gendered] Policy Agenda—are denied direct access to gender policy debates and thereby effectively politically silenced. Finally, I will suggest that as states increasingly subcontract feminist NGOs to advise on or carry out government women's programs, NGOs' ability to critically monitor policy and advocate for more thoroughgoing (perhaps more feminist?) reform may be jeopardized.

These developments deeply trouble many NGO activist-professionals and have infuriated their militantly 'autonomous' feminist critics. Many in both camps worry that growing numbers of feminist organizations seem to have been driven to focus their energies and resources on more technical, less contestatory activities, to the actual or potential detriment of more effective national or international policy advocacy and other modalities of feminist cultural-political intervention. I will conclude by suggesting that, despite adverse structural-political conditions, there is potential room for maneuver within the New *Gender* Policy Agenda and propose possible strategies for rearticulating the movement-activist and technical-professional faces of NGOs in the region.

This article draws on fieldwork and over 200 interviews conducted in Brazil, Chile, Peru and Colombia during 1997 and 1998,[4] as well as on previous research on Latin American participation in the preparatory processes for the recent string of United Nations Summits (see Alvarez 1998). I should make clear before I go any further that I am directly implicated in the story I am about to tell. During the three years (1993-1996) I served as Program Officer in Rights and Social Justice for the Ford Foundation in Rio de Janeiro, Brazil,[5] I evaluated, selected and funded gender-related research and advocacy projects, worked closely with a wide variety of feminist NGOs, and found myself—as never before in my fairly lengthy career as a US feminist internationalist activist and student of Latin American women's/ social movements—smack in the middle of transnational flows of feminist ideas and resources. The ensuing analysis therefore constitutes more than an academic exercise or an effort to solve a social scientific puzzle. It also grows out of my abiding concern as a Latina/Latin American/Latin Americanist activist-scholar to interrogate critically our always changing, multifaceted, and sometimes-contradictory cultural-institutional-academic practices as feminists.

Situating NGOs in the Contemporary Latin American Feminist Field

How and where Latin American activists practice their feminism changed markedly in the 1990s. Feminism—like many of the so-called new social movements that took shape in the region during the 1970s and 1980s—can today more aptly be characterized as an expansive, polycentric, heterogeneous discursive field of action which spans into a vast array of cultural, social and political arenas.[6] As I have argued elsewhere (Alvarez 1998), Latin American feminisms have undergone a notable process of decentering and diversification over the course of the past decade. That is, the reconfigured feminist movement field today spans well beyond social movement organizations, conventionally conceived. The 1990s saw a dramatic proliferation or multiplication of the spaces and places in which women who call themselves feminists act, and wherein, consequently, feminist discourses circulate. After over two decades of struggling to have their claims heard by male-dominant sectors of civil and political society and the state, women who proclaim themselves feminists can today be found in a wide range of public arenas—from lesbian feminist collectives to research-focused NGOs, from trade unions to Black and indigenous movements, from university women's studies programs to mainstream political parties, the state apparatus and the international aid and development establishments.

The diverse women who transit in this wide-ranging movement field interact in a variety of alternative and official publics and through a number of media. New, more formalized modalities of articulation or networking among the multiple spaces and places of feminist politics were consolidated during the 1990s. These range from region-wide identity and issue-focused networks, like the Afro-Latin American and Caribbean Women's Network and the Latin American Committee for the Defense of Women's Rights (CLADEM), to networks focused specifically on impacting the UN process, such as the Regional NGO Coordination established in preparation for the Beijing Summit.

NGOs have played a central role in setting up and sustaining these various forms of formal articulation among the vast range of actors who make up the feminist field. They have been crucial to articulating what I call social movement webs—the capillary connections among feminists and their sympathizers who now occupy a wide variety of social and political locations (Alvarez 1997; Alvarez, Dagnino and Escobar 1998). That is, in producing and circulating innumerable newsletters and publications, organizing issue-focused conferences and seminars, establishing electronic networks and a wide gamut of other communications media, NGOs have functioned as the key nodal points through which the spatially dispersed and organizationally fragmented feminist field remains discursively articulated.[7] As Jane Mansbridge suggests in the case of the US, the

> feminist movement ... is neither an aggregation of organizations nor an aggregation of individual members but a discourse. It is a set of changing, contested aspirations and understandings that provide conscious goals, cognitive backing, and emotional support for each individual's evolving feminist identity. (1995: 27)

Latin American NGOs have been vital in fashioning and circulating the discourses, transformational goals and ethical-political principles that are *consti-*

tutive of the movement, even as these are continually contested and resignified by the diverse women who today identify as feminists.

The Distinctive Features of Feminist NGOs

But just what exactly are feminist NGOs? What distinguishes them from non-feminist NGOs and from other actors in the broad-ranging feminist field? Though the concept of non-governmental organization is sometimes indiscriminately deployed in development discourse to refer to any social actor not clearly situated within the realm of the state, political society, or the market—from peasant collectives and community soup kitchens to research-oriented policy think tanks—among actors in the Latin American feminist field, the term 'feminist NGO' has come to denote particular kinds of groups with distinctive orientations and practices.

Indeed, in recent years, feminists in countries such as Brazil and Chile have ever more commonly drawn a sharp distinction between NGOs and 'the movement'. The former are typically characterized as having functionally specialized, paid, professional staff and sometimes a limited set of volunteers, receive funding from bilateral or multilateral agencies and (usually foreign) private foundations, and engage in pragmatic, strategic planning to develop reports or projects aimed at influencing public policies and/or providing advice or *asesoria* to the *movimiento de mujeres* (the grassroots women's movement) and varied services to low-income women. Though sometimes engaging in similar *asesoria* and policy-oriented activities, the latter is commonly understood to be made up of feminist groups or collectives that have largely volunteer, often sporadic, participants (rather than staff), more informal organizational structures, significantly smaller operating budgets, and whose actions (rather than projects) are guided by more loosely defined, conjunctural goals or objectives. But such a stark distinction between NGOs and the movement underplays the hybrid character of most feminist non-governmental organizations, ignores important differences in the timing and degree of movement NGOization in different countries, and obscures the diversity of NGO activities and practices.

Prevailing characterizations of NGOs—in both movement and scholarly discourses—often fail to capture the specificity of those operating within the feminist field. The academic literature most commonly defines NGOs as 'intermediary organizations' that 'are typically composed of middle-class, educated and professional people who have opted for political or humanitarian reasons to work with (or on behalf of) the poor and the marginalized' (Pearce 1997: 259). These grassroots support organizations (GRSOs) 'channel international funds to [member-serving grassroots organizations or] GROs and help communities other than their own to develop' (Fisher 1998: 4).

While feminist NGOs in most Latin American countries are typically made up of university-educated, middle-class, and most often white or *mestiza*, women (Tarrés 1997: 28), and many do work in some capacity with poor and working-class women's groups, they are distinct from non-feminist GRSOs in at least two key respects. First, most feminist NGOs do not see themselves as working only to 'help others' but also to alter gender power relations that circumscribe their own lives as women (see Lebon 1993, 1997, 1998; Soares 1998). In a comprehensive survey of 97 Mexican feminist NGOs, María Luisa Tarrés found that 'a strong identitarian component ... marked the logic of women's NGOs ... the space created by the NGO stimulates a re-elaboration of the identity of its members as social and political subjects' (1997: 4).

Second, the vast majority of NGO activist-professionals also view themselves as an integral part of a larger women's movement that encompasses other feminists (in other types of organizations and *sueltas* or independents) as well as the poor and working-class women for or on behalf of whom they profess to work. As one interviewee affirmed, 'In Peru, NGOs have a double identity ... we are centers and we are movement'.[8]

This double or hybrid identity led most professionalized feminist institutions to build horizontal linkages to a wide variety of organized expressions of the larger women's movements—from women in trade unions and urban community organizations to Church-linked mothers' clubs—while constructing vertical links to global and local policy-making arenas. And it has been this two-way political articulation that arguably fueled feminist NGOs' success in advancing a progressive gender policy agenda (Alvarez 1994). The actual or potential backing of sizeable, organized female constituencies proved crucial to feminist NGOs' ability to persuade political parties and government officials to endorse their women's rights and gender justice claims. Having a firm foot in the larger women's movement, in turn, kept NGOs accountable to other actors in the feminist field. The growing predominance of more technical-advisory activities, I will argue below, may be distancing NGOs from movement constituencies vital to successful advocacy.

Intra-Regional Variations in the NGOization of the Feminist Field

The degree of NGOization of the feminist movement and the extent to which NGOs' technical face supersedes movement-oriented activities varies significantly among countries in the region[9], reflecting the distinctive political environments in which feminisms unfolded, the country-specific priorities and preferences of international donors, and the particularities of feminist movement development in a given locality. In Brazil, for example, a sharper contrast between NGOs and 'the movement' is today drawn by many activists because early feminist groups were mostly of the more informal, feminist collective variety. Relatively few early groups received external funding or had paid administrative or professional staff. The process of institutionalization of the feminist movement in the form of more formal, professionalized groups—which only in the late 1980s came to refer to themselves as NGOs (Landim 1993)—accompanied the pace of Brazil's protracted and phased political transition process. The gradual liberalization of the political environment in which social movements operated and the gendered political opening promoted by some opposition-controlled state governments in the early to mid-1980s prompted growing numbers of feminists to formalize their organizations and develop greater policy expertise by the end of that decade (Lebon 1993; Heilborn and Arruda 1995; Alvarez 1990, 1994; Soares et al. 1995; Soares 1998). Fully 50 per cent of Brazilian NGOs were created between 1980 and 1990 (Lebon 1997: 7).

In Chile—where the heinous 17-year Pinochet dictatorship and shock-treatment-induced poverty made opposition movements favoured recipients of international humanitarian aid and liberal foundation funds—many second-wave feminist groups, who formed an integral part of that opposition, appear, by contrast, to have been able to institutionalize their organizations fairly early on. Given state repression and government indifference to the hardships neoliberalism heaped upon poor women, most of those early feminist NGOs centered their attention on supporting the survival struggles of women of the popular classes and organizing with them against the Pinochet dictatorship (Frohmann and Valdés 1995; Gaviola et al. 1994; Chuchryk 1994; Schuurman and Heer 1992; Schild 1994). Since the return of civilian rule and a new 'post-social democratic' brand neoliberalism in 1989, many Chilean feminists I talked with suggested that those links to the base have been largely severed, for reasons I shall explore further below.

In yet another variation, most Colombian feminists I interviewed concurred with Maruja Barrig's assessment that 'as compared to other countries in the region, the feminist movement has not expressed itself principally through NGO channels', but rather 'small activist organizations prevail ... which participate as such in various activities of the movement, in a *volunteer capacity*' (Barrig 1997b; see also Luna and Villareal 1994; Villareal 1994). The clientelism, corruption and *narcodemocracia* that permeate the Colombian regime, the historically weak presence of the state in much of the national territory, and the endemic political violence that flows from the above was hardly conducive to setting up specialized NGOs aimed at influencing public policy. Still, the post-1986 political decentralization, coupled with the 1991 Constitution which mandates state consultation with civil society in development planning, have fueled a process of increased institutionalization in various Colombian social movement fields. And, as I shall discuss below, there also seems to have been a marked increase in state subcontracting of NGO services for policy execution and social services delivery. Several Colombian feminist activists I talked with emphasized that 'there are two types of NGOs here: some are "historic", others more recent, which emerge after the Constitutional Assembly process, and are sometimes narrowly focused, opportunistic, and very nepotistic'.[10]

Variations in Latin American Feminist NGOs Practices and Activities

While scholars have attempted to classify NGOs into distinct types or generations—distinguishing among those engaged in charity, relief and welfare activities, those pursuing small-scale development projects, and those committed to community organization, mobilization and empowerment (Clarke 1998: 42), I maintain that most Latin American feminist and non-feminist NGOs are amalgams of these types. In any given context and over time, moreover, the activities prioritized by feminist NGOs also have varied significantly.

As in the Chilean case, most if not all NGOs emerging early in Latin American feminism's second wave focused their activities on popular education and women's empowerment or provided services and *asesoria* (advice) to poor and working-class women's organizations. Some still do. MEMCH—an umbrella organization of popular women's groups 'gone NGO' since the return of civilian rule in Chile—continues to view itself as a 'bridge between feminism and the popular classes'[11] and offers a variety of training courses and other services to women from the urban periphery. *Tierra Nuestra* runs a School for Grassroots Women Leaders in Santiago's southern zone and promotes the 'autonomous organization' of the 64 grassroots women's groups with whom they continue to work.[12] Similarly, Colombia's current post-Beijing coalition, coordinated by the Bogotá-based NGO, *Dialogo Mujer*, proclaims its intention to foster a 'popular feminism of diversity'.[13] Tarrés found that fully 90 per cent of Mexican feminist NGOs provide direct services to their targeted publics and 'the majority claims to be oriented toward women of the popular sectors, whether they be urban residents, peasants or indigenous women' (1997: 19, 18).

Some feminist NGOs, such as CFEMEA in Brazil and *Casa de la Mujer* in Colombia, today also center their work on promoting and monitoring gender-related legislation. The latter group, for example, has worked closely with Afro-Colombian Senator Piedad Córdoba and other women parliamentarians on both women's issues and non-gender-specific public policies so that they might 'integrate gender to their general programmatic agenda'.[14] Still others seek to articulate grassroots work with policy-focused or more macro forms of cultural-political intervention, pursuing rights advocacy, not just to promote more progressive policies but also to *engender* cultural change. Afro-Brazilian feminist NGOs, like São Paulo-based *Geledés* and *Fala Preta*, for example, promote consciousness-raising programs for Black youth and women, while advocating for racially-sensitive gender policies and gender-sensitive and anti-racist jurisprudence and public health policies.[15] *Themis*, a feminist NGO based in the southern Brazilian city of Porto Alegre, offers legal training courses for grassroots women community leaders and organizes specialized workshops on gender, race, class and the law for judges and other legal professionals, while also engaging in litigation to advance feminist jurisprudence.[16] The regional feminist legal rights network, Latin American Committee for the Defense of Women's Rights (CLADEM)—of which *Themis* forms part—claims to work to develop a radical critique of the law, to be more than a pressure group, to intervene in the culture, and promote women's empowerment. CLADEM spearheaded a transnational Campaign for a Universal Declaration of Human Rights with a Gender Perspective, organized to mark the fiftieth anniversary of that UN Declaration, for example, but their stated objective was not only to impact the UN, but also to use the commemorative occasion as a 'vehicle through which to educate the general public about women's human rights'.[17]

While many feminist NGOs continue to struggle to provide *asesoria* and promote *conscientización* (consciousness-raising) among popular women's organizations and strive to push gender policy beyond the narrow parameters of Latin America's actually existing democracies, however, the material resources and political rewards for doing so appear to be drying up. The global and local premium is increasingly placed on NGO gender policy assessment, project execution, and social services delivery. Amid the heterogeneous actors that today constitute the expansive feminist movement field, specific types of NGOs and NGO activities have attained particular prominence. To the potential detriment of NGOs' movement-oriented advocacy, alternative development and empowerment activities, growing numbers are concentrating on technical-advisory activities. I now turn to the factors—largely external to the feminist movement field—which are propelling this shift.

The Expansion of Local and Global Demand for Professionalized Feminism

A key factor in NGOs' heightened focus on technical-advisory activities has been growing state and IGO demand for specialized knowledge about women and gender—expertise increasingly supplied by the most technically adept, professionalized feminist organizations. Thanks in part to the success of local and global NGO feminist lobbying, there has been a veritable deluge of gender-focused policies and programs in recent years (see Htun 1998) and many governments today brandish more progressive discourses about women's rights. At least rhetorically, most Latin American states now profess a commitment to gender equity and have adopted an impressive number of policies, programs and plans focused on women.

Colombia's 'White Book on Women' asserted the Samper administration's avowed pledge to 'Pay Society's Debt to the Colombian Woman' (Presidencia de la República de Colombia 1994). And the Chilean government—the putative 'jaguar' of development in the region—professes that 'overcoming discrimination against women ... has been necessitated by the government's three fundamental guidelines for the current period—strengthening democracy, national economic development and modernization' (SERNAM 1994: 5). National leaders from Fujimori to Cardoso to Zedillo have echoed such pledges to enhance gender equity and have similarly declared their intention to 'promote women' and 'incorporate them into development'. During the regional preparatory process for the Beijing Summit, a wide gamut of long-standing feminist-inspired reforms—ranging from more equitable participation in public and family life to reproductive rights—made their way into the language of the Latin

American and Caribbean Platform for Action and were thereby elevated to the status of norms of regional governance.

Governments appear to have begun to translate some of those norms into legislation. Laws establishing quotas to ensure women's representation in elected office have been passed in countries such as Argentina, Brazil, and Peru and are presently under discussion in Chile and Bolivia, for example (Jones 1998). Sixteen states have adopted legislation and some have set up specialized police precincts to deter 'intra-familial violence' (Americas Watch 1991; Blondet 1995; Nelson 1996).

The many local feminist NGOs who focused their energies on promoting women's legal rights consequent to democratization certainly had a major hand in fostering this apparent gendered political opening. And the 'global women's lobby' —in which Latin American feminist NGOs have increasingly participated since they hosted the Women's Forum at the Earth Summit in Rio in 1992 (Sikkink 1995; Keck and Sikkink 1998)—has been instrumental in fostering what feminist international relations scholars have dubbed an 'emergent international women's regime' (Kardam 1997: 2). The increased gendering of international regimes, in turn, has brought new pressures to bear on local states, which further helps account for the recent flood of gender-focused policies and programs. As one Chilean interviewee put it, 'globalization requires that the state demonstrate sensitivity to gender ... resources come tied to that'.[18]

In virtually all countries in the region, specialized state machineries charged with proposing and monitoring (though seldom implementing) gender-focused programs and policies have been established (Waylen 1996; Lind 1995; Schumaher and Vargas 1993; Friedman 1997). In some cases, such as those of Chile's *Servicio Nacional de la Mujer* (SERNAM) and Brazil's *Conselho Nacional dos Direitos da Mulher* (CNDM), significant sectors of the feminist movements actively advocated the creation of state women's offices—though the ultimate mandate, design and performance of the specialized agencies actually created typically fell far short of feminist expectations (Valenzuela 1997; Schumaher and Vargas 1993). In other cases, such as the *Consejería para la Juventud, la Mujer, y la Família* established in Gaviría's Colombia or Fujimori's recently created *Ministério de Promoción de la Mujer y del Desarrollo Humano* (PROMUDEH), the founding of such women's state institutions appears to have been motivated by more pragmatic, when not outright opportunistic, considerations—such as the fact that bilateral and multilateral grants and loans now often require evidence of government sensitivity to women's role in development.

Gendered Citizens or Gender Experts?

Most governments have adopted this gendered dimension of the New [Global] Policy Agenda and many now view poor women's integration into the market as crucial to neoliberal 'development'. Gender therefore has come to be seen as a key technical dimension of state efforts to privatize social welfare provision, rationalize social policy and mount 'poverty alleviation programs (PAPs) to ameliorate the negative fallout of structural adjustment policies (SAPs) and to contain social discontent' (Craske 1998: 104). While, as noted above, feminist rights advocates have scored significant victories in areas such as political representation and violence against women, much recent Latin American 'policy with a gender perspective' forms an integral part of what we might call gendered 'social adjustment' strategies—'programs targeted at those groups [particularly poor women] most clearly excluded or victimized by SAPs' (Alvarez et al. 1998: 22). In the name of promoting gender equity, many states have mounted social adjust-ment programs targeting the poorest of poor women, such as those aimed at women heads-of-household in Chile, Colombia and Peru or temporary agro-export workers in Chile (Waylen 1996; Lind 1995; Schumaher and Vargas 1993; Friedman 1997). And feminist NGOs now are increasingly summoned to supply the expertise governments need to evaluate and implement such 'gender-sensitive' programs.

Despite the local and global feminist lobbies' central role in advocating for the changed international gender norms that help foster gender-friendly state dis-courses, then, the terms of women's incorporation into neoliberal development are not necessarily feminist-inspired. One Colombian local government official neatly summed up how feminists' political indictment of women's subordination is often translated or tergiversated by state bureaucrats: 'now things have changed, it's no longer that radical feminism of the 1970s, now it's policies with a gender perspective'.[19] Among many staff members of the women's government machineries I interviewed, gender seems to have become part of the lexicon of technical planning, a power-neutral indicator of 'modernity' and 'development' rather than a power-laden field of unequal relations between women and men (Largo 1998; Sánchez 1996; Alvarez 1999). As the Director of SERNAM in the Santiago Metropolitan Region emphasized in our conversation, 'our work is as technical as possible ... and there is a great deal of work to be done on the operational side of gender'.[20]

Since targeted social adjustment programs require specialized knowledge about female populations heretofore largely ignored by state and IGO bureaucracies alike, the new imperative to incorporate gender into PAPs and other forms of neoliberal development planning seems to have led states and IGOs to tap local and transnational feminist NGOs for their technical capabilities and 'gender expertise'. In an era of state downsizing, the gender-planning competency of government bureaucracies have not been expanded and many states have relied instead on contracting private consulting firms and NGOs to advise them on gender matters. Even Chile's SERNAM—which with its over 350 employees is perhaps the largest of the region's specialized state machineries—regularly turns to feminist NGOs to conduct research on indicators of gender inequality, draft policy statements, or evaluate the effectiveness of its various targeted social programs. As women's offices in most of the rest of the region typically lack staff with requisite gender expertise and are generally understaffed and underfunded, global pressures and the technical exigencies of gender planning increasingly have led many to rely on feminist NGOs to provide gender policy assessments and evaluate targeted women's programs.[21]

In many cases, the policy or program evaluations solicited of NGOs differ little from those provided by private consulting firms or academic gender specialists. That is, governments typically hire specialized NGO research teams to conduct policy impact studies or needs assessments surveys, but seldom encourage, much less require, wider political debate with the civil society constituencies with the highest stakes in gender-focused programs or with other actors in the feminist field. NGOs are most often consulted as experts who can evaluate gender policies and programs rather than as movement organizations that might facilitate citizen input and participation in the formulation and design of such policies. Feminist NGOs' technical involvement in policy assessment, then, does not necessarily translate into effectual gender policy or women's rights advocacy and, as I will suggest below, NGOs' growing contractual relationship with the state may in fact compromise their effectiveness in advocating for feminist reforms.

Representatives of or Surrogates for Women's Organizations in Civil Society?

The recent turn toward feminist NGOs is also inspired by many neoliberal governments' professed intention to promote 'the incorporation and participation of all civil society in the task of generating new gender social relations' (SERNAM 1994: 7). And among the diverse organizations that make up feminist civil society, NGOs are now often hailed as key 'intermediaries' for female social constituencies.

During the Cairo and Beijing Summits, for example, many Latin American governments invited select feminist NGOs to participate in the official preparatory process, thereby presumably heeding the UN's call for greater civil society participation in those processes. Some NGOs, along with gender specialists from the academy, were also contracted to prepare studies evaluating progress toward gender equity over the last two decades. And in keeping with the New Policy Agenda's view of NGOs 'as vehicles for "democratisation" and essential components of a thriving "civil society"' (Hulme and Edwards 1997a: 6), a veritable UN-Summits bonanza of grant funds was channeled from northern-based private donors and bilateral and multilateral agencies to those feminist NGOs willing and able, and judged to be technically competent, to work as intermediaries in promoting the involvement of civil society in the official and parallel preparatory processes for these world conferences.

Despite governments', donors' and IGOs' professed zeal for encouraging a 'thriving civil society', however, the criteria adopted in determining which NGOs would participate in the preparatory process or which would be consulted or funded seldom prioritized the extent to which such organizations actually functioned as intermediaries or conduits for the larger civil society constituencies officials presumed them to represent. In most countries, those NGOs who possessed policy-specialized staff, had previous experience in the UN process, and earned handsome foreign funding—irrespective of their links to larger social constituencies—were usually the ones selected to participate in the official preparatory processes. Governments and donors alike seldom required more than token consultations with NGOs' presumed constituencies—such as a public conference or seminar—as evidence of intermediation. Those funded or consulted were typically those feminist NGOs judged best able to 'maximize impact' with monies allotted or to have the technical capabilities deemed necessary for policy evaluation rather than those judged most politically capable of meaningfully involving women citizens in the UN process.

Typically non-membership organizations, most Latin American feminist NGOs are, of course, acutely aware of the fact that they don't represent anyone. Yet for many local states and IGOs alike, professionalized NGOs appear to have become convenient surrogates for civil society. In the Chilean case, María Elena Valenzuela argues that: 'SERNAM has privileged interlocution with institutions made up of experts and professionals which have contributed through evaluations and studies to design the themes and options of public policy' and further maintains that 'through this strategy SERNAM has tried to make up for its lack of interlocution with grassroots women's organizations, whose demands are expressed in mediated form through the knowledge produced by NGOs' (1997: 22).

That is, the more professionalized, technically adept NGOs seem to have become privileged interlocutors of states and IGOs on gender policy matters. In pronouncing them intermediaries, neoliberal governments effectively have circumvented the need to establish public forums or other democratic mechanisms through which those most affected by gender policies might directly voice their needs and concerns. And, as I shall argue below, NGOs and other women's movement organizations openly critical of government incumbents are seldom among the states' designated 'partners' in the implementation of gender and social welfare programs and policies.

Neoliberal States and the Boom in NGO Sub-Contracting

A discourse of state and civil society's 'co-responsibility' for social welfare pervades neoliberalism's recent quest to establish partnerships with NGOs. As virtually all but targeted or 'emergency' social programs are slashed, governments have promoted 'self-help strategies for combating poverty and providing welfare at the local level' (Craske 1998: 105; Barrig 1996). Civil society in general, and NGOs in particular, are enjoined to help implement such strategies and take on 'the responsibilities now eschewed by neoliberalism's shrinking state' (Alvarez et al. 1998: 1).

Among the most striking local examples I found of the growing tendency to rely on professionalized organizations in civil society to implement government programs was the 'NGO-state Coalition' discourse of the municipality of Santiago de Cali in Colombia. In a brochure entitled, 'The Social Face of Cali', the local government celebrated 'the existence of a great number of non-governmental organizations' in the city while stressing

that over the years, the work of many of these NGOs has become more complex. To their initial ideological convictions, they have incorporated an ever more technical professional dimension in approaching their work, such that along with promoting the development of social subjects, they are equally interested in generating new institutional forms. (Santiago de Cali 1997: 6)

The same document goes on to state that

NGOs are professionalizing themselves and they are beginning to introduce efficiency criteria in their work, which allows them in their contractual relation with the Administration to develop and execute social projects directed as the most vulnerable populations. (Santiago de Cali 1997: 8)

According to David Hulme and Michael Edwards, such discourse is fully in keeping with the shrinking state role in the realm of social policy—a key feature of the New Policy Agenda:

[M]arkets and private initiative are seen as the most efficient mechanisms for achieving economic growth and providing most services to most people ... because of their supposed cost-effectiveness in reaching the poorest, official agencies support NGOs in providing welfare services to those who cannot be reached by markets.... NGOs have a long history of providing welfare services to poor people in countries where governments lacked the resources to ensure universal coverage in health and education; the difference is that now they are seen as the preferred channel for service-provision in deliberate substitution for the state. (1997a: 6)

In interviews with Cali public officials, I learned that NGOs had become a panacea in the city government's efforts to become 'more than an *executor* ... a coordinator and orienting force in/of social policies' (Santiago de Cali 1997: 6). The local Secretary of Social Welfare and Community Action raved about how efficient it was to hire NGOs to execute government programs: 'I could contract 1,000 public servants' but instead 'I hire 200 NGOs.... There are no resources ... and that way we can do more in the social realm' (Lind 1995: 145).[22] The head of municipal Division for Women and Gender stressed, 'We don't execute or implement anything.... We work with NGOs, but not with all of them.[23]

Since, as I was told, most feminist groups in the city didn't fit the requisite technical profile, municipal officials turned to GRSOs with 'women's programs', as well as the local university's women's studies centre for technical assistance on gender matters. The Division of Women and Gender contracted three NGOs—charged with assessing poor women's health needs, promoting community participation, and training health personnel in 'gender perspectives'—to set up its Program for Integral Women's Health (which, despite its title, focused on birth control). Other NGOs were hired to train 'vulnerable' women heads-of-household in hotel and gastronomical services and the care of children and the elderly, for the municipality's Work Training Program.

In Chile, 'training with a gender perspective' (*capacitación con perspectiva de género*)—offered by feminist and non-feminist NGOs, women's GROs, private consulting firms, and many government agencies—has become a major growth industry. Much of this involves job training programs aimed at the poorest of the poor, particularly women heads-of-household, in an effort to keep them from slipping through the wide fissures at the bottom of the bottom of the neoliberal economic barrel. As one former feminist activist who now coordinates the Women's Office in one of Santiago's poorest municipal sub-divisions told me, 'Chile's subsidiary state tries to promote people with entrepreneurial capacity' to compete in the free market; those deemed to be lacking that capacity are simply further economically marginalized or disenfranchised.[24] Another argued that 'the Chilean state has begun to work only with social pathologies'. Like many other neoliberal Latin American governments, it has recodified policies toward women by treating the structural and cultural consequences of unequal gender power relations and market-induced exclusion as though they were 'extreme situations'. Violence against women is thus seen as a pathological condition rather than as an expression of women's subordination; and while women heads-of-household have always existed, their 'situation' is now framed as a social ailment that must be cured to achieve 'modernization'.[25]

Most feminists I talked with in Santiago were acutely aware of the problematic motives driving the burgeoning local *capacitación* market, but many also noted that diminishing funding from private donors and bilateral and multilateral agencies has pushed NGOs to increase their supply of training programs and other sub-contracted services. Indeed, the Chilean government's much-touted economic success story has led many donors to redirect funds away from local NGOs towards others in 'needier' societies in the South or East. And those agencies that still work in Chile now often channel funds for gender programs into SERNAM, which in turn contracts NGO services, while reserving some (relatively limited) funds to distribute to NGOs and researchers through grant competitions. Verónica Schild maintains that

> [o]ften, NGOs are put in the position of having to compete with SERNAM for funding.... As a result of ... changing priorities of foreign and domestic funding, most women's NGOs, and indeed most local or community-based NGOs, are either scrambling to survive or disappearing altogether. Those that remain are increasingly dependent on government-funded programs to survive. (1998: 105)

Barrig estimated that state funds today account for between ten and 25 per cent of the operating budgets of many Chilean feminist NGOs (1997a: 12).

In the case of Colombia, Barrig found that 'depending on the size and mission of the institution, as well as its technical profile, 40-50 per cent of the budget of NGOs comes from state sources' (1997b: 10). In Brazil, this trend is as yet less accentuated. As of 1993, only 3.2 per cent of feminist NGO monies came from Brazilian government sources (Lebon 1998: 267). But there, too, sub-contracting may be on the rise; diminishing international funding has also led many Brazilian feminist NGOs to pursue contracts with state and municipal governments. And at the federal level, the Cardoso administration's social adjustment program, *Comunidade Solidária*, has proclaimed a desire to work in partnership with NGOs to improve social services and provide job training for the poor.

While in cases such as that of Chile, donors' shifting regional priorities have pushed NGOs toward greater reliance on state contracts and consultancies, donors also have had a strong hand in the recent turn toward more technical, less movement-oriented kinds of activities in many countries in the region. My fieldwork, and my experience at the Ford Foundation, suggested that funding for projects centered on feminist mobilization and *concientización* has become more difficult to secure. The global donor community or what the NGO world dubs 'international cooperation' has changed its priorities over time: 'The '60s was the decade of development and the green revolution, the '70s one of solidarity. The '80s was the partnership decade, and now, in the '90s, what prevails is professionalism, impact, results' (Reich cited in Lebon 1998: 276). The factors behind this reorientation are well beyond the scope of the present essay. But again my experience as part of the donor community confirms this heightened emphasis on visible impact and quantifiable project results. In insisting on measurable outcomes and national or even transnational 'policy relevance', donors (however inadvertently and sometimes reluctantly) have helped reorient the activities and internal dynamics of many NGOs.[26]

I am not trying to suggest that there's something intrinsically wrong with feminist NGOs sub-contracting their services as experts or executors of government programs or abiding by donors' exigencies to demonstrate measurable impacts or results—especially when organizational survival and personal liveli-hoods are increasingly at stake. Nor am I endorsing the facile populism that often pervades social movement discourse, which invokes radical egalitarian ideals to proclaim it immoral and anti-democratic for some actors to play specialized roles within heterogeneous movement fields. However, I am suggesting that the above-outlined trends increasingly threaten to de-hybridize the heretofore dual identity of most Latin American feminist NGOs. And as I argued above, it is precisely that hybrid identity that up to now has formed the mainstay of feminist NGOs' critical ability to contest pathologized versions of neoliberal state policies 'with a gender perspective', advocate for alternative understandings of women's rights, and promote gendered social justice into the twenty-first century.

A Growing Chasm Between the Technical-Professional and Movement-Activist Faces of Feminist NGOs?

The competitive local and global gender projects markets, coupled with the shifting exigencies of international cooperation, may make it increasingly difficult for Latin American feminist NGOs to maintain the delicate balance between movement-oriented, contestatory activities and their expanding technical-advisory relationship to donors, states and IGOs. Executing state programs for 'at-risk' women or evaluating the effects of fashionable 'policies with a gender perspective' still brings many feminist NGOs into regular contact with the poor and working-class women's organizations that were once their core constituencies. But the nature of those linkages seems to be changing. Professionalized feminist groups are now perhaps more typically present in Santiago's *poblaciones* or São Paulo's *favelas* to administer short-term training courses or conduct surveys to assess the poverty levels of female-headed households. And as many interviewees noted, this has worked to distance feminist NGO activist-professionals from *las mujeres*.

The movement side of NGO identity is being challenged by their contractual relationships to states and donors who expect visible, short-term results on gender projects. Such exigencies may undermine NGOs' ability to pursue more process-oriented forms of feminist cultural-political intervention—such as consciousness-raising, popular education or other strategies aimed at transforming those gender power relations manifest in the realms of public discourse, culture and daily life—forms of gendered injustice that defy gender planning quick-fixes.

The technical-professional face of NGOs simultaneously has been foregrounded by shifting donor and IGO expectations and state sub-contracting. While the policy-relevant knowledge produced by NGOs sometimes has enabled feminists to mount credible challenges to pathologized gender policies, there is growing concern within the feminist field that the critical voice of the states' privileged interlocutors on gender policy may be increasingly muted. Comparative studies suggest that 'the ability of NGOs to articulate approaches, ideas, language, and values that run counter to official orthodoxies … may be compromised' and their willingness 'to speak out on issues that are unpopular with governments will be diluted by their growing dependence on official aid' (Edwards and Hulme 1996: 7). Sabine Lang's compelling analysis of the political effects of the NGOization of feminism in Germany, where the state has become the major source of funding for many feminist organizations, similarly suggests that increased reliance on state funding may lead NGOs to lose their critical edge: 'If NGOs don't want only to engage in social repair work, but actually want to change structural features of a certain political agenda, how successful can they be when they are dependent on exactly the structures that need to be transformed?' (1997: 112-113).

Many feminists I interviewed maintained, moreover, that irrespective of their technical competence, NGOs that refuse to play by the rules of the game or whose discourses and practices run counter to the official orthodoxies of the day may be losing out in the gender projects market and are often silenced or marginalized from the public debate. Others further noted that, despite official claims to the contrary, less-than-technical criteria are too often employed by governments when sub-contracting services or hiring NGOs as gender experts: 'the relationship with the state has been privatized'. When feminist NGOs are critical of the government, they are, predictably, less likely to get contracts or grants, which some claim results in a tendency toward 'self-censorship beyond even that which the state requires of you'.[27] Resource allocations and contracts are thus skewed towards those deemed to be politically trustworthy. Those resources, in turn, provide some NGOs with greater access to national and global policy microphones than others. Moreover, as Schild argues in the case of Chile,

> vital information [about state contracts or funding for women's projects] circulates in a network that is highly stratified and that has expanded to women in government ministries and other agencies, at the same time marginalizing others who are closer to the grass roots. These 'popular' women's NGOs are quite literally struggling to survive. (1998: 106-107)

Many feminists I talked with, including activist-professionals from the very NGOs most regularly summoned for state or IGO gender consultancies, project or policy assessments, or *capacitación*, seemed acutely aware of this growing bias in favour of particular types of feminist organizations and activities. Some were critical of the increased 'valorization of institutionalized NGOs' while 'the rest are not even consulted'.[28] Recent scholarly analyses of NGOs would seem to confirm the bias perceived by many in the feminist field: 'the popularity of certain forms of NGOs (large, able to absorb donor funding, quiescent) with donors [and, I would add, local states] may lead to a widening rift between well-resourced service providers and poorly-funded social mobilization agencies' (Hulme and Edwards 1997b: 281). Such a rift is increasingly in evidence in the contemporary Latin American feminist movement field.

Busting the NGO Boom? Maneuvering Within the New Gendered Policy Agenda and Rearticulating the Activist and Professional Dimensions of Feminist NGOs

The most vehement critics of feminist NGOs are the *feministas autónomas*[29]—a recent, relatively small, but highly vocal political current within the Latin American feminist field—who claim that NGOs have 'institutionalized' the women's movement and 'sold out' to the forces of 'neoliberal patriarchy'. During the seventh regionwide Latin American and Caribbean Feminist meetings or *Encuentros* since 1981, held in Cartagena, Chile, in November 1996, Chilean *autónomas* who organized the gathering brought their scathing critique of 'professionalized feminism' into the centre of debate within the regionwide feminist field.[30]

At the Cartagena meeting, the *autónomas* proclaimed NGOs to be 'decorative and functional complements of patriarchal policies' who constitute a 'gender technocracy'.[31] Accusing NGOs of having 'indecent relations with the state',[32] they denied the women they pejoratively dub '*las institucionales*' (the institutionalists) membership in the feminist fold: 'we do not think that NGOs as NGOs, that is, as institutions … are constitutive parts of the movement. We believe there may be feminist women working in these institutions but little by little the institutionalized and technocratic tendencies will destroy them'.[33] Others affirmed 'that these institutions are not neutral, that they belong to the system and sustain it, and that money thereby becomes a political instrument'.[34]

This kind of Manichean logic is belied by the heterogeneity of origins, the diversity of practices and the hybrid identity that still characterizes many feminist NGOs, most of whose members are quite self-consciously grappling with some of the very contradictions so vehemently condemned by the *autónomas*. Indeed, many women the *autónomas* identified with 'institutionalized feminism' expressed concern that 'the women's movement's agenda is becoming indistinguishable from that of the government'. Others even echoed their radical critics' claim that some feminist institutions were 'being functional as NGOs; it's not good or bad, it's just a reality. But we must ask ourselves, functional to an agenda constructed by whom?'[35]

Most expressed an urgent need to reassess their current practices as feminists, to rearticulate the two faces of NGOs' heretofore dual identity. Still, many were distressed that the weight of the New Gender Policy Agenda was forcing NGOs to privilege technical-advisory activities and to neglect other dimensions of 'movement work' so central to feminist visions of social transformation shared by most NGOers and others in the feminist field.[36]

I would submit, by way of conclusion, that feminist NGOs are hardly doomed to become a part of what some critics have dubbed the 'anti-politics machine' of development (Ferguson 1994) or the 'community face of neoliberalism' (Petras 1997). Blanket assessments of feminist NGOs as handmaidens of neoliberal planetary patriarchy, as the *autónomas* would have it, fail to capture the ambiguities and variations in both the local implementation of the New Gender Policy Agenda and in and among NGOs themselves.

Such variations would surely influence just how much room may be available for NGOs to maneuver within the confines of the restructured late modern, post-transition, and post-Beijing terrain of local and global gender politics. The extent to which NGOs' contractual relationship to the state constrains their critical capacity, for instance, is likely to vary in different global and local political conjunctures and according to the specific characteristics of local states. Barrig's findings (1997b) suggest that Colombian NGOs' autonomy seems to have been significantly less compromised, despite a growing dependence on state funding, in large part due to the Colombian state's own lack of institutionalization and consequent lack of disciplinary or regulatory capacities. The highly institutionalized, legalistic and rigorously disciplinary contemporary Chilean state, by contrast, may more narrowly constrain NGOs' ability to advocate for more feminist gender policies and sustain a dual identity while doing business with the government.

To enhance their room for maneuver (or *jogo de cintura*, as the Brazilians might put it—loosely translated as 'swing of the hips'), however, feminists would have to devise collective strategies to resist the de-hybridization of NGOs and enable them perhaps to serve as more genuine intermediaries for larger civil society constituencies. To attain both goals, NGOs would have to reaffirm their commitment to widely consulting other actors in the feminist field when they themselves are tapped for policy assessments or project administration by governments and IGOs. Beyond the token policy seminar, this might entail NGO involvement in the establishment or revitalization of on-going public forums open to the full range of actors in the feminist movement field and their democratic allies in civil society. Most feminists I interviewed expressed an urgent need for more regularized public spaces in which feminists of all stripes could regularly debate and critique prevailing 'policies with a gender perspective', demand accountability from NGOs regarding their state-contracted and donor-funded projects, and perhaps even (re)invent more transgressive public interventions that would move beyond the policy realm and thereby help revitalize the movement face of NGOs. Towards the end of the 1990s, some local feminist NGOs, like the Centro Flora Tristán in Lima, had begun investing renewed energies in revitalizing just such spaces.

In navigating the inevitably muddy waters of neoliberal state gender politics, many NGO activist-professionals suggested that it *is* still possible to retain a dual identity while doing business with particular governments on *proyectos puntuales* (punctual or specific projects). But many insisted that it is imperative for feminists to continually evaluate and interrogate their contractual and political relationship with official arenas rather than adopt rigid, 'principled' positions *a priori*. Successfully negotiating such *jogos de cintura puntuales*, however, would be more feasible if NGOs can invoke collective gendered citizenship claims and count on the support of other sectors of civil society within and without the feminist field than when they try to 'go it alone' in local and global gender projects markets. This, many women suggested, would require enhanced horizontal NGO accountability to the larger feminist field and to popular women's movement constituencies.

Many also expressed a pressing need for NGOs to devise ways of negotiating collectively with states and donors, not just about resources and time-lines for projects, but also to secure longer-term programmatic lines of action and set more movement-oriented project priorities. Funding agencies and government bureaucrats alike too often simply 'expect contracted outputs to be achieved and are less interested in a learning process.... Time and space for reflection may be reduced...' (Edwards and Hulme 1996: 7). As public advocates for women's citizenship, feminist NGOs rightfully might also insist that donors and state officials allow them the political space to more thoroughly and meaningfully involve broader sectors of movement and civil society constituencies in their technical evaluations of gender policies and programs, allowing them more time for consultation, genuine interlocution and critical reflection than impact- or results-driven project timetables typically permit. Such measures might help draw a clearer political line between feminist NGOs established to pursue the public interest and private consulting enterprises or individuals who market their policy expertise, thereby enabling NGOs to serve as more effective intermediaries of the societal constituencies which governments claim they want NGOs to represent.

Finally, those of us in the North who consider ourselves part of the so-called 'global women's movement' could take IGOs, northern states and donors to task on their professed intention to promote a 'thriving civil society' that would foster gender equity and expand democratization in Latin America. If as my findings and other critical studies suggest, donors have had a strong hand in skewing the feminist movement field toward more technical-professional endeavors, then they might surely tilt the scales at least a bit more in the other direction. Those of us who are social scientists and area specialists could summon our own 'technical expertise' to argue that increased NGO involvement in social service delivery, project execution and policy assessment does not exhaust their potential contributions to 'strengthening civil society'. Establishing funding criteria that would strengthen rather than obstruct Latin American feminist NGOs' historically hybrid political identities and enhance their ability to be more genuine intermediaries would surely be a step in the right direction.

Reprinted with permission from Taylor and Francis Ltd. and the International Feminist Journal of Politics *1 (2) (1999): 181-209. Available online: http://www. tandf.co.uk/journals.*

Sonia E. Alvarez is Professor of Politics at the University of California at Santa Cruz, where she also is affiliated with the Latin American and Latino Studies and Women's Studies Departments and the Chicano/Latino Research Center. She is the author of Engendering Democracy in Brazil: Women's Movements in Transition Politics *(Princeton) and co-editor of* The Making of Social Movements in Latin America: Identity, Strategy, and Democracy, *with Arturo Escobar (Westview) and* Cultures of Politics/Politics of Cultures: Re-visioning Latin American Social Movements, *with Evelina Dagnino and A. Escobar (Westview). Her writings on feminisms, social movements, and democratization have appeared in* Signs, Feminist Studies, Revista Estudos Feministas, Estudios Latinoamericanos, International Feminist Journal of Politics, Debate Feminista, Meridians, Revista Mora, *and a number of edited collections and social movement publications. She is currently completing a new book,* Looking for Feminism in Movement: Cultural Politics, Policy Advocacy and Transnational Organizing in Latin America, *under contract with Duke University Press.*

Notes

[1] I use the term institutionalization in the Weberian sense to denote the rationalization and routinization of an organization's procedures and norms.

[2] For a comparative overview of the emergence, development and dynamics of

feminisms in Latin America, see Jaquette (1994); Jaquette and Wolchik (1998); Nijeholt, Vargas and Wieringa (1996); Olea Mauleón (1998).

[3] Ferree and Martin similarly argue that formal feminist institutions or organizations in the US 'are an amalgam, a blend of institutionalized and social movement practices' (1995: 7-8). For a compelling analysis of the hybrid character of feminist NGOs and the most comprehensive ethnographic study of Brazilian feminist NGOs to date, see Lebon (1998).

[4] Research in Chile, Peru, and Colombia during July and August 1997 formed part of a commissioned study supported by a grant from the Ford Foundation—Andean and Southern Cone Office in Santiago de Chile. I am deeply grateful to the feminist movement activists and NGO professionals who conceded interviews or otherwise gave graciously of their time to this project.

[5] The ideas contained in this essay, of course, are my own and do not necessarily reflect those of the Ford Foundation.

[6] In her analysis of contemporary feminisms in India, Raka Ray argues that women's movements operate within political fields shaped by distinctive political cultures and particular distributions of power. She maintains that 'a political field can be thought of as a structured, unequal, and socially constructed environment *within* which organizations are embedded and *to* which organizations and activists constantly respond' (1999: 6, emphasis in the original). In my own conception (see Alvarez 1998, 1997), movements themselves constitute fields in a similar sense: they construct alternative publics in which particular 'ways of doing politics' and cultural-political meanings are fashioned and continually contested and in relation to which people who identify with the movement and are situated in a wide range of social and political spaces constantly renegotiate their political identities and practices.

[7] Ferree and Martin (1995) make a similar point regarding the contributions of institutionalized feminist organizations to the US women's movement.

[8] Interview 35, Lima, Peru, August 19, 1997. Not all NGO professionals I interviewed, however, shared in this hybrid identity. Some understood NGOs as providing 'a critical voice of a technical and professional character that contributes to the movement' (Interview 10, Santiago de Chile, 10 July, 1997).

[9] I thank Maruja Barrig for suggesting that I emphasize and elaborate upon local variations in rates and degrees of NGOization in distinct national feminist fields.

[10] Interview 45, Santa Fé de Bogotá, Colombia, 22 August, 1997.

[11] Interview 4, Santiago de Chile, 8 July, 1997.

[12] Interview 17, Santiago de Chile, 11 July 1997.

[13] Interview 39, Santa Fé de Bogotá, 21 August, 1997.

[14] Interview 49, Santa Fé de Bogotá, 20 August, 1997.

[15] Interviews BR 98-6 and 7, 1 September 1998; Interview BR 98-8, 3 September, 1998.

[16] Interview BR 98-2 and 3, Porto Alegre, 24 August, 1998.

[17] Interview 34, Lima, Peru, 16 August, 1997.

[18] Interview 1, Santiago de Chile, 8 July, 1997.

[19] On social adjustment and anti-poverty programs targeting women, see Barrig (1996); Craske (1998); Schild (1998); Ríos Tobar (1998).

[20] Interview 48, Santiago de Cali, 25 August, 1997.

[21] Interview 20, Santiago de Chile, 14 July 1997.

[22] On feminist NGOs relationship to the state, see also Friedman (1997); Schild (1998); Frohmann and Valdés (1995); Valdés and Weinstein (1997); Craske (1998); Barrig (1997a, b).

23 Interview 48, Santiago de Cali, 25 August, 1997.

24 Interview 51, Santiago de Cali, 26 August, 1997.

25 Interview 29, Santiago de Chile, 17 July 1997.

26 During one of our several working sessions in Lima in August of 1997, Maruja Barrig attributed the first part of this formulation to a Chilean feminist NGO researcher; I owe the latter insight regarding the recodification of gender policies to Maruja.

27 On NGOs' relationship to donors, see Hulme and Edwards (1997a, 1997b); Lebon (1998); Motta (1995); Barrig (1997a).

28 Interview 34, Lima, Peru, 16 August, 1997.

29 Interview 13, Santiago de Chile, 10 July, 1997.

30 Interviews 33, 5, 26 and 32, Santiago de Chile, July 1997.

31 Long-brewing tensions surrounding the growing NGOization and institutionalization of feminisms in the region came to a head during the VII *Encuentro*. The regional *Encuentros* had always served as 'historical markers, highlighting the strategic, organizational, and theoretical debates that have characterized the political trajectory of contemporary Latin American feminisms' (Sternbach et al. 1992:208). And this one proved to be a veritable watershed, giving rise to three distinctive, and seemingly antagonistic, political currents or tendencies within the Latin American feminist field: the *feministas autónomas*, those pejoratively dubbed the '*feministas institucionales*' by their *autónoma* foes, and a third grouping (encompassing the vast majority of Encuentro participants) who provocatively referred to themselves as '*Ni Las Unas, Ni Las Otras*' ('neither one nor the other'). On the debates triggered by the Encuentro, see special issues of *Cotidiano Mujer* (Uruguay), nos. 22 (May 1996) and 23 (March 1997); *Enfoque Feminista* (Brazil), No. 10, Ano VI (May 1997); *Brujas* (Argentina), 16, 24 (March 1997); and *Feminária* (Argentina) 10, 19 (June 1997) and Olea Mauleón 1998.

32 Speech delivered at the VII Latin American and Caribbean Feminist Encuentro, Cartagena, Chile, November 1996.

33 In her presentation on the dynamics of the VII Encuentro on a panel on 'Feminist NGOs and Global Civil Society: Critical Perspectives', at the 1997 Congress of the Latin American Studies Association, Guadalajara, México, April 19-21, feminist historian, Marysa Navarro, aptly captured in this interpretive phrase the often vituperative nature of the *autónomas'* critique of NGOs.

34 Speech delivered at the VII Latin American and Caribbean Feminist Encuentro, Cartagena, Chile, November 1996.

35 Speech delivered at the VII Latin American and Caribbean Feminist Encuentro, Cartagena, Chile, November 1996.

36 Interview 37, Santa Fé de Bogotá, 20 August 1997.

References

Alvarez, S. E. (1999) 'En qué *estado* está el feminismo? Reflexiones teóricas y perspectivas comparativas'. *Estudios Latinoamericanos*, 12.

Alvarez, S. E. (1998) 'Latin American feminisms "go global": trends of the 1990s and challenges for the new millenium', in S. E. Alvarez, E. Dagnino and A. Escobar (eds.), *Cultures of Politics/Politics of Cultures: Re-visioning Latin American Social Movements*, Boulder, CO: Westview Press, 293-324.

Alvarez, S. E. (1997) 'Reweaving the fabric of collective action: social movements and challenges to "actually existing democracy" in Brazil', in R. G. Fox and O. Starn (eds.), *Between Resistance and Revolution: Cultural Politics and Social Protest*, New Brunswick, NJ: Rutgers University Press, 83-117.

Alvarez, S. E. (1994) 'The (trans)formation of feminism(s) and gender politics in democratizing Brazil', in J. S. Jaquette (ed.), *The Women's Movement in Latin America: Participation and Democracy*, Second edition. Boulder, CO.: Westview Press, 13-63.

Alvarez, S. E. (1990) *Engendering Democracy in Brazil: Women's Movements in Transition Politics*. Princeton: Princeton University Press.

Alvarez, S. E., E. Dagnino and A. Escobar (1998) 'The cultural and the political in Latin American Social Movements', in S. E. Alvarez, E. Dagnino and A. Escobar (eds.), *Cultures of Politics/Politics of Cultures: Re-visioning Latin American Social Movements*, Boulder, CO: Westview Press, 1-29.

Americas Watch (1991) *Criminal Injustice: Violence Against Women in Brazil*. New York: Human Rights Watch.

Barrig, M. (1997a) 'De cal y arena: ONGs y movimiento de mujeres en Chile', Photocopy.

Barrig, M. (1997b) 'La larga marcha: movimiento de mujeres en Colombia', Photocopy.

Barrig, M. (1996) 'Women, collective kitchens and the crisis of the state in Peru', in J. Friedman, R. Abers, and L. Autler (eds.), *Emergences: Women's Struggles for Livelihood in Latin America*, Los Angeles: Center for Latin American Studies, University of California, Los Angeles, 59-78.

Blondet, C. (1995) 'Out of the kitchens and onto the streets: women's activism in Peru', in A. Basu (ed.), *The Challenge of Local Feminisms: Women's Movements in Global Perspective*, Boulder, CO.: Westview Press, 251-275.

Chuchryk, P. (1994) 'From dictatorship to democracy: the women's movement in Chile', in J. S. Jaquette (ed.), in *The Women's Movement in Latin America: Participation and Democracy*, Second edition. Boulder, CO: Westview Press, 65-107.

Clarke, G. (1998) 'Non-governmental organizations (NGOs) and politics in the developing world', *Political Studies* 46, 36-52.

Craske, N. (1998) 'Remasculinization and the neoliberal state in Latin America', in V. Randall and G. Waylen (eds.), *Gender, Politics, and the State*, London: Routledge, 100-120.

Edwards, M. and D. Hulme (1996) 'Introduction: NGO performance and accountability', in M. Edwards and D. Hulme (eds.), *Beyond the Magic Bullet: NGO Performance and Accountability in the Post-Cold War World*, West Hartford, CT: Kumarian Press, 1-20.

Ferguson, J. (1994) *The Anti-Politics Matching: 'Development', Depoliticization, and Bureaucratic Power in Lesotho*, Minneapolis: University of Minnesota Press.

Ferree, M. M. and P. Y. Martin (1995) 'Doing the work of the movement: Feminist organizations', in M. M. Ferree and P. Y. Martin (eds.), *Feminist Organizations: Harvest of the New Women's Movement*, Philadelphia: Temple University Press, 3-33.

Fisher, J. (1998) *Nongovernments: NGOs and the Political Development of the Third World*, West Hartford, CT: Kumarian Press.

Friedman, E. (1997) 'Unfinished transitions: the paradoxical political opportunities of women's organizing in Latin American democratization', Ph.D. dissertation, Stanford University.

Frohmann, A. and T. Valdés (1995) 'Democracy in the country and in the home: the women's movement in Chile', in A. Basu (ed.), *The Challenge of Local Feminisms: Women's Movements in Global Perspective*, Boulder, CO.: Westview Press, 276-301.

Gaviola, E., E. Largo and S. Palestro (1994) *Una História Necesária: Mujeres en Chile: 1973-1990*, Santiago de Chile: Akí & Aora Ltda.

Gruhn, I. V. (1997) 'NGOs in partnership with the UN: a new fix or a new problem for African development?', *Global Society*, 11, 3,325-337.

Heilborn, M. L. and A. Arruda. (1995) 'Legado feminist e ONGs de mulheres: notas preliminares', in M. da Graça Ribeiro das Neves e D. Martins Costa (eds.), *Gênero e Desenvolvimento institucional em ONGs*, Rio de Janeiro: IBAM/ENSUR/NEMPP; Madrid: Instituto de la Mujer.

Htun, M. (1998) 'Equal rights for women in Latin America: problems and prospects', paper prepared for the Women's Leadership Conference of the Americas, Inter-American Dialogue, International Center for Research on Women. Photocopy.

Hulme, D. and M. Edwards (1997a) 'NGOs, states and donors: an overview', in D. Hulme and M. Edwards (eds.), *NGOs, States and Donors: Too Close for Comfort*, New York: St. Martin's Press/Save the Children.

Hulme, D. and M. Edwards (1997b) 'Conclusion: too close to the powerful, too far from the powerless?' in D. Hulme and M. Edwards (eds.), *NGOs, States and Donors: Too Close for Comfort*, New York: St. Martin's Press/Save the Children.

Jaquette, J. S. (ed.) (1994) *The Women's Movement in Latin America: Participation and Democracy*, Boulder, CO: Westview Press.

Jaquette, J. S. and S. L. Wolchik (eds.) (1998) *Women and Democracy: Latin America and Eastern Europe*, Baltimore: Johhs Hopkins University Press.

Jones, M. P. (1998) 'Gender quotas, electoral laws, and the election of women: lessons from the Argentine provinces', *Comparative Political Studies* 31, 1, 3-21.

Kardam, N. (1997) 'The emerging international women's regime', photocopy.

Keck, M. and K. Sikkink (1998) *Activists Beyond Borders: Transnational Advocacy Networks in international Politics*, Ithaca, NY: Cornell University Press.

Landim, L. (1993) 'A invenção das ONGs: Do serviço invisível à profissão sem nome', Ph.D. diss., Universidade Federal do Rio de Janeiro/Museu Nacional, Programa de Pós-Graduação em Antropologia Social.

Lang, S. (1997) 'The NGOization of feminism', in J. C. Scott, C. Kaplan and D. Keates (eds.), *Transitions, Environments, Translations: Feminisms in International Politics*, New York: Routledge.

Largo, E. (ed) (1998) *Género en el Estado, Estado del Género*, Santiago de Chile: ISIS Internacional.

Lebon, N. (1998) 'The labour of love and bread: professionalized and volunteer activism in the São Paulo women's health movement', Ph.D. dissertation, University of Florida.

Lebon, N. (1997) 'Volunteer and professionalized activism in the São Paulo women's health movement', Paper presented at the XXI International Conference of the Latin American Studies Association, Guadalajara, México, 17-19 April.

Lebon, N. (1993) 'The Brazilian feminist movement in the post-constitutional era: assessing the impact of the rise of feminist non-governmental organizations', *Florida Journal of Anthropology*, 18, 17-26.

Lind, A. C. (1995) 'Gender, development and women's political practices in Ecuador', Ph.D. diss., Cornell University, Ithaca, New York.

Luna, L. G. and N. Villareal (1994) *História, género y política: movimiento de mujeres y participación política en Colombia, 1930-1991*, Barcelona: Universidad de Barcelona/ Comisión interministerial de Ciencia y Tecnologia.

Mansbridge, J. (1995) 'What is the feminist movement?', in M. M. Ferree and P. Y. Martin (eds.), *Feminist Organizations: Harvest of the New Women's Movement*, Philadelphia: Temple University Press, 27-34.

Motta, P. R. (1995) 'ONGs Sem Fins Lucrativos: estratégia de Sobrevivência por Meios

Comerciais', in M. da Graça Ribeiro das Neves e D. M. Costa (eds.), *Gênero e Desenvolvimento Institucional em ONGs,* Rio de Janeiro: IBAM/ENSUR/NEMPP; Madrid: Instituto de la Mujer.

Nelson, S. (1996) 'Constructing and negotiating gender in women's police stations in Brazil', *Latin American Perspectives,* 23, 1, 131-54.

Nijeholt, G. L., V. Vargas and S. Wieringa (1996) *Triángulo del Poder,* Bogotá: Tercer Mundo Editores.

Olea Mauleón, C. (ed.) (1998) *Des(encuentro) y Busquedas: El Movimento Feminista en America Latina,* Lima: Edicione Flora Tristan.

Pearce, J. (1997) 'Between co-option and irrelevance? Latin American NGOs in the 1990s', in in D. Hulme and M. Edwards (eds.), *NGOs, States and Donors: Too Close for Comfort,* New York: St. Martin's Press/Save the Children.

Petras, J. (1997) 'NGOs and imperialsm', *Monthly Review,* 49, 7, 10-27.

Pisano, M. (1996) *Un Cierto Deparpajo,* Santiago de Chile: Ediciones Número Crítico.

Presidencia de la República, Colombia (1994) *Libro Blanco de la Mujer: Propuestas Básicas.* Photocopy.

Ray, R. (1999) *Fields of Protest: Women's Movements in India,* Minneapolis: University of Minnesota Press.

Ríos Tobar, M. (1998) 'The contested terrain of gender policies in Chile: the case of the Programa para Mujeres Trabajadoras Temporeras', paper presented at the XXI international Congress of the Latin American Studies Association, Chicago, September 24-26.

Sánchez, O. A. (1996) 'Las políticas públicas para las mujeres', in M. C. López (ed.), *Mujer, Poder y Estado: Memórias del Encuentro realizado en Santafé de Bogotá, Mayo de 1995,* Medellín: Corporación para la Vida, Mujeres que Crean.

Santiago de Cali, A. (1997) *El Rostro Social de Cali,* Cali: Secretaría de Bienestar Social y Gestión Comunitária, Oficina de Coordinación Social PROCALI.

Schild, V. (1998) 'New subjects of rights? Women's movements and the construction of citizenship in the 'new democracies''', in S. E. Alvarez, E. Dagnino and A. Escobar (eds.), *Cultures of Politics/Politics of Cultures: Re-visioning Latin American Social Movements,* Boulder, CO: Westview Press, 93-117.

Schild, V. (1994) 'Recasting "popular" movements: gender and political learning in neighborhood organizations in Chile', *Latin American Perspectives,* 21, 2, 59-80.

Schumaher, M. A. and E. Vargas (1993) 'Lugar no governo: alibi ou conquista?' *Revista de Estudos Feministas,* 1, 2, 348-365.

Schuurman, F. J. and E. Heer (1992) *Social Movements and NGOs in Latin America: A Case-Study of the Women's Movement in Chile,* Fort Lauderdale: Verlag Breitenbach Publishers.

Servicio Nacional de la Mujer (1994) *Equal Opportunities Plan for Chilean Women, 1994-1999,* Santiago de Chile: SERNAM.

Sikkink, K. (1995) 'Transnational networks on violence against women', paper presented at the XIX international Congress of the Latin American Studies Association, Washington, D.C., September 28-30.

Soares, V. (1998) 'Feminismo e ONGs', Photocopy.

Soares, V., A. A. Alcantara Costa, C. M. Buarque, D. Dourado Doura and W. Sant'Anna. (1995) 'Brazilian feminism and women's movements: a two-way street', in A. Basu (ed.), *The Challenge of Local Feminisms: Women's Movements in Global Perspective,* Boulder, CO.: Westview Press, 302-323.

Sternbach, N. S., M. Navarro-Aranguren, P. Chuchryk and S. E. Alvarez (1992) 'Feminisms in Latin America: from Bogota to San Bernardo', in A. Escobar and S. E. Alvarez (eds.),

The Making of Social Movements in Latin America: Identity, Strategy, and Democracy, Boulder, CO: Westview Press, 207-239.

Tarrés, M. L. (1997) 'La difícil construcción de las nociones de democracia y ciudadanía desde las ONGs de mujeres en México', paper presented at the conference on 'New Concepts of Democracy and Gendered Citizenship in Latin America: Local, National and Global Perspectives', Guadalajara, México, 14-16 April.

Valdés, T. and M. Weinstein (1997) 'Corriendo y descorriendo tupidos velos', in *Chile 96: Análisis y Opiniones,* Santiago: FLACSO-Chile.

Valenzuela, M. E. (1997) 'Las mujeres y el poder: la acción estatal desde una perspectiva de género en Chile', paper presented at the conference on 'New Concepts of Democracy and Gendered Citizenship in Latin America: Local, National and Global Perspectives', Guadalajara, México, 14-16 April.

Villareal Méndez, N. (1994) 'El camino a la utopía feminista en Colombia, 1975-1991', in M. León (ed.), *Mujeres y Participación Política: Avances y Desafíos en América Latina,* Bogotá: Tercer Mundo Editores, 181-204.

Waylen, G. (1996) 'Democratization, feminism, and the state in Chile: the establishment of SERNAM', in S. M. Rai and G. Lievesley (eds.), *Women and the State: International Perspectives,* London: Taylor & Francis.

ORGANIZING FOR DOMESTIC WORKER RIGHTS IN SINGAPORE

THE LIMITS OF TRANSNATIONALISM

LENORE LYONS

The forces of globalization increasingly compel feminist activists to engage internationally, either through involvement in transnational networks and social movements, or by incorporating understandings of the 'global' into local and national practices. Globalization collapses both time and space, thus fundamentally altering the types of political and economic relationships that states maintain with both citizens and a range of 'others'. For this reason, Rochelle Ball and Nicola Piper assert that non-government organizations (NGOs) 'will increasingly play a pivotal role in lobbying nationally and transnationally for greater state and multilateral institutional accountability to both national and global citizens' (2002: 1031). However, as differently situated actors with diverse agendas and priorities come together to address women's rights within a transnational frame they face a range of challenges and contradictions. Rather than simply transcending the 'national', transnational feminist activists must pay particular attention to the roles played by nation-states and national governments in mediating the relationship between local and transnational groups. This embeddedness of the national within transnationalism is often overlooked in romanticized accounts of global civil society.

This article examines the limits of transnational feminist activism through a case study of domestic worker rights in Singapore. This work builds on my decade-long research on the feminist movement in Singapore and my activist involvement in the Singaporean women's organization, the Association of Women for Action and Research (AWARE). I argue that the Singaporean state inhibits attempts by local feminist organizations to engage transnationally whether through links with international NGOs, or by confronting the forces of globalization locally. Singaporean activists have creatively responded to these challenges, but their actions remain constrained by the imperatives of the nation-state.

The first part of this article briefly surveys the growing literature on feminist transnational activism, before examining the issues facing domestic migrant workers in Southeast Asia. In the second part of the paper I provide an overview of the history of the feminist movement in Singapore with particular emphasis on the constraints of working within a state-defined sphere of civil society, and the implications this has for attempts by Singaporean feminists to engage transnationally. The article ends with a case study of The Working Committee 2, a loose network of Singaporean activists working to address the rights of foreign domestic workers in Singapore.

Transnational Feminism and Global Civil Society

Although women's movements have a long history of engagement in the international arena (Daley and Nolan 1994; Rupp 1997; Rupp and Taylor 1999), it was not until the 1990s that women's rights advocates began to organize on an unprecedented scale transnationally (Friedman 2003).[1] A number of recent studies have sought to document the diverse activities of such groups (Meyer and Prügl 1999; Basu 2000; Mitter and Rowbotham 2000; Moghadam 2000; Mackie 2001; Sperling, Ferree and Risman 2001; Naples and Desai 2002). This work forms part of a growing body of research on the role of transnational NGOs, advocacy networks and social movements in the emergence of global civil society (i.e., Guarnizo and Smith 1998; Keck and Sikkink 1998; Della Porta, Kriesi and Rucht 1999; Anheier, Glasius and Kaldor 2001). For Valentine Moghadam, the creation of transnational feminist networks is indicative of the emergence of 'global feminism', defined as 'the discourse and movement of women aimed at advancing the status of women ... through transnational forms of organizing and mobilizing' (2000: 62). Examples of such networks include Development Alternatives with Women for a New Era (DAWN) and Women Living Under Muslim Laws (WLUML). These groups

> engage in information exchange, mutual support and a combination of lobbying, advocacy and direct action toward the realization of their goals of equality and empowerment for women and social justice and societal democratisation'. (Moghadam 2000: 62)

Their emergence can be seen as a direct response to the processes of globalization.

On a cautionary note, Vera Mackie (2001: 188) reminds us that the 'transnational public sphere, if it can be said to exist, is a gendered, raced, classed and ethnicized public sphere'. It is not unsurprising then, that the relationship between 'grass-roots' and/or community-based activists and transnational groups is often fraught. A number of studies have begun to document the numerous problems facing transnational feminist activists, including: the dominant role played by women's groups from the North; the disproportionate amount of attention and support from international agencies that is directed to more 'well-known' Third World

NGOs; the enormous resources and energy required to organize transnationally; the particular skill-sets needed to be effective (such as international legal or scientific expertise, and knowledge of the rivalries and practices of inter-state political bargaining); and the varied value systems and priorities of differently situated actors (Basu 2000; Mitter and Rowbotham 2000; Moghadam 2000; Sperling et al. 2001). In their work, Valerie Sperling, Myra Marx Ferree and Barbara Risman (2001) identified a number of strategies used by local and transnational activists to build cross-cultural, trans-national alliances or coalitions. These strategies may include ethical principles, organizational structures, leadership models, language policies and forged common identities.

Opportunities for transnational activist groups to advocate on behalf of women's rights are frequently constrained by states that tightly control access to the politically sensitive arena of civil society. Local and transnational groups must pay attention to the complexities and contradictions of civil society as they consider what kind of alliances to forge and resources to accept. Despite the important role played by the state, few studies have focused their attention on the limitations posed to feminist transnationalism by local state forces (see, however, Gurowitz 2000; Uhlin 2001). Instead, there is a tendency for scholars and policy-makers to unproblematically project a romance of 'more' civil society as ballast against coercive state power and its excesses (Phillips 1999). This partly explains the continuing commitment of international funding agencies towards strengthening civil society and thereby addressing 'women's rights'. In these approaches, civil society is often treated as a monolithic whole with a unity of purpose rather than as a space occupied by a range of actors with divergent agendas (Howell and Mulligan 2003). In some contexts, local activists may find it politically safer to avoid transnational interactions, or to restrict their involvement to groups with similar goals and objectives. For example, the Malaysian group, Sisters in Islam, distances itself from western feminist models of global sisterhood, preferring instead to forge strategic alliances with women's organizations in other Muslim countries (Ong 1996). This example points to the need for feminists to pay closer attention to the local content of debates about 'feminism', 'women's rights', 'human rights' and 'civil society', if transnational activism is to be successful.

Female Migrant Domestic Workers

Large segments of the world's population are increasingly mobile. Women migrate within national boundaries and across international borders for many reasons. While many migrate by choice as workers, wives and mothers (Piper and Roces 2002), others find themselves victims of displacement or trafficking (Ucarer 1999). Within southeast Asia, the increasing feminization of transnational migration is associated with labour movements into the domestic service sector by women from the Philippines, Indonesia, Malaysia, Burma and Thailand. There are no precise figures on the numbers of transnational female migrants from southeast Asia working as domestic workers.[2] As an indicator, however, some estimate that there are between 4.2 to 6.4 million Filipinas working abroad as domestic helpers and entertainers (Wee and Sim 2003: 2). While these women typically migrate to the Middle East, Japan, Europe and North America as domestic workers, large numbers also find employment in the rapidly developing countries of the region. As increasing numbers of women in Hong Kong, Singapore and Malaysia enter paid employment outside the home, demand for relatively cheap female migrant labour to perform household tasks has risen. In Singapore, for example, women's labour force participation is 53.9 per cent (Singapore Department of Statistics 2003). There are currently over 140,000 foreign domestic workers in Singapore (Chiam 2003). Huang and Yeoh (2003) estimate that there are almost equal numbers of women from the Philippines and Indonesia working as domestics, with a significant minority from Sri Lanka. This equates to approximately one foreign domestic worker to every seven households.

Numerous studies have documented the tenuous position of female migrant workers in relation to labour laws and citizenship rights in the Asia-Pacific. Migrant workers face difficult working conditions, poor remuneration, and constant surveillance by both the state and their employers (i.e., Huang and Yeoh 1996; Lim and Oishi 1996; Shah and Menon 1997; Yeoh and Huang 1997; Lindio-McGovern 2001). Despite their dependency on the labour and remittances of migrant workers, sending and receiving states have been slow to address these workers' welfare. For this reason, NGOs have begun to play a significant role in both disseminating information and providing assistance to migrant workers. While some migrant-worker NGOs are associated with local or transnational women's movements, others are affiliated with religious groups, unions or civil rights groups. Some adopt gender-specific responses to the plight of domestic workers, while others organize around class or work (i.e., women's role as workers) as well as race/ethnicity or nationality (i.e., advocating on behalf of women with a common country of origin).

The most visible of these are Filipino migrant worker groups based in Hong Kong, Japan and the Philippines (Law and Nadeu 1999; Ball and Piper 2002; Law 2003; Piper 2003). Filipino migrant worker groups have received the most scholarly attention not only because of the significant proportion of female domestic 'maids' from the Philippines who work in the region, but also because in comparison with other national groups, Filipinos have the strongest transnational advocacy networks (Piper 2003). Although Singapore is a major receiving country for female migrant labour in the region, groups such as these are noticeably absent. In part, their absence can be explained by the presence of a strong, authoritarian state and a relatively weak NGO sector. This has meant that for many years, the plight of domestic workers in Singapore has remained largely unaddressed.

Participating in Singapore's 'Civil Society Experiment'

To understand the forces that impact on the ability of international agencies and transnational groups to advocate for foreign worker rights in Singapore, it is necessary to examine the relationship between the state and civil society. After achieving independence in 1965, the Singaporean government embarked on a program of widespread social and economic transformation aimed at boosting economic growth and maintaining social and political stability. The cornerstone of this program is a model of strong government built on a limited social welfare network and an emphasis on technological innovation aimed at maintaining a competitive edge in the global market place (Rodan 1993). Such an approach has seen Singapore outstrip its neighbours in terms of both economic growth measures and social/lifestyle indicators. During this period, the People's Action Party (PAP) maintained its political dominance such that the government, the state and the political party are synonymous in terms of both everyday governance and public sentiment. Michael Haas (1989) argues that despite a parliament modelled on Westminster-style democracy, the PAP has effectively restricted the growth of a participatory parliamentary system, and instead fostered a 'mass society' characterized by a lack of political institutions between the state and the people; Singapore lacks an effective civil society.

Since the mid-1990s, however, the PAP government has sought to encourage the growth of a more active citizenry through the promotion of 'civic society'. The party's absolute hold on all parliamentary seats began to decline in 1981.[3] Amongst the leadership the loss of seats, combined with a decline in the PAP's share of the vote, was attributed to alienation amongst the middle-class. In an effort to win back the support of these voters, the PAP embarked on a range of initiatives intended to provide alternative avenues for public involvement in policy debate, thereby undercutting other potentially threatening political alternatives. Likening the all-pervasive power of the PAP to that of the banyan tree, Minister for Information and the Arts, Brigadier General George Yeo reflected that:

The problem now is that under the banyan tree, very little else can grow. When state institutions are too pervasive, civic institutions cannot thrive. Therefore, it is necessary to prune the banyan tree so that other plants can grow (qtd. in Worthington 2003: 7).

Chua Beng Huat (2000) notes that the use of the term 'civic' was favoured by the government because of its emphasis on the civic responsibilities of citizens as opposed to the rights of citizenship implied by the concept of civil society. The discourse of civic society also stresses the positive attributes of 'civility, kindness and public orderliness' exemplified in state sponsored courtesy and graciousness campaigns (Lee 2002). More recently, the term 'civic society' is used interchangeable with 'civil society'; however, the precise meanings attached to both terms remain deliberately ambiguous (Chua 2000).

In developing its vision statement for the new millennium (referred to as Singapore 21), the PAP government identified 'active citizenry' as one of the five pillars on which the Singaporean society of the future will be built:

The hallmark of Singaporeans in the twenty-first century will be active participation in civic life. This will be built upon a foundation of mutual respect and trust between the public and people sectors, and enlightened by commitment to the values and principles that underpin Singapore. (S21 Facilitation Committee 2003)

This vision of civic or civil society requires Singapore's 'active citizens' to inform themselves of issues and challenges facing the country; offer feedback and suggestions in a thoughtful manner with the aim of making things better; and help to implement what they suggest. The PAP expects those engaged in civil society to support state-defined 'national values'. These values are: 1) placing nation before community and society above self; 2) upholding the family as the basic building block of society; 3) resolving major issues through consensus instead of contentions; 4) stressing racial and religious tolerance and harmony; and 5) regard and community support for the individual (see Chua 1995: 32). Consequently, some subjects are always 'off-limits' or fall within what the governing elite refers to as 'out-of-bounds markers' (OB markers). Ho Kai Leong describes these as 'issues that are too sensitive to be discussed in public for fear of destabilizing or jeopardizing public peace and order' (2000: 186). The ruling PAP government is responsible for determining the limits of the OB markers, a task that it largely performs retrospectively with the result that what actually constitutes 'unacceptable political engagement' is unclear. In 1995, Prime Minister Goh Chok Tong commented :

Use your common sense. On government policy, ministerial salaries, COEs [Certificates of Entitlement] and so on, you are free to debate that, no problem whatsoever. If you are to venture into areas that touch on religious sensitivity, on race, then we would pull you back very early before you cause problems for the ground or for the community. ('PM: debate welcomed but govt will rebut malicious arguments' 1995)

Negotiating the constraints of state-defined civil society continues to be a fraught process for Singapore's NGOs. In embarking on the 'civil society experiment' both the state and the NGOs themselves are engaged in a constant process of 'testing the boundaries' between acceptable and unacceptable behaviour.

The state also limits the parameters of civil society through legislation. While the Singapore Constitution guarantees freedom of association (Article 14) in principle, organizations with more than ten members or committees with more than five members are required to register under the *Societies Act* or the *Companies Act* (Tanaka 2002: 208). The Registrar of Societies is empowered to exercise discretion with regard to registration and accreditation, and requires all registered groups to have a formal organizational structure and membership. All registered organizations are expressly prohibited from engaging in 'political activity' and must restrict their activities to issues outlined in their constitutions. Individuals who participate in groups that are not officially registered face the threat of arrest and imprisonment for participating in 'illegal assemblies'. The government has effectively used the *Societies Act* to suppress the activities of a number of local groups (Tanaka 2002: 209).

The legislative framework also works to limit the opportunity for international NGOs to participate in Singapore's civil society. Foreign-based NGOs find it difficult to become formally registered in Singapore, and without registration and accreditation, cannot operate on the ground. In addition, locally-based NGOs are extremely wary of receiving funding from overseas sources for fear that this may result in government suspicion about their activities (Perera and Ng 2002). This has resulted in a very small international NGO presence in Singapore, and very few transnational linkages between local, regional and global groups.

In addition to the *Societies Act*, the government also uses the *Internal Security Act* (ISA) to discipline the actions of groups it sees as politically threatening. The ISA was introduced during British colonial rule and was originally used against suspected communists. It provides the state with the means to arrest and detain without trial those individuals or groups that in its view threaten the national security.

The *Internal Security Act* and the *Societies Act* are significant deterrents to the emergence of a broad-based and diverse feminist movement. Instead, the feminist movement in Singapore can be characterized as a 'one organization movement' (Lyons 2004) dominated by the Association of Women for Action and Research (AWARE). AWARE[4] was established in 1985 in response to a series of government policies known as the 'Great Marriage Debate' aimed at encouraging graduate women to marry and have more children (Lyons-Lee 1998). These policies prompted a backlash amongst middle-class women and formed a crucial rallying point around which the organization was formed. AWARE's stated goals are to promote: 1) the awareness and participation of women in all areas; 2) the attainment of full equality; and 3) equal opportunities for women (AWARE 1990). Through research, discussion and support, it aims to make men and women more aware of the barriers that each faces as a result of gender discrimination. In addition to its research work, AWARE also runs workshops and seminars, and operates a volunteer helpline service. The organization is publicly recognized as a feminist group, even though it rarely uses the term to describe its own activities. The majority of members are uncomfortable about using the label 'feminist' for either themselves or the organization. The meanings attached to feminism are closely tied to the debate over western versus Asian values. In public discourse, feminism is described as a western ideology associated with radical lesbian man-haters and/or sexually promiscuous women with a 'chip on their shoulders'. [5]

While there are many other 'women's organizations' in Singapore, these tend to be formed on the basis of professional affiliation, ethnicity, religion, interest, service provision, or are local chapters of international organizations (e.g. the YWCA). The Singapore Council of Women's Organizations (SCWO) is a state-sponsored umbrella group that acts as a federation of all these groups. The SCWO holds regular forums and workshops aimed at examining and improving the status of women. It is involved in the development of government policy through its research and legislative arm (Singapore Council of Women's Organizations 2002). Given the diversity of organizations that are associated with the SCWO, the organization is careful not to present itself as feminist in either goals or orientation. This has led some critics to suggest that the SCWO is a conservative mouthpiece for government policy that is not directed towards the goal of improving women's social or legal status (Lyons 2004). While informal groups and networks do emerge, they tend to operate by word-of-mouth and with almost no public profile. In this environment, AWARE thus continues to be the public face of feminism in Singapore.

AWARE adopts a cautious and conservative approach to its activities. Working within the framework provided by the 'out-of-bounds markers', members are never completely sure how the organization's statements will be received and are forced to respond carefully (Lyons 2000a, 2000b). Fear of negative perceptions or closure means that AWARE tempers its public statements or limits its activities to avoid criticism. Issues of sexuality and the rights of lesbians, religion and the role of Shariah Law, or class-based social divisions are all designated as 'off-limits' by the organization. Instead, AWARE has focused on equal employment opportunities for women, access to equal educational opportunities for girls, and changes to domestic violence law. As Chua (1995: 208) comments, AWARE's demands 'do not challenge the fundamental premise of the regime although they do bring out anomalies in existing state practices'. AWARE's activities remain essentially reformist in nature. In many ways, this is a successful means of state control—AWARE ends up policing its own behaviour; the Singapore government is most adept in utilizing group and individual self-regulation as a means of control.

This picture of civil society in Singapore, however, is overly pessimistic. There is no doubt that the Singapore government has effectively stifled the growth of an independent and vibrant sphere of NGO activity. Nonetheless, a number of organizations continue to test the OB markers. Among these was the short-lived 'The Working Committee' or TWC that was formed in late 1998 and disbanded a year later.[6] TWC operated as an informal network of individuals and representatives of NGOs and voluntary welfare organizations (VWOs). Its goal was to build links between differently situated civil society actors, and thereby participate in both re-assessing and re-invigorating the sphere of civil society in Singapore. Unlike other NGOs, the TWC was not formally registered through the *Societies Act*, but operated as a loose affiliation of individuals and organizations. During this time, it organized workshops, open houses,[7] public forums, and a conference. By deliberately limiting its life span to one year, and focusing its activities on 'network building' rather than pursuing the interests of a particular client or membership group, TWC was able to avoid the otherwise restrictive requirements of registration under the *Societies Act*. Not only did it facilitate greater information sharing amongst Singaporean NGOs and VWOs, but it also acted as a focal point for broader public discussion of the meaning of civil society. As I argue below, it was also an important alternative model of civil society engagement for other groups and has provided an opportunity for previously banned topics to be dealt with.

Advocating for Domestic Worker Rights

For many years, the plight of women working as domestics in Singapore has remained 'out-of-bounds'. Like many taboo topics, the issue of domestic workers has not been publicly identified by the state in its official statements as a topic that is 'off-limits', but its association with the 'Marxist conspiracy' has meant that few NGOs have been willing to address it. In May 1987, 22 people (including several AWARE members) were arrested under the *Internal Security Act* for threatening the state and national interests (Rodan 1993). Those arrested included Catholic social workers and lay workers at the Geylang Catholic Center for Foreign Workers. Among the issues that they were concerned with were higher wages, social security benefits, job security and employment conditions for all foreign workers (Mauzy and Milne 2002). At the time of their arrest, the government's official statements claimed that Catholic organizations were 'a cover for political agitation' to 'radicalise student and Christian activists' (qtd. in Haas 1989: 59). The Catholic Center for Foreign Workers was subsequently closed. Of those arrested, some were later released, while others were detained for varying periods. Those charged had to admit to being a Marxist as a condition of their release. They were 'rehabilitated' with an agreement not to enter into politics.

AWARE was silent on the arrests, and many members still believe that they narrowly escaped arrest and the closure of the organization. In interviews I conducted with AWARE members in the mid-1990s, the Marxist conspiracy was still fresh in their memories. Many AWARE members interpreted the arrests as a clear signal that domestic worker rights were off-limits and that for AWARE to address the issue would be extremely risky. AWARE's failure to engage with the domestic worker issue since the late 1980s, however, cannot be solely attributed to its fear of closure. As Nirmala PuruShotam has clearly pointed out, there is a remarkable alliance between the middle-class values espoused by the PAP and AWARE which centres around a 'shared language' of 'fears of falling and the normal family ideology' (1998: 144). This group has experienced rapid upward class mobility since the 1960s and clings to a normative family model as a means of shoring up their class position (i.e., fear of falling back into the working class). This produces a situation in which the predominant voice of 'moderate feminism' in AWARE 'arises and takes shape within a constantly shifting continuum of compliance with and resistance to patriarchal ideologies and practices' (PuruShotam 1998: 145). The majority of AWARE members are middle-class and it is widely acknowledged within the organization that many members employ domestic workers. My own research on AWARE members' attitudes towards feminism and social change suggests that a significant group hold conservative views on sex roles and family structures, and are thus supportive of the traditional association of household labour with 'women's work' (Lyons 1999). For these busy women, hiring a live-in domestic worker is a pre-requisite for juggling career and family responsibilities. Engaging with the question of maids would require AWARE members to address the contentious topics of class and sex/gender roles, issues that the organization has carefully avoided in its public statements and activities.

AWARE's silence was also consistent with its claim not to speak on behalf of 'other' women. In their dealings with a range of others (including non-AWARE members and non-Singaporeans), AWARE members adopt an ethical framework of 'respect' (Lyons 2000b, 2001). The decision not to speak about religion or sexuality is therefore seen not only as a strategic move to avoid state wrath, but also as a validation of the very principle of respect. For example, behind the relegation of religion as a taboo topic by AWARE, is a strong belief in the need to respect women's religious convictions. This principle extends to AWARE's decision not to make public statements about the status or rights of women in other countries. On one of the few occasions in which AWARE broke its self-imposed silence on foreign women, it found itself the target of a backlash against its own failure to take a stand on the issue of foreign domestic workers in Singapore.[8]

The labour movement has also been silent on issues surrounding migrant labour in Singapore. Most independent unions were closed down or weakened in the 1960s, and replaced by a state-sponsored National Trades Union Congress (NTUC) that acts as an umbrella group for affiliated organizations that are largely supportive of the government's economic and labour policies (Rodan 1996).

In the absence of a local or international NGO presence in Singapore to deal with the rights of domestic workers, religious groups and foreign embassies stepped in and filled the void. Their actions, however, were largely ad hoc. During the 1990s, concerned about the linkage between Catholicism and the Marxist conspiracy, Christian churches were extremely careful in their public dealings with domestic workers. As the numbers of Indonesian foreign workers rose, several mosques began to provide support and training services to Muslim domestic workers through their women's programs.[9] Both groups acted informally to assist 'runaway' domestics to contact embassy officials when they needed assistance. These ties became stronger in the 1990s as increasing pressure was placed on sending countries by overseas workers and their families to address the needs of their citizens working abroad. In Singapore, these claims were crystallized around the arrest and execution of a Filipina domestic worker, Flor Contemplacion, in 1995. Contemplacion was found guilty of murdering another domestic worker and her four-year old charge. The execution caused a diplomatic rift between the Philippines and Singapore as speculation mounted over her guilt.[10]

As a result of this, and other cases, migrant worker welfare became a significant issue for bilateral relations between receiving and sending countries throughout s outheast Asia. The Philippines Government established the Overseas Workers Welfare Administration (OWWA) as part of the Department of Labour and Employment. The OWWA runs a range of services for overseas Filipino workers, including refuges for domestic workers in a number of countries. In Singapore, the

OWWA half-way house for runaway domestic workers operates through the Philippines Embassy. In 1998, the Catholic Archdiocese of Singapore established the Commission for Migrants and Itinerant People (CMI). One of its goals is to reach out to 'strangers' (including migrant workers, foreign students, travellers and refugees) 'who have experienced injustice, oppression and alienation' (The Commission for Migrants and Itinerant People 2001). In addition to services aimed as assisting domestic workers, the CMI has also worked with the Singapore Ministry of Manpower to run workshops for employers on 'How to Establish a Harmonious Working Relationship with your Foreign Domestic Helper'. Both groups operate in partnership with the Singaporean government to address the question of individual treatment of domestic workers by employers, rather than dealing with broader questions of labour law, immigration law, or citizenship rights.

The Working Committee 2

As the numbers of domestic workers entering Singapore has risen, so too have reports of physical and sexual abuse of domestic workers by their employers, domestic worker deaths, as well as incidents of assault or theft carried out by domestic workers. Despite concerns about overstepping the OB markers in relation to maids, the increasing visibility of these issues has made them difficult to ignore. In December 2001, a 19-year old Indonesian woman, Muawanatul Chasanah, died after months of brutal assault by her employer Ng Hua Chye. Ng's neighbour, Mr Neo, was quoted in the media as saying: 'Even if I knew, I wouldn't have called the police, it's not my business. He can do what he wants, that's his problem' (Ho and Chong 2002). These comments prompted a number of Singaporeans to meet informally with the goal of addressing attitudes towards and treatment of domestic workers in Singapore. Modelling themselves on TWC, The Working Committee 2 (TWC2) emerged in late 2002.

TWC2's aim was to 'promote respect for domestic workers through education, and secure better treatment of domestic workers through legislation and other means' (TWC2 2003a). Like its predecessor, TWC2 was formed as an ad-hoc group of individuals and organizations with a one-year limited life-span. International Day to Eliminate Violence against Women on 25 November 2003 marked the culmination of its year-long efforts. Braema Mathi, a Nominated Member of Parliament[11] and member of AWARE, chaired the committee. The TWC2's membership was multi-racial, reflecting the major ethnic groups in Singapore (Chinese, Malay, Indian and Others—a euphemism for Europeans and Eurasians). It included women and men, a wide distribution of age groups, as well as foreign nationals, including some domestic workers. Both AWARE and the SCWO were listed as 'partner' organizations, and TWC2 web-site and bulletin board were hosted on the AWARE web-site. Although AWARE supported TWC2's activities, it did not take a public stance in relation to the issue of domestic worker rights or incorporate similar activities into its own agenda.

TWC2's activities were organized under the banner 'Dignity Overdue: Respecting the Rights of Maids', and included workshops, public forums, and exhibitions. The issue of domestic worker 'rights' focused on three interrelated topics— reducing demand for domestic workers; employment contracts (including wages and conditions); and treatment by employers (built around a notion of respect for human dignity). Consistent with other NGOs in Singapore, rather than adopting a direct lobbying role in relation to legislative change, TWC2 focused its activities on public education. For this reason, part of the group's activities were focused on drawing attention to the gendered division of labour within the home, and finding alternative solutions to Singapore's reliance on the labour of domestic workers. For example, the art-installation 'houseWORK project' brought together a range of artists who drew attention to the issue of household labour by asking participants to bring along their clothes to be ironed on stage (Teng 2003). The TWC2 also drew attention to the problems facing Singaporean families, such as the lack of childcare or after-school care, the lack of nursing homes or alternative facilities for the care of the elderly or disabled, and the lack of family-friendly workplace policies within both the public and private sectors.

In relation to employment contracts, TWC2 encouraged employers to provide a day off per week to their employees. Members organized a 'Sunday Off Campaign' that included a Block Party[12] for workers and their employers, and a photograph exhibition of domestic workers on their days off (Tee 2003). Members also used the forum pages in the local media to raise the issue of standardized contracts for foreign domestic workers (Price and Lim 2003). These, and other initiatives, were successful in raising public awareness of the issues surrounding conditions of work. The PAP government, however, continues to argue that the matter of working conditions is an issue to be negotiated between individual employers (or agents) and employees because of the individual nature of the duties required in each household (Tan 2003a, 2003b).

TWC2's interest in the treatment of domestic workers focused on the issue of violence. The group's activities culminated with a series of events focused on International Day to Eliminate Violence against Women and Singapore's first 'White Ribbon Campaign'.[13] TWC2 focused the campaign on the foreign domestic worker because

> she is the most vulnerable woman in our homes. She is a guest worker, here at our invitation, to support our families and earn an honest living for their own families. Help agencies get one new case of abuse every week. Every act of violence against her is a shame on us. (TWC2 2003b)

Although this campaign could have provided an important opportunity to address the intersection between domestic violence against all women, and the 'private' nature of violence against domestic workers, it remained largely focused on migrant women. The campaign was thus supportive of the state's own interest in developing a gracious and more civic-minded citizen, in contrast to the image of the 'ugly Singaporean' conjured up by images of domestic worker abuse. The interrelated issues of citizenship, marriage, residence and family migration, were largely unaddressed. In part, this reflects concerns about overstepping the state's OB markers. But, it also points to an inability to address violence as an issue of power embedded in social relations, rather than as an individual, isolated act. The focus on violence also means that the rights of the vast majority of workers who do not face violence in the workplace, were also overlooked.

After the TWC2 was disbanded in November 2003, a new group consisting of former members announced that they would establish a Maid Resource Centre to deal with

> all issues relating to maids, whether these are raised by workers, employers or recruitment agencies. ... It plans to be a one-stop centre for maids, providing information on the industry, a training centre for skills upgrading, as well as a coordination point to link workers, employers, foreign embassies and employment agencies. (Hooi 2003)

In signalling its intentions to extend the TWC2's work, this group raises the possibility of a stronger, more formalized NGO presence in the field of domestic worker rights. At this stage, it is too early to tell whether they will be successful, and what implications this will have for both domestic worker rights and the expansion of civil society in Singapore. It may be that the 'maid-economy' is now such a public issue for discussion and debate, that a more formal NGO presence and/or the incorporation of domestic worker rights into pre-existing NGO activities (such as those of AWARE) will not be seen to overstep the OB markers.

Conclusion

The feminization of migrant labour clearly is a transnational issue and many groups are working to improve the status of female migrant workers both globally and regionally. This study, however, points to problems that transnational activists face as they attempt to advocate across national borders. Singapore is a major receiving country of migrant labour in the region, and like women elsewhere, domestic workers there face a range of problems. Transnational actors seeking to advocate on their behalf not only face legal barriers to cross-border activism, but also the constraints of working in a narrowly defined sphere of civil society. For their part, local activists are understandably wary of associating too closely with international groups, and limit their activities in ways that support state-defined 'out-of-bounds markers'. The Working Committee 2 tests the boundaries of these markers through its activities. It marks one of the first attempts by local NGOs and activists in Singapore to address a transnational issue. However, it has done so by focusing specifically on 'national' issues and deliberately avoiding affiliations or alliances with non-Singaporean based networks or organizations. While the TWC2's activities are creative, ultimately they remain non-confrontational and consensual. The group lacks radical potential because its members fail to address the substantive issues of class, gender and ethnicity that underpin the demand for domestic migrant labour, as well as the factors that constrain the rights of these workers.

In the rush to celebrate the emergence of global civil society, we must stop to remind ourselves that transnationalism does not transcend difference but is embedded within it. For transnational activism to be successful, feminists must consciously delineate the boundaries of their engagement, paying close attention to the different situations 'on the ground' in those places where they seek to forge alliances. Like locally-based groups such as the TWC2, transnational activists need to develop creative responses to the limitations imposed by state forces. They must also seek ways of supporting the efforts of local groups without jeopardizing their activities. Recognizing the limitations of transnationalism is thus the greatest challenge facing the future of global feminism.

Lenore Lyons is Deputy Director of the Centre for Asia-Pacific Social Transformation Studies (CAPSTRANS) at the University of Wollongong, Australia. She is currently working on a study of gender, the state and civil society in Singapore, and on a collaborative project on domestic worker rights in Southeast Asia. She has published widely on the women's movement in Singapore, and cross-cultural feminist methodology. Her most recent publication is A State of Ambivalence: The Feminist Movement in Singapore, *Brill Academic Publishers, Leiden, 2004.*

Notes

1   Transnationalism can be defined as 'regular activity crossing national borders that involve at least one nonstate actor', in contrast to 'international' activism which primarily involves state actors (Clark, Friedman and Hochstetler 1998: 3).

2   Data on transnational migration in the region is extremely difficult to verify due to the large numbers of 'illegal' or 'unofficial' migrants.

3   However, the number of opposition held seats has since remained less than five per cent of the total.

4   In 2003, AWARE had a membership of over 600. Membership is open to female Singaporean citizens and permanent residents. Men and non-citizens may participate in some activities as 'Friends of AWARE'. For a discussion of AWARE's goals and activities see Lyons (2004).

5   See Lyons (1999) for a more detailed discussion of the debates around the meaning of feminism within AWARE.

6   For a discussion of the TWC see Singam et al. (2002).

7   For example, visits to the premises of affiliated NGOs.

8   In 1998, AWARE presented a petition to the Indonesian Embassy decrying the treatment of ethnically Chinese women in Indonesia who were raped during a series of racial clashes that year. In receiving the petition, a spokeswoman for the Indonesian Embassy pointed out that Indonesian women were frequent victims of violent abuse while working as domestic workers in Singapore, an issue that AWARE had not addressed (Zakaria 1998).

9   Such activities include religious instruction as well as English language tuition.

[10]   For a discussion of this case, see Hilsdon et al. (2000) and Yeoh, Huang and Gozalez III (1999).

[11]   The Nominated Member of Parliament (NMP) scheme was introduced in 1990 to co-opt alternative non-partisan voices into parliament. NMPs are nominated by members of the public, NGOs or VWOs, and appointed by the government for a term of 3 years. While NMPs share the same parliamentary privileges and immunities as normal MPs, they have limited voting rights and do not play a role in the running of town councils.

[12]   Block here refers to a housing apartment block, the main form of housing in Singapore.

[13]   The White Ribbon Campaign is an international program organised by men where ribbon wearers pledge 'never to commit, never to condone and never to remain silent about violence against women' (White Ribbon Campaign 2003).

References

Anheier, H., M. Glasius and M.Kaldor (eds.) (2001) *Global Civil Society*. Oxford: Oxford University Press.

AWARE 1990 *Association of Women for Action and Research Declaration and Constitution.* Singapore.

Ball, R. and N. Piper (2002) 'Globalization and regulation of citizenship: Filipino migrant workers in Japan', *Political Geography,* 21, 1013-34.

Basu, A. (2000) 'Globalization of the local/localization of the global: mapping transnational women's movements', *Meridians: Feminism, Race, Transnationalism,* 1, 1, 68-84.

Chiam, C. (2003) '186 maid agencies accept rules set by Jakarta', *The Straits Times,* 30 July.

Chua, B. (2000) 'The relative autonomies of the state and civil society', in G. Koh and O. G. Ling (eds.), *State-Society Relations in Singapore,* Singapore: Institute of Policy Studies and Oxford University Press, 62-76.

Chua, B. (1995) *Communitarian Ideology and Democracy in Singapore,* London: Routledge.

Clark, A. M., E. J. Friedman and K. Hochstetler (1998) 'The sovereign limits of global civil society: A comparison of NGO participation in UN world conferences on the environment, human rights, and women', *World Politics,* 51, 1, 1-35.

Daley, C. and M. Nolan (eds.) 1994 *Suffrage and Beyond: International Perspectives,* Auckland: University of Auckland Press.

Della Porta, D., H. Kriesi and D. Rucht (eds.) (1999) *Social Movements in a Globalizing World,* New York: St Martin's Press.

Friedman, E. J. (2003) 'Gender the agenda: the impact of the transnational women's rights movement at the UN conferences of the 1990s', *Women's Studies International Forum,* 26, 4, 313-331.

Guarnizo, L. E. and M. P. Smith (1998) 'The locations of transnationalism', in L. E. Guarnizo (ed.), *Transnationalism From Below,* New Brunswick: Transaction, 3-34.

Gurowitz, A. (2000) 'Migrant rights and activism in Malaysia', *Journal of Asian Studies,* 59, 863-88.

Haas, M. (1989) 'The politics of Singapore in the 1980s', *Journal of Contemporary Asia,* 19, 1, 48-77.

Hilsdon, A. M., M. Macintyre, V. Mackie and M. Stivens (eds.) (2000) *Human Rights and Gender Politics: Asia Pacific Perspectives,* London: Routledge.

Ho, K. L. (2000) *The Politics of Policy-Making in Singapore,* Oxford: Oxford University Press.

Ho, K. and E. Chong (2002) 'Starved battered dead ... nine months of maid abuse went unnoticed', *The Straits Times,* 20 July.

Hooi, A. (2003) 'Permanent centre for maids', *The Straits Times,* 4 December.

Howell, J. and D. Mulligan (2003) 'Editorial', *International Feminist Journal of Politics,* 5, 2, 157-61.

Huang, S. and B. Yeoh (2003) 'The difference gender makes: state policy and contract migrant workers in Singapore', *Asian and Pacific Migration Journal,* 12, 1-2, 75-97.

Huang, S. and B. Yeoh (1996) 'Ties that bind: state policy and migrant female domestic helpers in Singapore', *Geoforum,* 27, 4, 417-93.

Keck, M. E. and K. Sikkink (1998) *Activists Beyond Borders: Advocacy Networks in International Politics,* Ithaca: Cornell University Press.

Law, L. (2003) 'Sites of transnational activism: Filipino non-government organizations in Hong Kong', in S. Huang (ed.), *Gender Politics in the Asia-Pacific Region,* London: Routledge, 205-21.

Law, L. and K. Nadeu (1999) 'Globalization, migration and class struggles: NGO mobilization for Filipino domestic workers', *Kasarinlan,* 14, 3-4, 51-68.

Lee, T. (2002) 'The politics of civil society in Singapore', *Asian Studies Review,* 26, 1, 97-117.

Lim, L. L. and N. Oishi (1996) 'International labor migration of Asian women: distinctive characteristics and policy concerns', *Asian and Pacific Migration Journal,* 5, 1, 85-116.

Lindio-McGovern, L. (2001) 'The globalization of labor and the politics of foreign debt in the Philippines: the experience of overseas Filipino domestic workers', paper presented at the Annual Conference of the Association of Asian Studies. Washington DC, 4-7 April.

Lyons, L. (2004) *A State of Ambivalence: The Feminist Movement in Singapore,* Leiden: Brill Academic Publishers.

Lyons, L. (2001) 'Negotiating difference: Singaporean women building an ethics of respect', in S. Schacht and J. Bystydzienski (eds.), *Forging Radical Alliances Across Difference: Coalition Politics for the New Millennium,* London: Rowman and Littlefield Publishers, 177-90.

Lyons, L. (2000a) 'The limits of feminist political intervention in Singapore', *Journal of Contemporary Asia,* 30, 1, 67-83.

Lyons, L. (2000b) 'A state of ambivalence: feminism and a Singaporean women's organization', *Asian Studies Review,* 24, 1, 1-24.

Lyons, L. (1999) 'Believing in equality: the meanings attached to "feminism" in Singapore', *Asian Journal of Women's Studies,* 5, 1, 115-39.

Lyons-Lee, L. (1998) 'The "graduate woman" phenomenon: changing constructions of the family in Singapore', *Sojourn: Journal of Social Issues in Southeast Asia,* 13, 2, 1-19.

Mackie, V. (2001) 'The language of globalization, transnationality and feminism', *International Feminist Journal of Politics,* 3, 2, 180-206.

Mauzy, Diane K. and R. S. Milne (2002) *Singapore Politics Under the People's Action Party.* London: Routledge.

Meyer, M. K. and E. Prügl (eds.) (1999) *Gender Politics in Global Governance,* Lanham: Rowman and Littlefield.

Mitter, S. and S. Rowbotham (2000) 'Bringing women's voices into the dialogue on technology policy and globalization in Asia', *International Feminist Journal of Politics,* 2, 3, 382-401.

Moghadam, V. (2000) 'Transnational feminist networks: collective action in an era of globalization', *International Sociology,* 15, 1, 57-85.

Naples, N. A. and M. Desai (eds.) (2002) *Women's Activism and Globalization: Linking Local Struggles and Transnational Politics,* London: Routledge.

Ong, A. (1996) 'Strategic sisterhood or sisters in solidarity? questions of communitarianism and citizenship in Asia', *Indiana Journal of Global Legal Studies,* 4, 107-36.

Perera, L. and T. Ng (2002) 'Foreign funding: Managing conflicting views', in L. Perera, (ed.), *Building Social Space in Singapore: The Working Committee's Initiative in Civil Society Activism,* Singapore: Select Publishing, 93-6.

Phillips, A. (1999) 'Who needs civil society? A feminist perspective', *Dissent,* Winter, 56-61.

Piper, N. (2003) 'Feminization of labor migration as violence against women: international, regional, and local nongovernmental organization responses in Asia', *Violence Against Women,* 9, 6, 723-45.

Piper, N. and M. Roces (eds.) (2002) *Wife or Worker? Asian Women's Marriage and Migration,* Boulder: Rowman and Littlefield.

'PM: Debate welcomed but govt will rebut malicious arguments', (1995) *The Straits Times,* 24 January.

Price, I. A. and C. Lim (2003) 'Let's have affordable alternatives', *The Straits Times,* 3 October.

PuruShotam, N. (1998) 'Between compliance and resistance: women and the middle-class way of life in Singapore', in M. Stivens (ed.), *Gender and Power in Affluent Asia,* London: Routledge, 127-66.

Rodan, G. (1996) 'State-society relations and political opposition in Singapore', in G. Rodan (ed.), *Political Oppositions in Industrialising Asia,* London: Routledge, 95-127.

Rodan, G. (1993) 'Preserving the one-party state in contemporary Singapore', in G. Rodan (ed.), *Southeast Asia in the 1990s: Authoritarianism, democracy, and capitalism,* St Leonards: Allen and Unwin, 76-108.

Rupp, L. J. (1997) *Worlds of Women: The Making of an International Women's Movement,* Princeton: Princeton University Press.

Rupp, L. J. and V. Taylor (1999) 'Forging feminist identity in an international movement: A collective identity approach to twentieth century feminism', *Signs,* 24, 2, 363-86.

S21 Facilitation Committee (2003) *Singapore 21,* Online: http://www.singapore21.org.sg/ [Accessed 4 June 2003].

Shah, N. and I. Menon (1997) 'Violence against women migrant workers: issues, data and partial solutions', *Asian and Pacific Migration Journal,* 6, 1, 5-29.

Singam, C., T. C. Kee, T. Ng and L. Perera (2002) *Building Social Space in Singapore: The Working Committee's Initiative in Civil Society Activism,* Singapore: Select Publishing.

Singapore Council of Women's Organizations (SCWO) (2002) *Aims and Objectives,* Home Page. Online: http://www.scwo.org.sg/about_aims.html [Accessed 4 July 2002].

Singapore Department of Statistics (2003) *Key Stats,* http://www.singstat.gov.sg/keystats/ annual/indicators.html [Accessed 9 March 2004].

Sperling, V., M. M. Ferree and B. Risman (2001) 'Constructing global feminism: transnational advocacy networks and Russian women's activism', *Signs,* 26, 4, 1155-86.

Tan, J. (2003a) 'Go for individual contracts', *The Straits Times,* 5 August.

Tan, J. (2003b) 'Law does protect maids', *The Straits Times,* 21 August.

Tanaka, Y. (2002) 'Singapore: subtle NGO control by a developmentalist welfare state', in S. Shigetomi (ed.), *The State and NGOs: Perspectives from Asia,* Singapore: Institute of Southeast Asian Studies, 200-221.

Tee, H. C. (2003) 'They're maid like you and I', *The Straits Times,* 22 October.

Teng, Q. X. (2003) 'Dignity for maids: forum to highlight the plight of foreign domestic workers', *Today,* 5 July.

The Commission for Migrants and Itinerant People (2001) *About Us,* Online: www.migrants.org.sg/aboutus.htm [Accessed 5 December 2003].

The Working Committee 2 (TWC2) (2003a) *Our Objectives,* Online: www.aware.org.sg/twc2/who.shtml [Accessed 5 December 2003].

The Working Committee 2 (TWC2) (2003b) *White Ribbon Campaign Singapore (2003),* Available at: www.aware.org.sg/twc2/wrc.shtml [Accessed 5 December 2003].

Ucarer, E. M. (1999) 'Trafficking in women: alternative migration or modern slave trade?' in M. K. Meyer and E. Prügl (eds.), *Gender Politics in Global Governance*, Lanham: Rowman and Littlefield, 230-44.

Uhlin, A. (2001) 'The transnational dimension of civil society: migration and independence movements in Southeast Asia', in B. Beckman, E. Hansson and A. Sjoegren (eds.), *Civil Society and Authoritarianism in the Third World. A Conference Report*, Stockholm: PODSU/Stockholm University.

Wee, V. and A. Sim (2003) *Transnational Labour Networks in Female Labour Migration: Mediating Between Southeast Asian Women Workers And International Labour Markets.* Hongkong: Southeast Asia Research Centre (SEARC), Working Paper Series, No. 49.

White Ribbon Campaign (2003) *About Us,* Available at: http://www.whiteribbon.ca/about_us/ [Accessed 5 December 2003].

Worthington, R. (2003) *Governance in Singapore,* London: Routledge Curzon.

Yeoh, B. and S. Huang (1997) 'Spaces at the margins: foreign domestic workers and the development of civil society in Singapore', paper presented at the International Conference on Women in the Asia-Pacific Region: Persons, Power and Politics, Singapore, 11-13 August.

Yeoh, B. S. A., S. Huang and J. Gonzalez III (1999) 'Migrant domestic female workers: debating the economic, social and political impacts in Singapore', *International Migration Review,* 33, 1, 114-136.

Zakaria, Z. (1998) 'Surprise invite for AWARE as petition delivered', *The Straits Times,* 10 September: 30.

III.
WOMEN'S LOCAL STRUGGLES AND FEMINIST POLITICS

THE CURSE OF NAKEDNESS

NIGERIAN WOMEN IN THE OIL WAR

TERISA E. TURNER AND LEIGH S. BROWNHILL

In 2002-2003 popular movements shut down much of Nigeria's huge oil industry[1] and faced US military intervention. Women who were at the forefront forged strategic connections with insurgents worldwide. This article examines the period in three parts.

First, between July 2002 and February 2003 women's organizations occupied ChevronTexaco's export terminal and several flow stations. Their weapon was their nakedness. In much of Africa, women throw off their clothes in an ultimate protest to say 'this is where life comes from. I hereby revoke your life'. Nakedness by elderly women, in particular, is used in extreme and life-threatening situations. Women wielding the weapon of the exposed vagina could be killed or raped. It is therefore with knowledge of the act's life and death implications that women enter into such protest. Women who go naked implicitly state that they will get their demands met or die in the process of trying. Naked protests multiplied around the world as women were inspired by the Nigerian example to 'bare all' to resist the Bush attack on Iraq. Global boycotts of oil companies proliferated.

Second, between January and July 2003 waged Nigerian men joined the peasant women's shutdown of the oil industry by organizing strikes. This mobilization culminated in an eight-day national general strike.

Third, in the July-September 2003 period, women again seized oil facilities and shut down the oil companies after oil union 'male dealers' sabotaged the general strike. In response to oil-company demands the Nigerian and US military intervened.

Three questions are addressed in this article. First, why were women at war with the international oil companies in Nigeria? Second, how were anti-oil company campaigns internationalized by women and third, with what implications? We begin with a brief treatment of the theoretical framework within which we pose these questions.

First, women are at the forefront of social movements because, despite their being largely unwaged, capital exploits them as it commodifies and uses up 'free' nature, social services, built space and the production of paid and unpaid work (Brownhill and Turner 2003; Benjamin and Turner 1992). All these 'values' are integral to the subsistence or life-centred political economy in which the needs of all are addressed through collective, cooperative and autonomous activity including producer-organized trade or direct deals (Bennholdt-Thomsen and Mies 1999). Communal land-holding and social relations essential to such a life-centred political economy remain resilient in much of the Niger Delta. Oil company operations since 1957 have been destroying the social and physical basis of subsistence. In 2002 women who are responsible for farming, fishing, feeding and life sustenance stood up against corporate destruction.

An examination of Nigerian women's occupation and shut-down of oil company facilities in the Niger Delta reveals a pattern of resistance involving two distinct social constructions. Women first broke up 'male deals' between some of their own menfolk and personnel of the oil companies and state. Second, they formed alliances with other men, often their grandsons, and in this 'gendered class alliance', successfully evicted the world's largest corporations from their land (Turner et al. 2001; Turner 1997; Nore and Turner 1980). Both of these social de- and re-constructions had national and international expressions. The global reach of cross-class 'male deals' is immediately apparent in the oil industry. In breaking these, Nigerian women built international solidarities and systemic coordinations with women and men similarly pitted against the commodification and war brought by oil majors and their corporate-state allies. In sum, to theorize women's war against big oil is to recognize the erasure of subsistence which corporate commodification entails and both the imperative and the capacities of life-producers to stand against it.

The second question—how were international solidarities forged and what is their anatomy?—is here theorized by reference to the systemic, global realities of capitalist organization and markets. The international oil companies bring two groups of people—those resident on oil reserves and those who consume oil—into one organization, i.e., the organization of the oil corporations themselves and of the oil market that they define. Because the oil companies bring these two groups into one global organization, the groups, by acting together, have the power to destroy the corporations by simultaneously denying them crude oil and product purchases. When residents of oil producing communities stop production at the same time as consumers boycott oil companies by refusing to buy their products, the two groups engage in a simultaneous global 'production-consumption oil strike'. Such a strike has the potential to annihilate the capacities of oil companies to make profits or exercise the power of accumulation. The crucial point here is that the popular organization with this potential to annihilate capital is not 'the party', or 'the forum'. Rather it is the international organization of the oil corporations themselves and of the oil market that they define. Embraced also within this organization are those engaged in the work of social reproduction and of the defence and restoration of nature (Dyer-Witheford 1999).

This conception challenges those constructions of 'globalization from below' which are limited to liberal declarations or protestations for reform. A much more fertile form of anti-imperial, transformational 'globalization from below' was promoted by Nigerian women who, in defending their subsistence life economy, denied strategic crude oil to globally dominate capital. Their explicitly feminist actions provoked women outside Nigeria to defend subsistence as life-affirmation in the context of global anti-war mobilization. This historically unprecedented world-wide 'no to war' movement boosted already-existing campaigns to boycott the oil companies which were at the same time facing shutdowns in Nigeria as women and their rural allies denied crude oil to the majors. This embryonic world-scale production-consumption oil strike foreshadows a future of globally coordinated strikes and boycotts that not only shut down oil corporations but re-start the petroleum system on a new, subsistence-positive basis. The systemic impetus to globalization from below revealed by the Nigerian insurgency is embodied in the corporate organizational and oil market ties that bind together all the world's people engaged in producing and consuming oil. The exploited, waged and unwaged, are 'organized, united and disciplined' by the 'process of production itself'. By privileging waged workers, most critical analysts (for example, Fagan 2002) have silenced or misconstrued the essential powers of the unwaged in this new crystallization of social forces which is asserting a global 'life economy civil commons' (McMurtry 2002). The hitherto silenced actors in the system of oil company organization and markets are the women who live in the communities built over hydrocarbon reserves.[2] Their paramount strategic importance is the reason for their silencing. In 2002-2003 Nigerian peasant women broke this silence and bequeathed 'a gift to humanity' in the form of a tremendous impetus toward 'a world transformed'.

The third question—what were the implications of the women's internationalized war against the oil companies?—can be pursued by theorizing 'direct deals'. We saw above how producer-consumer oil strikes have the potential to deny corporations their profits. Those who engage in producer-consumer oil strikes can take one further step. They can use their control over physical crude oil production sites, on the one hand, and their control over consumption on the other, to negotiate direct deals for the sale and purchase of oil. The crucial point here is that the very organization bequeathed by large corporations can be appropriated by producers and consumers and used against profit and for life support. This takes us to the connections between subsistence and capitalist relations. Those who live on oil reserves, such as the Niger Delta women and their allies, took control of oil facilities to defend and extend a subsistence commoning way of life. They thereby entered into oil company-organized alliances with people elsewhere who were attacking the same oil companies through other means, especially boycotts. Through these alliances and channels, direct deals can be negotiated so as to provide those defending subsistence with the means to succeed. Because these direct deals are autonomously organized for mutual benefit, they support the building of subsistence by both parties involved. This globalized defence, re-invention and building of subsistence is the central implication of the women's internationalized war against the oil companies.

This vision of revolutionary transformation involves the selective merging of two sets of social relations. On the one hand, the organization of transnational corporations is used by those it organizes to support life instead of profits. This use signals a shift in power within corporate organizations in favour of 'commoners'. This shift in power gives 'commoners' social relations which are global. On the other hand, this set of social relations, extracted from capitalist firms and markets, is merged with subsistence social relations in those autonomous communities that seek to re-invent a global commons.

Part 1: Women Seize Oil Facilities–July 2002 to February 2003

We no go 'gree o', we no go 'gree,' Chevron people we no go 'gree![3]

On 8 July 2002, after ChevronTexaco ignored their June correspondence, some 600 women occupied the US oil giant's 450,000 barrels a day (b/d) Escravos export terminal and tankyard. In their ten-day take over, the Itsekiri women negotiated 26 demands with corporate management. These included a demand that the government and oil companies meet with rural women and establish a permanent tripartite body for the resolution of problems related to oil operations. They signed a memorandum of understanding committing ChevronTexaco to the upgrading of 15 members of the communities who are contract staff to permanent staff status; the employment of one person from each of the five Ugborodo villages every year; the building of one house each for the elders—the Oloja Ore and the Eghare-Aja—in the communities; provision of vital infrastructure; a monthly allowance of N50,000 at least for the elderly aged 60 years and above and the establishment of income-generating schemes (Okon 2002). However, the most fundamental demand, that ChevronTexaco must go, was not countenanced by the company negotiators.

Why were women 'at war with Chevron?' Christiana Mene of the Escravos Women Coalition explained that

> We want Chevron to employ our children. If Chevron does that we the mothers will survive, we will see food to eat. Our farms are all gone, due to Chevron's pollution of our water. We used to farm cassava, okro, pepper and others. Now all the places we've farmed are sinking, we cannot farm. We cannot kill fishes and crayfish. That is why we told Chevron that Escravos women and Chevron are at war. (qtd. in Abiola 2002).

International petroleum corporations had reduced the once-rich subsistence economy of the Niger Delta to a polluted wasteland. Women could no longer train their children in peasant pursuits nor look forward to being fed in their old age. Because the oil companies had imposed a fundamental 'death economy' on the Delta's seven million people, the women warriors demanded the majors get out completely. They exposed their naked bodies, and most particularly their vaginas, to impose on oil company male dealers 'social death' through ostracization that was widely believed to lead to actual demise.[4] Death was imminent, a 'regular guest at the table', because the majors had destroyed subsistence. This imminence produced in the women warriors a fearless emotional state of existential liberation, a willingness to die in the cause of expelling ChevronTexaco, Shell, ExxonMobil and the others. As Queen Uwara, deputy chairperson of the Escravos Women Coalition stated,

A mother gets old someday, she becomes weak; the same with the father. It is your son and daughter who will be feeding you. If our children are not given work then the mothers cannot survive. They employ other tribes to work here, this time we cannot allow this kind of situation.... Chevron brought soldiers and police to threaten us when we were at Chevron yard. If Chevron wants to kill us, we are no longer afraid. We women have taken over the yard. But we are not afraid because Chevron is on our land. All we want is for Chevron to leave our land. (ERA 2002a)[5]

The women's bold strike at ChevronTexaco's export terminal immediately inspired at least twelve additional takeovers. Even before the Escravos group concluded negotiations, well over 1,000 women occupied six ChevronTexaco flow stations including Abiteye, Makaraba, Otuana and Olera Creek (Wamala 2002). One hundred women paddled a massive 'canoe' five miles into the high seas to take over the company's production platform in the Ewan oilfield. ChevronTexaco evacuated its staff, shut down production and refused to negotiate with the women because, according to the US major, 'they are not from our host community' ('Nigerian women seize platform' 2002). The positive results of the women's takeovers encouraged youth to occupy six Shell flow stations in western Niger Delta on 20 September 2002 ('Protests disrupt Warri ouput' 2002). On 26 September 2002, in an environment of growing anti-war activism, Nigeria's Environmental Rights Action (ERA) and the Ecuadorian affiliate of OilWatch International called for a boycott against ChevronTexaco (Osouka, Martnez and Salazar 2002). The ChevronTexaco boycott, like the million-strong UK-based 'StopEsso' boycott of ExxonMobil, which began in 2001 and continues today, connected consumer action with the resistance of oil producing communities.

The subsistence way of life 'was sweet' and was under dire threat from highly destructive oil company production 'on the cheap'. On 22 July 2002 a spokes-woman for occupiers of ChevronTexaco's Abiteye flow station, Felicia Itsero, 67, told ERA researchers that:

We are tired of complaining, even the Nigerian government and their

Chevron have treated us like slaves. Thirty years till now, what do we have to show by Chevron, apart from this big yard and all sorts of machines making noise, what do we have? They have been threatening us that if we make noise, they will stop production and leave our community and we will suffer, as if we have benefited from them. Before the 1970s, when we were here without Chevron, life was natural and sweet, we were happy. When we go to the rivers for fishing or forest for hunting, we used to catch all sorts of fishes and bush animals. Today, the experience is sad. I am suggesting that they should leave our community completely and never come back again. See, in our community we have girls, small girls from Lagos, Warri, Benin City, Enugu, Imo, Osun and other parts of Nigeria here every day and night running after the white men and staff of Chevron, they are doing prostitution, and spreading all sorts of diseases. The story is too long and too sad. When you go (to ERA) tell Chevron that we are no longer slaves, even slaves realise their condition and fight for their freedom. (ERA 2002b)

By 2003, even the International Monetary Fund (IMF) recognized that the conditions against which Delta insurgents were protesting and seeking to reverse had reached life-threatening proportions. In a 2003 report, the IMF revealed that:

Between 1970 and 2000, the poverty rate, measured as the share of the population subsisting on less than $1 per day, increased from close to 36 percent to just under 70 percent. This translates into an increase in the number of poor from about 19 million in 1970 to a staggering 90 million in 2000.... These developments, of course, coincided with the discovery of oil in Nigeria.... Over a 35-year period, Nigeria's cumulative revenues from oil (after deducting the payments to the foreign oil companies) have amounted to about US$350 billion at 1995 prices. In 1965, when oil revenues per capita were about US$33, per capita GDP was US$245. In 2000, when oil revenues were US$325 per capita, per capita GDP remained at the 1965 level. In other words, all the oil revenues—US$350 billion in total—did not seem to add to the standard of living at all. Worse, however, it could actually have contributed to a decline in the standard of living. (Sala-i-Martin and Subramanian 2003: 4)

The *Guardian* of 3 May 2003 reported that:

Poverty on the Delta is now extreme and communities are desperate for development and work, complaining that none of the billions of dollars earned from oil found under their land has reached them. Many schools have no teachers or books, hospitals and health centres are ill-equipped to deal with malaria and other equatorial diseases that are rife, and many communities have no electricity. Unemployment is 80 per cent or more in some places, sanitation is almost non-existent, housing is atrocious, and the death rate amongst children is very high. (Vidal 2003)

A June 2002 report by the Trade and Community Sub-committee of the Nigeria's federal House Petroleum Resources Committee found the Delta's oil communities to be 'exploited, misused, abused, polluted, underdeveloped, and almost completely dead; like a cherry fruit sucked and discarded' (qtd. in Eluemunor and Awom 2002). The operations of transnational oil companies were responsible for 'the dearth of social amenities in the host communities, the high unemployment, environmental degradation, and even prostitution'. Perhaps most damning were the report's findings on 'civil unrest.' It blamed

> some oil companies for encouraging and sponsoring civil unrest in the Niger Delta by engaging in divide and rule tactics by supporting some passive traditional rulers or even communities against radical ones, thus fuelling discord in the region. (qtd. in Eluemunor and Awom 2002)

In July 2002 the majors made specific promises to the insurgent women. Because ChevronTexaco and Shell were slow to implement their undertakings, 4,000 Warri women demonstrated on 8 August 2002 at the companies' regional headquarters only to be attacked by police and soldiers. Protester Alice Youwuren stated:

> We were just singing, we didn't destroy anything. We were peaceful. The police and soldiers misbehaved. Look at me, seven armed men pounced on me and reduced me to nothing. I found myself in a Shell clinic a day after the protest. (qtd. in Okon 2002)

The United Nations Integrated Regional Information Network (IRIN) (2002) reported that Shell police killed at least one woman. Shell later 'dismissed reports in the local press ... which claimed that a security agent at the scene shot dead an unarmed protestor. "To the best of our knowledge, the protests at our offices went without any major incident",' Shell stated ('Shell denies killing protestor' 2002).

In an ultimatum published worldwide, the 4,000 August 8th women demon-strators gave the Anglo-Dutch giant ten days to pay their hospital bills. Otherwise the women would subject Shell to the curse of nakedness (Adebayo 2002).

By 12 November 2002 the movement against corporate globalization expanded dramatically to oppose the impending US military attack on Iraq. Women in California were explicitly inspired by how the Nigerian women who captured Escravos 'shamed the men and won their cause'. They introduced a new anti-war tactic (Ivan 2002). With their naked bodies they wrote gigantic letters to spell 'Peace', photographs of which circulated the globe via the internet and print media to instigate still more nude demonstrators to enact variations (Rosen 2003). In the weeks that followed, naked protests proliferated. Organizers sent photos of their demonstrations to the California women's website. Naked anti-war protestors marched in Buenos Aires, Argentina on 1 March 2003. At this point the Nigeria-inspired anti-oil naked protests had taken place on all seven continents (see Baring Witness 2003).

The Lysistrata Project emerged in January 2003. Project organizers set up a website which provided several versions of the script of Aristophane's 2,400 year old feminist anti-war drama, *Lysistrata*. In the play women from two warring states unite to deny their menfolk sexual and domestic services until the men make peace. The organizers invited anti-war people worldwide to present the play in their own schools, workplaces and communities on 3 March 2003. Versions of *Lysistrata* were staged in 1,029 venues in 59 countries. Among the theatrical activists were unnamed 'international journalists' who staged a version in Arbil, Iraq on the eve not of war but of massacre. The organizers described the Lysistrata Project as 'the first-ever worldwide theatrical act of dissent'. In the meantime, on 15 February 2003 some 50 million people marched against Bush's attack on Iraq in the largest-ever global anti-war demonstration.

Between July 2002 and February 2003, the numbers of women engaged in naked protests grew from a few thousand in the Niger Delta to several hundred thousand worldwide. The world's first global use of protest theatre elaborated the nudity message: women were revoking the very lives of men who destroyed subsistence. Moreover, women were withdrawing all subsistence life support services, especially sex, food and other housework. The unwaged work of women in sustaining life was juxtaposed (by women *and allied men*) to the waged work of men engaged in sustaining profits through depredation and war. Insofar as this challenge was at once global and conscious, it transcended the idea that 'another world is possible' to embody the actually existing alternative.

The high level of Nigerian resistance to the US war against Iraq forced the corrupt Obasanjo government to stay out of the 'coalition of the willing'. Obasanjo suffered retaliation in the form of a temporary US withdrawal of some military backing that shored up his unpopular regime. The opening created by women's takeovers in the oil belt was seized by largely male trade unionists to launch a series of strikes. This extension of insurgency by the unwaged majority to the 30 per cent of the wage-earning workforce is the focus of part two.

Part 2: February to July 2003 Strikes—'Pirates, Monsters, Miscreants and Street Urchins'[6]

By March 2003 Nigeria was 'on the verge of collapse due to strikes' by the Academic Staff Union of Universities, the Department of Petroleum Resources, the Nigerian Union of Railway men, workers of the University College Hospital, Ibadan and the Central Working Committee of Freight Forwarders of Nigeria (Ajaero 2003). Oil workers at TotalFinalElf struck for ten days in March.

In Warri oil communities, over 100 people were killed in March 2003 in struggles to take over oil facilities, expel oil contractors and protest unequal political representation. Shell and ChevronTexaco shut in a total of 817,500 b/

d and by 25 March had evacuated most of their expatriate staff (Nzeshi 2003). As community protests continued, oil workers took over four off-shore oil platforms operated by the US giant Transocean, under contract to the majors. On 16 April, oil workers on board the rig MG Hulme staged a wildcat (but union-supported) strike after Transocean fired five union officers who were organizing against the firm's racist practice of transporting Nigerian workers in boats (thereby making them vulnerable to community wrath) versus expatriates in helicopters. On 19 April workers took over Transocean's three other deep-sea oil platforms in solidarity (Oyawiri 2003). Striking workers held the platforms and over 200 foreign and Nigerian oil workers employed by Halliburton, Schlumberger, TotalFinaElf and Shell. The strike ended on 2 May, just as British mercenaries and the Nigerian navy prepared to end the siege with force (Vidal 2003).

In June, Obasanjo, under pressure from the World Bank, announced a 55 per cent increase in the price of oil products. The National Labour Congress (NLC) called a general strike for 30 June 2003 to reverse the price increase. On 2 July, the third day of the strike, 'Ijaw and other pro-Niger Delta activists' announced their intention to 'close down all the oil flow stations in the Niger Delta and sack all the oil companies operating in the area [and] target the oil terminals in Forcados and Bonny' (Ebonugwo 2003).

Leaders of the two oil workers' unions responded to the possibility of a community shut-down of oil by backing away from participation in the general strike.[7] Male dealers in charge of the oil unions were capable of rescinding a strike threat by waged workers. But they were not capable of controlling community occupations of oil facilities. Despite this strategic faultline, by Monday 7 July, day eight of the general strike; waged and unwaged workers in the informal sector had forged sufficient unity to challenge the government's grip on power. The following account of the 'day of rage' draws on reports by Mike Ebonugwo (2003) and Godwin Ifijeh (2003).

By 7 July, the populace had 'fully thrown its weight behind the NLC's call for civil disobedience, following government's failure to effect a reversal of the new prices after a five-day ultimatum'. On day eight the general strike was 100 per cent effective in Lagos. On Monday 7 July, an Oodua Peoples' Congress (OPC) spokesman told the *Vanguard* (2003) that 'the OPC was in support of the strike and was taking part in its enforcement...'.

From as early as 7:00am, pro-labour protesters, made up of youths, students, artisans, suspected members of the Oodua Peoples' Congress (OPC) led by NLC officials and members of the United Action for Democracy (UAD) broke into the street to protest.... The fury knew no bounds with anger visibly written on the faces of the protesting youths.... They claimed that they had exhausted food and cash at home after a week of being home for the strike action, denouncing the government for offering to peg petrol price at N35 [US$.26 per litre]. Nothing short of the old price of N26 [US$.20], they said, would be acceptable to them, stating that even the N32 [US$.24], being negotiated by the NLC with government would not make any significant reduction in prices of goods and transport fares. ('We shoot to maim—police ... people died—NLC' 2003)

In a country in which 70 per cent of the population lives on less than US$1 per day, these fuel price increases marked a major degradation of living standards. The price of one litre of gasoline moved from a fifth to a quarter of daily cash income for almost three-quarters of the population.

In Lagos, 'area boys' mounted barricades, made bonfires of disused tires and dumped waste on roadsides. They smashed vehicles, robbed drivers who were found on the road and hijacked motorcycles from deliverymen, shouting, 'don't you know there's a strike today?' (Ebonugwo 2003) Some 'hoodlums took advantage of the attendant anti-fuel hike protests to unleash terror and mayhem on hapless commuters and motorists' (Ebonugwo 2003) and 'had gone ahead to rape some ladies who dared to venture out in the early hours of the morning' (Ebonugwo 2003). People ran helter-skelter to flee the streets. Members of the public reportedly 'vowed not to leave their homes again until the NLC called off the strike' (Ifijeh 2003).

Those police who turned on the public 'were beaten back by protesters, who wielded weapons of all sorts. They had asked the police to retreat in their own interest or they would meet them force for force' (Ifijeh 2003).

Women were pivotal in the shutdown because they controlled food transport and sale. 'Workers engaged in the informal sector; traders, artisans were the heroes and heroines of the strike.... The informal sector, especially market women played a significant role in the strike' ('Tit-bits' 2003). The highly organized market women and traders kept the markets closed for nine days. Millions of urban residents without refrigeration began to run out of food after three days. By Monday, day eight, the government's power was severely compromised; markets remained closed, sections of the police were on the side of the general strikers, while those remaining loyal to the government were being trounced by 'area boys' and were unable to contain civil disobedience. Activists across the Niger Delta were mobilizing to shut down flow stations, occupy the oil export terminals and 'sack' the oil companies. George Bush was scheduled to arrive in the country four days later, on Friday 11 July.

By day nine of the strike it appeared that power, as C. L. R James used to say, 'was rolling around in the streets' (James and Turner 1971). There were three possible solutions to the crisis. The first was to maintain the status quo of imperialist 'democracy' by acquiescing to the government's and World Bank's fuel price hike. This entailed calling off the general strike. The second was combined action by waged and unwaged workers to shut down the oil industry within the context of the general strike. This resolution would involve the expulsion of the oil companies, the convening of a national sovereignty conference and the possibility of a revolutionary move towards resource control by national and local communities. The third option for crisis resolution was yet another military coup.

Ochereome Nnanna (2003) characterized the strike as 'a great historic struggle of the Nigerian people'.

The real challenge to 'imperial democracy' and oil company control over the economy came from the potentially revolutionary combination of waged and unwaged workers who had the power to expel oil companies from the Niger Delta. To forestall this combination, the Obasanjo regime almost certainly threatened a coup. After Monday July 7th's militant protests, and faced with the likelihood of a coup, union bureaucrats broke the strike and urged people to return to work. NLC leaders opted for the maintenance of 'corporate rule' democracy and quickly settled with Obasanjo on a gasoline price hike of 31 per cent.

Three observations may be made about the general strike and the sectoral strikes that preceded it. First, in these largely men's strikes, the demands were about terms of labour commodification, not about the defence of subsistence against it. Second, peasants and other informal sector, unwaged people responded positively to the general strike call, but oil workers did not. Third, of the three possible solutions to the political crisis caused by the general strike, the trade union bureaucrats chose bourgeois democracy with a barely veiled military presence immediately behind the throne, which began to usurp elected governors in a 'creeping coup' throughout the country and especially in the oilbelt.

As the national mobilization of the general strike wound down, the Delta insurgency intensified. Labour aristocrats in the oil unions had refused to endorse the general strike. The women of the Delta nullified this betrayal by forcing oil workers off the job. This culmination of a year of growing insurgency is the focus of part three.

Part 3: Women Assert Community Control in the Delta, July–September 2003

On 10 July 2003, the day before US President Bush's arrival in Nigeria, women took over many petroleum companies' facilities in the Niger Delta including Amukpe, Sapele West and Imogu-Rumuekpe. Some 80 unarmed peasant women, ranging in age from 25 to 60, drove oil workers out of the Amukpe flow station, took possession of all vehicles, changed the facility's locks, installed their cooking equipment, made their infants and toddlers comfortable and began 'running shifts' of several dozen women each. The women demanded that Shell keep promises made earlier—employ local people, provide domestic amenities including water and electricity and remove a recently installed chain-link fence that impeded their agricultural product processing. Finally, they said Amukpe would be a 'no-go zone for oil companies' if Shell failed to honour past and present demands.

Within days the Delta was substantially under the control of a network of indigenous clan-based organizations. On 1 August 2003 one source reported that 'there have been several women's actions here ... the whole place is full of such actions, which are symptomatic of the state of the collapse of the Nigerian state and environmental decay' (IOWG 2003a). The government and oil companies were denied profits from a total of some 1.1 million barrels a day or over a third of Nigeria's estimated overall production capacity of 3.3 million b/d because communities had shut-in 817,500 b/d of oil production and were siphoning off another 300,000 b/d to sell on their own accounts (Oduniyi et al. 2003; 'EIA warns oil prices could stay high if Iraqi oil fails to come back' 2003; 'Vienna' 2003). Villagers' actions denied the government an estimated US$11 million a day and cost the oil companies an estimated minimum of US$2.5 million a day in foregone profits alone.

The oil companies demanded military intervention. Civil society organizations in an open letter to Bush, opposed US troop involvement. The broad coalition, including Niger Delta Women for Justice, told Bush that:

> The corporations have been flaring death-dispensing gas into the atmosphere of local communities, mangling fishing waters and farmlands with oil from old and broken pipelines they have refused to maintain and repair, cutting down forests and abolishing fresh water sources. We have seen them march alongside Nigerian soldiers they pay with blood money, into villages and hamlets killing, maiming and raping young men and women whose only crime is that they dared raise their voice to protest the wanton destruction of their lives and sources of livelihood. (ERA 2003)

In July 2003, the Washington D.C. based Institute for Policy Studies reported that the Pentagon planned 'to move between 5,000 and 6,500 troops from bases in Germany to various countries in Africa with the express purpose of protecting US oil interests in Nigeria' (Nuri 2003). Furthermore, 'according to the *Wall Street Journal*, US officials claim that a key mission for US forces [in Africa] would be to ensure that Nigeria's oil fields are secure' (Nuri 2003). By September 2003 US troops were in the Delta. The *Vanguard* reported that 'Right now we are co-habiting the Niger Delta with the Marines and US Naval patrol boats of different sizes' (Igho 2003).

The Nigerian government and international media rationalized and justified military intervention by reference to 'ethnic conflict' in a 'failed state'. Oil companies were notorious for 'engineering' conflict. As Nimmo Bassey (2002), director of Nigeria's ERA asked, 'How can peace find a foothold on these shores when communities that have lived at peace for centuries are engineered to live in suspicion of each other and in conflict with one another while others plunder their resources?'

By fomenting division, oil companies fulfilled Zbigniew Brzezinski's imperative to 'keep the barbarians from coming together' (1997: 40). The *Economist*, in a May 2003 review of Paul Collier's 2003 World Bank report, *Breaking the Conflict Trap: Civil War and Development Policy*, endorsed Collier's resuscitation of the old imperialist rationale that military peacekeeping was the only route to stability and hence to poverty alleviation. Washington had planned the West African military incursion, apparently since at least 2000, in tandem with its attack on Iraq. Bush's State Department head of policy planning, Richard Haass (2000) argued back in 2000 that the United States, 'No. 1 superpower', should multiply its military interventions in order to enhance its global strategic assets: 'Imperial understretch, not overstretch appears to be the greater danger of the two'.

But in Nigeria, as in Iraq, it is unlikely that the US can succeed in actually controlling the oil industry through force of arms or legal manoeuvres such as Presidential Directive 13303 which gives US oil companies immunity from prosecution for their actions in Iraq (Kerr 2003; Girion 2003). The Delta has a long history of success in repelling invasion by sea. Allusions to a contemporary chapter were made by the chairman of Burutu local government area of Delta state, Asupa Forteta, who on 18 July 2003 decried the 'high level of brigandage and turbulence being witnessed in the riverine communities and waterways'. Forteta sought to stamp out 'anti-social vices such as piracy, hostage taking, oil pipeline vandalisation, and so on'. The military advantage enjoyed by residents indigenous to the Delta was underlined: 'Those behind these dastardly acts are people that you and I know; strangers cannot effectively operate in our terrains because of its peculiarity'. Hidden in chairman Forteta's declamation was the insight that only members of oil communities could defend the Delta or carry out illegal bunkering because only they could 'effectively operate in our terrains' (Delta State Government 2003).

After activists established control over much of the western Delta's oil production infrastructure by March 2003, did they secure and sell crude on the international market? Are villagers and ex-oil workers not only shutting down the industry, but also restarting it on their own account by marketing crude and products? These questions are sharpened by press reports in 2003 of armed Delta youth overcoming the Coast Guard and 'rescuing' an impounded illegal bunkering vessel. Does this confrontation foreshadow, in part, the future content of the struggle for 'resource control'? Are peasants going beyond the sacking of oil companies to start up the lifting and sale of crude on a new basis? Are they defending the process by force of arms? Government's armed forces lost most confrontations in the byzantine mangrove swamps of the Delta's riverine zones. The combined forces of the oil companies, federal and state governments and all their law enforcement agencies had not, by September 2003, suppressed the Delta militants, in part because 'strangers cannot effectively operate in our terrains' (Delta State Government 2003). Many militants were said to be armed by 'illegal oil traders' or those positioned to buy guns with proceeds from that trade. Is the future of twenty-first century subsistence on the Delta enclosed in the potential for direct producer-consumer deals in oil?

In early September 2003 Delta activists held the oil installations and continued to shut-in some 40 per cent of oil production. Their capacities to withstand military attacks have to do with the high level of community solidarity, explicit support from women who control food supplies and trade, and the extremely complex and inaccessible nature of the mangrove swamp terrain. The 'resource control' revolutionaries are well-armed. Buyers abound for 'parallel market' crude. Solidarity with Delta commoners goes deep, reaching back to pro-Biafra campaigns in the 1960s, anti-apartheid cooperation in the 1970s, networks to stop oil to the racist regime in South Africa in the 1980s, to boycott Shell mobilizations in support of the Ogoni struggle in the 1990s and in the 2000s, and the groundswell of anti-war nude militancy after women seized ChevronTexaco's Escravos oil terminal in 2002.

Beyond international solidarity is the deepening of relations fundamental to global alternatives to corporate rule. Direct producer-consumer oil deals are central to these alternatives. Nigerian insurgents may already be fashioning direct deals. Since 1985 Nigerians have organized oil barter or 'countertrades'. Supplies of Nigerian crude would make possible popular, ecologically-sound, citizens' control of refineries in Trinidad and Tobago, in South Africa, in Cuba and elsewhere. These visions of the future inform the strategizing of commons environmentalists and 'resource control' activists.

ChevronTexaco, Shell, ExxonMobil and the other oil companies in Nigeria may visit the Delta peoples with terrible military carnage. International vigilance and readiness to hold the corporations accountable are deterrents. The majors seek direct control over Nigerian, West African, Middle Eastern, Asian and Latin American petroleum reserves. Instability in oil producing countries, and shutdown petroleum facilities are not necessarily shunned by the majors. They can be turned to a profit.

The oil companies are in the business of making profits. Violence, military attacks and instability drive up prices even if they do not impose actual shortages of crude on the world market. Higher prices mean higher profits. Shimon Bichler and Jonathan Nitzan (2002) have demonstrated that when major oil companies' profits fall below the average, war is fomented and profits recover. Their analysis argues that the oil companies want and possibly promote strife in producing societies. This is especially the case in the 2000s when, they argue, the majors are pursuing an accumulation strategy based on stagflation (stagnation of the economy, inflation in prices). Higher oil product prices can only be imposed on the consumer under crisis conditions (war on terrorism, suspension of civil liberties). This accumulation strategy is a corporate weapon against deflation and the implosion of the capitalist system. It is in this international strategic framework that the struggles in Nigeria's oil belt can best be analysed and understood.

Conclusion: 'Stand Up Now'

I call upon the Ogoni people, the peoples of the Niger Delta, and the oppressed minorities of Nigeria to stand up now and fight fearlessly and peacefully for their rights. History is on their side, God is on their side. For the Holy Quran says in Sura 42, verse 41: 'All those who fight when oppressed incur no guilt, but Allah shall punish the oppressor'. Come the day. (Ken Saro-Wiwa cited in Okonta and Oronto 2001: 209).

Two themes considered in this conclusion are the roots of insurgents' power in subsistence and corporate organization, and direct producer-consumer deals.

In 2003, Barbara Epstein argued that it is only by 'draw[ing] out the connections between production and consumption under capitalism' that the global anti-war movement can gain 'staying power, the capacity for its different elements to coalesce, and a meaningful political praxis' (116). This article has drawn out those global 'connections between production and consumption' as they emerged through conscious praxis at the community and world levels in the period July 2002 to September 2003. It has treated the genesis, successes and possible futures of these global gendered class alliances by relating them to the defence and re-invention of the commons and the subsistence political economy, North and South (Bennholdt-Thomsen and Mies 1999).

The central focus in this concluding assessment is on the *sources* of insurgent power. Power arose from defending the social relations of subsistence and attacking the social relations of commodification. The unwaged were and are integrated inextricably into both. Women and their allies were able to achieve a remarkable degree of success by commanding and exercising power grounded in their own life-centred political economy and in the enclosing oil-death economy. The two foundations of insurgent peasant power were subsistence itself and the organization bequeathed by the transnational oil corporations. Both groundings were at once national and international.

First, the unwaged, peasants, indigenous people and women were firmly ensconced on the commons. These subsistence life grounds provided the means through which to satisfy most life needs. These are the same grounds and commons that capital sought to enclose, commodify and destroy. The commons, then, were both a site of struggle and a crucial source of the power for Escravos and all Niger Delta communities in their war against the oil transnationals. Central to the continued existence of the commons in the Niger Delta are the village, trade and clan-based organizations that prosecuted the insurgency. Over the past decade, through processes of direct democracy, each 'nationality' formulated declarations that contain demands and programs. A fundamental universal demand is 'resource control'. More recently coalitions of these clan-based organizations have been formed and are calling for 'a national sovereignty conference' to remake the Nigerian political economy. Autonomous village organizations, linked to each other through regional solidarity networks, coordinated pan-Delta defence against Nigerian and US military counterinsurgency and took over some of the administration of their own communities. Prominent among the many cross-cutting solidarity networks were Chicoco, which brought together some 27 ethnic groups of small farming and fishing peoples and the pan-Delta, international Niger Delta Women for Justice.

In August 2000, twelve Niger Delta women representing several women's organizations and federations met in Banjul, the Gambia, and resolved that:

1) Oil exploration, production and all other activities be suspended with

immediate effect until amenities such as pipe borne water, electricity, safe water transportation systems, functional health centres, scholarship schemes and schools are provided in the Niger Delta;

2) All laws inimical to the development of the Niger Delta people be repealed, including a total rejection of the 1999 constitution;

3) All victims of oil spillages and fire disasters be compensated and treated;

4) All qualified youths in the Niger Delta be gainfully employed by the government and multinationals and those summarily dismissed be reinstated;

5) The percentage of interest payable on micro credit loans should be determined by participating women;

6) The multinationals and government desist from making allegations of sabotage without proper investigations of any spill and stop the indiscriminate employment of youths of the Niger Delta for cleaning up exercises without appropriate protection, as a result of which their life spans are reduced drastically;

7) The Niger Delta women be empowered economically, in order that they may claim their right to political empowerment;

8) A law be enacted making it mandatory for oil companies to take responsibility for the welfare of any child and mother of such child born out of company's staff's promiscuous activities;

9) Forthwith, any act that will further devastate the environment (our aquatic and ecological environment) be stopped immediately and all devastated environments be cleaned up;

10) Henceforth, all oil companies and sub-contractors adhere to all regulations and laws that apply to global environment standards, and Environmental Impact Assessment reports must be made public;

11) We be represented in all decision-making processes that affect us in the Niger Delta;

12) We totally support all the declarations of the ethnic nationalities of the Niger Delta for resource control, self-determination and true federalism;

13) All those unjustly detained should be released with immediate effect; and

14) The only solution to peace in the Niger Delta is justice. (Niger Delta Women for Justice 2000)

The subsistence political economy supported the unwaged majority. While insurgents frequently charged oil companies with holding communities hostage, in reality, peasants were food self-sufficient. As all were reminded during the general strike, women controlled strategic urban food sources. Most low-waged workers relied for their needs on African women engaged in subsistence production and trade. At the same time, oil companies ravaged the environment and made it increasingly untenable for anyone or anything to survive in the vicinity of oil wells, pipelines, flares and other production and export facilities. These facts go a long way towards explaining why women were at the forefront of Nigeria's 2002-2003 oil wars. They 'held their ground' to defend subsistence against the most powerful corporations in the world. They did so peacefully; armed with actual, considerable power to give and deny life. This moral high-ground gave women warriors the capacity to visit public relations catastrophes on oil majors which, in 2003 were struggling to annex Iraq's 250 billion barrels of oil behind the thin veil drawn by their seconded personnel in the White House. In the highly developed subsistence political economy of Nigeria, the threat of women's naked protests had a Hydra-like power to force men to stop and flee in fear (Linebaugh and Rediker 2000). It was a power that eroded the surety of the male deal between Nigerian men and the oil 'corporate male gang' (McMurtry 2001). When women made international connections and took naked protests to the global stage, their aim was precisely to break down the bonds of the global male deals that were driving Bush's neoconservative Imperial America toward new oil wars.

This brings us to the second source of the power of the emergent global gendered class alliances against the oil-war machine: the corporations themselves. Insurgents in Nigeria's oil war built links with other national and international actors in three integrated arenas: the parallel market, boycotts, and the coordinated assertion of community control over petroleum resources. As oil companies consolidated and militarized their global control over oil resources, they bound more closely the interests, capacities and experiences of people in all parts of the world (Other Shell Report 2003).[8] US military adventurism in Iraq, Venezuela and Nigeria has produced sharper and deeper national opposition to foreign petroleum capital and its drive to privatize especially the upstream industry. Second, it has forged tighter international unity amongst the resistance to US military interference in the three countries. Both effects have multiplied possibilities for coordination against imperial oil and for popular, international control over a restructured oil industry.

Oil companies' environmental racism impelled communities to enforce resource control. They organized joint producer-consumer actions against oil companies and oil-wars. These began with Nigerian women's 2002 ChevronTexaco takeovers and continued with international boycotts from September 2002, women's naked protests in California in November 2002 and the 50 million strong global anti-war demonstration of 15 February 2003. These global actions were extended by the creation of a national producer-consumer alliance against big oil in Nigeria during the general strike of June-July 2003. Throughout the period, the demands of Niger Delta women continued to present the most far-reaching challenges to corporate oil power.[9] They used nakedness and direct occupation of oil facilities to break the male deal. Their explicit demand was that the oil companies 'should leave our community completely and never come back again' (ERA 2002b).

Direct deals are alternatives to market control by the majors. In Nigeria were barrels shut in and then sold on the international and national markets? Was the buoyancy of the parallel market in Nigerian oil a central motivation for US military intervention?[10]

The crucial gendered and ethnicized class unity demonstrated in producer-consumer joint actions is a precondition for going beyond oil production shutdowns. If Nigerian oil workers, indigenous communities and other democratic organizations in the future move beyond shutdowns to running the oil industry on their own, the widely articulated goals of reparations for the environmental debt owed Nigeria, pollution cleanup and wise use of petroleum wealth could be realized. A kind of reparations would be won to the extent that oil workers and indigenous organizations were able to sell or barter oil directly. Direct deals would enable a Nigerian 'sovereign national convention' to use the proceeds to support life, and stop the current practice of revenue theft and the use of foreign exchange from oil sales to service ever-increasing levels of International Monetary Fund, World Bank and Paris Club debt.

In 2001, the noted oil economist Michael Tanzer encouraged direct deals via multi-state oil barter:

> By developing a multilateral barter exchange system for Third World commodities, such a strategy could secure reliable revenues for the oil-exporting countries, while providing the oil-importing countries with a steady flow of oil, and with export outlets at fair prices for their own commodities. (2001: 24)

This analysis of Nigerian women's shutdown of major oil companies in 2002-2003, and the alliances they forged at home and abroad has explained 'why women are at war' by arguing that they were defending subsistence. It has accounted for the sweep of the insurgency's growth by reference to the force of oil companies as agencies for the organization, unity and discipline of those caught in corporate nets. Women worldwide, by asserting life against the corporate death economy, are impelling the movements against neo-imperial war for corporate rule to champion a subsistence life economy alternative. The future of the oil component of this new set of social relations lies in the elaboration of direct deals between producers and consumers who have a track record of coordination in wresting resource control from oil corporations.

A version of this study was presented at the 56th Annual United Nations Department of Public Information/NGO Conference, 'Human Security and Dignity: Fulfilling the Promise of the United Nations', New York, 8-10 September 2003.

The authors wish to acknowledge funding for fieldwork in Nigeria from the Canadian International Development Agency (CIDA) and from the Canadian Social Science and Humanities Research Council.

Terisa E. Turner is associate professor of sociology and anthropology at the University of Guelph in Ontario, Canada. Leigh S. Brownhill is a Ph.D. candidate at the University of Toronto. They are co-founders of First Woman: The East and Southern African Women's Oral History and Indigenous Knowledge Network. First Woman's central activity is the recording of the life stories of elderly Mau Mau women in Kenya. Terisa Turner and Leigh Brownhill are co-directors of the International Oil Working Group, a non-governmental organization registered with the Department of Public Information at the United Nations Secretariat in New York. In 2001 they co-edited Gender, Feminism and the Civil Commons, *published as a special issue of the* Canadian Journal of Development Studies *available at www.uoguelph.ca-terisatu.*

Notes

1. In 1999 the major oil companies active in Nigeria and their share of crude oil production were Shell, 40 per cent; Mobil (now ExxonMobil), 25 per cent; Gulf (now ChevronTexaco), 21 per cent; and Agip (now TotalFinaElf), 12 per cent. Two per cent of production was shared by Ashland (of the USA), Deminex (Germany), Pan Ocean (Switzerland), British Gas, Sun Oil (USA), Conoco (USA), Statoil (Norway), Conoil (Nigeria) and Dubril Oil (Nigeria). The Nigerian National Petroleum Corporation (NNPC) had a 55-60 per cent joint venture interest in the majors' operations. The United States took about 40 per cent of Nigeria's exports. The remainder was exported to Spain, South Korea, India, France, Japan, China, Taiwan, the Philippines and Thailand (Frynas 2000; Okonta and Douglas 2001).

2. An exception to the silencing of women and more broadly, analysis of gender relation, is Sokari Ekine's 2001 oral history-based account of Niger Delta women's experiences with the oil companies and their military defenders, *Blood and Oil: Testimonies of Violence from Women of the Niger Delta.*

3. This is a chant sung by women during their occupation ChevronTexaco's Abiteye flow station in July 2002 (cited in Okon 2002). It echoes Fela Anikulapo-Kuti's 'No Agreement', originally released in 1977 by Fela Anikulapo-Kuti and The Africa 70.

4. Many men subjected to this 'social execution' believe they will actually die when exposed to such a serious threat. According to one Nigerian source, 'In a lot of the rural communities here, the practice of throwing off the wrapper is a common [form of censure, given the] belief among the women folks here that it goes with some magical powers to inflict curses ranging from death to madness on its foes. In the 1980s it was very prevalent among the Gokana people of Ogoni' (IOWG 2003b). In 2003 the 1993 Ogoni declaration that Shell is 'persona non grata' in Ogoniland remained in force.

5. In September 2002, during a speech to oil industry executives gathered in Rio de Janeiro, Brazil for the seventeenth World Petroleum Congress, ChevronTexaco's chairman and chief executive officer David O'Reilly made reference to the Nigerian village women's seven occupations. In contrast to Queen Uwara's testimony that 'Chevron brought soldiers and police to threaten us when we were at Chevron yard' (ERA 2002a), O'Reilly stated that the oil company's Nigerian representatives had handled the situation 'with great sensitivity' and that he was 'proud of their efforts' to reach an understanding with the women ('Strong partnerships are key for success of big oil, says Chevron's O'Reilly' 2002).

6. These words were used in Nigerian press accounts of the strikes during this period. 'Pirates' and 'miscreants' referred to those who sold oil products on the parallel market and who stopped oil vessels on the high seas and the Delta creeks to demand payment for passage. 'Hydra-headed monster' was used in a discussion of conflict in oil

communities to describe three ethnic groups in the Delta; Ijaw, Itsikeri and Urhobo (Nzeshi 2003). Nzeshi blamed conflict on the ethnic groups rather than identifying destruction and enclosure of the commons, competition for jobs, revenues and resources as well as the divisive tactics of the oil companies themselves. At the same time Nnimmo Bassey, Executive Director of ERA, described Shell's giant new Floating Storage Production and Off-loading (FPSO) vessel as 'a monster rearing its head' (Kpor 2002). 'Street urchins' were part of the multitudes who participated in the general strike of 30 June to 8 July. Nnanna (2003) stated that the leader of the Nigerian Labour Congress, Oshiomhole, 'should take adequate judicial note of those very important Nigerians, whom the police often foolishly describe as "street urchins". Those are the people that give industrial struggles such as we have just passed through their potent striking power. They are the people who get shot at for coming out to express the feelings of the people, even if sometimes a little bit exuberantly. Those "street urchins" are Nigerian youths united irrespective of tribe, religion, region or party affiliation, against obnoxious official policy. The police would not grade them as "street urchins" if their demonstration was in favour of the government of the day for any reason. They would then become "patriotic Nigerian youths".' The multitudes also included market women, traders, artisans, other informal sector workers, religious leaders, bank workers, concerned professionals, trade unionists, 'area boys' or unemployed urban youth, teachers, university lecturers, students, the governors of Lagos, Kano and Sokoto States, unemployed people, villagers and subsistence farmers and fishers.

7   On 3 July, day four of the strike, the oil workers' junior staff union NUPENG had begun 'removing staff from posts' but NUPENG called off the strike action on 4 July, day five of the national action. Then on 5 July, day six of the strike, the Trade Union Congress called off its strike action. This immediately prompted the senior oil staff union, PENGASSAN, to cancel its participation in the general strike which it had intended to begin on Sunday 6 July ('Nigerian oil operations continue, as unions consider proposal' 2003).

8   On the one hand, Nigerian women and their allies, by expelling the majors from the Delta, cut out of the world market some 800,000 b/d. They thereby raised prices and the overall take of the majors and OPEC governments. In the first quarter of 2003 Shell and ChevronTexaco scored their highest profits ever. 'Exxon, the world's largest oil group, reported the biggest quarterly corporate profits in history at $7bn.' (Gow 2003). Price hikes by the weapondollar-petrodollar coalition were supported by non-oil corporations. These were keen to impose stagflation and dispel the nightmare of deflation by forcing on 'terrorized' consumers the oil cost hikes embodied in their commodities.

On the other hand, on a *national* basis, insurgents forced net losses on Shell, ChevronTexaco, the other international subsidiaries and the Nigerian government. The Nigerian government losses from the shut-in of 1 March (assuming that it continued to the end of 2003) of some 800,000 b/d and the diversion of some 200,000 b/d onto the parallel market were an estimated minimum of US$3.366 billion (assuming an average crude oil price of US$25/b minus a $3/b production cost). Oil companies operating in Nigeria lost US$765 million (assuming US$22/b for crude and a US$5/b refining margin). Thus, the Niger Delta oilfield takeovers (if they persisted throughout the last ten months of 2003) would have reduced government oil income (including windfalls from higher prices) by 19 per cent. We estimate that the takeovers also reduced the oil companies' income by 25 per cent.

⁹ The Other Shell Report demanded that Shell 'send skilled and experienced international officials to meet with representatives at the sites where people living nearest to Shell are experiencing difficulties, and resolve these [environmental and health] problems'. The report called for Shell to 'support national and international laws that allow affected communities to hold companies like Shell accountable for their negative impacts' (Other Shell Report 2003: 5).

¹⁰ After Venezuela and Cuba struck barter deals whereby Cuba got oil in exchange for medical services and generic drug manufacturing processes, the US objected. Iraq's barter deal with India which secured the oil exporter grain and bought India crude was met in July 2002 with US and British opposition through the UN oil sales program and in 2003 through US military attack. Nigerian direct deals were under attack by the US oil companies, the Nigerian government and by September 2003, by the US military. The US regime, on behalf of the oil majors, has opposed oil barter with all its tremendous subsistence-promoting potential. But imperial America has even more vigorously opposed public control of oil and gas exploration, production and reserves through state-owned corporations.

References

Abiola, A. C. (2002) 'Chevron ignores demand of women for employment and clean environment', *ERA Field Report*, 103, 14 July, eraction@infoweb.abs.net.

Adebayo, S. (2002) 'N-Delta women give Shell 10-day ultimatum on demands', Women of Nigeria International (WONI) and Women's International League for Peace and Freedom (WILPF) Email List Serv, November 14.

Ajaero, C. (2003) 'Grinding on the wheels of strikes', *Newswatch*, 8 March, posted to www.allAfrica.com.

Baring Witness (2003) Online: www.baringwitness.org.

Bassey, N. (2002) 'What peace in the world today?', paper presented at the conference marking the International Day of Peace, Benin City, Nigeria, 21 September, eraction@infoweb.abs.net.

Benjamin, C. S. and T. E. Turner (1992) 'Counterplanning from the commons: labour, capital and the "new social movements"', *Labour, Capital and Society*, 25, 2, 218-248.

Bennholdt-Thomsen, V. and M. Mies (1999) *The Subsistence Perspective: Beyond the Globalised Economy*, London: Zed Books.

Bichler, S. and J. Nitzan (2002) *The Global Political Economy of Israel*, London: Pluto.

Brownhill, L. S. and T. E. Turner (2003) 'Mau Mau Women rise again: land take-overs and the new anti-imperialism', *Canadian woman studies/ les cahiers de la femme*, 23, 1, 168-176.

Brzezinski, Z. (1997) *The Grand Chessboard: American Primacy and its Geostrategic Imperatives*, New York: Basic Books.

Delta State Government (2003) 'Burutu LG boss launches anti-piracy team', *Delta State Government News*, 18 July, www.Deltastate.gov.ng.

Dyer-Witheford, N. (1999) *Cyber-Marx: Cycles and Circuits of Struggle in High-Technology Capitalism*, Chicago: University of Illinois Press.

Ebonugwo, M. (2003) 'Bad price for fuel price hike', *Vanguard*, 2 July.

'EIA warns oil prices could stay high if Iraqi oil fails to come back' (2003) Energy Intelligence, *Oil Daily*, 11 July, www.energyintel.com.

Ekine, S. 2001. *Blood Sorrow and Oil: Testimonies of Violence from Women of the Niger Delta*, Oxford, UK: Centre for Democracy and Development.

Eluemunor, T. and U. Awom (2002) 'Oil firms indicted over huge joint venture fraud', *Daily Independent*, June 24-30: 1.

Environmental Rights Action (ERA) (2003) 'Press statement: groups oppose us troops deployment to Niger Delta', 11 July, Ijaw_National_Congress-owner@yahoogroups.com.

Environmental Rights Action (ERA) (2002a) 'Confronting Chevron: women stare down the barrel', Environmental Testimonies #28, 13 July, eraction@infoweb.abs.net.

Environmental Rights Action (ERA) (2002b) 'Protesting women continue occupation of Chevron flow-stations', Environmental Rights Action, 22 July, eraction@infoweb. abs.net).

Epstein, B. (2003) 'Notes on the antiwar movement', *Monthly Review*, 55, 3, 109-116.

Fagan, C. (2002) 'Bush's search for black gold', *International Socialist Review*, November/ December.

Frynas, G. (2000) *Oil in Nigeria: Conflict and Litigation between Oil Companies and Village Communities,* London: Lit Verlag.

Girion, L. (2003) 'Immunity for Iraqi Oil Dealings Raises Alarm', *The Los Angeles Times*, 7 August.

Gow, D. (2003) 'Shell doubles its earnings', *The Guardian*, May 3, http:// www.guardian.co.uk/Print/0,3858,4661014,00.html

Haass, R. (2000) www.brook.edu.

Ifijeh, G. (2003) 'When fuel price hike protest went wild', *This Day,* 10 July, posted to www.allafrica.com on 11 July.

Igho, E. (2003) 'Niger Delta: death versus development', *Vanguard*), 4 September, posted to www.allAfrica.com

Integrated Regional Information Network (IRIN) (2002) 'Nigeria: woman shot dead during protest at transnationals' offices', IRIN News, United Nations Office for the Coordination of Humanitarian Affairs, 15 August, www.irinnews.org.

International Oil Working Group (IOWG) (2003a) Interview #1 with Nigerian source, 1 August.

International Oil Working Group (IOWG) (2003b) Interview #2 with Nigerian source, 2 August.

Ivan, G. (2002) 'West Marin women strip for peace,' *Point Reyes Light,* 14 November.

James, C. L. R. and T. E. Turner (1971) Personal communication.

Kerr, S. J. (2003) 'The end?' *ZNet,* 6 August.

Kpor, C. (2002) 'Why ERA opposes Shell's offshore FPSO vessel', *Daily Independent*, 24-30June: B2.

Linebaugh, P. and M. Rediker (2000) *The Many-Headed Hydra: Sailors, Slaves, Commoners and the Hidden History of the Revolutionary Atlantic,* Boston: Beacon.

Lysistrata Project. (2003) Online: www.lysistrataproject.org.

McMurtry, J. (2001) 'The life-ground, the civil commons and the corporate male gang', *Canadian Journal of Development Studies*, 22, 819-854.

McMurtry, J. (2002) *Value Wars: The Global Market Versus the Life Economy*, London: Pluto.

Niger Delta Women for Justice (2000) 'Communique and fourteen resolutions issued by the consultative meeting of Niger Delta Women', Banjul, the Gambia, August, www.ndwj.kabissa.org.

'Nigerian oil operations continue, as unions consider proposal' (2003) *International Oil Daily*, 8 July, www.energyintel.com.

'Nigerian women seize platform' (2002) *International Oil Daily*, 19 August, www.energyintel.com.

Nnanna, O. (2003) 'A struggle, not just a strike', *Vanguard*, 10 July.

Nore, P. and T. Turner (eds.) (1980) *Oil and Class Struggle*, London: Zed.

Nuri, J. J. (2003) 'US troops move to Africa to protect oil interests', Institute for Policy Studies, 9 July, posted at www.corpwatch.org/bulletins/PBD.jsp?articleid=7449.

Nzeshi, O. (2003) 'Okerenkoko: battle on the jungle island', *This Day*, March 25, posted to www.allAfrica.com.

Oduniyi, M., F. Ugwoke and L. Okenwa (2003) 'Warri refinery shut down, PENGASSAN threatens fresh strike', *This Day*, 27 March, posted to www.allAfrica.com

Okon, E. (2002) *A Report of the Niger Delta Women Justice (NDWJ) on the Delta Women Siege on the American Oil Company, Chevron-Texaco in Delta State of Nigeria*, Port Harcourt: Niger Delta Women for Justice, August, www.ndwj.kabissa.org.

Okonta, I. and Oronto D. (2001) *Where Vultures Feast: Shell, Human Rights, and Oil in the Niger Delta*, San Francisco: Sierra Club Books.

Osouka, A., E. Martnez and L. Salazar (2002) 'Boycott Chevron-Texaco', *OilWatch*, 26 September, posted to www.corpwatch.org.

Other Shell Report (2003) *Failing the Challenge: The Other Shell Report 2002*, London: Friends of the Earth, www.foei.org/media/2003/0423.html

Oyawiri, L. (2003) 'Rivers hostages: Britons may take legal action', *This Day*, 14 May, posted to www.allAfrica.com.

'Protests disrupt Warri output' (2002) *International Oil Daily*, 23 September, www.energyintel.com.

Rosen, R. (2003) 'Peace buffs', *San Francisco Chronicle*, February 18, www.sfgate.com/cgi-bin/article.cgi?file=/chronicle/archive/2003/02/18/ED89714.DTL

Sala-i-Martin, X. and A. Subramanian (2003) 'Addressing the natural resource curse: an illustration from Nigeria', *IMF Working Paper WP/03/139*, International Monetary Fund, Washington D.C, July.

'Shell denies killing protester.' (2002) *International Oil Daily*, 14 August, www.energyintel.com.

StopEsso (2003) Online: www.stopesso.com.

'Strong partnerships are key for success of big oil, says Chevron's O'Reilly' (2002) *International Oil Daily*, 5 September, www.energyintel.com.

Tanzer, M. (2001) 'Solidarity at the pump: a proposal for the oil exporting nations of the Third World', *NACLA Report on the Americas*, 34, 4, 17-24.

'Tit-Bits' (2003) *Vanguard*, 10 July.

Turner, T. E. (1997) 'Oil workers and oil communities in Africa: Nigerian women and grassroots environmentalism', *Labour, Capital and Society*, 30, 1, 66-89.

Turner, T. E., L. S. Brownhill, A.Brisibe, S. Ekine, I. Lott, E. J. Okon, A. Opurum-Briggs and D. Barikor-Wiwa (2001). 'Fightback from the commons: petroleum industry and environmental racism', paper presented at the United Nations World Conference Against Racism, Racial Discrimination, Xenophobia and Related Intolerance, Durban, South Africa, 31 August-7 September, http://www.uoguelph.ca/~terisatu/.

Vidal, J. (2003) 'Oil rig hostages are freed by strikers as mercenaries fly out', *The Guardian*, 3 May, http://www.guardian.co.uk/Print/0,3858,4661001,00.html.

'Vienna' (2003) *Platts Oilgram*, 31 July, www.platts.com.

Wamala, I. (2002) 'Nigerian Women take on the oil companies', *Women and Environments*, 56/57, Fall, 38.

'We shoot to maim—police ... people died—NLC' (2003) *Vanguard*, 31 July.

'WE ARE THAT MYTHICAL THING CALLED THE PUBLIC'

MILITANT HOUSEWIVES IN THE US DURING THE GREAT DEPRESSION

ANNELISE ORLECK

The crisis conditions created by the Depression of the 1930s moved working-class housewives and mothers across the United States to organize on a scale unprecedented in US history. From New York City to Seattle; from Richmond, Virginia, to Los Angeles; and in hundreds of small towns and farm villages in between, poor wives and mothers staged food boycotts and anti-eviction demonstrations, created large-scale barter networks and lobbied for food and rent price controls. Militant and angry, they demanded a better quality of life for themselves and their children. Echoing the language of trade unionism, they asserted that housing and food, like wages and hours, could be regulated by organizing and applying economic pressure. By organizing themselves as class-conscious mothers and consumers, they stretched the limits both of working-class and women's organizing in the US

This was not the first time Americans were treated to the spectacle of housewives demanding food for their families. Since the early nineteenth century, hard times in New York, Philadelphia and other major cities had moved housewives in immigrant neighbourhoods to demonstrate for lower food prices. But never before had Americans seen anything this widespread or persistent. Housewives' activism, like that of every other group of Americans during the Depression, was profoundly influenced by Franklin Roosevelt's New Deal. During the early years of the Depression, prior to the 1932 presidential election, housewives organized to stave off imminent disaster. Their focus was on self-help—setting up barter networks, gardening cooperatives and neighbourhood councils. After 1933, the tactics and arguments used by militant housewives reflected their acceptance of Roosevelt's corporatist vision. By the mid-1930s, poor and working-class housewives, like farmers and factory workers, had begun to see themselves as a group that could, by organizing and lobbying, force the New Deal state to respond to their needs.

Press coverage reflected the ambivalence with which many Americans greeted the idea of politically organized housewives. Both mainstream and radical editors took their movement seriously. Housewives' strikes and demonstrations were featured in major newspapers and national magazines. Still these publications could not resist poking fun at the very idea of a housewives' movement. Writers never tired of suggesting that, by its very existence, the housewives' movement emasculated male adversaries. A typical headline ran in the *New York Times* in summer 1935 at the height of housewives' activism nationwide. 'Women picket butcher shops in Detroit suburb', it blared. 'Slap. Scratch. Pull hair. Men are chief victims' ('Buyers trampled by meat strikers' 28 July 1935). A more pointed headline, about Secretary of Agriculture Henry Wallace, ran a few weeks later in the *Chicago Daily Tribune*: 'Secretary Wallace beats retreat from five housewives' (20 August 1935). Underlying this tone of ridicule was a growing tension over the fact that housewife activists were politicizing the traditional roles of wives and mothers.[1]

In New York City neighbourhoods, organized bands of Jewish housewives fiercely resisted eviction, arguing that they were merely doing their jobs by defending their homes and those of their neighbours. Barricading themselves in apartments, they made speeches from tenement windows, wielded kettles of boiling water and threatened to scald anyone who attempted to move furniture out on to the street. Black mothers in Cleveland, unable to convince a local power company to delay shutting off electricity in the homes of families who had not paid their bills, won restoration of power after they hung wet laundry over every utility line in the neighbourhood. They also left crying babies on the desks of caseworkers at the Cleveland Emergency Relief Association, refusing to retrieve them until free milk had been provided for each child. These actions reflected a sense of humour but sometimes housewife rage exploded. In Chicago, angry Polish housewives doused thousands of pounds of meat with kerosene and set it on fire at the warehouses of the Armour Company to dramatize their belief that high prices were not the result of shortages (*Working Woman* April 1931, June 1931, April 1933, June 1935; *New York Times*, 30 Jan.-28 Feb. 1932; *Detroit Free Press*, 6-9 Aug. 1935; *Chicago Daily Tribune*, 18 Aug. 1935).

This activity was not simply a reaction to the economic crisis gripping the nation. It was a conscious attempt on the part of many housewives to change the system that they blamed for the Depression. In Seattle in 1931, urban and farm wives orchestrated a massive exchange of timber and fish from western Washington for grain, fruits and vegetables from eastern Washington. As a result, tens of thousands of families had enough food and fuel to survive the difficult winter of 1931-32. Similar barter networks were established in California, Colorado, Ohio and Virginia in which housewives gathered and distributed food, clothing, fuel and building materials (see *The Atlantic* October 1932; *Collier's* 31 Dec. 1932; *Literary Digest* 11 Feb. 1933; *The Nation* 1 Mar. 1933, 19 Apr. 1933; *Survey* 15 Dec. 1932, July 1933; *Saturday Evening Post* 25 Feb. 1933; *Commonweal* 8 Mar. 1933; *Good Housekeeping* March 1933).

Understanding their power as a voting bloc, housewives lobbied in state capitals and in Washington, D.C. They also ran for electoral office in numerous locales across the country. In Washington State and in Michigan, housewife activists were elected in 1934 and 1936 on platforms that called for government regulation of food prices, housing and utility costs. And in Minnesota, in 1936, farm wives were key players in the creation of a national Farmer-Labour Party (*Working Woman* June 1935; *Woman Today* April 1936; *New York Times* 10 Apr. 1936; *Party Organizer* September 1935).[2]

These actions were not motivated by desire on the part of poor wives and mothers to be relieved of their responsibilities in the home—although certainly many were attracted by the excitement and camaraderie of activism. These were the actions of women who accepted the traditional sexual division of labour but who found that the Depression had made it impossible for them to fulfil their responsibilities to the home without leaving it.

Housewife activists argued that the homes in which they worked were intimately linked to the fields and shops where their husbands, sons and daughters laboured; to the national economy; and to the fast-growing state and federal bureaucracies. Mrs Charles Lundquist, a farmer's wife and president of the Farmer-Labour Women's Federation of Minnesota, summed up this view in a 1936 speech before a gathering of farmers and labour activists:

Woman's place may be in the home but the home is no longer the isolated, complete unit it was. To serve her home best, the woman of today must understand the political and economic foundation on which that home rests—and then do something about it. (*Woman Today* April 1936)

The extent and variety of housewives' activism during the Depression suggests that this view of the home was widely accepted by Black as well as white women, farm as well as urban women. The housewives' rebellions that swept the country during the 1930s cannot be seen as only spontaneous outcries for a 'just price'. Like so many others during the Depression, working-class housewives were offering their own solutions to the failure of the US economic system.[3]

Roots of a Housewives' Uprising

This article focuses primarily on urban housewives' organizing, but it should be noted that farm women played an essential role in Depression-era housewives' activism. Apart from organizing on their own behalf—establishing farmer-labour women's committees and food-goods exchanges with urban women—farm women provided urban women with information about the gap between what farmers were paid and what wholesalers charged. This profit-taking formed the basis for activists' critique of what they called 'food trusts'. Farm wives' activism during the 1920s and 1930s must be studied before a full assessment of this phenomenon is possible. However, because of space limitations, this article focuses on three of the most active and successful urban housewives' groups: the

New York-based United Council of Working-Class Women (UCWCW), the Seattle-based Women's Committee of the Washington Commonwealth Federation, and the Detroit-based Women's Committee against the High Cost of Living.

An examination of these three groups illustrates that although there were some important regional differences in housewives' political style and focus, there were also commonalities. Most significantly, each had a strong labour movement affiliation. Housewives' activism developed in union strongholds, flourishing in the Bronx and Brooklyn among the wives and mothers of unionized garment workers; in Detroit among the wives and mothers of United Auto Workers' (UAW) members; and in Seattle, among the wives of unionized workers who had begun to argue the importance of consumer organizing during the 1920s.[4]

This union link is important for several reasons. Union husbands' fights for higher wages during the 1910s had resulted in a fairly comfortable standard of living for many families by World War I. But spiralling inflation and the near-destruction of many trade unions during the 1920s eroded the working-class quality of life. By 1929 it had become increasingly difficult, even for families of employed union workers, to make ends meet.[5]

The militance of the Depression-era housewives' movement was an outgrowth of this sudden and rapid decline in working-class families' standard of living. But it was also rooted in women organizers' own experiences in trade unions. There are no statistics detailing exactly how many housewife activists were formerly union members. However, in all the areas where housewives' organizations took hold, it was common for women to work for wages before marriage. And given the age of most leading activists in New York, Seattle and Detroit, their working years would have coincided with the years of women's labour militance between 1909 and 1920.[6]

Certainly the key organizers of the housewives' movement were all labour leaders before the Depression. In Seattle, Jean Stovel and Mary Farquharson were active in the American Federation of Labour (AFL) before they became leaders of the Women's Committee of the Washington Commonwealth Federation. Detroit's Mary Zuk was the daughter of a United Mine Workers' member and was raised on the violent mine strikes of the 1920s. As a young woman she migrated to Detroit to work on an automobile assembly line and was fired for UAW organizing before founding the Detroit Women's Committee against the High Cost of Living. In New York, Rose Nelson was an organizer for the International Ladies' Garment Workers' Union (ILGWU) before she became co-director of the United Council of Working-Class Women. And the career of the best-known housewife organizer of the 1930s, Clara Lemlich Shavelson, illustrates the importance of both labour movement and Communist Party (CP) links. Only the New York organizers had explicit CP ties, although charges of CP involvement were levelled against nearly all the housewife leaders (*Woman Today* July 1936; *Mary Farquharson Papers* n.d.; Frank 1988).

Shavelson's career also roots the housewives' rebellions of the 1930s in a long tradition of Jewish immigrant women's agitation around subsistence issues.

Because few immigrant or working-class families in the early twentieth century could afford to live on the salary of a single wage earner, wives, sons and daughters contributed to the family economy. Clara Lemlich Shavelson's mother ran a small grocery store. Other immigrant women took in boarders, ran restaurants, peddled piece goods and took in washing or sewing. Their experience with small-scale entrepreneurship gave them a basic understanding of the marketplace that carried over to their management of the home. This economic understanding was deepened by their exposure to unionist principles through their husbands, sons and daughters and sometimes through their own experience as wage workers.[7]

These experiences nourished a belief among working-class women that the home was inextricably bound in a web of social and economic relationships to labour unions, the marketplace and government. That view of the home was expressed in a series of food boycotts and rent strikes that erupted in New York, Philadelphia, Paterson, New Jersey and other East Coast cities between the turn of the century and World War I. Clara Lemlich came of age on Manhattan's Lower East Side where married women led frequent food boycotts and rent strikes during the first decade of the twentieth century. Long before she made the famous speech that set off the massive 1909 shirtwaist makers' strike, 'I am one of those who feels and suffers...I move that we go on a general strike!', (Orleck 1995: 60) Lemlich was aware that the principles of unionism could be applied to community activism.[8]

Blacklisted by garment manufacturers after the 1909 strike, fired from her new career as a paid woman's suffrage advocate after conflicts with upper-class suffragists, Lemlich married printer Arthur Shavelson in 1913 and immediately began looking for ways to channel spontaneous outbursts of housewives' anger into an organizational structure. During World War I, the US government made her task easier by mobilizing housewives in many city neighbourhoods into Community Councils for Defence. Now, when housewives decided to protest rapidly increasing food prices, they had an organizational structure to build on and halls in which to meet. In 1917 and 1919 Shavelson and other community organizers were able to spread meat boycotts and rent strikes throughout New York City by winning support from the community councils, as well as synagogue groups and women's trade union auxiliaries (*New York Times* 3, 4, 7-10, 12-15 May; 17 June; 4-6 Sept. 1919; *Daily Worker* 23 May 1927; Tax 1984).

By 1926, when Shavelson established the United Council of Working-Class Housewives (UCWCH), she was working under the auspices of the Communist Party. However, Shavelson's insistence on organizing women made her a maverick within the CP, as she had been in the labour and suffrage movements. The male leadership of the CP expressed little interest in efforts to win working-class wives to the party. And the women who ran the UCWCH put no pressure on women who joined the housewives' councils to also join the CP.[9]

Around the same time that the united councils were founded, non-Communist organizers like Rose Schneiderman of the Women's Trade Union League (WTUL) and Pauline Newman and Fania Cohn of the ILGWU were also trying to bring housewives into the working-class movement. In the twenty years since the 1909 shirtwaist strike—the largest strike by US women workers to that time—these labour organizers had run up against the incontrovertible fact that working-class women lacked the economic power to achieve their social and political aims unless they allied themselves with more powerful groups such as middle-class women or working-class men (New York WTUL 1922, 1926, 1928; Women's Auxiliary Conference 30 June-1 July, 1928; *Mary Van Kleeck Papers*, n.d.; *Fania Cohn Papers*, n.d.; Klueg 1927).

Seeking a way to maximize working-class women's economic power, they decided to organize women both as consumers and as workers. As workers, women were segregated into the lowest-paid, least-skilled sectors of the labour force. Economic deprivation and discrimination in male-dominated labour unions limited their power, even when they organized. But as consumers, US working-class women spent billions of dollars annually. Organized as consumers, even poor women could wield real economic power. By the late 1920s, women organizers were ready to try to link the home to labour unions and government in a dynamic partnership—with wage-earning women and housewives as full partners.[10]

That goal brought women organizers into direct conflict with male leaders in the trade union movement and in the CP, who were unwilling to accept the home as a centre of production or the housewife as a productive labourer. Nor did they see a relationship between production and consumption. Poor housewives, whatever their political stripe, understood that relationship implicitly. They responded to the neighbourhood organizing strategy because they saw in it a chance to improve day-to-day living conditions for themselves and their families.[11] Jean Stovel explained the surge of militance among Seattle housewives this way: 'Women', she said, 'have sold the idea of organization—their own vast power—to themselves, the result of bitter experience. We are that mythical thing called the public and so we shall demand a hearing' (*Women Today* July 1936).

It is important to distinguish the aims of veteran women's organizers from the aims of the majority of women who participated in housewives' protests. For the most part, these housewives had no intention of challenging the traditional sexual division of labour. Nor were they interested in alternative political philosophies such as socialism or communism. But, desperate to feed, clothe and shelter their families, poor women challenged traditional limits on acceptable behaviour for mothers and wives. In so doing, they became political actors (Kaplan 1982).

From Self-Help to Lobbying the Government

Between 1926 and 1933 housewives' self-help groups sprang up across the US In cities surrounded by accessible growing areas (such as Dayton, Ohio; Richmond, Virginia; and Seattle, Washington), housewives and their husbands created highly developed barter networks. Unemployed workers, mostly male, exchanged skills such as carpentry, plumbing, barbering and electrical wiring. Women—some workers' wives, others unemployed workers themselves—organized exchanges of clothing and food. These organizations grew out of small-scale gardening collectives created by housewives during the late 1920s to feed their communities (*The Atlantic* October 1932; *Collier's* 31 Dec. 1932; *Literary Digest* 11 Feb. 1933; *The Nation* 1 Mar. 1933, 19 Apr. 1933; *Survey* 15 Dec. 1932, July 1933; *Saturday Evening Post* 25 Feb. 1933; *Commonweal* 8 Mar. 1933; *Good Housekeeping* March 1933).

In Seattle, unemployed families organized quickly in the aftermath of the 1929 stock market crash; but then this was an unusually organized city, described by a local paper in 1937 as 'the most unionized city in the country'. In 1919, Seattle had been the first city in the US to hold a general strike. During the 1920s, Seattle's labour unions again broke new ground by calling on working-class women and men to organize as consumers. When the Depression hit, Seattle's vast subsistence network was described in the national press as a model of self-sufficiency, 'a republic of the penniless', in the words of *The Atlantic* (Parry 1932). By 1931-32, 40,000 Seattle women and men had joined an exchange in which the men farmed, fished and cut leftover timber from cleared land, while the women gathered food, fuel and clothing. The women also ran commissaries where members could shop with scrip for household essentials. By 1934, an estimated 80,000 people state wide belonged to exchanges that allowed them to acquire food, clothing and shelter without any money changing hands (Parry 1932; *New York Times* 7 June, 3 Sept. 1936; *The Woman Today* July 1936; *Ladies' Home Journal* Oct. 1934; *Seattle Post-Intelligencer* 11 Jan. 1937; *American Mercury* Feb. 1937).

In larger cities like New York, Chicago, Philadelphia and Detroit, self-help groups also sprang up during the early years of the Depression, but housewives there had little chance of making direct contact with farmers. Rather than establishing food exchanges, they created neighbourhood councils that used boycotts and demonstrations to combat rising food prices. And, rather than rehabilitating abandoned buildings for occupation by the homeless, as the unemployed did in Seattle, housewives in larger cities battled with police to prevent evictions of families unable to pay their rents (*Working Woman* June-September 1931).[12]

Tenant and consumer councils in those cities took hold in neighbourhoods where housewives had orchestrated rent strikes and meat boycotts in 1902, 1904, 1907, 1908, and 1917.[13] They organized in the same way as earlier housewife activists had done—primarily through door-to-door canvassing. Boycotts were sustained in the latter period, as in the earlier one, with picket lines and street corner meetings. Even their angry outbursts echoed the earlier housewives' uprisings: meat was destroyed with kerosene or taken off tracks and thrown to the ground. Flour was spilled in the streets, and milk ran in the gutters (Hyman 1980; Frank 1985; Kaplan 1982).

But although its links to earlier housewives' and labour union struggles are important, the 1930s housewives' revolt was far more widespread and sustained, encompassing a far wider range of ethnic and racial groups than any tenant or consumer uprising before it. The earlier outbursts were limited to East Coast

Jewish immigrant communities, but the housewives' uprising of the 1930s was nationwide and involved rural as well as urban women. It drew Polish and native-born housewives in Detroit, Finnish and Scandinavian women in Washington State, and Scandinavian farm wives in Minnesota. Jewish and Black housewives were particularly militant in New York, Cleveland, Chicago, Los Angeles and San Francisco (Nelson Raynes 1987, 1989).[14]

The 1930s housewives' movement can also be distinguished from earlier housewives' actions by the sophistication and longevity of the organizations it generated. Depression-era housewives moved quickly from self-help to lobbying in state capitals and Washington, D.C. Leaders like the 'diminutive but fiery' Mary Zuk of Detroit displayed considerable skill in their use of radio and print media. Their demands of government—regulation of staple food prices; establishment of publicly owned farmer-consumer cooperatives—reflected a complex understanding of the marketplace and the potential uses of the growing government bureaucracy (*Detroit Free Press* July-August 1935).

Leaders of these groups also demonstrated considerable sophistication about forming alliances. Shortly after Roosevelt was elected president, hostilities between Communist and non-Communist women in the labour movement were temporarily set aside. AFL-affiliated women's auxiliaries and CP-affiliated women's neighbourhood councils worked together to organize consumer protests and lobby for regulation of food and housing costs. This happened in 1933, well before the CP initiated its Popular Front policy urging members to join with 'progressive' non-Communist groups and well before the Congress of Industrial Organizations extended its hand to Communists to rejoin the labour movement.[15]

This rapprochement highlighted the desperation that gripped so many working-class communities during the Depression. Although anti-Communist charges were levelled against housewife organizers throughout the Depression, such accusations did not dampen the enthusiasm of rank-and-file council members. To many non-Communists in the movement, the question of who was Communist and who wasn't did not seem terribly relevant at a time when millions faced hunger and homelessness. Detroit housewife leader Catherine Mudra responded this way to charges of Communist involvement in the Detroit meat strike of 1935: 'There may be some Communists among us. There are a lot of Republicans and Democrats too. We do not ask the politics of those who join. All we want is to get prices down to where we can feed our families' (*New York Times* 6 Aug. 1935).

Despite this tolerance of Communist leadership, housewife organizers affiliated with the CP were careful not to push too hard. Party regulars like Clara Lemlich Shavelson were open about their political beliefs, but they did not push members of the housewives' councils to toe the party line. And they organized as mothers, not as Communists. Shavelson did not use the name Lemlich, which still reverberated among New York City garment workers who remembered her fiery speech in 1909. Instead, she organized under her married name and made sure to point out her children whenever they passed by a street corner where she was speaking (Shaffer 1989)[16].

Seasoned organizers like Shavelson sought to build bonds between women in the name of motherhood. They understood that when appealed to as mothers, apolitical women lost their fears about being associated with radicalism in general and the CP in particular. Meeting women organizers day after day, in the local parks with their babies, in food markets and on street corners, shy housewives gained the confidence to express their anger. The deepening Depression hastened such personal transformations. Once all sense of economic security had dissolved, temperamentally conservative women became more open to radical solutions. Sophia Ocher, who was a member of a Mother and Child Unit of Communist organizers in the Bronx, wrote that, 'work among these women was not difficult for there was the baby, the greatest of all issues, and there were the women, all working-class mothers who would fight for their very lives to obtain a better life for their babies' (*Party Organizer* 10 July 1937: 36).

In New York, ethnic bonding between women facilitated the growth of housewives' councils. Although many community organizers like Shavelson, Rose Nelson Raynes, Sonya Sanders and Sophia Ocher were CP members, they were also genuine members of the communities they sought to organize, familiar with local customs, needs and fears. They addressed crowds of housewives in Yiddish as well as English. And steering clear of Marxist doctrine, they emphasized ethnic and community ties in their speeches, likening housewives' councils to the women's charitable associations traditional in East European Jewish culture.[17]

Conscious of the hardship of poor women's lives, the organizers never hesitated to roll up their sleeves and help out. In one Bronx neighbourhood, Sonya Sanders created an entire neighbourhood council by winning over one resistant housebound woman. After Sanders came into the woman's house when she was sick, cleaned it, bathed the children and prepared a kosher dinner for the family, the woman gave up her suspicion of Sanders and became an enthusiastic supporter. She invited all her friends to come to her home and listen to Sanders discuss ways to fight evictions and high prices. Before long a new neighbourhood council was born. Of course, successes like these were predicated on the shared ethnicity of organizer and organized. The ploy would not have worked as well if Sanders did not understand the laws of *kashrut* or know how to cook Jewish-style food (*Party Organizer* 11 March 1938: 39-40).

This strength was also a weakness. As a result of New York's ethnic balkanization, the city's neighbourhood councils were not ethnically diverse. Organizers tended to have most success organizing women of their own ethnic group. The United Council of Working-Class Women (UCWCW), founded and run by Jewish immigrant women, was primarily composed of Jewish immigrant housewives; owing to the CP's strength in Harlem, Black women were the second largest group; small numbers of Irish and Italian housewives also joined.

'We never intended to be exclusively a Jewish organization', Rose Nelson Raynes (1987) recalls,

But we built in areas where we had strength. Maybe it was because of the background of so many Jewish women in the needle trades, maybe it was because of the concentration of immigrants from the other side, I don't know. But there was a feeling in the Jewish working class that we had to express ourselves in protest of the rising prices.

As in New York, the Detroit and Seattle housewives' actions were initiated by immigrant women of a particular ethnic group—Polish Catholics in Detroit and Scandinavian Protestants in Seattle. Because those cities were less ghettoized than New York, organizers were more successful in creating coalitions that involved Black as well as white women; Protestants, Jews and Catholics; immigrants and native born. However, ethnic differences were not unimportant, even outside New York. For example, American-born Protestants in the Detroit housewives' councils were far less confrontational in their tactics than their Polish, Jewish or Black counterparts. They signed no-meat pledges rather than picketing butcher shops and handed in petitions rather than marching on city ball.[18]

Women had different reasons for joining housewives' councils in the 1930s, but those who stayed did so because they enjoyed the camaraderie, the enhanced self-esteem and the shared sense of fighting for a larger cause. During an interview in her Brighton Beach apartment, 88-year-old Rose Nelson Raynes offered this analysis of why the councils inspired such loyalty:

> Women were discriminated against in all organizations in those years and the progressive organizations were no exception. When women joined progressive organizations with men they were relegated to the kitchen. There was a need on the part of the mother, the woman in the house. She wanted to get out. There were so many things taking place that she wanted to learn more about. So women came to our organization where they got culture, lectures. Some developed to a point where they could really get up and make a speech that would meet any politician's speech today. It came from the need, from the heart. We felt we wanted to express ourselves, to learn to speak and act and the only way was through a women's council.

The Meatless Summer of 1935

Depression-era organizing against high food prices reached its peak during the summer of 1935. Working-class women activists from Communist and non-Communist organizations convened two regional conferences the previous winter, one for the East Coast, another for the Midwest, to coordinate protests against the sales tax and high cost of living. Representatives from AFL women's union auxiliaries, parents' associations, church groups, farm women's and Black women's groups attended. By that summer, they had laid plans for the most ambitious women's consumer protest to that time (*Working Woman* March 1935).

It began when the Chicago Committee against the High Cost of Living, headed by Dina Ginsberg, organized massive street meetings near the stockyards to let the meat packers know how unhappy they were with rising meat prices. New York housewives in the UCWCW quickly raised the ante by organizing a citywide strike against butcher shops (*Chicago Daily Tribune* 18 Aug. 1935; *Working Woman* August 1935).

On May 22 women in Jewish and Black neighbourhoods around New York City formed picket lines. In Harlem, according to historian Mark Naison (1983), the meat strike 'produced an unprecedented display of coordinated protest by black working-class women' (149). The strike lasted four weeks. More than 4,500 butcher shops were closed down by housewives' picket lines. Scores of women and men around the city were arrested. The New York State Retail Meat Dealers Association threatened to hold Mayor Fiorello LaGuardia responsible for damage to their businesses as a result of the strike. The mayor, in an attempt to resolve the strike, asked federal officials to study the possibilities for reducing retail meat prices (*New York Times* 27-31 May; 1, 2, 6, 10-12, 14-16 June 1935).

Nelson Raynes (1987), city-wide coordinator of the meat strike, describes what happened next:

It was successful to a point where we were warned that the gangsters were going to get us. We decided to call the whole thing off but first we organized a mass picket line in front of the wholesale meat distributors. About three, four hundred women came out on the picket line. It was supposed to be a final action. But instead of being the wind-up it became a beginning.

Housewives across the US promptly joined in. Ten thousand Los Angeles housewives, members of the Joint Council of Women's Auxiliaries, declared a meat strike on June 8th that so completely shut down retail meat sales in the city that butchers cut prices by the next day. In Philadelphia, Chicago, Boston, Paterson, St. Louis and Kansas City, newly formed housewives' councils echoed the cry of the New York strike: 'Stop Buying Meat until Prices Come Down!' (*Working Woman* June 1935; *New York Times* 15, 16 June 1935).

On June 15, a delegation of housewives from across the country descended on Washington, D.C., demanding that the Department of Agriculture enforce lower meat prices. Clara Lemlich Shavelson described the delegation's meeting with Secretary of Agriculture Henry Wallace:

The meat packers and the Department of Agriculture in Washington tried to make the strikers' delegation believe that the farmer and the drought are to blame for the high price of food. But the delegation would not fall for this. They knew the truth. (*Working Woman* August 1935)

The Polish housewives of Hamtramck, Michigan, a suburb of Detroit, did not believe Wallace's explanation either. A month after the end of the New York strike, 32-year-old Mary Zuk addressed a mass demonstration of housewives gathered on the streets of Hamtramck to demand an immediate reduction in meat prices. When the reduction did not come by that evening, Zuk announced a meat boycott to begin the following day (*Detroit Free Press* 27 July 1935; *New York Times* 28 July 1935).

On July 27, 1935, Polish and Black housewives began to picket Hamtramck butcher shops, carrying signs demanding a twenty per cent price cut throughout the city and an end to price gouging in Black neighbourhoods. When men, taunted by onlookers who accused them of being 'scared of a few women', attempted to cross the lines, they were 'seized by the pickets, their faces slapped, their hair pulled and their packages confiscated'. A few were knocked down and trampled'. That night Hamtramck butchers reported unhappily that the boycott had been 95 per cent effective (*Detroit Free Press* 28 July 1935; *New York Times* 28 July 1935).

Within a matter of days the meat boycott spread to other parts of Detroit, as housewives in several different ethnic communities hailed the onset of 'a general strike against the high cost of living'. Jewish women picketed kosher butcher shops in downtown Detroit neighbourhoods. Protestant women in outlying regions such as Lincoln Park and River Rouge declined to picket or march but instead set up card tables on street corners to solicit no-meat pledges from passing housewives (*Detroit Free Press* 29-31 July 1935; *New York Times* 30 July 1935).

Housewives also sought government intervention. Detroit housewives stormed the city council demanding that it set a ceiling on meat prices in the metropolitan area. 'What we can afford to buy isn't fit for a human to eat', Joanna Dinkfeld told the council. 'And we can't afford very much of that' (*Detroit Free Press* 1 Aug. 1935). Warning the council and the state government that they had better act, Myrtle Hoaglund announced that she was forming a state wide housewives' organization. 'We feel that we should have united action', she said. 'We think the movement of protest against present meat prices can be spread throughout the state and the nation' (*New York Times* 4 Aug. 1935). As evidence, she showed the city council bags of letters she had received from housewives around the country, asking her how to go about organizing consumer boycotts.

Throughout August the meat strikers made front-page news in Detroit and received close attention in major New York and Chicago dailies. The women staged mass marches through the streets of Detroit, stormed meat-packing plants, overturned and emptied meat trucks and poured kerosene on thousands of pounds of meat stored in warehouses. When these actions resulted in the arrest of several Detroit women, hundreds of boycotters marched on the city jails, demanding the release of their friends. Two hours after her arrest, Hattie Krewik, 45 years old and a mother of five, emerged from her cell unrepentant. A roar went up from the crowd as she immediately began to tell, in Polish, her tale of mistreatment at the hands of police. By the end of the first week in August, retail butchers in Detroit were pleading with the governor to send in state troops to protect their meat (*Detroit Free Press* 3-5 Aug 1935).

Although without a doubt the butchers suffered as a result of this boycott, the strikers in Detroit, like the strikers in New York, frequently reiterated that the strike was not aimed at retail butchers or at farmers. It was aimed, in Clara Shavelson's words, at the 'meat packer millionaires'. To prove that, in the second week of August, a delegation of Detroit housewives travelled to Chicago where they hooked up with their Chicago counterparts for a march on the Union stockyards.

Meeting them at the gates, Armour and Company president R. H. Cabell attempted to mollify the women. 'Meat packers', he told them, 'are not the arbiters of prices, merely the agencies through which economic laws operate'. The sudden rise in prices, he explained, was the fault of the Agricultural Adjustment Administration which had recently imposed a processing tax on pork (*Chicago Daily Tribune* 18 Aug. 1935; *Newsweek* 17 Aug. 1935; *Saturday Evening Post* 2 Nov. 1935).

'Fine', Mary Zuk responded. The housewives would return to Washington for another meeting with agriculture secretary Wallace. On August 19, 1935, Zuk and her committee of five housewives marched into Wallace's office and demanded that he end the processing tax, impose a twenty per cent cut on meat prices, and order prompt prosecution of profiteering meat packers (*New York Times* 20 Aug. 1935). Wallace, perhaps sensing how this would be played in the press, tried to evict reporters from the room, warning that he would not speak to the women if they remained. Zuk did not blink. She replied: 'Our people want to know what we say and they want to know what you say so the press people are going to stay'. The reporters stayed and had a grand time the next day reporting on Wallace's unexplained departure from the room in the middle of the meeting (*New York Times* 20 Aug. 1935). 'Secretary Wallace beats retreat from five housewives', the *Chicago Daily Tribune* (20 Aug. 1935) blared. *Newsweek* reported it this way:

> The lanky Iowan looked down into Mrs. Zuk's deep-sunken brown eyes and gulped his Adam's apple.
>
> Mrs. Zuk: 'Doesn't the government want us to live? Everything in Detroit has gone up except wages'.
>
> Wallace fled. (31 August 1935)

In the aftermath of Zuk's visit to Washington, *Newsweek* reported housewives' demonstrations against the high price of meat in Indianapolis, Denver and Miami. The *New York Times* reported violent housewives' attacks on meat warehouses in Chicago and in Shenandoah and Frackville, Pennsylvania. And Mary Zuk, the 'strong-jawed 100 lb. mother of the meat strike', became a national figure. The Detroit post office announced that it was receiving letters from all over the country addressed only to 'Mrs. Zuk-Detroit' (*Detroit Free Press* 6-7, 9 Aug. 1935; *Newsweek* 31 Aug. 1935; *New York Times* 19 Aug., 1, 5 Sept. 1935).

Although boycotts and strikes continued to be used as a tool in the housewives' struggle for lower prices, the movement became more focused on electoral politics as the decade wore on. Both Shavelson and Zuk used the prominence they'd gained through housewife activism to run for elected office. Shavelson ran for New York State Assembly in 1933 and 1938 as a 'real' mother fighting to maintain an American standard of living for her own family as well as for other families'. She did not win but she fared far better than the rest of the CP ticket (Shaffer 1989; Melvin Getson 1989).

Zuk ran a successful campaign for the Hamtramck City Council in April of 1936. Although the local Hearst-owned paper warned that her election would be a victory for those who advocate 'the break- up of the family', Zuk was swept into office by her fellow housewives. She won on a platform calling for the city council to reduce rents, food prices and utility costs in Hamtramck. After her election she told reporters that she was proof that 'a mother can organize and still take care of her family' (*Detroit Free Press* 10 Apr. 1936; *New York Times* 10 Apr. 1936; *Woman Today* July 1936).

In some ways what the Hearst papers sensed was really happening. Zuk's campaign represented an express politicization of motherhood and the family. On Mother's Day, 1936, 700 Zuk supporters rallied outside the city council to demand public funding for a women's healthcare clinic, childcare centres, playgrounds and teen centres in Hamtramck. They also called for an end to evictions and for construction of more public housing in their city. The government owed this to mothers, the demonstrators told reporters (*Woman Today* July 1936).

Two years earlier, in Washington State, the Women's Committee of the Washington Commonwealth Federation (WCF) had successfully elected three of its members to the state senate—Mary Farquharson, a professor's wife; and Marie Keene and Katherine Malström, the wives of loggers. Their campaign had been built around a Production-for-Use initiative to prohibit the destruction of food as a way of propping up prices. Such waste, they said, was an outrage to poor mothers in the state, who had been fighting the practice since the beginning of the Depression. The ballot measure also proposed a state distribution system for produce so that farmers could get a fair price and workers' families could buy food directly from farmers. Led by Katherine Smith and Elizabeth Harper, committee members collected 70,000 signatures to put the measure on the 1936 ballot (*Woman Today* July 1936; *New York Times* 7, 13 June; 5, 26 July; 3, 9, 10, 13 Sept.; 1, 9 Nov. 1936; 'A few honest questions and answers about initiative 119' n.d.).

The Production-for-Use initiative failed by a narrow margin but it made national news as columnists across the country speculated on the impact it might have had on the US economic system. Other WCF campaigns were more successful, however. The most important of these was the campaign to create publicly owned utilities in Washington State. Washington voters were the only ones to approve state ownership of utilities, but voters in localities across the country endorsed the creation of city and county utility companies during the 1930s ('A few honest wuestions and answers' n.d.; *The Nation* 28 Nov. 1934, 19 Aug. 1939).

Housewife activists also kept their sights on the federal government during this period. From 1935 to 1941, housewives' delegations from major cities made annual trips to Washington, D.C. to lobby for lower food prices. These trips stopped during World War II but resumed afterward with a concerted campaign to save the Office of Price Administration and to win federal funds for construction of public housing in poor neighbourhoods (*Woman Today* March 1937; *New York Times* 4 Dec. 1947; 20 May; 20 July; 3-31 Aug. 1948; 24, 26-28 Feb.; 25, 26 May; 14 June; 18 Aug. 1951).

The alliance of housewives' councils and women's union auxiliaries continued to grow through the late 1930s, laying the groundwork for two more nationwide meat strikes in 1948 and 1951. These strikes affected even more women than the 1935 action because housewives now had an organizing tool that enabled them to mobilize across thousands of miles: the telephone. 'We have assigned 58 women ten pages each of the telephone directory', said one strike leader in Cincinnati. In August of 1948, housewives in Texas, Ohio, Colorado, Florida, Michigan and New York boycotted meat. And during the winter of 1951, a housewives' meat boycott across the country forced wholesalers dealing in the New York, Philadelphia and Chicago markets to lower their prices. In New York City alone, newspapers estimated one million pounds of meat a week went begging. Fearing for their own jobs, unionized butchers, then retailers, and finally even local wholesalers, called on the federal government to institute price controls on meat (Nelson Raynes 1989; *New York Times* 3, 5, 8-11, 19, 28, 31 Aug. 1948; 24, 26-28 Feb.; 14 June 1951).

But even as these actions made front-page news across the country, the housewives' alliance was breaking apart over the issue of Communist involvement. As early as 1933, the Washington State legislature had passed a bill requiring that Seattle take over the commissaries created by the unemployed two years earlier. Conservative politicians claimed that Communists had taken control of the relief machinery in the city and were seeking to indoctrinate the hungry. In 1939, Hearst newspapers charged that the housewives' movement nationwide was little more than a Communist plot to sow seeds of discord in the American home. The Dies Committee of the US Congress took these charges seriously and began an investigation. US entry into World War II temporarily ended the investigation but also quelled consumer protest because the government instituted rationing and price controls (*New York Times* 26 Feb. 1933; *The Woman Today* March 1937; *The Nation* 5, 12 June 1937; 18 Feb. 1939; *Business Week* 11 Nov. 1939; *Forum* October 1939; *The New Republic* 1 Jan. 1940).

Investigations of the consumer movement began again soon after the war ended. During the 1948 boycott, housewife leaders were charged by some with being too friendly to Progressive party presidential candidate Henry Wallace. In 1949, the House Committee on Un-American Activities began investigating the organizers of a 1947 housewives' march on Washington, and in 1950 they were ordered to register with the Justice Department as foreign agents. By the early 1950s national and local Communist-hunting committees had torn apart the movement, creating dissension and mistrust among the activists (*New York*

Times 23 Oct. 1949; 7 Jan. 1950).

The unique alliance that created a nationwide housewives' uprising during the 1930s and 1940s would not re-emerge, but it laid the groundwork for later consumer and tenant organizing. Housewives' militance politicized consumer issues nationwide. 'Never has there been such a wave of enthusiasm to do something for the consumer', *The Nation* wrote in 1937. Americans have gained 'a consumer consciousness', the magazine concluded, as a direct result of the housewives' strikes in New York, Detroit and other cities. The uprising of working-class housewives also broadened the terms of the class struggle, forcing male union leaders to admit that 'the roles of producer and consumer are intimately related' (*The Nation* 5, 12 June 1937; *The New Republic* 8 Apr. 1936).

Housewives' groups alleviated the worst effects of the Depression in many working-class communities by bringing down food prices, rent and utility costs, preventing evictions, and spurring the construction of more public housing, schools and parks. By the end of World War II, housewives' activism had forced the government to play a regulatory role in food and housing costs. Militant direct action and sustained lobbying put pressure on local and federal politicians to investigate profiteering on staple goods. The meat strikes of 1935 and of 1948 through 1951 resulted in congressional hearings on the structure of the meat industry and in nationwide reductions in prices. The intense anti-eviction struggles led by urban housewives and their years of lobbying for public housing helped to convince New York City and other localities to pass rent-control laws. They also increased support in Congress for federally funded public housing (*New York Times*, 20, 24, 25 Aug. 1935; 20 May; 20 July; 3-31 Aug. 1948; 24, 26-28 Feb.; 25, 26 May; 14 June; 18 Aug. 1951).

Perhaps an equally important legacy of housewives' activism was its impact on the consciousness of the women who participated. 'It was an education for the women', Brooklyn activist Dorothy Moser (1987) recalls, 'that they could not have gotten any other way'. Immigrant women, poor native-born white women, and Black women learned to write and speak effectively, to lobby in state capitals and in Washington, D.C., to challenge men in positions of power, and sometimes to question the power relations in their own homes.

By organizing as consumers, working-class housewives not only demonstrated a keen understanding of their place in local and national economic structures, they also shattered the notion that because homemakers consume rather than produce, they are inherently more passive than their wage-earning husbands. The very act of organizing defied traditional notions of proper behaviour for wives and mothers—and organizers were often called upon to explain their actions.

Union husbands supported and sometimes, as Dana Frank (1988) argues in her study of Seattle, even instigated their wives' community organizing. However, that organizing created logistical problems—namely who was going to watch the children and who was going to cook dinner? Some women managed to do it all. Others could not. Complaining of anarchy in the home, some union husbands ordered their wives to stop marching and return to the kitchen. In November

1934, *Working Woman* magazine offered a hamper of canned goods to any woman who could answer the plaint of a housewife whose husband had ordered her to quit her women's council.

First prize went to a Bronx housewife who called on husbands and wives to share childcare as 'they share their bread. Perhaps two evenings a week father should go, and two evenings, mother'. The same woman noted that struggle keeps a woman 'young physically and mentally' and that she shouldn't give it up for anything. Second prize went to a Pennsylvania miner's wife who agreed with that sentiment. 'There can't be a revolution without women. No one could convince me to drop out. Rather than leave the Party I would leave him'. And an honourable mention went to a Texas farm woman who warned, 'If we allow men to tell us what we can and cannot do we will never get our freedom' (*Working Woman* March 1935). The prize-winning essays suggest that, like many women reformers before them, Depression-era housewife activists became interested in knocking down the walls that defined behavioural norms for women only after they had personally run up against them. [19]

In defending their right to participate in a struggle that did not ideologically challenge the traditional sexual division of labour, many working-class housewives developed a new sense of pride in their abilities and a taste for political involvement. These women never came to think of themselves as feminists. They did, however, begin to see themselves as legitimate political and economic actors. During this period, poor wives and mothers left their homes in order to preserve them. In so doing, whether they intended to or not, they politicized the home, the family and motherhood in important and unprecedented ways.

Reprinted with permission from Feminist Studies *19 (1) (Spring 1993): 147-172.*

Annelise Orleck is the author of Common Sense and a Little Fire: Women and Working Class Politics in the United States, 1900-1965 *(1995),* Soviet Jewish Americans *(1999) and co-editor of* The Politics of Motherhood: Activist Voices from Left to Right *(1997). She is also the author of* Storming Caesar's Palace: How Black Welfare Mothers Fought Their Own War on Poverty *(forthcoming: 2005). She teaches history, gender and women's studies at Dartmouth College.*

Notes

1   *New York Times, Newsweek, The Nation, The New Republic, Saturday Evening Post, Harper's, Christian Century, Business Week* and *American Mercury* all covered and commented on housewife organizing. The *Detroit Free Press* also provided detailed coverage of housewives' activism in their cities. *Working Woman*, the monthly publication of the Women's Commission of the Communist Party, was invaluable. Although extremely dogmatic in its early years, the magazine is one of the most complete sources available on working-class women during the Depression. The two main archives consulted for this paper were the Tamiment Library in New York City

     and the Robert Burke Collection in the Manuscripts Division of the University of Washington Library, Seattle.

2   Meridel Le Sueur describes the radicalization of one of those farm women, Mary Cotter, in her 1940 short story, 'Salute to Spring'.

3   Selected sources on housewife activism early in the Depression include: *Working Woman* 1931-35. See *New York Times* 23, 30 Jan.; February; 22 Mar.; 22 May; 7 June; 7, 11 July; 13-26 Sept.; 9 Oct.; 7, 21 Dec. 1932; January-February; 23, 30 Mar.; 13, 24 May; 1, 2, 8 June; 2, 31 Aug.; 7, 9, 26 Sept.; 9 Dec. 1933. See *The Atlantic* October 1932; *The Nation*, 1 Mar. 1933; 19 Apr. 1933; 14, 18 Mar. 1934; *The New Republic* 15 Nov. 1933; *Ladies' Home Journal* October 1934.

4   For information on the links between union activity and community organizing in New York City neighbourhoods between 1902 and 1945, see Orleck (1989) on Seattle politics in the post-World War I period, see Acena (1975); Frank (1988).

5   A *Working Woman* study in the winter of 1931 reported that even among those workers still employed in the big cities of the US, income had declined 33 per cent, but food prices had decreased only seven per cent (3 March 1931).

6   Rose Nelson Raynes (1987), one of the chief organizers of the UCWCW, recalls that in 1931, when she first became involved with the organization, most of the women were older than 35. *New York Times* reports of arrests in anti-eviction actions and consumer boycotts between 1931 and 1935 show that all the women were married and the vast majority were between the ages of 30 and 42. *Detroit Free Press* accounts of arrests in the 1935 meat strike list the majority as having been between the ages of 28 and 48. In 1932, T. J. Parry, writing about members of the food exchanges in Seattle, commented that most of them were 'near life's half-way mark or beyond'.

7   In *The Jewish Woman in America*, Charlotte Baum, Paula Hyman and Sonya Michel (1976) review some of the voluminous immigrant literature highlighting the entrepreneurship of Jewish immigrant mothers. See Orleck (1995) 'Chapter 1', for a fuller analysis of the literature on working-class women's entrepreneurship, their conception of home, and their involvement in activism around tenant and consumer issues in the first decade of the twentieth century.

8   Paula Hyman (1980) makes this point in her essay on 'Immigrant Women and Consumer Protest: The New York City Kosher Meat Boycott of 1902'. See also *New York Times* May-June 1902; 13 July-2 Sept. 1904; 30 Nov.-9 Dec. 1906; 26 Dec. 1907-27 Jan. 1908. These sources indicate that many of the women involved were the wives and mothers of garment workers.

9   CP women complained consistently in the *Party Organizer* during the 1930s that CP men were hindering or ignoring their efforts at organizing women in urban neighbourhoods. See particularly the August 1937 issue in which Anna Damon, head of the CP Women's Commission, lashes out at CP leaders for undercutting her efforts with Black women in St. Louis.

10   A study by the American Federation of Women's Auxiliaries of Labour estimated in 1937 that US women in union households spent $6 billion annually. See *Working Woman* March 1937.

11   Robert Shaffer (1979) notes that the national CP leadership condemned CP feminist theorist Mary Inman particularly for her assertion that the home was a centre of production and that housewives did productive labour. See also Inman (1949).

12   For anti-eviction activity, see *New York Times* almost daily in February 1933, as well as well as 1, 2, 13 Mar.; 28 May; 7 June; 7 July; 13, 15-18, 20, 26 Sept.; 7, 21 Dec. 1932; 6, 12, 17, 28 Jan.; 1, 22 Feb.; 8, 23, 30 Mar.; 13, 24 May; 1, 2, 8 June; 2, 3 Aug.;

7, 9, 26 Sept.; 9 Dec. 1933.

[13] Identifiable links to these earlier events, in addition to Clara Lemlich Shavelson include Dorothy Moser (1987), another New York activist of the 1930s, who remembers her mother's involvement in the 1917 boycotts. Judging from the age of the women arrested in New York and Detroit actions (see *New York Times* and *Detroit Free Press*, 1931-1935), mostly in their forties, most of the 1930s' activists were old enough to remember earlier actions.

[14] *Working Woman* June, July, and August 1935; *Woman Today* July 1936; *New York Times, Chicago Daily Tribune, Detroit Free Press, Newsweek*, and the *Saturday Evening Post* also provided coverage of housewife actions. See particularly, *New York Times* 28 July; 4, 6, 11, 18, 24, 25 Aug. 1935; *Saturday Evening Post* 2 Nov. 1935; *Chicago Daily Tribune* 18, 20, 21 Aug. 1935; *Newsweek* 17, 31 Aug. 1935.

[15] In 1933, pleased with the success of their neighbourhood organizing strategy, the UCWCW, the umbrella organization for New York housewives' councils, began working to build a coalition with other New York women's organizations, many of which had previously been quite hostile to anyone with CP affiliations. This was an important turning point in the housewives' movement (see *Working Woman* October 1933, December 1933).

[16] 'Who Is Clara Shavelson?' is a leaflet Shavelson distributed during her 1933 campaign for New York State Assembly in the 2nd Assembly District to emphasize that her identity as a mother would be central to her legislative agenda. (courtesy of her daughter Rita Margulies).

[17] Brighton Beach, Brooklyn, where Clara Shavelson organized, is a perfect example of this strategy. Shavelson built on a highly developed network of Jewish women's religious and cultural associations to create the effective Emma Lazarus Tenant's Council during the 1930s (see Orleck 1995, Chapter 6).

[18] Information on the New York UCWCW comes from interviews with Raynes, 8 October 1987, and 17 February 1989. Also, both *New York Times* and *Working Woman* coverage of New York City housewives' actions from 1932 to 1937 show that the most consistently militant sections of the city were Jewish immigrant communities. Information on the composition of the Seattle housewives' groups was drawn from membership lists of the Renter's Protection, Cost of Living and Public Ownership committees of the Women's League of the Washington Commonwealth Federation. Information on the composition of the Detroit housewives' movement comes from the *Detroit Free Press*, 26 July-25 August 1935 when housewife activists made the paper, quite often the front page, almost every day.

[19] Frank (1988) argues that, during the 1920s, working-class women in Seattle resisted their husbands' and brothers' calls to consumer action, because they resented their exclusion from meaningful participation in governance and policy making of the labour unions.

References

'A few honest questions and answers about initiiative 119', (n.d.) Leaflet of the Washington Commonwealth Federation, Robert BurkeCollection, Manuscript Division of the University of Washington Library, Seattle

Acena, A. (1975) *The Washington Commonwealth Federation: Reform Politics and the Popular Front*, Ph.D. diss., University of Washington, Seattle.

'Buyers trampled by meat strikers', (1935) *New York Times*, 28 July.

Baum, C., P. Hyman, and S. Michel (1976) *The Jewish Woman in America*, New York: New American Library.

Fania Cohn Papers (n.d.) New York Public Library.

Frank, D. (1985) 'Housewives, socialists, and the politics of food: the 1917 New York cost-of-living protests', *Feminist Studies,* 11, Summer, 255-85.

Frank, D. (1988) *At the Point of Consumption: Seattle Labour and the Politics of Consumption, 1919-1927*, Ph.D. diss., Yale University.

Hyman, P. (1980) 'Immigrant women and consumer protest: the New York City kosher meat boycott of 1902', *American Jewish History*, 70, September, 91-105.

Inman, M. (1949) *Thirteen Years of CPUSA Misleadership on the Women Question*. Los Angeles, CA: self-published.

Kaplan, T. (1982) 'Female consciousness and collective action: the case of Barcelona, 1910-1918', *Signs*, 7, Spring, 545-66.

Klueg, G., (1927) Personal correspondence to Fania M. Cohn. *Fania Cohn Papers*, New York, New York Public Library, 7 August.

Le Sueur, M. (1940) *Salute to Spring*, New York: International Publishers.

Mary Farquharson Papers (n.d.) boxes 12-14, folders 30 and 94, Burke Collection, University of Washington Library.

Mary Van Kleeck Papers (n.d.) Sophia Smith Collection, Smith College, Northampton, Massachussettes.

Melvin Getson, S. (1989) Personal interview, 17 February.

Moser, D. (1987) Personal Interview, 8 October.

Naison, M. (1983) *Communists in Harlem During the Depression*, New York: Grove Press.

Nelson Raynes, R. (1987) Personal Interview, 8 October.

Nelson Raynes, R. (1989) Personal interview, 17 February.

New York Women's Trade Union League (WTUL) (1928) *Annual Report*, Tamiment Library.

New York Women's Trade Union League (WTUL) (1926) *Annual Report*, Tamiment Library.

New York Women's Trade Union League (WTUL) (1922) *Annual Report*, Tamiment Library.

Orleck, A. (1995) *Common Sense and a Little Fire: Women and Working Class Politics in the United States, 1900-1965,* Chapel Hill: University of North Carolina Press.

Orleck, A. (1989) *Common Sense and a Little Fire: Women and Working Class Activism in the 20th Century United States.* Unpublished Ph.D. dissertation. New York University.

Parry, T. J. (1932) 'Republic of the penniless', *The Atlantic,* October.

Renter's Protection, Cost of Living, and Public Ownership Committees of the Women's League of the Washington Commonwealth Federation Information (n.d.) Burke Collection, folders 30, 94, 182, 183, 188. University of Washington LIbrary.

'Secretary Wallace beats retreat from five housewives', (1935) *Chicago Daily Tribune*, 20 August.

Shaffer, R. (1979) 'Women and the Communist Party, USA, 1930-1940', *Socialist Review*, 45, May-June, 73-118.

Shaffer, M. (1989) Personal interview, 11 March.

Tax, M. (1984) *Women's Councils in the 1930s*, paper presented at the Berkshire Conference on the History of Women, Smith College, June.

Women's Auxiliary Conference. (1928) 'Summary of speeches', Unity House, Forest Park, Pennsylvania, 30 June-1 July.

SOLIDARITY, PATRIARCHY AND EMPOWERMENT

WOMEN'S STRUGGLES AGAINST ARRACK IN INDIA

REKHA PANDE

Sara babus *(liquor contractors) we salute you. Ruling ministers, we pray, please listen. My grandfather drank and drank and destroyed himself, my father drank and fell in a ditch, they increased our difficulties and starved our stomachs, but you enjoy all comforts. We don't want* sara *that spoils our liver, that ruins our homes.* (Song used by women in anti-arrack protests)

The women's movement against *arrack* (a locally-produced liquor) in the state of Andhra Pradesh can be described as one of the most extraordinary social uprisings of contemporary India. It began when rural women sought to address what they viewed as one of the root causes of widespread domestic violence: their husbands' daily drinking habits and government policy on liquor. This article is based on interviews I, and four research assistants, conducted during 1994-1995 with over one thousand women involved in the anti-arrack movement, as well as our participation in many of the women's meetings and marches. What started as a small local movement quickly spread across the entire state. The struggle against arrack is important because of the efforts by activists to make links across issue areas and for the extent to which it challenged notions of political apathy, especially amongst rural women. Despite the hurdles, the movement achieved considerable success especially in the face of a recalcitrant state.

In India, the issue of violence against women came into sharp focus in the 1980s with the widespread coverage by the mass media of growing incidents of torture of brides, of dowry deaths and of the localized populist protests against these crimes (Kishwar and Ruth 1984). The only large-scale indicator of violence against women, in the public sphere, is the data published annually by the National Crimes Record Bureau, Ministry of Home Affairs, Government of India, which every year reveals a shocking increase in crimes against women (*Crimes in India*

1995, 1996 1997, 2000). Andhra Pradesh, the fifth largest populated state in India, is no exception. A report by the Bureau Police Research and Development (*Crimes in India* 1997), in a comparative analysis of crimes against women in the various states, ranks Andhra Pradesh second highest for dowry deaths, fourth for rape of girls below the age of sixteen, and seventh for molestation. These statistics are based on reported cases. For every case reported, there are several that are not in the name of family honour.

Definitions of domestic violence in India rest not only upon the nature of relationship between the perpetrator and the victim but also upon culturally accepted norms of behaviour. Most of the public discourse equates domestic violence only with dowry deaths. Such an understanding undermines the daily psychological, physical and sexual abuse confronted by women in their day-to-day lives. Women do not discuss domestic violence with their parents or other relatives who, even if aware of the violence taking place, do not deem it their place to intervene. Often a woman's family feels helpless to stop the abusive husband. Women also rarely talk to neighbours or seek external help because they are socialized to believe that doing so would disgrace the "honour" of both families.

It is remarkable then that in the 1990s, in the state of Andhra Pradesh, women who had been experiencing domestic violence for years took it upon themselves to deal with one of its main causes publicly and, in the process, started a movement which questioned the government policy on liquor, *arrack*. The rural women of Andhra Pradesh who for centuries have been marginalized from every sphere of life, exploited by landlords, and made targets of domestic and social violence, suddenly rose in revolt. They had a simple demand: '*No selling and drinking of liquor in our village*'. This demand that started as an agitation soon became a movement involving thousands of women. This movement was instrumental in bringing the issue of domestic violence in India to the public platform.

The Background

Deceitful sara, *deceitful* sara. *It swallowed our house*, maava *[term of endearment used to plead with husband]. Please don't drink useless* sara*! Don't drink* maava*! Our kids roam with torn clothes and you don't feel ashamed. Don't drink* maava, *useless* sara, *don't drink* maava*!* (Song used in anti-arrack protests)

During the last two decades, liquor contractors, a powerful lobby in Andhra Pradesh, have dominated the socio-political and economic fabric of India because of their association with arrack. Arrack is rectified spirits obtained by distilling fermented molasses. As a result of the Green Revolution, the sugarcane cultivation in India increased which in turn led to an increase in sugar production and its by-product molasses. In Andhra Pradesh, this liquor is made and supplied by the government through a network of contractors and intermediaries who bid at annual auctions to purchase the arrack as well as the licence to sell it. When the Telugu Desam Party came into power in 1982, the arrack trade received a big boost due to an aggressive packaging and marketing campaign to promote sales of the liquor.

The process of making arrack costs the government one rupee per litre. It is then sold to the contractors at auction, usually at Rs.10.60 to Rs.11 per litre. They in turn dilute it and pack it into sachets (small plastic bags) that they then sell for Rs.60 to 90 per litre (Rs.45 is equivalent to $1). The contractors use hired gangs of musclemen, *goondas*, to maintain their monopoly in the liquor trade, to pay bribes to police and excise officials, and to protect their territories from rival contractors or tribal or other communities who traditionally distill liquor at home.

Government revenues from excise on arrack and Indian Made Foreign Liquor (other kinds of locally produced spirits bottled and sold in previously used foreign liquor bottles) increased from Rs.390 million in 1970-71 to Rs.812 billion in 1991-92. This is the result of a deliberate policy implemented by the government in Andhra Pradesh, *Varun Vahini* (the "flooding of liquor" program)—the door-to-door delivery of liquor in villages to encourage purchases of alcohol and thus add to the state coffers. Previously, the arrack could only be purchased outside the village in the *sara* (liquor) compound. Men would go to the compound to purchase a drink usually in the evenings after they finished their work. The *Varun Vahini* program made it possible for the men to purchase alcohol on their doorstep. In 1991-92, the annual average family income in the State of Andhra Pradesh was Rs.1,840, of which Rs.830 was spent on liquor. Men were thus spending a significant portion of their income on the purchase of liquor and as time passed this eroded the family economy (Balgopal 1992).

Literacy and the Anti-Arrack Movement

What should I tell about sara, *sister? what should I tell about my husband? The whole days labour goes for buying* sara *packets. He comes with the* sara *smell and saw pickle in the plate, asked for egg.... And threw the plate. The heart is burning the stomach is starving but my husband's mouth is filled with* sara. (Song used in anti-arrack protests)

Women in Andhra Pradesh were able to articulate their concerns about arrack in the space provided by adult literacy classes. The National Literacy Mission (NLM) officially began its operation in Nellore District in January 1991. This program was implemented in a very innovative way. At the core of the program was recognition of development as an instrument of change and empowerment of women. A three-pronged approach was adopted to spread the message of literacy. Committees were set up to write and prepare primers dealing with contemporary issues as reading material to be used for the target groups. Cultural committees were also organized to convey the meaning and need for literacy in the popular performances of songs, dance-dramas and street plays. The pre-implementation programs consisted of distributing pamphlets and putting up posters as well as a number of *padyatras* (walking through the village on foot, meeting and talking to people). The cultural troupe, *Kalajatras,* gave thousands of performances in an idiom and language understood by the village folk. The themes included problems encountered in daily life because of illiteracy, exploitation of labour, low wages, untouchability, dowry, heavy drinking, and wife beating.

As the purpose of the program was not just gaining literacy but also development and empowerment, the post-literacy programs consisted of the formation of *Jana Chetana Kendras* (Centres for People's Awareness) where villagers could discuss their problems. The *Kendras* were very popular especially among the women as they became a space where they could share their experiences with other women.

The anti-arrack agitation was sparked by a number of incidents. Some senior officials associated with the literacy programs had gone to Dubagunta, a small village 80 kilometers from the town of Nellore. As the officials planned the literacy program together with a group of villagers, two inebriated men confronted them, shouting that the officials had no business coming to teach in their village as they were happy the way they were. The women present at the meeting were very angry at the behaviour of the men and forced them to leave, vowing that they would attend literacy classes.

When the literacy classes started, one of these primers contained a story, *Seeta Katha* (The Story of Seeta). Seeta, the wife of an alcoholic, commits suicide after failing in her efforts to reform her husband. In Dubagunta, a lot of discussion followed the reading of the primer. Slowly some women opened up and stated that they had also contemplated suicide but could not do this because of their children. Many others spoke about the violence they faced daily, attributing it to their husband's alcoholism. These women had a very simple solution: if the arrack shops were closed, the men would not be able to purchase arrack. The next day, these women marched in protest and were successful in closing the village arrack shop.

The Dubagunta episode was soon quoted in another literacy primer, under the title, *Adavallu Ekamaithe* (If Women Unite). The lesson read thus,

This is not a story. This is the achievement of women who have studied in the evening school. Our village is Dubagunta. We are wage earners. We produce gold from earth. But what is the use? All our hard-earned money is spent on toddy and arrack. When our men folk do not have money, they sell away rice, butter, ghee or anything that fetches them arrack.... They take away everything they can lay their hands on.... Apart from drinking they abuse us, pick fights with us, slap our children. They make our day-to-day existence miserable.... Then we read the story of Seethama's death. We started thinking. Who is responsible for her death? We then told the *sarpanch* to close the arrack shop.

So next day hundreds of us marched out of the village and stopped a cart of toddy. We told the owner to throw away the liquor and all of us would contribute Rs.1 to compensate his loss. He was terrified. That is all. From that day no toddy has entered our village.

When the Jeep carrying arrack arrived in the village we gheraoed [surrounded] it and threatened the owner we would lodge a complaint with the collector. This sent a shiver down his spine. He closed his shop. Now we became strong and got confidence. We realized that this victory was possible only through education. This year no one dared participate in the arrack auction.

This lesson had an electrifying impact on women. Women in many other villages felt that if women in Dubagunta had succeeded so could they. In many villages women's committees were formed. First they tried to stop their husbands and other male relatives from drinking but found that this was a difficult goal to achieve while the liquor shops continued to exist in the village. Their fight then turned into a larger battle that involved the contractor, the excise department and the state itself. The women wanted to know why their village did not have drinking water and schools for their children but plenty of arrack shops. Why, they demanded, was the government so keen on supplying arrack?

Domestic violence due to the consumption of arrack was a problem shared by all the women. The anti-arrack agitation soon became a movement that spread like wildfire all over the state. The three districts of Nellore, Chittoor and Kurnool took the lead and from here the movement spread into the urban areas of Hyderabad and Secunderabad.

The Anti-Arrack Movement in Nellore District

Sister listen! Oh, brothers, listen! You should all come forward to stop sara! *Chase* sara *and mend your family! Shout that we shouldn't have* sara *and that it shouldn't be in the village!* (Song used in anti-arrack protests)

Nellore is one of the richest agricultural districts in the coastal region of Andhra Pradesh. Paddy, sugarcane and groundnuts are grown extensively in this district and agriculture flourishes though continuous floods and cyclones also take a heavy toll on crops. The 1990s also saw the rapid development of shrimp farming, controlled by big corporations. But, the land used for the shrimp farms became increasingly saline and could no longer be used for agriculture. Soon after, the corporations involved closed the shrimp farms. This adversely affected the agricultural labourers when the government withdrew its farming subsidies. As the men turned to drinking, the women found it difficult to make ends meet and the incidence of domestic violence increased.

Hundreds of the women we interviewed and who were participating in the agitation had similar stories to tell. The majority were victims of domestic violence. Many of these women had lost the economic help of their husbands, brothers or brothers-in-law who did nothing but drink all day. Women had to sell their *saris*, utensils, and even the *Tali* (a marriage sign worn by the women, consisting of a gold piece tied to a thread on a chain around their necks), to supply arrack. If the women refused to part with their things, the men became violent (Pande 1997).

The men were not contributing to the family income and the women's burden increased as the government's New Economic Policy abolished the subsidized rice program. They focused their anger on arrack.

In Nellore District many women came together and mobilized others in the fight against arrack. Meetings were organized in Saipeta and Kavali. Women faced the armed *goondas* of arrack contractors without fear. The police resorted to *lathi* charges (charging the women with wooden sticks and caning them) to bring the situation under control. The women retaliated by throwing chilli powder and stones at the police. Many of the women were charged with disturbing the peace. The women were not afraid of the police charges as such but dealing with the charges was time-consuming as it involved travel outside the village and this disturbed the women's daily routine.

In one of the subsequent protests, when a police sub-inspector verbally abused one of the women protesting against arrack on the Bombay highway in the district, the women joined together and staged a six-hour *dharna,* sitting on the highway and blocking traffic until the sub-inspector apologised and finally agreed that their cause was just and he would also sympathise with them and if need be join them in their struggles.

There were reports of contractors offering bribes to villagers for their co-operation to re-open the arrack shops. Amounts ranging between Rs.20 and Rs.2,000 had been offered. Some villagers were offered bribes in the form of water, schools and temples for their villages. The women thus decided that they would each contribute one rupee per person so the contractor did not suffer financial loss, but they would not allow the arrack shops to be open in their villages. Soon 200 shops were shut down and another 300 shops were partially closed (Pande 1997).

At first, the liquor contractors did not take the movement seriously, believing it would soon die a natural death and that they could reopen the arrack shops and go on with their business. However, as the movement spread in many villages, the contractors became alarmed and began to attack the women and file complaints against them. A group of contractors filed a claim in the High Court against the loss of their livelihood. They boycotted the auctions and demanded the repayment of rental fees as shops were closed and they had no revenues. They also demanded guarantees for the protection of their business in future. They challenged government officials to open at least 50 per cent of the shops closed due to the women's struggle.

The opposition parties also stepped in and demanded a policy decision by the government on the auctions in the wake of the anti-arrack movement launched by women in Nellore district. Throughout the agitation the government maintained they could not close arrack shops because the revenues from the sale of arrack was used to subsidize government welfare programs. Women of Nellore district were not convinced by the argument that the government could not run welfare programs like rice subsidies without revenues earned from the sale of arrack. Some women declared, 'We are willing to contribute our one day's wages for the government upkeep, but let the government close down the arrack shops first'.

Jagruti, an organization based in Nellore, filed a public interest writ petition. The organization secretary, G. Goplakrishnaiah Murthy, pointed out that the Supreme Court had ruled that no private individual or group could sell liquor. He contended that this law should be applied to the government as well and maintained that the sale of liquor by the government, even with regulatory measures, was a violation of the fundamental rights guaranteed in the constitution.[1]

As a result, Justice D. J. Jagannadha Raju stayed the arrack auction in the district on 21 September 1992. Bowing to pressure from the contractors, however, the stay was lifted on 23 September 1992 and the district administration scheduled another auction on 26 September 1992. Thousands of women gathered at the auction centre on the morning of the 26th. They attempted to prevent the officials and contractors from entering the building but were unsuccessful. The protestors then broke the police barricades, jumped the walls of the stadium and rushed into the office of the official responsible for the arrack auctions in the district. The contractors left immediately and the auctions were postponed indefinitely.

A state-wide conference on the anti-arrack struggle was scheduled to take place on September 28, 1992 in Hyderabad. Many women left Nellore for Hyderabad on September 27. The district administration announced on the evening of the 27th that auctions would be conducted the next day, September 28, 1992. Upon discovering this, however, the women postponed their trip and thousands more gathered at the stadium in Nellore where the auction was to take place. They expressed their resentment through songs and street plays. During that protest, women helped each other with childcare and other household chores to facilitate their presence at the stadium. As a result, the auctions were postponed once more and finally cancelled. In all, the auctions were postponed more than 30 times. Newspapers reported the government's subsequent decision to sell the arrack directly through the excise department in the district.

Meanwhile the village women found support for their demands from various organizations, intellectuals and lawyers who openly came out in favour of their demands. Nellore Bar Association decided that it would not take up any case filed against the participants of the movement. Soon an Anti-Arrack Movement Coordination Committee (*Sara Vyatireka Udyama Samnvya*) was formed to coordinate this movement in the district and it had the support of many left-wing organizations, political parties, student unions and women's groups.

In Dubagunta, nearly 90 per cent of the men were alcoholics. Rosamma, one of the women who led others in the village to close their local arrack shop, told us their village had such a bad reputation no one would offer their daughter in matrimony to any of the villagers. 'Who would give a girl in marriage in a village of drunkards?' she asked. After the ban on arrack things changed, however, and many of the villagers began to show a keen interest in literacy programs (Pande 1997). A special savings program, *Podupu Lakshmi* (Goddess of Thrift), was introduced by the District administrator. By each contributing one rupee daily, the women were able to save about Rs.60,000, which was then used in the village for extra bore wells, a community hall and a paved road to the nearest town (Pande 1997).

Anti-Arrack Movement in Chittoor District

Chase sara! *If all the women become one, no power can stop them.... All sisters in our village and all the sisters who feel bad, walk to the front with us, shoulder to shoulder, to chase this* sara, *useless* sara. (Song sung in anti-arrack protests)

The women's anti-arrack campaign in Nellore District in 1991 inspired women in the Eastern *mandals* (townships) of Chittoor District, adjacent to Nellore District. This movement spread throughout the entire district of Chittoor. The Dubagunta women became a role model for the women in this district and their success in closing the arrack shops led to stronger, more militant, women's groups. The anti-arrack agitation in Chittoor District started with the closing of one arrack shop in Ingamala village in 1991. Almost all the newspapers covered the incident. This had a significant impact on all the women of Chittoor. Women started organizing themselves by forming village committees. They decided to prevent the vans carrying arrack into the villages through *Rasta Roko* (stopping all roads—the women would lie on the roads blocking vehicles from passing). Soon there was hardly a *mandal* in Chittoor District that was free from the anti-arrack agitation. The women in village committees also mobilized to stop arrack auctions and an anti-arrack committee was formed comprised of different organizations.

This committee organized many meetings to discuss the movement and to lead it in a peaceful and progressive way. In many villages anti-arrack marches were organized. These marches and protests forced vehicles carrying arrack to retreat. In order to demonstrate to the Mandal Revenue Officer (MRO) how liquor had impacted on their families, three women threw away their *mangal sutras* (marriage symbols) in a telling gesture. A postcard movement was organized in which 5,000 post cards were mailed from each *mandal* to the Chief Minister of the state requesting the ban of arrack. With the help of the school children, the women also wrote letters to the Prime Minister demanding prohibition. Many women took their husbands to the local temples forcing them to take a vow that they would give up liquor. Anyone breaking the vow would be penalized with Rs.2,000 (Pande 1997).

The women of Chittoor, despite the police warnings and the attacks of *goondas*, were unwavering in their commitment to the movement. They picketed arrack shops and, in some cases confiscated and/or set fire to arrack barrels and sachets. Some kept watch on the men in the village who were vulnerable to drink. They would remain awake at nights and take turns to see that arrack was not brought to the villages. Some would get up early to follow their husbands who would buy arrack secretly on the pretext of going to the toilet.

Some of the slogans heard throughout this district were:

We don't want arrack but water to drink.

Nobody can stop the women's struggle.

We don't want Panasalas, (liquor shops) but Pathasalas (schools).

A step into the arrack shop is a step to death.

Give up arrack and go back to your families. (Pande 1997).

The Anti-Arrack Movement in Kurnool District

Each and every village spread the message of quitting sara. *Each and every mother's heart will speak of its abolition. Each and every woman should agitate and it should be written in the annals of Indian history.* (Song used in anti-arrack protests)

Kurnool District is in the Rayalseema region. In this region faction and gang leaders are very powerful forming an almost parallel government. Many of them are liquor contractors. The gang leaders collect illegal taxes from different sources in their region and have acquired a lot of power. Stone mining is an important industry. The stones are used as flooring tiles in construction. Many villagers informed us that these gang leaders would collect Rs.150 per lorry, Rs.50 per tractor and Rs.20 per bullock cart from those transporting stones from the district to other areas. They collect land taxes of Rs.100 to Rs.300 for each irrigated acre. The people pay these illegal taxes to avoid repercussions and this has become a way of life. The gangs maintain their own courts and deliver their own justice using any means necessary to maintain their supremacy. There is rivalry among the gang leaders and *goondaism*. In 1991-92, newspapers reported many murders in this district.

When liquor auctions were announced, it was well-known that the government intended to auction rights to 360 million litres of sara hoping to earn a revenue of Rs.210 billion per year. Gang leaders of the districts came to the town of Kurnool with their private armies to participate in the arrack auctions. Hundreds of women marched in protest to stop the auctions. They sat down for four hours in front of the Excise Office demanding that the auction be cancelled. When the district administration refused, the women jumped over the walls and rushed into the excise office. The *sara* contractors escaped on seeing the anger of the women. The women also lay down in front of the collector's car and refused to let it move.

This agitation and its success attracted people's attention to the anti-arrack movement. Many organizations came forward and gave support to the movement. The district administration announced the arrack auctions would take place again on September 21, 1992 at 11:00 am. Fearing the wrath of women, however, they conducted the auctions at 9:00 am knowing this was a time when they would be busy with their household chores and would thus not be able to do anything about it. When the women later found out they became angry and gathered at the auction centre for two hours in the afternoon. Since the auction was not completed that day, the next arrack auction was scheduled for September 23. This time the women finished their household chores very early and started gathering in front of the office from 8:00 am onwards. They sat down in front of the gates and prevented the staff from entering the building. The police were called in but the women were successful in having the auctions postponed.

It was not easy for the women to walk out of their homes and join in the protests. Most had children who had to be fed and their households depended on their completing chores like hauling water from various distances. Many women were also daily waged labourers, thus participating in a march meant that they did not get paid on that particular day. In spite of these hardships, the cause brought the women together and they supported each other by helping with everyone's daily chores. For example, women who had older children offered to help those with infants (Pande 1997).

The police and the local and district governments were taken aback by the women's solidarity and courage. *Stree Vimukthi*, (Progressive Organization of Women or POW) stepped in and helped the women in their struggle to close arrack shops in the villages. They campaigned throughout the district by conducting meetings, processions and *dharnas* (sit-ins) in front of government offices and arrack shops. It became clear that interfering in the arrack auctions was not enough, and that the only lasting solution lay in the closure of the arrack shops.

The women had become revolutionary in their battle against the sale of *sara*. The faction leaders of the district were shocked at the momentum gained by the anti-arrack movement. They feared this would break their traditional hold over their 'fiefdom'. They tried to deal with the agitators by sending their henchmen to attack the women in the movement. They even threatened the husbands asking them to control their wives and restrict their activity. Women spoke out openly against the faction leaders, criticizing their actions. They would not rest until all the *sara* shops were closed in their villages.

When the Chief Minister Shri Kotla Vijaya Bhaskar Reddy came to Srisailam on official business, the women gathered in front of the building where he was staying. Nearly 500 women held a *dharna* in front of the guesthouse with a demand to meet the Chief Minister. The Chief Minister had to cancel his appointment as he did not want to use police force in front of the press and media that had collected in large numbers. Having no alternative the Chief Minister agreed to meet with the women. The women demanded he commit to implementing prohibition. They shouted slogans and asked for a ban on the sale of arrack. The media coverage of this event was extensive.

The women had come to understand their collective strength and were ready to take on the local *goondas,* the arrack contractors, the police, the government officials and the state itself (Pande 2000). There was no stopping them.

The Movement in Urban Areas

Hyderabad became a meeting point of all the groups in the districts. The government was forced to bow down to the pressure and took the bold decision of banning arrack from October 1, 1993. It meant a huge revenue loss and, by 1995, the State incurred an annual loss of approximately Rs. 600 crores (or six billion Rupees) equivalent to almost two billion US dollars.

The Excise Department was entrusted with the job of preventing smuggling of arrack from neighbouring states, bootlegging, and the adulteration of toddy (another locally-produced spirit with low alcohol content) to make it more potent. In order to create awareness among the people, the Information Department launched a massive publicity campaign promoting the ban on arrack. Once again many cultural groups performed publicly in each village and through dance performances, plays, film screenings, slide shows and art exhibits the government demonstrated how arrack was causing problems for the average person and why they had banned it. Within a few weeks, posters against drinking were plastered all over the city. The government tried hard to regain the good will of the people.

The women's groups were happy with the government's efforts but soon saw their troubles return. As a result of the ban on arrack, the following year there was a substantial increase in the consumption of toddy that had not been banned. Toddy was also being adulterated with drugs like diazepam or chemicals like chloral hydrate that had lethal side effects. Since Indian Made Foreign Liquor (also marketed and sold by the government) and toddy were not banned, the number of shops selling these spirits increased. Women began to feel that their struggle, in reality, had not achieved much.

Total Prohibition

Many women's groups felt total prohibition was the only solution. Women's groups agreed to take up this issue under a common platform irrespective of any particular ideology and formed a Joint Action Forum. They collected signatures, arranged meetings in the slums, organized rallies, marches and picketing, starting their battle all over again.

On October 2, 1994, when India celebrated the birthday of Mahatma Gandhi, the father of the Nation, the women activists of Hyderabad decided that they would picket in front of the statue of Gandhi and prevent the ruling party leaders from garlanding the monument as was the tradition. As most of the women protesting that morning were from the urban areas, Telugu Desam's leader (the opposition party) N. T. Rama Rao joined them. He proclaimed that if his party were elected to power he would declare a total prohibition. Soon press photographers and television crews surrounded him. The police tried to move the protesters and when they refused the police again used a *lathi* charge, beating the women back. Hundreds of women were arrested. The next day newspapers carried photographs of women being caned by the police. The activists decided that they would go ahead with their demands by staging a protest to prevent the government from conducting ceremonial functions on November 1, the official day celebrating the formation of Andhra Pradesh.

The ruling Congress party did not want to oppose the women and be a target of criticism by everyone nor did it want to annoy the powerful liquor barons as state elections were around the corner. It tried to buy time by appointing various committees to look into the details of implementing prohibition. N. T. Rama Rao emerged as the biggest advocate of prohibition. Public memory being very short, nobody questioned him though it was under his leadership in 1982 that arrack was packaged and sold in sachets, making it more readily and widely available in order to increase government revenues. Women's groups went along in the hope of gaining a victory on the prohibition front. Since the elections were scheduled to take place in December, prohibition became a big issue with all the political parties vying to gain women's votes. Thus, a political party successfully appropriated the women's movement.

The Telugu Dasam party was elected with a thumping majority with 214 seats in an assembly of 294. On December 12, 1994, at the swearing in ceremony, N. T. Rama Rao again reiterated his commitment to total prohibition and declared that on January 1, 1995 prohibition would be implemented. An ordinance was soon promulgated to amend the *Andhra Pradesh Excise Act* and the manufacturing, distribution, selling and consumption of liquor became illegal and punishable by law. The women had, for the time being, achieved their victory.

Aftermath

Total prohibition was no doubt a populist measure for the government to get women's votes and, coupled with other populist measures like subsidized rice for people living below the poverty line and cheap electricity for farmers, ensured a majority for the party in the legislature. However, implementing and sustaining prohibition proved to be difficult for the newly-elected government.

In a coup within the Telugu Desam party, Chandra Babu Naidu, the son-in-law of the Chief Minister, N. T. Rama Rao and a member of the Cabinet wrested power from his father-in-law. The new government of Chandra Babu Naidu was sworn in 1995. The new government found itself in a catch-22 situation. It could not remove the ban on prohibition and annoy the women who had supported the party wholeheartedly, nor however could it deal with the worsening financial situation, a result of the loss of revenues from the sale of arrack. The period following 1995 saw an increase in taxes on water, electricity rates and other necessities. The women's anti-arrack movement and the prohibition were blamed for these developments.

Opinion on the prohibition policy became divided. Women's groups felt that this policy had resulted in many positive changes in the rural areas. There was a reduction in domestic violence and an increase in savings that significantly improved the people's standard of living. They felt strongly that the government needed to reduce its expenditures and look for other sources of revenue.

Another equally strong lobby felt that the government had no right to impose its rules and regulations on the social habits of private individuals. Questions were raised about the freedom of the people to decide for themselves. They did not like the financial burden of the state being passed onto the individual through heavy taxation.

By November 1995, the government's policy on liquor began to sag and prohibition was lifted. Today there is no prohibition in the state of Andhra Pradesh, though the price of liquor is very high compared to other states. Interestingly, the lessons in the literacy primers that sparked the original agitation are no longer used in the literacy programs.

Conclusion

The house where no one drinks is a house full of flowers of joy. We will no longer be quiet and we will no longer be beaten. We will shout and drive away sara! *Oh, brother, please stop drinking. Please don't go near the crematorium.* (Song used in anti-arrack protests)

Once total prohibition was achieved women's collectives dispersed. When prohibition was lifted by the government, women could not regain their earlier momentum. Women found that they lacked support from other quarters once political parties had appropriated the movement. Many of the left-wing groups distanced themselves from the movement because it was no longer seen as an achievement of women but was instead associated with the aims of a political party. Yet, the movement cannot be considered a failure. Given the various hurdles, the movement in and of itself was a considerable achievement, especially in the face of a recalcitrant state.

The literacy classes provided the space for this movement. Women used the literacy classes to hold discussions with other women and to articulate the challenges they faced. Initially, women who bore the guilt and shame of being beaten by their husbands did not speak for fear of being ostracized or stigmatized. However, these meetings provided them with the opportunity to share their experiences of financial problems and their husband's alcoholism as a major cause of domestic violence.

The movement was spontaneous, loosely organized and flexible in structure. There was no formally organized leadership. In the absence of a single leader many women in organizations, as well as women based in the villages, exhibited leadership qualities by effectively mobilizing other women. There were no detailed plans or pre-determined agendas. Women took action on the spot depending on the situation. Whether it was deciding to stop an arrack van from coming into the village, burning arrack sachets, marching in processions, submitting petitions, or punishing the village drunk, the women stopped the men from drinking. The women's strength lay in their large numbers and once they realized this they were increasingly able to mobilize other women to participate in their struggle.

The greatest achievement of the movement was in raising awareness in rural areas of issues such as domestic violence and empowering women to take control of their life situation. This has gone a long way to strengthening many democratic movements like *Panchayati Raj* (Movement for Local Self Government) which are currently working at the grassroots level in India today. Many of the self-help groups that were formed in Andhra Pradesh, inspired by women's mobilization against arrack, are also doing extremely well and have become role models for other states in India. Today many women's groups in Andhra Pradesh have successfully organized women around issues of domestic and public violence, land rights, poverty, environmental protection and globalization.

Through their participation in the anti-arrack movement, women became aware of their strengths and their ability to effect change in their villages and in society as a whole. Most importantly, their struggles against arrack brought the issue of violence against women to the public platform, allowing them to deal with the issue of domestic violence openly and publicly, and implement a strategy that had a significant impact on the sale of arrack in the region. The solidarity they built during that time, and continue to share today, is a crucial component in their continuing struggle for women's equality and human rights in India.

I would like to acknowledge the assistance received from the Department of Women and Child Welfare, Ministry of Human Resources, Government of India in providing the funds to carry out this project. I would also like to thank those hundreds of women we interviewed in the three Districts of Nellore, Kurnool and Chittoor who allowed us to become a part of their struggle. I would also like to acknowledge many of the women in Hyderabad and Secunderabad who were part of this movement and allowed me to participate in their meetings and discussions and have now become good friends.

Rekha Pande has been involved with women's issues for more than two decades. She is the co-editor of the Feminist Journal of International Politics *and is a member of the Core Advisory Group, Sensitization and Capacity Building Towards Eliminating Child Labour, MCR-HRD Institute, Government of Andhra Pradesh. She is also a Member of the National Resource Group of the Mahila Samakhya Programme (Education for Women's Equality), Ministry of Human Resource Development, Government of India. She has authored two books, (with Sub hash Joshi),* Gender Issues in the Police *(2000) and* Succession Struggle in the Delhi Sultanate *(1990) and has published articles in history and women's studies journals both in India and abroad.*

Notes

[1]   Article 47 of the Constitution states: '…It is the duty of the state to raise the level of nutrition and the standard of living and to improve public health—the state shall

regard the raising of the level of nutrition and the standard of living of its people and the improvement of public health as among its primary duties and in particular, the state shall endeavour to bring about prohibition of the consumption except for medical purposes of intoxicating drinks and drugs which are injurious to health'.

References

Article 47, Constitution of India. Online: http://www.ccsindia.org/RP01_6.html

Balgopal, K. (1992) 'Slaying of a spirituous demon', *Economic and Political Weekly*, 27, 46, 2457-2461.

Crimes in India (2000) Report, Crimes Record Bureau, Government of India.

Crimes in India (1997) Report, Crimes Record Bureau, Government of India.

Crimes in India (1996) Report, Crimes Record Bureau, Government of India.

Crimes in India (1995) Report, Crimes Record Bureau, Government of India.

Kishwar, M. and V. Ruth (eds) (1984) *In Search of Answers*, London: Zed Books.

Pande, R. (1997) *A Women's Movement: The Anti-Arrack Movement in Andhra Pradesh, Project Report,* Department of Women and Child Welfare, Ministry of Human Resources, Government of India, New Delhi.

Pande, R. (2000) 'From anti-arrack to total prohibition: the women's movement in Andhra Pradesh, India', *Gender Technology and Development*, 4, 1, 131-144.

COMING TO TERMS WITH THE PAST
IN BANGLADESH

NAMING WOMEN'S TRUTHS

BINA D'COSTA

Uncovering the truth from a shroud of erroneous national consciousness is a prerequisite for a nation's reconciliation. The wounds will only begin to heal when the victims are able to narrate their stories. The strategic use of rape as a genocide tactic makes the 1971 war for independence in Bangladesh a particular case study of gendercide and rape as a war-crime (Brownmiller 1975; Copelon 1995; Manchanda 2001). During the conflict an estimated 200,000 Bengali women were raped by soldiers (Copelon 1995: 197; Manchanda 2001: 30). Of those, some 25,000 were forcefully impregnated (Brownmiller 1975: 84). Yet, women's narratives that directly speak to the war crimes of 1971 have been excluded from the official construction of history-making. In this context, certain narratives were privileged and valorized while other narratives were silenced in order to create an 'acceptable' national story (Matsui 1998; Puja 1998).

National interpretations of rape and forced impregnation of women saw these experiences as being less about women themselves then about the challenge to Bengali nationalist and masculine identity. Bangladesh's lack of interest and failure to hold the perpetrators responsible for the war crimes led to a 'brittle peace' in the post-war state and growing frustration and resentment among its citizens about the fabrication of history through textbooks and government-sponsored media to serve the need of regimes. Bangladesh's history has been written and revised during each change of political regime, a process further complicated by the influence of military and religious elites. Eventually the reinstatement of some of the infamous pro-Pakistani political leaders who were directly responsible for the genocide committed in 1971 led to the construction of separate and parallel histories: one that exists in the official discourse and others that exist in micro-narratives, in memory and in lived experience.

While the gender aspects of this deliberate suppression of women's experiences of sexual violence during conflict have been investigated by feminist researchers (Menon and Bhasin, 1998; Butalia 1998 in South Asia for example), what remains is the question of how to bargain with a hostile state without compromising the agenda for justice, should suppressed stories come out. Local initiatives by Bangladeshi feminist or civil society organizations made several attempts to organize a platform for these silenced voices to be heard but they remain marginalized and unstable. The Peoples' Tribunal proceedings in 1993 discussed later in this article and the oral history report published by Ain-O-Shalish Kendro, a Bangladeshi human rights organization, in 2001 (Akhter, Begum, Hossain, Kamal and Guhathakurta 2001) are two examples where pro-liberation[1] civil society and the feminist human rights organizations made efforts to bring in women's voices. What strategies can feminists and activists use to create a stronger platform for action? Is there a way of applying feminist theorizing and activism around women's experiences in war zones, including mass rapes, in order to seek redress for historic wrongs? When the wall of silence that surrounds abuses of women's human rights breaks down with testimonies and evidence, how do we then translate emotions and passions into practical actions? This article addresses these questions by focusing on the vulnerability of women survivors of the 1971 war whose needs the state failed to address in a responsible and responsive manner and by exploring the impact of the state's 'managing' of the 1971 history on the lives of those women. I will argue that regional collaboration with other feminist and human rights organizations in India and Pakistan is an essential and strategic tool to create a platform that will not only provide the space for women to speak but also a network for action.

Context 1971: *Birangona*

Anti-colonial nationalism reached its highest peak of intensity in the Indian subcontinent after War II. Finally, on 3 June 1947, the British Government announced the 'Mountbatten Plan', a policy statement that recognized the inevitability of the partition of India. The Plan was implemented with the birth of Pakistan on 14 August 1947 under the provisions of the British *Indian Independence Act 1947*. Pakistan was comprised of five provinces in two regions: Punjab, Sindh, the North-West Frontier Province (NWFP), Baluchistan in West Pakistan and East Pakistan that became Bangladesh later on.

During their 24 years of union, the two regions of Pakistan enjoyed an uneasy partnership marked by intermittent regional, economic, political and cultural conflicts. Tension reached its zenith after a national election in 1970 escalated into an armed conflict in March 1971. For over nine months the Pakistani Army tried to subdue a rebellious civilian population. A guerilla insurgency continued under the leadership of *Muktibahini* (Liberation Army) in full force until 3 December 1971 when Inida stepped in primarily due to a refugee crisis across the border. Finally, Pakistan surrendered to a joint Bangladesh-India force and on 16 December Bangladesh emerged as a sovereign nation-state.

Estimates of loss of life during the war (excluding natural disasters) ranges from 200,000 to 1.5 million (LaPorte 1972: 105). Estimates of the number of dislocated and displaced refugees vary but the Pakistani Government cited a figure of two million while the Indian figure is ten million (LaPorte 1972: 105). Estimates by the United Nations and the World Bank support the Indian figure (*The New York Times* 1971). The national Liberation War of Bangladesh was also a story of women. Although the exact number is unknown, women participated as active combatants in the war. Women also assisted the freedom-fighters in a range of ways such as hiding them in their houses in times of crisis and providing them with food and medicine. When men in local communities fled the areas in fear of army persecution or to fight in the guerrilla warfare, women took care of the families. After the war, the widows were responsible for children and the elderly.[2] Finally, women were also the targets of rape and forced impregnation by the Pakistanis.

Birangona was the term introduced by the first Prime Minister of Bangladesh, Sheikh Mujibur Rahman ('Mujib'), to 'acknowledge' the 'sacrifice' of women for the freedom of Bangladesh in 1971. The literal translation of the word is 'war heroine'. Originally its use was intended to honour all women—political activists, freedom fighters, rape survivors and so on—who participated in the national struggle (Kamal 2001: 16). The term *Birangona* was intended to give these women an honorary status and to provide them with equal access to privileges in the public sector such as the education and employment rights granted to male freedom fighters (Pereira 2002). Unfortunately, rather than doing justice to the women, or effectively granting them a special status, the term labelled them as 'fallen' women. The word *Birangona* became a distinct marker or a boundary that identified these women as victims of rape and often subjected them to mockery. As Faustina Pereira (2002) points out, by its very nature, the term *Birangona* was a restrictive privilege. So strong was the stigma of rape in Bangladesh that most women did not take advantage of the title, 'because to do so would be tantamount to focusing on the scar of rape on the victim, thus forcing her to risk a social death' (Pereira 2002: 62).

On the other hand, the presence of *Birangona* women is a stinging reminder to the state of how the norm of *purdah*, or female seclusion, collapsed during the war when men were unable to defend their women. Not only were the women left unprotected during the war, but many were abandoned by their families after the war.

Over the years, as a response to this complex situation, concerned Bengalis, especially the cultural elites of the country, coined a new term: *nari jodjhya*, or, women combatants. Nonetheless, without an informed plan of action to change the patriarchal traditions and societal norms from which the stigma emanates, introduction of new or innovative terms did not prove adequate to positively address the situation of the *Birangona* women. Furthermore, *jodhya* implies active combat and thus does not apply to the many women whose lives were changed dramatically by a war that they neither initiated nor actively participated in. It also blurs the category between women combatants who were in the frontline and women who were victims of rape. Their battle with the structural violence did not end after the war was over (D'Costa 2002b). Their sacrifice has virtually gone undocumented (not unnoticed) and remains unaddressed.

As part of my Ph.D. research since 1999, I contacted several of the *Birangona* women, social workers and government officials who worked with the women. Although I received a variety of information from families and friends of the women, there were only twelve with whom I was able to establish some form of contact. However, none of the conversations were taped. Except for one woman, a combatant who was captured and kept under the army guard, none of the other interviews were carried on for a longer period of time or in detail. Most of the thoughts expressed in this paper are from my own personal experience as a Bangladeshi woman growing up with narratives that ran parallel to the government's version of history, from interviews with the local and international social workers, freedom-fighters and from conversations with people who experienced the war directly.

Responses to *Birangona*

Men who fought in the war were referred as *muktijodhya, mukti* meaning freedom and *jodhya* meaning combatant. The most common translation is 'freedom-fighters'. Acknowledging the courage and sacrifice of the *muktijodhya* men, the government awarded them with public service quotas to enter into various government departments. Bangladeshis commemorated them through patriotic songs, poems and literature. On the other hand, women were not beneficiaries of any actual or symbolic rewards. Although neither men nor women participated in the Liberation War with some form of benefits in mind, the governments ill-planned and biased policies created frustration within the community. I should note, however, that immediately after the independence of the country *Birangona* women did meet with some positive responses. *Muktijodhya* in formal and informal conversations with me suggested that they helped the women rescued from the rape camps in any way they could, such as offering them food, water and medicine, and taking them to health care units or back to their families. One of the freedom-fighters I spoke with clearly stated, 'We always treated the women with respect and we were genuinely concerned about their suffering' (D'Costa 2000b). In contrast, the initial responses of the women's families were not positive. In middle-class families, the issue of rape was treated with secrecy and many families never revealed their daughters were 'taken' by the Pakistani army. A shroud of silence covered their stories. Some families took pregnant women to clinics for abortions.

One respondent commented:

It still remains as a scar in my heart. The government allowed abortion on a mass scale. They did not want any Pakistani child. Either they were to be aborted or to get out of the country as soon as possible. We had incubators and we were prepared to take the premature babies. (D'Costa 2000c)

Those families that could afford to exile their daughters to neighbouring India or one of the western countries preferred to do so in order to quietly get rid of their family 'shame'. If the women were in an advanced stage of pregnancy, they were left in rehabilitation centres or clinics to give birth after which the babies were given up for adoption. When I asked Geoffrey Davis[3] who worked as a physician in Bangladesh immediately after the war if there were some women who were reluctant to have abortions or give up their babies for adoption he said 'Well ...a few of them did...' When asked if he knew what happened to them he answered, 'I have no idea. ISS [International Social Service] was there to get as many babies as they could. Because there were less and less babies available for adoption in America and Western Europe and they wanted as many babies as they could get' (D'Costa 2002a). Some 25,000 cases of pregnancy were reported after the war. However, to my knowledge no official or unofficial statistics exist that indicate the number of women who had abortions or the number of babies sent to other countries.

Three related concerns in Bangladesh contributed to the silence surrounding rape. First, because reintegration into society was given the highest priority, rape as war crime and crimes against humanity received no significant attention from the government and its elite segments. Second, the post-war diplomacy between India, Pakistan and Bangladesh compromised the trial of war-criminals and their collaborators which had serious consequences for seeking justice in post-war Bangladesh.[4] Third, the gradual rehabilitation of Bengali collaborators of the Pakistani Army into the Bangladesh political scenario at both local and state government levels silenced the micro-narratives through direct or indirect coercion. In particular, with the lifting of the ban on extremist religious political parties (Jahan 1995: 97), the *Birangona* issue was buried further and there was no coordinated and sustained feminist movement/consciousness to make available a 'pro-women' political language.

In addition, while in the Pakistani context 'purity' meant creating a 'proper' Muslim identity that would fit the Muslim Pakistani imagination, in the context of Bangladesh it meant 'purging' the state of the Pakistani blood. Children were vivid reminders of the attack on a 'pure' Bengali identity. Therefore, the Bangladeshi state responded to the issue of wartime pregnancy in a way it perceived as legitimate: it exercised its authority over women's bodies and their maternal role through abortion and adoption programs. The needs of the women were insignificant in this nationalist construction of identity. Clinics, international adoption agencies and religious organizations acted as surface mechanisms for the state and often also against the wishes of some of the women, thereby victimizing them for a second time. As far as Bangladesh was concerned, the task of flushing out 'impure' Pakistani blood was necessary for the honour of the new nation. The abstract notions of purity and honour are dangerous rationales for which women often pay heavily. The appropriation of birth, denying it and, when possible, stopping it through state abortions, demonstrates the power of the state over women's bodies when women have little or no control of their reproductive rights (Das 1995: 55-83).

Women are symbolically distanced from birth by the nation-state's narrative. The abortion and adoption programs carried out by the Bangladesh Government following the war indicate the forcible appropriation of women's bodies for the interest of the nation.

In the context of the mass suicide of women during 1947 Partition[5] Urvashi Butalia (1998) argued that these actions were approved because women were protecting the purity of the community whose borders they constituted. Similarly, in 1971, the issue of 'choice' became even more problematic in terms of the complex intersections of gender, religion and national interests in which women were trapped.

Social workers, government officials and medical staff working in the rehabilitation centres and clinics were, like the *Muktijodhya*, genuinely compassionate towards the survivors. Dr. Geoffrey Davis recalled many women's stories.

> Some of the stories they told us were appalling. Being raped again and again and again by large Pathan soldiers. You couldn't believe that anybody would do that! All the rich and pretty ones were kept for the officers and all the other ones were distributed among the other ranks. And the women had it really rough. They did not get enough to eat. When they got sick, they got no treatment. A lot of them died in those camps. There was an air of disbelief about the whole thing ... but the evidence clearly showed that it did happen. (D'Costa 2002a)

When I asked Dr. Davis if the social workers and the medical personnel involved respected women's choices to either have abortion or to go through with the pregnancy, he replied,

> Nobody wanted to talk about it. You could ask questions and get an answer. Quite often it would be that they couldn't remember. And the men [in their families] didn't want to talk about it at all! Because according to them the women had been defiled [emphasis mine]. And women's status in Bangladesh was pretty low anyway. If they had been defiled, they had no status at all. They might as well be dead.... (D'Costa 2002a)

An employee who had worked in the rehabilitation centres and was particularly involved in the adoption programs commented, 'There was a wound. We tried to rehabilitate them, tried to accept the situation they were in. And we would never write names, neither addresses. Stigma would remain if people knew' (D'Costa 2000c).

The attitudes and decisions taken by the social workers and medical staff in the rehabilitation centres reflect patriarchal, traditional values about family, community norms and state policies and they thus endorsed decisions to reintegrate women into society as soon as possible by keeping their trauma and ordeal a secret, contributing to the silencing in official documents and personal narratives.

In the aftermath of the war in Bangladesh, there was no large-scale protest or demonstration by the women's organizations to demand justice on behalf of the *Birangona*. There also existed a vast power discrepancy between the *Birangona* women and the social workers, government officials or others who were involved in the rehabilitation programs for the women undertaken by the government. The shame and stigma attached to sexual violence were not challenged. Instead there was an implicit charity-focused approach that denied women the opportunity to voice their protests if they were unwilling to go ahead with the state's prescribed policies. Women were cast as victims and only as victims did they deserve the state's assistance.

The Bangladesh government gradually eradicated the programs principally designed for *Birangona* women. Initially, in 1972, in response to women's initiatives, it set up the Women's Rehabilitation Organization to institutionalize women's rehabilitation programs and place them under the management of the National Central Women's Rehabilitation Board which coordinated the government's postwar policies. In 1974, the name of the board was changed by legislation to the Bangladesh Women's Rehabilitation and Welfare Foundation (Gafur 1979: 555).[6] Eventually, the government changed the profile of the Foundation and merged it under the Women's Division of the Women's and Children Affairs Ministry. Programs such as those 'to free women from the *unchosen* [my emphasis] curse of motherhood' (Gafur 1979: 555) and to encourage men to marry *Birangona* (Gafur 1979: 429) reveal that patriarchal and traditional beliefs played out in decisions made in relation to *Birangona* rehabilitation programs (D'Costa 2003). The state-sponsored abortion and adoption programs prioritized the national identity as Bengalis and identified children carrying Pakistani blood as liabilities. In an atmosphere filled with nationalistic passion and hatred towards Pakistanis, *Birangona* women who were already vulnerable relied on the state's prescribed policies and were unable to articulate resistance if they had any.[7] Since the pregnant body was a vivid reminder of the Pakistani father, *Birangona*'s reproductive rights belonged to the nation. The primary goal of the state in relation to *Birangona* was to reintegrate the women into the traditional gender roles they had previously performed as housewives, mothers or daughters. Women's silence guaranteed that the state's rehabilitation programs remained unchallenged. This silence also ensured that the elite narrative construction of the past gained official acknowledgement.

Revisiting the Past

The 1971 war in Bangladesh led to a complete breakdown of state and community. The question of justice assumed great urgency but there was no common understanding of how to achieve it. In the absence of legal norms or any nationally organized political forces, there were several individual and local efforts to respond to the demands for justice. The most successful of all these efforts were led by a single woman, Jahanara Imam. Rumi, her son, participated in the war as a *muktijodhya* (freedom-fighter) and was brutally tortured and killed by the Pakistani army in 1971. Her book *Ekatturer Dinguli* (*Those Days of '71*) is an autobiographical record of the violence of 1971.

Popularly known as *shahid jononi* (martyr mother), Jahanara Imam, chairperson of the *Ghatok Dalal Nirmul Committee* (Committee for the Elimination of Killers and Collaborators) (Kabir 1993) began a crusade in January 1992 directed against Golam Azam (Ghosh 1993: 703-704), possibly the most notorious collaborator with the Pakistani army in Bangladesh.[8] Under Imam's leadership, intellectuals, students, freedom-fighters (both men and women) of the 1971 war, war widows and families—especially those of children whose parents had been killed during the war—formed a pro-liberation organization, *Projonmyo Ekattur* (Generation '71), which together with *Birangona* demanded a People's Tribunal to bring Golam Azam and other war criminals to trial. By February 1992, the National Coordinating Committee for Realization of Bangladesh Liberation War Ideals and Trial of Bangladesh War Criminals of 1971, which integrated the political parties in opposition and cultural elites of Bangladesh, was formed to hold the People's Tribunal. In Imam's words: 'Prompted by our commitment to the values of the Liberation War and love for our country and aggrieved by the failure of the government to try the war criminals...' the Committee decided to unearth 'evidence of complicity of all collaborators of war crimes, crimes against humanity, killings and other activities' (qtd. in Ziauddin 1999).

After three months of intensive organizing and activism, the People's Tribunal was held in Dhaka on 26 March 1992. Nearly 200,000 people from across the country participated (*Dhaka Courier* 1992). This massive popular movement demonstrated that Bangladeshis were interested in seeking justice for 1971. Unfortunately, the quality of the Commission reports were very poor, the language emotive rather than reasoned, and they lacked details that would lead to any possible criminal prosecutions (Ziauddin 1999). After Imam's death in 1994, political differences significantly weakened the movement.

Despite the intervening years, the silence surrounding the rape of women in 1971 was still prevalent and the rapes remained well-guarded secrets within the affected families. Some viewed the 'digging into the past' as an unnecessary exercise that would cause them more pain and misery, especially because no organized effort to seek redress had occurred in the country. Moreover, various interest groups ignored the sensitive nature of the women's stories and the fact that disclosing their identities might contribute to the stigma they were forced to bear by their communities. For example, at the Dhaka People's Tribunal in 1992 mentioned above, the court was not able to hear the testimonies of victims and survivors of the 1971 war due to a government-sponsored assault[9] by the police on the organizers (Kabir 2000: 29). The Government also filed cases of treason against the organizers (Kabir 1999: 20) that stagnated the movements afterwards.

The three rape survivors who were brought in from the rural areas of Kushtia, a southern region in Bangladesh to provide testimonies were also unable to narrate their experiences. None of them had clear ideas about the tribunal proceedings, what their testimonies actually signified and what implications these public testimonies might have for their present lives (Begum 2001: 82, 86). The local activists who brought them to Dhaka had not asked them if they wanted to testify either (Begum 2001: 102) and they were thus left in the dark. Yet, their photos and stories appeared in newspapers the next day (*Dhaka Courier* 1992; Kabir 1993; Begum 2001). As a consequence, these women were excluded from participating in the life of their communities.[10] This experience had a significant impact on the women's increasing reluctance to speak with 'outsiders'.

Most women still do not feel comfortable in talking about the pain and trauma of 1971. Their discomfort is a combination of traumatic memories, traditional parameters of shame and purity, the stigma attached to the rape experience, the need to reintegrate into their society and to address basic requirements for survival. In combination, all these have led the women to create their own negotiated survival techniques 'just to get on with their lives' as one *Birangona* I interviewed in 1999 commented.

In 1994, Nilima Ibrahim, a prominent social worker appointed by the Prime Minister, Sheikh Mujibur Rahman, to coordinate the rehabilitation program, published a two-volume book, *Ami Birangana Bolchi*, the only available collection of testimonies of women survivors in print until 2001 when Ain-O-Shalish Kendro (Akhter et al. 2001) published its oral history report. In the preface of the 1998 edition Ibrahim writes,

> I promised my readers to publish the third volume of *Ami Birangona Bolchi* ("I, the Birangona"). However, I no longer want to do so, for two reasons. First, my physical condition: Writing about Birangona women affected me both physically and emotionally. Second, the present society's conservative mentality. They [society] do not hesitate to call the Birangona sinners. Therefore, I don't want to insult those women all over again who were not allowed to live an easy and normal life even 25 years ago.... In addition, many compassionate people requested me for their [*Birangona*] contacts. I believe, it wouldn't be right to rub salt on the wounds of those who we coldly banished from our community one day. [my translation]

Until her death in June 2002, Ibrahim refused to reveal any personal information about the women. In her conversation with me in 2000 she mentioned that she was very concerned about the renewed interest to publicize the stories of *Birangona* women. I realized that she still wanted to protect the women's privacy and did not want to cause any harm to them (D'Costa 2000a). This reaction was not surprising considering the way in which women's stories have been exploited or used without any legal, financial or moral support being offered in return.

Nevertheless, a small but significantly important number of *Birangona* were prepared to come forward and document their narratives. If an action-oriented network is organized to seek justice for crimes committed during the 1971 war, some *Birangona* would be interested in participating. In her interview with me, Halima Parveen, who fought in the war and was raped in captivity, indicated that she would testify and encourage other women to do so (D'Costa 2002b). Sharing their war memories in a woman-friendly environment sensitive to their traditional and cultural restrictions would faciliate the participation of many *Birangona* in this kind of network.

It has become customary in Bangladesh to demand an official apology from the Pakistani government and that war criminals be tried during the months of March and December. March and December hold special meaning in Bangladesh's history. On 26 March 1971 independence was declared and on 16 December 1971 the Pakistani army surrendered, marking the liberation of the country. Unfortunately, over the years these demands have not been successfully coordinated nor consistently presented.

For example, in December 1996, the Shommilito Nari Shomaj (SNS) (a broad network of feminist activists in Bangladesh) broadcast on Bangladesh Television four women's testimonies from Ibrahim's book. After the telecast a few *Birangona* contacted Nilima Ibrahim and the feminist network SNS to share their stories (D'Costa 2000a). There was a newspaper report on the communication between some *Birangona* and the SNS. It revealed that the SNS was approached by one of the women who bluntly said, 'I was raped by the Pakistani army in 1971'. When SNS activists asked the women who contacted them why they were coming forward after 26 years of silence, one woman replied, '… because now I am getting the courage to do so'. Several others gave similar explanations. One rape survivor stated, 'I was raped and I would like to tell my son about it but do not know how to do so' (Khan 1997). These women wanted the Pakistani government and its collaborators to be brought to trial internationally. It was the crucial factor in their decision to communicate with Ibrahim and other social workers whom they trusted. Despite the reactions to the *Birangona* as a result of the television show, with the memory of the People's Tribunal in 1992 still fresh in mind, women's groups remained sensitive in bringing the women into the public.

Although women's groups did not pursue the issue, *Birangona* continued their demands for justice. Ferdousi Priyobhashini, another courageous *Birangona* woman who came forward with her story stated: 'I am one of the 250,000 raped women of '71. I am telling you these stories because, those who killed three million Bengalis in '71 and raped 250,000 women, still have not been brought to justice' (qtd. in Priyobhashini 1999: 67).

Halima Parveen reiterated the demands of other women and commented, 'I will fight with even the last bit of strength I have in my body to demand justice from Bangladesh government and from Pakistan' (D'Costa 2002b). It is evident that despite the hardship and possible consequences of disclosure, if an appropriate forum is provided, women will come forward to speak.

Although making women visible is necessary, it is not enough, alone, to enable feminists to provide a full analysis of women's exploitation within the nation-state system (Waylen 1996; Rai 2002). While it is possible to arrive at a macro-level understanding of nationalism's gender-blind approach, without looking at micro-level and regional politics, a feminist scholarship of post-conflict situations will be unable to address the 'woman question' in diverse locations. Similar to other regions in South Asia, cultural and regional experiences of women vary immensely and women respond quite differently—and sometimes from contradictory positions—according to their backgrounds and politics. *Birangona*, especially those who live in rural areas, might lack the means to reflect upon and to articulate their own experiences except through the socially-accepted norms with which they are already familiar. Focusing on the lived reality of women and offering them choices so that they can decide themselves whether or not they have been silenced in the national history-making of the state may be more important. This might create social awareness that will serve as the driving force behind a common platform of action.

The Movement in Bangladesh and Feminist Organizing in South Asia

Despite holding fragmented and dispersed views, Bangladeshi women's organizations have successfully raised numerous feminist issues. The space of social activism is occupied by activists well versed in the social and political movements of South Asia, especially of India. As political activists, Bengali women contributed to the anti-colonial nationalist struggle for the independence of the Indian subcontinent. This experience of social and political activism continued to shape the character of the Bangladeshi feminist movement after 1971, which was also influenced by its own local historical struggle against patriarchy, religion, traditional practices and poverty.

In Bangladesh, women's rights activist groups raised women's issues in national and international policy levels, women's research and advocacy organizations, and developed and promoted public awareness. Various non-governmental bodies mobilized women at the micro-level, allowing them to engage and participate in networking. All these streams are also engaged in shared dialogues and may interchange roles for various purposes.

While discussing the gender dynamics of nationalism, Valentine Moghadam (1994: 2) observed that movements for national liberation were rarely extended to the autonomy and liberation of women. As I discussed earlier, the policies for the rehabilitation programs in Bangladesh after 1971 that were initiated irrespective of women's wishes and consent are examples of the ways women's rights are subsumed and subordinated to a national 'right'. Generally, women's liberation has been regarded as being unfavourable to the identity and existence of the national group. During the 1971 nationalist struggle, Muslim Bengali women went out onto the streets in active resistance. This liberating gesture served several purposes. It demonstrated to the Pakistani rulers that Bengali culture was different from West Pakistani traditions, that Bengalis shared similar cultural values irrespective of whether they were Hindu or Muslim, and that Bengali women were more liberated than West Pakistani women. Many Muslim Bengali women participated as activists in their country's national movement. Their unique cultural identity became their symbol and the use of the phrase 'Muslim Bengali woman' had a political rather than a religious connotation.

Although their political activism played a crucial role in achieving independence, after their country was born these women were encouraged to go back to their traditional roles as wives, mothers and daughters and as protected beings. Moreover, the national movement was not concerned with women's 'actual' emancipation. Therefore, the national Liberation War of Bangladesh failed to achieve freedom for all its citizens. National liberation rhetoric had served to consolidate emotion in order to create an active struggle against the Pakistani Army, using the situation of women. In reality, women were still seen to belong in the private sphere, which is a complex construction of traditional, religious and cultural values.

The image of Bengali women as 'cherished and protected mothers/wives/daughters' was, over the years, challenged by an awareness that women are subordinated in the hierarchical gender relations in Bangladesh, which denies them both social power and autonomy over their own lives. Traditionally, the honour of the family is linked to the virtue of its women, and men are responsible for protecting this honour (Kabeer 1998: 100). The experience of 1971 helped women to raise their concern about their subordination. The norm of female seclusion and the so-called 'safety' of the private sphere was shattered by the 1971 war when women could not be protected by their men against aggression and were then abandoned, through no fault of their own (Jahan 1995: 102).

Since the Liberation War, a Bengali ruling class comprising an unstable class alliance of an underdeveloped bourgeoisie, the military and the bureaucracy has been in power (Kabeer 1998: 99). Though regimes have changed, increasing impoverishment and social differentiation and a steady rise in aid dependency has persisted. At the same time, increased violence against women in both the public and private spheres has helped to develop a greater awareness of the position of women in Bangladesh. This awareness has also been informed by developing communication with other states and increased participation in transnational feminist programs, including attendance at international conferences, workshops and dialogues, and a significant interest worldwide in addressing gender inequality.

During both the anti-colonial movement against the British and the Bangladesh national liberation movement, Muslim Bengali women appeared in public and participated in protests, demonstrations and other forms of political campaigns for the freedom of their land. Their visibility became an important symbol in the Bengali national movement.

During the national movement of Independence for Bangladesh, women organized and participated in protests against the repressive measures taken by the military regime of Pakistan. The military regime detained numerous political activists and leaders without trial during 1966–70. A group of young women activists, most of whom were associated with leftist organizations, approached the Awami League (AL), the strongest political party in East Pakistan, and with the help of political leaders formed a joint women's action committee to organize protests by the wives and mothers of political prisoners for their release (Jahan 1995: 93). This eventually led to the formation of the *Mahila Parishad* (Women's Caucus), which is now the largest and most important women's organization in Bangladesh.

Both during the liberation struggle in 1971 and in the aftermath of the creation of Bangladesh, women activists enthusiastically expressed their solidarity in the construction of the new nation-state. However, as Rounaq Jahan (1995) observes, despite their significant role in the war, the new government soon marginalized women:

> Interestingly, the nascent women's movement did not work actively to mobilise support for these rape victims either. In reflecting on the reasons for this, women leaders offer a variety of perspectives. Many groups and individuals were still hesitant to challenge the society's strong patriarchal traditions and feared that doing so would invite backlash that could hurt the victims more. The groups were very new, with limited scope and membership, and as such still quite vulnerable. Even some organizations such as Mahila Parishad that later vocally and successfully challenged the government's stand on gender violence did not articulate a position on rape at this time. (95)

Some organizations and individuals also wished to remain 'apolitical', implying that even after more than three decades of independence the stories of women can make some powerful groups 'uncomfortable' and 'angry'. Cautioned by the drastic curtailment of women's rights in Iran and Pakistan that accompanied the rise of political power of Islamists (Jahan 1995: 98), the Bangladesh women's movement sought to build public opinion in support of secular politics. During the Decade of Women (1975-1985) Bangladesh governments invited women's groups to advise in preparing official reports for intergovernmental discussions and agreements that provided the opportunity to women's groups to articulate their positions in the government agenda (Jahan 1995: 98). With gender equity and poverty alleviation programs at the forefront of development planning, Banlgadeshi women researchers and NGO employees were invited to voice their opinions in international conferences and workshops. This opened up the possibilities of cross-border dialogues. To serve the interests of its development policies, governments encouraged this dialogue and the sharing of views and information with women's groups in other countries. Despite the changing political situation in Bangladesh, dialogues among women inside Bangladesh enabled them to create partnerships with women's organizations overseas in order to address specific issues, especially development and women's empowerment.

While an increase in women's status is essential for gender equity, the issue of violence against women has also been addressed strategically by women's organizations. For example, Ain-O-Shalish Kendro, Odhikar, Shaishob, Shakti and Nari Pakkha publicized cases of dowry-related family violence and murder, acid throwing and rape (inclusive of rape in police custody and rape of adolescents), creating a public outcry. Their history, activism and the contemporary politics of Bangladeshi nationhood within which a vibrant feminist movement thrived, saw these organizations adopt agendas that addressed violence against women, patriarchal dominance, common class problems, labour exploitation and unequal economic arrangements within specific national contexts. The activism of non-state actors organized into local networks has had a positive impact in agenda-setting, framing and spreading norms, and changing state practices.

The similarities of women's movements in the Indian subcontinent derives from the fact that India, Pakistan and Bangladesh have a shared colonial national past that utilized the situation of women for the existence of the nation state. Furthermore, regional workshops, conferences and academic exchanges between activists and scholars regarding women's rights have contributed to the growth of a shared and coherent women's networking and intellectual activism in South Asia. Based on common cultural and traditional backgrounds, and on the shared history of nation-building in different states, these networks have exchanged ideas, formulated strategies and developed new ways of addressing the historical abuse of women and seeking restitution in the present.

Women's movements in South Asia have a centuries-old history of resistance to colonialism and patriarchy. Salma Sobhan argues:

> Although not all women who are politically active are a part of it— choosing instead to belong to the women's fronts of various political parties, including those based in religion—it is possible to identify a mainstream South Asian Women's movement that cuts across national boundaries. The rights that women in South Asia are fighting for run the gamut from issues of elementary human rights and equality rights to issues that will decide whether or not this world survives. (2003: 26).

Feminist solidarity is rather fragile in the region because opportunities to meet are hard and resources for regional meetings are not easy to come by (Menon-Sen 2002: 132). Despite these barriers, South Asian women's groups recently held several regional dialogues affirming their commonalties. One outcome of regional dialogues among the feminist activists and women's groups of South Asia is the South Asian Feminist Declaration, the outcome of one of the first regional meetings of women's groups in January, 1989 in Bangalore, India, which is an expression of personal/political commitment to a broad-based South Asian Feminist Platform (Menon-Sen 2002: 133). It states:

> We come from different countries in South Asia—Bangladesh, India, Paki-

stan, and Sri Lanka. Divided by geopolitical boundaries, we are all bound together by a common South Asian identity. This identity expresses itself both in the linkages we have with each other and in the struggles each of us is involved with in the women's movement in our respective countries.

Feminist exchanges between South Asian feminists have created several coalitions, such as the South Asian feminist solidarity platform, the South Asian Network of Gender Activists and Trainers (SANGAT), which comprises activists from Bangladesh, India, Nepal, Pakistan and Sri Lanka. In 2001, SANGAT organized a workshop for various movements, to give them a platform to make their demands for reforms such as sustainable agriculture, right of information and self-government, and for protests against displacement of the population in the building of large dams (Menon-Sen 2002).

Radha Kumar's *The History of Doing: An Illustrated Account of Movements for Women's Rights and Feminism in India, 1800-1990* (1993) traces the construction of women's activism in various campaigns and struggles. Kumar argues that while the earlier reform discourse rationalized the family, the later discourse of nationalism created the archetypal mother figure. Women became socially useful for the nationalist movement, which saw the symbolic use of 'mother' as a rallying device, from the feminist assertions of women's power as mothers of the nation to the Gandhian celebration of the spirit of endurance and suffering embodied in the mother.

In pre-Partition India, the nationalist-feminist movement raised the issue of rape mainly to indicate the 'excesses' committed by the British state as a foreigner-colonizer. In post-Partition India, the left and far right raised the issue of rape to indicate the 'excesses' committed by the state and the ruling class (Kumar 1993: 128). Indian feminist campaigns against rape in the last two decades have focused on custodial and mass rape because of the scale and frequency of police rape in India.

The feminist understanding of rape as an expression of class and gender-based power was shouldered aside by the patriarchal view of rape as a violation of honour and the need to ensure the protection of women (Kumar 1993: 142) that is quite similar to Bangladesh. Despite their record of mobilizing against rape and domestic violence, the progressive women's movements in India have been unable to anticipate and counter either the incitement to or the acts of communal violence. Although communal violence of a gendered nature played a central role in the formation of the Indian nation, feminists such as Veena Das (1995), Urvashi Butalia (1995a, 1995b) and Ritu Menon (1998) initiated discussions of nation, violence and sexuality only in the mid-1990s. In reconstructing the gendered history of the Partition of India and Pakistan in 1947, Butalia (1995a, 1995b) and Ritu Menon and Kamla Bhasin (1996) discussed the symbolic use of violence suffered by women in the construction of the nation-state. This approach emerged mainly from discussions of the scholar-activist circle in India that spread to Bangladesh and Pakistan. Inspired by the scholar-activist feminist contribution of these dialogues, Ain-O-Shalish Kendro took the initiative to document women's testimonies from the 1971 Bangladesh Liberation War. Their oral history project (Akhter et al. 2001), which continues today, proved to be a very significant step toward examining the gendered construction of the Bangladeshi national identity. However, it also necessitated a research project on a broader scale.

Feminist scholars have established that women's bodies are charged with metaphorical meanings profoundly rooted in a social and cultural structure that is beyond the physical control of individual women (Brownmiller 1975; Seifert 1993). In times of conflict and violence, women's bodies often become the carriers of violent messages between different ethnic groups. The symbolism of female bodies being used to signal disorder in the imagined social and civil life has received increased scholarly attention since the recent Balkan wars (Stiglmayer 1994). Paola Melchiori suggests that this reproduces women's original role, 'a general exchange coin' that is the concealed basis of a social bond (Melchiori 1997: 7). Feminist scholars in various South Asian regions have also started to recast questions in relation to historical conflicts after interest in the symbolism of women's bodies was renewed.

While some of the key feminist activists in Bangladesh felt that silence about the incidence of war rape was necessary to erase the stigma suffered by the women, ironically this silence reinforced that stigma. This is where the current women's movement in Bangladesh could make a difference. It could raise public awareness of the *Birangona* issue and demand justice and reparation for the women, particularly through establishing linkages with the regional women's movements. By doing so, the Bangladeshi women's movement could also provide a way for Bangladeshi society to deal with a past that affects its present and future so strongly. It could provide a useful understanding about revising the way in which assistance is delivered to the women and their families. Without an important revision of the policy model designed to help these women, there will be no permanent solution.

Conclusion: The Need for Regional and Transnational Links

A growing body of work in feminist activism points to the importance of networking in the global space and the challenges faces by global activism of women (Keck and Sikkink, 1998; Thompson, 2002). Transnational feminist dialogues have developed insight and strategies at regional, local and national levels to promote women's human rights (Alvarez 1999; reprinted in this volume, pp. 122-148). Two successful examples of transnational networking are the Global Tribunal on Violations of Women's Human Rights held in Vienna in June 1993 (Bunch and Reilly 1994) and the Women's International War Crimes Tribunal on Japan's Military Sexual Slavery held in Tokyo in December 2000 (Puja 2001).

At the local level, the Bangladeshi feminist movement may gain insight from the strategies used to establish and maintain these networks, and formulate its own strategies within the boundaries of international and national laws. However, the first step towards seeking any form of justice needs to be a strong regional network for action within South Asia, especially with the Indian and Pakistani women's groups with expertise in charting women's experiences of partition. I suggest that the women's movement in Bangladesh could productively link with the regional movement in South Asia and transnational networks to design, and gain support for, a fact-finding project to document and produce a report comprising the narratives of women's experiences in 1971. This project could be an important step on the path of reconstructing history and addressing multiple truths in order to clear the way for justice.

There are several rationales for this approach. First is the need for an exchange of information. India, Pakistan and Bangladesh were all involved in the 1971 war and have documents in both government and non-government archives, which could be accessed, albeit not without difficulty, by local women's organizations. Indian and Pakistani women's groups would also prove to be invaluable in documenting memories, testimonies of army officials, social workers, historians and emergency staff who were in any way involved during and after the war. Their language skill, easier access in the local areas and knowledge of local cultural and traditional ways would be additional benefits for this process of investigation.

Secondly, Indian feminists already have a decade long experience in collecting testimonies of the Partition riots of 1947. A Bangladesh oral history project could benefit from a dialogue with Indian feminists where these experiences are shared and that model is used to develop Bangladesh's own. On the other hand new possibilities would open up for Indian feminists to collect testimonies of survivors of Partition violence in Bengal that were previously absent from Indian oral history project findings. This would have broader implications for the region as the 1947 Partition, the 1971 Bangladesh war of independence and recent Kashmir conflicts are inescapably linked and have gendered narratives of their own.

Finally, India is considered a significant threat to Bangladesh's security, a trump card used by political groups during elections. Pakistan is also viewed with distrust and often with dislike by Bangladeshis. If the feminists of the region join hands in peace, it might lead to a future of mutual respect and sharing of responsibilities in other areas. A feminist alliance might also release these countries that have remained prisoners of the past for far too long.

Bina D'Costa is the John Vincent Research Fellow (2003-04) at the Department of International Relations, Research School of Asia and Pacific Studies, the Australian National University. Her research areas include feminist theories of international relations; gender and governance; the theories of citizenship; conflict management and peace-building issues; and activism and transnational networking. She is continuing her work on issues of reconciliation, truth and justice in South Asia.

Notes

---

[1]   In Bangladesh, often the terminology pro-liberation and anti-liberation forces are used to distinguish between groups who are interested to pursue justice and who are

against any kind of focus on the 1971 war. This is also because many pro-liberation forces groups either participated in the national war or are sympathetic to it. On the other hand the anti-liberations forces worked as collaborators with the Pakistani army or are biased towards Islamic fundamentalist groups which have strong connections with Pakistan.

[2] This is particularly evident from one of the social workers I interviewed (who wishes to remain anonymous). I spoke with her in Kolkata, India in January, 2000. She played a major role in the rehabilitation of the women. They focused on female-headed households after the war as the numbers of these increased. She commented, 'We also did some rehabilitation work for women on the other side of the Buriganga (a river next to Dhaka city). All were Hindu women. No men, no grownup boys. The army killed all the men. They dug up a big hole where they buried all the men and also the grown-up boys. Women were left alone. We started a program for helping the women. I gave each women rupee to do some small business. They made a little extra. Afterwards they continued to work with that small savings. Then we gave them goose, ducklings, chicks and goats. For the next three years we helped them to stand on their own feet. That is how Jagoroni (a handicrafts shop in Dhaka city run by Catholic nuns) came into being. It was the Widows' Program.'

[3] I gratefully acknowledge Roger Kilham's assistance in tracking down Geoffrey Davis.

[4] After the war ended on 16 December 1971 with Indian army intervention, the three states involved in the war, India, Bangladesh and Pakistan began prolonged negotiation over the release of approximated 93,000 Pakistani Prisoners of War (POWs) including 15,000 civilian men, women and children captured in Bangladesh/East Pakistan (Burke 1973: 1037) but detained under Indian authority. The matter was complicated by the Bangladeshi Prime Minister Sheikh Mujibur Rahaman's insistence on trying 1,500 Pakistani POWs for war crimes and the Pakistani President, Zulfikar Ali Bhutto's, reluctance to agree to it (Burke 1973: 1037-1038). On 28 August, 1973, India and Pakistan signed a treaty with Bangladesh's support which provided repatriation of all POWs except 195 prisoners who Bangladesh insisted on prosecuting for genocide and other war crimes (*Statesman Weekly* 1973). Even these trials were not carried out at the end.

[5] The Partition of India in 1947 sparked violent communal riots between Hindus, Muslims and Sikhs. During March, 1947, four months before the actual Partition, some Sikh villages in Rawalpindi area of Punjab had been attacked in retaliation for Hindu attacks on Muslims in Bihar. The story of 90 women who drowned themselves by jumping into a well at Thoa Khalsa, a small village in Rawalpindi, when their men were no longer able to defend their honour is still discussed today in tones of admiration and respect. For details, see Butalia (1998: 146-184).

[6] I wish to thank Donald Biswas for this reference.

[7] It is not my contention that many *Birangona* did not want to go through abortions or the adoption programs. However, without recovering the voices of the women themselves, we cannot determine the extent to which they had any choice in the matter. Motherhood that previously belonged in private domain was then controlled by the state.

[8] Golam Azam is the most prominent leader of the of the Jama'at-i-Islami, an extremist Islamic nationalist party of Bangladesh (Kabir 1993: 11) that did not support the Liberation movement of Bangladesh which had its roots in secularism and Bengali national identity. The Jama'at members actively collaborated with the Pakistani army during the war (Jahan 1980: 58). As a consequence, along with some other religious

parties, it was banned after 1971 (Jahan 1995: 94). However, following significant political changes in Bangladesh, in particular with the Amendment in the Constitution in 1977 and the pro-Islamic tilt in Zia and Ershad regimes policies, Jama'at got back into Bangladesh politics. One of the earliest demands against Golam Azam was in March 1981 when Bangladesh Muktijodhya Shongshod, an association of freedom fighters, sought to try Golam Azam and other collaborators for war crimes in a People's Tribunal (Kabir 1993: 15-19). The ruling Bangladesh Nationalist Party (BNP) was unsettled by this as it had already started reinstating the collaborators into powerful ministerial positions. Following President Zia's request, Muktijodhya Shongshod postponed the movement against Golam Azam. In December 1991, Golam Azam was appointed the *ameer* (chairperson) of the Jama'at-i-Islami. This appointment sparked the first major nationwide movement against the 1971 war criminals that culminated in the 1992 Peoples' Tribunal.

[9] The Bangladesh Nationalist Party (BNP)-led government was against this symbolic tribunal. BNP won the election in February 27, 1991 with 168 seats (in a total of 330 seats) and formed the government with the support of Jama'at-i-Islami (see footnote 8 above). Although it lost the 1996 election to the relatively secure Awami League, BNP regained power after the October 1, 2001 election, leading the Four-Party Alliance with Jatiyo Party (Naziur-Firoz wing), Jama'at-I-Islami and the Islami Oikyo Jote. It should be noted that there are two ministers of Jama'at in the current cabinet who served as Pakistani collaborators in the Liberation War.

[10] The three women come from rural and traditional areas where *purdah* and *izzat* (honour) have very strong social meanings. The Tribunal organizers were not sensitive to this.

References

Akhter, S., S. Begum, H. Hossain, S. Kamal and M. Guhathakurta (eds.) (2001) *Narir Ekattur o Judhyo Porobortee Kothyokahini,* Dhaka: Ain-o-Shalish Kendro.

Alvarez, S. (1999) 'Advocating feminism: the Latin American feminist NGO "boom"', *International Feminist Journal of Politics,* 1, 2, 181-209. [Reprinted here pages 122-148]

Begum, S. (2001) 'Masuda, elijan, duljan, momena: kushtiar charjon grihobodhu', in S. Akhter, S. Begum, H, Hossain, S, Kamal and M, Guhathakurta (eds.), *Narir Ekattur o Judhyo Porobortee Kothyokahini,* Dhaka: Ain-o-Shalish Kendro, 80-107.

Brownmiller, S. (1975) *Against Our Will: Men, Women and Rape,* New York: Bantam Books.

Bunch, C. and N. Reilly (1994) *Demanding Accountability: The Global Campaign and Vienna Tribunal for Women's Human Rights,* New York: Centre for Women's Global Leadership and UNIFEM.

Burke, S. M. (1973) 'The post-war diplomacy of the Indo-Pakistani war of 1971', *Asian Survey,* 13, 11, 1036-1049.

Butalia, U. (1998) *The Other Side of Silence: Voices from the Partition of India,* New Delhi: Penguin Books India.

Butalia, U. (1995a) 'Muslims and Hindus, men and women: communal stereotypes and the partition of India', in T. Sarkar and U. Butalia (eds.), *Women and Right-Wing Movements: Indian Experiences,* London: Zed Books, 58-81.

Butalia, U. (1995b) 'A question of silence: Partition, women and the state', in R. Lentin (ed.), *Gender and Catastrophe,* London: Zed Books, 92-109

Copelon, R. (1995) 'Gendered war crimes: reconceptualising rape in time of war', in Julie

Peters and Andrea Wolper (eds.), *Women's Rights Human Rights: International Feminist Perspectives*, New York: Routledge, 197-214.

Das, V. (1995) *Critical Events: An Anthropological Perspective on Contemporary India.* Oxford: Oxford University Press.

Das, V. (1994) 'Moral orientations to suffering: legitimation, power, and healing,' in L. C. Chen, A. Kleinman and N. C. Ware (eds.), *Health and Social Change in International Perspective,* Boston: Harvard School of Public Health, 139-170.

D'Costa, B. (2003) *Gendered Nationalism: From Partition to Creation,* Ph.D. dissertation. Canberra: The Australian National University.

D'Costa, B. (2002a) Personal interview with Geoffrey Davis, Sydney, Australia, 1 June.

D'Costa, B. (2002b) Personal interview with Halima Parveen, Dhaka, Bangladesh, 25 Dec.

D'Costa, B. (2000a) Personal interview with Nilima Ibrahim, Dhaka, Bangladesh, 14 Jan.

D'Costa, B. (2000b) Personal interview with Respondent A,. Dhaka, Bangladesh, 16 Jan.

D'Costa, B. (2000c) Personal interview with respondent B, Kolkata, West Bengal, India, 7 Feburary.

Dhaka Courier (1992) 3-16 April, 14-16.

Gafur, M. A. (1979) *Shomaj Kolyan Porikroma.* Dhaka: Pubali Prokashoni.

Ghosh, P. S. (1993) 'Bangladesh at the crossroads: religion and politics', *Asian Survey,* 33, 7, 697-710.

Ibrahim, N. (1998) *Ami Birangana Bolchi,* Dhaka: Jagriti Prokashoni.

Imam, J. (1986) *Ekatturer Dinguli,* Dhaka: Sandhani Publications.

Jahan, R. (1980) *Bangladeshi Politics: Problems and Issues,* Dhaka: University Press Ltd.

Jahan, R. (1995) *The Elusive Agenda: Mainstreaming Women in Development,* London: Zed Books.

Kabir, S. (2000) *Ekatturer Gonohotya, Nirjaton ebong Judhyaporadhider Bichar.* Dhaka: Shomoy.

Kabir, S. (1999) 'Introduction' in S. Kabir (ed.), *Ekatturer Dushoho Smriti.* Dhaka: Ekatturer Ghatok Dalal Nirmul Committee, 7-30.

Kabir, S. (1993) *Gonoadaloter Potobhumi,* Dhaka: Dibyo Prokash.

Kabeer, N. (1998) 'Subordination and struggle: women in Bangladesh', *New Left Review,* 168, March/April, 95-121.

Kamal, S. (2001) 'Potobhumi', in S. Akhter, S. Begum, H. Hossain, S. Kamal and M. Guhathakurta (eds.), *Narir Ekattur o Judhyo Porobortee Kothyokahini,* Dhaka: Ain-O-Shalish Kendro, 14-20.

Keck, M. E. and Sikkink, K. (1998) *Activists Beyond Borders: Advocacy Networks in International Politics,* Ithaca: Cornell University Press.

Khan, N. (1997) 'War crimes against Bengali women by Pakistani army and their collaborators in 1971: the rape of a nation', *The Daily Star,* 12 December.

Kumar, R. (1993) *The History of Doing: An Illustrated Account of Movements for Women's Rights and Feminism in India, 1800-1990,* London: Verso.

LaPorte, R. (1972) 'Pakistan in 1971: the disintegration of a nation', *Asian Survey,* 12, 2, 97-108.

Manchanda, R. (2001) 'Where are the women in South Asian conflicts?', in R. Manchanda (ed.), *Women, War and Peace in South Asia: Beyond Victimhood to Agency,* New Delhi: Sage Publications, 9-41.

Matsui, Y. (1998) 'History cannot be erased, women can no longer be silenced' in I. L. Sajor, (ed.) *Common Grounds: Violence Against Women in War and Armed Conflict Situations,* Philippines: Asian Center for Women's Human Rights, 26-32.

Melchiori, P. (1997) 'Messages from Beijing' *Mediterranean, Summary No. 2.* Online:

http://www.medmedia.org/review/numero2/en/art4.htm Date accessed May 25, 2004.

Menon, R. (1998) 'Reproducing the legitimate community: secularity, sexuality, and the state in post-partition India', in P. Jeffrey and A. Basu (eds.), *Appropriating Gender: Women's Activism and Politicized Religion in South Asia,* New York: Routledge, 15-32.

Menon, R. and K. Bhasin (1998) *Borders and Boundaries: Women in India's Partition,* New Delhi: Kali for Women.

Menon, R. and K. Bhasin (1996) 'Abducted women, the state and questions of honour: Three perspectives in the recovery operation in post-partition India,' in J. Kumari and M. De Alwis (eds.), *Embodied Violence: Communalising Women's Sexuality in South Asia,* London: Zed Books, 1-31.

Menon-Sen, K. (2002) 'Bridges over troubled waters: South Asian women's movements confronting globalization', *Society for International Development,* 45, 1, 132-136.

Moghadam, V. (1994) 'Introduction: women and identity politics in theoretical and comparative perspective', in V. Moghadam (ed.), *Identity Politics and Women: Cultural Reassertions and Feminisms in International Perspective,* Boulder, CO: Westview Press, 3-26.

New York Times (1971) 17 October.

Pereira, F. (2002) *The Fractured Scales: The Search for a Uniform Personal Code,* Calcutta: Stree.

Priyobhashini, F. (1999) 'Onek mrityo dekhechi, nari nirjatoner kotha shunechi kintoo kokhonou bhabini ami tar shikar hobo', in S. Kabir (ed.), *Ekatturer Dushoho Smriti.* Dhaka: Ekatturer Ghatok Dalal Nirmul Committee, 67-86.

Puja, K. (2001) 'Global civil society remakes history: "The Women's International War Crimes Tribunal 2000"' *Positions: East Asia Cultures Critique,* 9, 3, 611-620.

Puja, K. (1998) 'Backlash against the Comfort Women issue: moves against history textbook references', in I. L. Sajor (ed.), *Common Grounds: Violence Against Women in War and Armed Conflict Situations,* Philippines: Asian Center for Women's Human Rights, 198-204.

Rai, S. M. (2002) *Gender and the Political Economy of Development: From Nationalism to Globalization,* Cambridge: Polity.

Seifert, R. (1993) *War Rape: Analytical Approaches,* Geneva: Women's International League for Peace and Freedom.

Sobhan, S. (2003) 'The women's movement of Southern Asia' in *Canadian Dimension,* 37, 1, 26.

South Asian Feminist Declaration Online: http://www.sacw.net/Wmov/sasiafeministdecla.html. Date accessed May 25, 2004.

Statesman Weekly (1973) September 1.

Stiglmayer, A. (ed.). (1994) *Mass Rape: The War Against Women in Bosnia-Herzegovina.* Lincoln: University of Nebraska Press.

Thompson, K. B. (2002) 'Women's rights are human rights' in S. Khagram, J. V. Riker and K. Sikkink (eds.), *Restructuring World Politics: Transnational Social Movements, Networks and Norms,* Minneapolis: University of Minnesota Press, 96-122.

Waylen, G. (1996) 'Analysing women in the politics of the Third World' in H. Afshar (ed.), *Women and Politics in the Third World,* London: Routledge, 7-24.

Ziauddin, A. (1999) 'What is to be done about the Pakistani war criminals and collaborators' *The Daily Star,* 3 December. Online: http://www.bangladeshmariners.com/HmdrRprt/what.html, last accessed on 5/24/04.

MISSIONARY WOMEN AND FEMINISM IN NORWAY, 1906-1910

LINE NYHAGEN PREDELLI

This article examines the troubled relations between the women's missionary movement and the feminist movement in early twentieth-century Norway. The fact that the effects of the women's missionary movement included the expansion of women's spheres of action and the changing of cultural assumptions about what women could accomplish is not disputed. However, contemporary scholars disagree on whether women in the missionary movement were supporting and promoting feminist ideas at the time (Nyhagen Predelli 2000). The debate on missionary women's links to feminism must be informed by careful research. This article is a contribution to that effort.

Missionary Women in Norway Gain Influence and Power

One of the major figures in the creation and sustaining of links between the missionary movement and the feminist movement in Norway was Bolette Gjør. Gjør gained an increasingly important position in the women's missionary movement. She contributed significantly and decisively to the establishment of a journal for women's missionary associations, to missionary women being granted voting and representational rights in the Norwegian Missionary Society (NMS) (founded 1842 and closely associated with the Lutheran State Church), and to the establishment of a school for women missionaries. In 1884, she became editor of the new journal *Missionary Readings for Women's Associations* (*Missionslæsning for Kvindeforeninger* or *MLK*). Missionary women lacked a national organization that could unite all the local associations, but the women's associations that were spread throughout the country shared a common bond through their subscription to *MLK*. The *MLK*, which was published as a supplement to the NMS journal *Norsk Missionstidende (NMT)*, was also instrumental in supporting and encouraging the loyalty of independent women's associations to the NMS. These associations were only loosely affiliated with the NMS, but despite the lack of formal organization, ties to the NMS were close and dependable. Bolette Gjør emphasized the need for loyalty toward the NMS, and as a gesture of her own loyalty, she informed the NMS leadership about the missionary women's plans.

The women's missionary movement gained a more important position within the NMS in 1904, when women were granted voting and representational rights (see Nyhagen Predelli 2000). The 1904 decision by the NMS General Assembly was an important development for missionary women who had long contributed most of the financial support for the NMS without having a say in how the money should be spent. At that time, some missionary women used a public display of loyalty and accommodation in combination with a more privately expressed resistance to the patriarchal principles of the NMS leadership's efforts to change the established gender regime.

The Norwegian feminist movement had its breakthrough in the 1880s, with organizing efforts, fierce debates and radical demands (Agerholt 1980; Hagemann 1999). In her position as editor of *MLK*, Gjør could draw upon the growing feminist movement for ideas and inspiration for her own agenda for missionary women. She could also draw upon the increasing power and influence that women gradually achieved within the missionary movement. In 1909, looking back on the history of the women's missionary movement, Gjør claimed that the women's associations established in the 1840s had been

> the first tender beginnings of a rising of women.... Wherever it reached, it had influence, [and] it helped to lift women's thoughts above the daily toil and struggle; helped many forward to a life in God, [and] became in many areas a liberation for women. (Gjør 1909:57)

The Conflict Between Missionary Women and NMS

The first international women's organization, the International Council of Women (ICW), was founded in the United States in 1888, after an initiative by Susan B. Anthony, May Wright Sewall, and others. Its purpose was to promote women's cooperation both nationally and internationally in order to secure equal rights and opportunities for women (McFadden 1999). In 1904, Gina Krog, the most prominent feminist in Norway from 1884 until her death in 1916, was instrumental in founding the Norwegian branch of ICW, the Norwegian National Council of Women (NNCW) (*Norske Kvinners Nasjonalråd*). The NNCW was established to promote cooperation between women's organizations in Norway and to represent Norwegian women in ICW, the global feminist organization. By 1914, a wide array of Norwegian women's organizations had become members of the NNCW (Krog 1914).

The women's missionary associations were urged to join the NNCW by Marie Michelet, a friend of Bolette Gjør. Michelet (1866-1951), who became the founder of the Association of Norwegian Housewives (*Norges Husmorforbund*), saw women's calling as a combination of the dutiful housewife and the dutiful citizen.[1] Her main concern was to promote a domestic ideology for women in which housewifery was elevated to a profession (see also Melby 1999). She envisioned women's contributions to society as deriving from both their professional lives as housewives and their participation in the public sphere. Michelet saw women's entrance into public life as God-given and wanted Christian women to invade the Norwegian feminist movement, take control of it, and mold it after Christian principles: 'Women, with Jesus as their watcher, can become a new leaven in society; if the feminist cause could come in under the scepter of Christianity, then this powerful movement would be won for the Church and for God's Kingdom'.[2]

Michelet (1946) saw a great opportunity in the women's missionary associations, which were spread around the country, numbering about 4,000 local chapters. If these chapters could be mobilized to join the NNCW, the position of Christian women in that organization would be significantly strengthened, and Christian women would have an opportunity to influence NNCW policies. Through Gjør, Michelet received an invitation to present her case at a meeting in the missionary Ladies' Committee (*Damekomiteen*) in Christiania (Oslo), in February, 1906. Michelet argued that missionary women ought to join the NNCW, as the direction of the women's movement in Norway would now to a large extent be determined by the NNCW. Michelet declared, 'We Christian women must invade the women's movement.... The women's cause becomes what we women make it to be; but if the good ones stay away, then the other ones will work, and if Christian women stay away, then the movement will become unchristian'.[3] Bolette Gjør and the Ladies' Committee were convinced by Michelet's arguments, and began working towards missionary women's inclusion in the NNCW.

In a newspaper article in *Morgenbladet*, Bolette Gjør stated that mission work by women had been 'the first and the largest rising of women in our country', and that mission women must take advantage of the opportunity to join the national movement of feminist women in Norway. Gjør also wrote to the NMS general secretary, Lars Dahle, and informed him about the plans. In her opinion, Christian women ought to use this chance to gain influence within the NNCW and possibly to have an impact on the development of the feminist movement *per se*. In order to be effectively represented within the NNCW, however, missionary women would have to come together in a national organization, with headquarters and leadership located in Christiania. Gjør had for some time wished to establish closer ties between missionary women through the founding of a national organization. Repeated communications from missionary women also underscored the need for a unifying, national leadership. Gjør emphasized that also local women's missionary associations could join the NNCW, but local associations could not compete with a national organization in terms of its potential for power and influence. The obvious advantage to the NMS, Gjør pointed out, was that the national organization and its member associations would commit themselves to work for and support only the NMS, to the disadvantage of competing mission societies.[4]

Gjør and her mission friends had reason to believe that the NMS leadership would approve of their association with the NNCW, as Lars Dahle, the powerful and influential general secretary of the NMS, had for a long time supported missionary women's rights within the NMS. Dahle commented that 'even the feminist movement contains something justifiable that now has to come forward' (1904: 350). Dahle had thus gained a certain reputation for being positive towards the linking of missionary women and women's rights, and he was thought of as a potential ally by missionary women. Marie Michelet declared Dahle to be 'the man to take the initiative in this case, because you have thrown a glove against the old pietist views of the woman'.[5]

Lars Dahle, however, was not interested in promoting the cause of missionary women seeking links with feminists. In a stern letter to Gjør, Dahle wrote that membership in the NNCW was quite foreign to the NMS leadership, and that missionary women were better off without getting involved in issues of women's emancipation. The NMS leadership would not deny individual women or local associations the right to become NNCW members. On the other hand, the leadership did 'not want our [mission] society as such to work towards such an association, which is also why—if there should be any question about it—it could not permit that any of the society's magazines be used toward [such a purpose]'.[6] The women's associations were not officially a part of the NMS, but a struggle for organizational control was initiated when the NMS leadership in effect censored Gjør by forbidding her to write about the links between missionary women and feminist women in mission magazines. This left Gjør without an opportunity to explain or defend her own position in the only magazines that were sure to reach the majority of mission women around the country.

While Gjør saw opportunities for missionary women to become influential within feminist circles, Dahle and the NMS leadership were afraid that missionary women would simply be co-opted into the feminist movement and gradually lose interest in the mission cause. Instead of seeing missionary women as able to recruit mission supporters among feminists, Dahle envisioned a situation in which 'many honest mission women could suffer damage in their own spiritual life and mission life by getting in a more intimate contact with the mixed society of the common feminist organization [NNCW]' (1906: 570). Dahle was afraid that missionary women would not be able to convert feminists to Christianity, and that feminists would instead make Christian women become secular. He had quite a negative view of missionary women's independence, religious strength, and possibilities for organizational survival and success within a feminist environment. Moreover, Dahle (1906) was adamant that the feminist cause should under no circumstance be linked with the missionary cause, as the two were simply incompatible. Such a merger would not only threaten women's commitment to the missionary cause, but also the integrity of proper life within the mission, especially that of women.

Despite strong opposition from the NMS leadership, Gjør decided to go ahead with her plans to form a national organization for missionary women, *Misjonsarbeidernes Ring,* or MAR, and to make that organization a member of the NNCW. MAR was formed in April 1907, and consisted at that time of four member associations: The Ladies' Committee, two chapters from the Female Teacher's Missionary Associations (*Lærerinnenes Misjonsforbund*), and the local women's missionary associations in Finstad and in Storelvdalen (*Damekomiteens protokoll* no. 2).[7] The decision to found MAR, which constituted an act of independence by missionary women, must have been a difficult one, as it conflicted with these women's deep sense of loyalty towards the NMS. The missionary women risked alienating the NMS leadership, but, at the same time, they believed in their cause so wholeheartedly that they could not abstain from challenging the views of the NMS leadership. In April 1907, Gjør again wrote Dahle, insisting that MAR had been founded with the best interests of the mission in mind, and in full loyalty to the NMS (*Damekomiteens protokoll* no. 2). Realizing that her actions constituted a contestation of the views of the NMS leadership, Gjør sought to explain her position by pointing to her gender:

It is not easy to take a step where you know that you go against the tide and even act against the NMS leadership, but it could also be that men do not look too clearly on this thing, which is fully a feminist issue, especially in a time where those women's strengths are awakening that before lay dormant. (*Damekomiteens protokoll* no. 2)

The controversy between Gjør and the NMS leadership now reached beyond the sphere of mission circles, as it received national attention in newspapers and in feminist and religious journals. The editors of the religious journal *Norsk Kirkeblad* condemned the NMS leadership's treatment of missionary women, and charged that women had silently to endure the patriarchal principles by which the NMS was run (*Norsk Kirkeblad* 1907a: 101-102). Although missionary women had gained the right to vote at the NMS General Assembly, the editors charged that 'all in all the relationship is as patriarchal as before, the NMS leadership, that is, Lars Dahle, commands, and mission women are treated as minors even when they have something to say' (*Norsk Kirkeblad* 1907a: 101). They found it to be particularly scandalous that the NMS leadership had 'forbidden [Mrs. Gjør] to present the case in her own journal [*MLK*], and this despite the fact that Lars Dahle had permitted the publication of a letter arguing for the opposite opinion in the *Misjonstidende* [Missionary Tidings]' (*Norsk Kirkeblad* 1907a: 101).

Lars Dahle reacted quickly to the accusation of censorship by writing to both *Norsk Kirkeblad* and Bolette Gjør.[8] He was adamant that the NMS leadership had not forbidden Gjør to write about MAR and the NNCW in her own journal, as the *MLK* was not the property of Gjør herself, but the property of the Norwegian Missionary Society (*Norsk Kirkeblad* 1907b: 149-151). Although she was the paid editor of the *MLK,* Gjør was not allowed to write or print whatever she pleased.

In his reply, Dahle also emphasized that the NMS leadership had only given advice to mission women in this case, and not an order (*Norsk Kirkeblad* 1907b: 150).[9] The most important task for women's associations was, according to NMS leadership, to work for the conversion of 'heathens' to Christianity; a task which differed substantially from the main purpose of the NNCW and feminism (Dahle 1906: 569-570; see also *NMT* 1907: 47-48).

It is interesting to speculate on why Dahle, who had been positive towards giving women new rights within the NMS, was so hostile towards missionary women seeking to influence the feminist movement in a Christian direction. One reason may be the strict demarcation between religious and secular spheres that was upheld by representatives of religious forces in Norway from the 1870s onward. The introduction of a naturalistic, scientific world view inspired by Charles Darwin, competing with Biblical explanations of past, present and future developments, led to a separation and conflict between religious and secular movements, a conflict between explanatory paradigms that was influential well into the twentieth century (Oftestad, Rasmussen and Schumacher 1993). From its inception in the 1870s and 1880s, the women's feminist movement was thought of as being associated with secularism. The religious camp saw it as working towards the dissolution of both society and Christianity (Agerholt 1980). In light of these considerations, it is not surprising that Lars Dahle and the NMS leadership had misgivings about missionary women joining the feminist cause. From the religious point of view, it was Christian women's eagerness to join a secular movement that needed explanation, not the hostility of the NMS towards the feminist women's movement.

Another reason for Dahle's opposition to a link between missionary women and feminist women can be found in the internal organization of the NMS. The 1904 decision to grant women voting and election rights within the NMS did not come without a major conflict between conservative forces promoting a strict reading of the Bible and more liberal forces that were open to alternative interpretations of scriptural texts. The NMS leadership had to juggle the interests of both sides, and recommended that women should not be eligible for seats on the national and regional executive boards. The NMS leadership could thus give recognition to those who argued against women's participation, while at the same time pushing through a major, democratic transformation that gave women the right to vote, to serve as representatives at regional and national assemblies, and to be elected members of local executive boards.[10] In order to take the sting out of the organizational changes, the NMS leadership was careful to note that these organizational changes were not a result of the 'spirit of the times', stemming from the growing feminist movement.

As a result of these developments, Gjør found it necessary to write about MAR and the NNCW in journals and newspapers that were not controlled by the NMS. Ironically, the issue probably received more attention this way. Gjør published an appeal to missionary women about the NNCW in the magazine *Urd*.[11] In her appeal, Gjør continued to emphasize missionary women's opportunity to influence youth in a Christian way through the establishment of direct ties to the NNCW, the need for a national organization of mission women, MAR, and her continued loyalty towards the NMS (Gjør 1907: 166).[12] In Gjør's opinion, the 'mission to the heathens' had a special position, as it was 'the first rising of women in our country, and—perhaps without knowing it—it has more than anything else worked towards the great goal of emancipating women' (1907: 166). A missionary feminist, Gjør believed that missionary work by women had simultaneous effects of emancipation for women at home, through women's participation in the missionary movement, and for women abroad, through the conversion of women to Christianity.

Dahle (1907) had a very different view. He disputed Gjør's and Michelet's interpretations, and insisted that the women's missionary movement had nothing to do with the feminist cause.[13] In a letter published as a response to Michelet, Dahle (1907) asked: 'Does she really think that our female missionaries or our more than 3,000 women's associations are fruits of the feminist issue?' Quite the contrary, Dahle argued, the women's associations had been working long before the appearance of a feminist movement in Norway, 'and would without a doubt have made it just as well without it'.

The Development of MAR and its Reception by the Missionary Movement

Gjør and the new organization for missionary women, MAR, gained sympathy and support from within and outside the mission. Both Gjør and Michelet mention the support of some Lutheran State Church ministers as important.[14] It has been argued that representatives of the Norwegian State Church were uniform in their disapproval of the feminist movement (Lein 1981), but an examination of the case of democratic rights for missionary women within the NMS has shown that a high number of those who spoke in favour of women's rights were members of the clergy or other church servants (Nyhagen Predelli 2000). It is therefore not surprising that Gjør and her friends managed to mobilize some Church support for the inclusion of Christian women in the NNCW.

Although Gjør had hoped that MAR would become a national organization of missionary women, it would not be fair to call it a great success in organizational terms. Only a few of the several thousand local women's missionary associations joined the organization, which had as its goals 'to strengthen and develop interest and knowledge about the mission among its members', 'to promote a closer affiliation between associations working for the mission' and 'to inform missionary workers about the work that is done by and for women in our country'.[15] Interestingly, the organizational laws passed in 1909 did not mention that MAR sought to be accepted as a member of the NNCW. The original draft of laws, however, presented the goal of MAR as 'represent[ative of] the work by missions for heathens in the NNCW and in the ICW'.[16] The change in emphasis is an indication of the strong opposition that MAR was met with from both the missionary movement and the feminist movement, and of its lack of organizational success.

Contributing to MAR's lack of success was the publication of an appeal to all local women's missionary associations by 233 women arguing against MAR and NNCW membership.[17] About 67 out of these 233 women were married to ministers, pastors, bishops and other men employed by the State Church. Many of the women were allegedly leaders of local women's mission associations.[18] Not surprisingly, Gabrielle Dahle, wife of NMS general secretary Lars Dahle, was among the women who signed. The fact that so many churchmen's wives had signed the appeal was used later by opponents of MAR to indicate the seriousness and legitimacy of missionary women's resistance to MAR and feminist issues. One missionary woman declared, 'we must believe that our country's bishop's wives, parish dean's wives, and minister's wives have the best understanding of and insight into this question, and we must therefore respect their opinion'.[19] The main argument forwarded against MAR was that local women's associations had always considered the NMS as its collective centre, and the signatories found 'no reason whatsoever to seek another organization, and that even less now when women have won the right to vote at the NMS regional and general assembly meetings'.[20] The appeal had serious negative effects for MAR, as many missionary women became uneasy about it, and decided not to join the organization.

Gjør published a reply to the appeal by the 233 missionary women in which she declared herself unwilling to give up her work for MAR. She also asked missionary women who were negative towards MAR to respect the women who chose to join the organization. Gjør did not believe that MAR would be the cause of any break-ups within local women's associations. Having realized the extent of the opposition against MAR, Gjør sought to comfort missionary women by stating that 'anyhow, the Ring [MAR] will be small against the women's associations' thousands [of members]'.[21]

At the time of its founding in April 1907, MAR consisted of four local women's missionary associations. A year later, nine local missionary associations had joined, bringing the total up to thirteen. The following year was 'extraordinarily quiet' according to Bolette Gjør, and MAR only gained the membership of two local associations.[22] In addition, a few individual women had become affiliated with MAR. The MAR leadership remained quite stable, as five of the six members from the original leadership stayed on.[23] The following year proved to be slightly more positive, as MAR could list 35 local women's associations and ten individual women as members.[24] The number of affiliated associations increased largely because the organization of female teachers' mission work, Lærerinnenes Misjonsforbund (LMF), together with seventeen of its local associations, had joined. Counting all of its own individual members and all individuals with membership in its affiliated associations, MAR had by then reached a membership of 850 women.[25] By comparison, the women's missionary movement that defined itself as part of the NMS had a membership of 87,500 women in 1905 (Tjelle 1990). MAR was thus not particularly successful in terms of membership recruitment. The negative reactions towards MAR by the NMS leadership certainly worked against organizational growth. Furthermore, Bolette Gjør and her allies probably underestimated the resistance towards linking missionary work and feminist work that existed among women around the country. Gjør and Michelet defined the problem of recruitment as one of understanding: missionary women, especially those in the countryside, would be convinced of the rightfulness of a link with NNCW if only they could get the necessary information. If any information got out, however, it was of the negative kind. The lack of an opportunity to explain the cause in mission journals contributed to the lack of growth experienced by MAR.[26] As a result, MAR was much more successful in recruiting local missionary associations that were not affiliated with the NMS, and about half of MAR's membership actually came from the LMF. In 1910, MAR called on its members to subscribe to the LMF journal *Missionshilsen*; an indication of LMF's increasingly important position within MAR.[27]

MAR continued to experience difficulties in recruiting members. In 1911 the total membership had increased with four new local associations, bringing the total up to 39. Throughout its four years of existence, the main activity of MAR, in addition to its attempt to join the NNCW, had been to establish a library of mission literature and to make its books available to its members. The 1911 annual report declared, 'as an organization, MAR has not done a lot for the mission. The main thing has been to start the "traveling library". But we hope that we eventually will do more'.[28] If not an outright admission of failure, this statement suggests that MAR experienced problems in defining its role alongside the existence of local NMS affiliated women's associations and other independent organizations like the LMF. MAR had failed completely in its attempt to constitute a common, national umbrella organization for all the local women's missionary associations that defined themselves as loyal to the NMS. By 1912, no more than 22 NMS-affiliated women's associations, in addition to about seventeen LMF-affiliated associations, had membership in MAR (see 'Missionsarbeidernes Ring. Aarsberetning 1911-1912': 23). Two years later, only seventeen local women's associations, plus the LMF, were members of MAR (Høgh and Mørck 1914: xxxii).

The Reception of MAR by Feminists

The issue of missionary women's alliance with feminist women through membership in the NNCW and the ICW was not only controversial within the women's missionary movement and within the NMS. Feminist women also had doubts about whether such an alliance would benefit their work. The NNCW was divided in half on the issue of membership (Michelet 1946: 288), and the lines were drawn between secular and religious feminists.[29] Christian feminists were positive towards increased involvement by religious women in the NNCW.

When the NNCW received the first MAR application for membership in the spring of 1907, a mixed environment of hostility and friendliness towards MAR had been created among NNCW leaders. In its reply to Gjør's request for MAR membership, the NNCW leadership declared that

> the International Council of Women is not the right arena for mission work for the heathen, as the ICW does not adhere to any faith and rests on a pillar of tolerance. At the international meetings [of the ICW], representatives of different religious societies—both Jewish and heathen—have been present— and at this very moment one is seeking to establish national councils among Chinese, Japanese and Turkish women.[30]

In her reply to the NNCW leaders, Gjør confirmed her knowledge of the ICW policy of religious freedom and tolerance, and stated that MAR had no intention to evangelize within the NNCW and the ICW.[31]

The NNCW leaders were, however, not convinced of the justifiability of MAR membership. Quoting an article by Henny Dons, a member of the MAR leadership, emphasizing the importance of a Christian dimension to NNCW work, the NNCW leaders worried about the consequences of MAR inclusion (see *Husmoderen* 1907: 58-59). Would there be a take-over of the organization by Christiania women? The size of the women's missionary movement was probably a threat, but it would only be a realistic threat if missionary women were to form several organizations which all applied for NNCW membership. The NNCW leadership continued to be afraid of missionary propaganda (see *Nylænde* 1907a: 214; *Nylænde* 1907b: 372-373). Having expressed these doubts, the NNCW asked its branches to vote on the issue and report the results back by June 12, 1907. When the results were in, the inclusion of MAR had received a majority of the votes, but the majority was not large enough for membership to go through. The necessary two-thirds majority had not been reached.[32]

Because MAR had been very close to achieving inclusion, the issue was forwarded to the agenda of the NNCW National Assembly meeting in Trondheim, in July, 1907.[33] According to the journal *Nylænde* (1907a: 213-214), some NNCW branches had submitted last-minute votes that supported MAR inclusion and actually secured the necessary two-thirds majority. Tension between the two camps was high, and both Bolette Gjør and Henny Dons arrived to mobilize support for MAR inclusion. At that time, Bolette Gjør was under the impression that MAR would be accepted as a member by the NNCW national meeting (*Husmoderen* 1907: 262).

Some delegates thought the issue had already been decided through the late branch votes, but the NNCW leadership insisted that the National Assembly cast a vote. First, both sides were given the opportunity to present their arguments. On the one hand, the fact that the purpose of the NNCW was to gather all Norwegian women, or all the organizations that Norwegian women worked for, made it difficult to exclude missionary women. After all, the women's missionary movement constituted the largest mobilization of Norwegian women at the time. Moreover, the opposition to missionary women's inclusion from the missionary movement itself, especially from the NMS, was mentioned as an indication of the courage with which some missionary women had approached the NNCW. Missionary women had also promised to abstain from mission propaganda (*Nylænde* 1907a).

The other side, however, made MAR's inclusion an issue with international ramifications. According to its laws, the ICW did not adhere to any religious faith, and promoted tolerance and neutrality among its members. Marie Michelet (1946: 303) has asserted that Gina Krog, the feminist leader of the NNCW, interpreted this to mean that the ICW refused religious and political organizations the right to become members. Krog herself was apparently more worried that MAR was not representative of the women's missionary movement, as only a few missionary associations had become MAR members.[34] The opponents were also worried that the acceptance of Christian organizations would force the acceptance of members adhering to competing faiths, or even organizations working against Christianity (*Nylænde* 1907a). The ICW itself, however, was a meeting place where members of various religious faiths abstained from promoting religious causes. The opposition from the NNCW leadership was thus not so much a result of hostility towards the inclusion of MAR *per se* as resulting from the fear that MAR would not accept ICW's 'tolerance clause' and would actually promote the cause of Christianity. The previously mentioned journal article by Henny Dons had been interpreted to mean the MAR envisioned Norwegian women presenting themselves as united in the support of Christianity in the international arena. MAR constituted only a small fraction of the wider women's missionary movement, and Gjør's guarantee that it would abstain from evangelization was thus not worth that much. Furthermore, there were fears that missionary women would take control of the NNCW; a situation that could arise if several organizations of mission women were to apply for NNCW membership. Gina Krog (1907) expressed fears that missionary women could 'invade the [NNCW] and, if they choose to, take all power or break up our organization' (373; see also *Nylænde* 1907a). Had all the women's missionary associations either been formally affiliated with the NMS or members of MAR, the issue would have been different. In those cases, there would have been no threat of a massive influence by Christian women in the NNCW, as each member organization only had two votes at the National Assembly meeting.

The end result at the NNCW national meeting was that MAR acceptance won 37 votes, while 24 votes were cast for exclusion. MAR was thus formally excluded from the NNCW, as the votes in favour of acceptance did not meet the required two-thirds majority. This voting requirement was not standard in the NNCW, and in an effort to reduce the chances of MAR inclusion, the NNCW board argued at the last minute that an extra-ordinary two-thirds requirement was needed (Tokheim 1975: 79; see also Michelet 1946: 303). The resulting vote showed that MAR lacked a meager three votes in order to get accepted.

Bolette Gjør vowed to continue her efforts to make MAR into a larger organization of mission women. She was satisfied that many feminist women at the NNCW national meeting had declared support for MAR inclusion and this encouraged her not to give up her efforts. Gjør made it clear, however, that MAR was not only concerned with NNCW membership: 'We are not dependent on our inclusion in the NNCW' (*Husmoderen* 1907: 263), thus signaling that the existence of MAR was entirely justified by its goal to gather all missionary women under one organization.

Several nationally prominent feminists signed and published an appeal in support of Bollete Gjør's work towards having missionary women represented in the NNCW.[35] They argued that an inclusion of missionary women would greatly increase the NNCW's claim to be representative of all Norwegian women, as women's missionary associations were spread around the country and had many branches in rural areas. Gjør herself published a 'thank-you note' to all her supporters (*Husmoderen* 1907: 294-295). It had been a difficult time, she noted, especially because of the lack of understanding within the missionary movement itself. She also stated, however, that when a group of mission women dared to oppose the resistance from the missionary movement and actually applied for NNCW membership, they were met with a similar lack of understanding from within the ranks of the women's movement.

The debate about MAR continued in various journals and newspapers, while Gjør actively sought to clarify the future possibilities for MAR membership in the NNCW.[36] The question was lifted to an international level, as Gjør wanted the ICW itself to declare whether or not missionary women were welcome. Marie Michelet, who was going to the ICW board meeting in Geneva, was asked to bring along the following letter:

During our work for the mission we have felt more and more that as well as the women's movement, the women's mission work in our country demands that these so familiar working-branches ought not to be kept in opposition to each other as they now are, but together try to solve those problems that our time gives women in our country to take up. As we think that the ICW has given us that basis on which such a cooperation might be practicable, we have organized our mission ring and tried to be admitted into NKN [NNCW] but here we are refused because the spirit and the laws of the ICW are supposed to be understood thus, that work for Christian and political propaganda has no place in the ICW. We now ask you to put this question before the president of the council now at Geneva, hoping to get a clear answer of it: Is it against the principles of the ICW to admit mission workers in the national council when these are willing to submit to the laws as well as those of the ICW as those of the respective national council?...[37]

The answer obtained by Michelet read as follows:

Absolutely not. The spirit of the ICW is that all organizational work should be admitted as long as it obeys the basic principle of our constitution, and does not bring up questions about religious or political conflicts. We think that actually all our national councils have members of that kind. (1946: 312)

With the full support of the ICW board, Michelet could return to Norway with the message that there was nothing in the ICW laws or 'spirit' that prevented missionary women from becoming members of the NNCW, and, through the NNCW, becoming part of the ICW.

At the NNCW National Assembly meeting in Stavanger in 1910, MAR was finally accepted as a member. The vote showed unanimous support for MAR inclusion (Michelet 1946). Gina Krog must have realized that her arguments had been weakened by the ICW board statement. She suggested that MAR finally had become a national, representative organization of missionary women (Tokheim 1975).[38] Whether this was truly the case is another matter, as MAR at the time consisted of 35 local associations, with 18 of these coming from the missionary teacher's organization (LMF). In 1910, Henny Dons was elected member of the NNCW board, and missionary women finally got a say in the formulation of NNCW policies. Christian feminists also increased their influence in the NNCW when Nicoline Hambro, a religious feminist, was elected leader after the death of Gina Krog in 1916 (Michelet 1946). Bolette Gjør, who died in 1909, did not experience the victory that was a direct result of her relentless effort to get missionary women interested in feminist politics and to gain the feminist movement's acceptance of feminist-oriented missionary women.

Conclusion

In Norway, parts of the women's missionary movement of the early twentieth century established direct links with the feminist movement. Although the majority of Norwegian missionary women, especially those in rural areas, were either indifferent or opposed to linking mission work with feminist work, a significant number of women shared views that are characteristic of what has been called 'relational feminism' (Offen 1988). However, the fact that missionary women's associations were women-only was not enough for their application for NNWC membership to be universally welcomed. MAR gained membership only in 1910 after a bitter struggle which divided the NNWC. Certainly, members had reasons to be cautious. As we have seen, Marie Michelet called for the invasion of the women's movement by Christian women, and envisioned Norwegian women as presenting a united, Christian front on the international arena in the ICW.

The Norwegian experience of links between Christian and/or mission women and the feminist movement is not atypical in Nordic countries. In Denmark, Christian missionary women worked actively towards giving women the political right to vote, and in 1908 formed an association with the specific purpose of working towards this goal (Rømer Christensen 1995; Michelet 1946). Inger Hammar (1999) has shown that the pioneers of the women's movement in Sweden embraced Christianity as a basis of their emancipatory ideology. The women's missionary movement contributed significantly to the betterment of women's positions in Norwegian society. Nevertheless, the mixed response to MAR's 1907 application for membership of the NNCW shows that, for many members, feminism was not reducible to women's activism, even when beneficial to women. Principles of autonomy, diversity, inclusiveness and tolerance were non-negotiable for these feminists.

Research for this project was funded by the National Science Foundation and the Haynes Foundation of the United States, and by the Research Council of Norway.

Reprinted with permission from Nordic Journal of Women's Studies (NORA) 9 (1) (2001): 37-52.

Line Nyhagen Predelli received her Ph.D. in 1998, and her book Issues of Gender, Race, and Class in the Norwegian Missionary Society in Nineteenth-Century Norway and Madagascar *was published recently by the Edwin Mellen Press. She continues to write about gender and religion and has recently completed a research project on gender relations among Muslim immigrants in Oslo, Norway. Currently she has a dual appointment as a researcher at the Centre for Research in Social Policy at Loughborough University, England, and the Norwegian Institute for Urban and Regional Research.*

Notes

1   See Marie Michelet's letter to Lars Dahle (1907), University Library of Oslo; Marie Michelet's papers, Ms 40 1835, packet XXI a, III.

2   Marie Michelet's letter to Lars Dahle (1907); Michelet's papers, Ms 40 1835, packet XXI, III. Unless otherwise noted, all translations from the Norwegian are by author.

3   Memo from the meeting of the Ladies' Committee, February 15, 1906. Michelet's papers, Ms 40 1835, packet XXI.

4   Gjør in a letter to Dahle, February 1906, *Damekomiteens protokoll* no.2; see also Michelet's papers, Ms 40 1835, packet XXIa.

5   Marie Michelet's letter to Dahle, undated (the words 'sent in 1907' have been added). Michelet's papers, Ms 40 1835, packet XXIa.

6   Lars Dahle's letter to Gjør of March 20, 1906. *Damekomiteens protokoll* no.2.

7   Bolette Gjør, Hanna Hærem, Mrs. Jensen, Henny Dons, Mrs. Johnnsen, Mrs. Klavenæs, and Mrs. Hansen were elected to the MAR leadership (*Damekomiteens protokoll* no.2).

8   For the letter to Gjør of April 24, 1907, see *Damekomiteens protokoll* no.2.

9   The NMS leadership had, however, explicitly 'advised against' membership in the NNCW (Dahle 1906).

10   Women became eligible for seats on national and regional executive boards in the NMS in 1939.

11   Gjør sent the appeal to other journals as well, but it is unclear whether it was published elsewhere. Michelet wrote a personal note on her copy: 'Mrs. G was not allowed to

write this in her own journal' (Ms 40 1835, packet XXI).

12 The appeal was also published as a special offprint (*Særaftryk af 'Urd' No. 14*) found in *Damekomiteens protokoll* No.2.

13 See Michelet's papers, Ms 40 1835, packet XXI. See also letter from Lars Dahle to Bolette Gjør, December 22, 1908. *Damekomiteens protokoll* no. 2.

14 See letter from Bolette Gjør to Lars Dahle, December 30, 1908, *Damekomiteens protokoll* no. 2, and letter from Marie Michelet to Lars Dahle, 1907, Michelet's papers, Ms 40 1835, packet XXI. See also the supportive letter from vicar Gustav Jenssen to Marie Michelet, May 7, 1907 in Michelet's papers, Ms 40 1835, packet XXI. Another minister in favour of women's emancipation was Harald Olstad, who wrote an article about the Church and the feminist movement in *Urd* in 1907.

15 *Love for 'Missionsarbeidernes Ring'*, Michelet's papers, Ms 40 1835, packet XXI. These laws were agreed to in 1909.

16 See letter '*Til formanden*', where the original MAR application for NNCW membership is referred to, Michelet's papers, Ms 40 2835, and Dons (1907).

17 The appeal was apparently published in several daily newspapers in early July, 1907 (see Michelet 1946: 302). A copy of the appeal is found in Marie Michelet's papers, Ms 40 1835, packet XXI.

18 See article by A. D. Bassøe, 'Missionskvinde foreningerne og Misjonsringer', in *Kristeligt Ugeblad* 1908, Michelet's papers, Ms 40 1835, packet XXI.

19 As referred by Gustava Amlund in her letter to Marie Michelet of February 4, 1908, Michelet's papers, Ms 40 1835, packet XXI.

20 From an article in *Morgenbladet*, December 1907. See Michelet's papers.

21 Bolette Gjør: '*Kvindeforeningernes stilling til norske kvinders nationale raad*'. The article is found in *Damekomiteens protokoll* no. 2. There is no indication as to where it was published.

22 *Aarsberetning for Missionsarbeidernes Ring. Fra 1ste April 1908-1ste April 1909*, Michelet's papers, Ms 40 1835, packet XXI.

23 These were Bolette Gjør, Hanna Hærem, Mrs. Jensen, Mrs. Klaveness, and Ms. Henny Dons.

24 *Aarsberetning for Missionsarbeidernes Ring: Fra 1. April 1909-1. April 1910*, Michelet's papers, Ms 40 1835, packet XXI.

25 See *Aarsberetning* (1909-1910, 4 and 8) for the number of affiliated associations and individuals. See also *Aarsberetning* (1910-1911).

26 The NMS leadership was criticized by Michelet for not having mentioned the name of Bolette Gjør in its journal in connection with the proposal for missionary women to join the NNCW. See *NMT* no. 24 (1906, 568-571) and *NMT* no. 3 (1907, 71). Michelet charged that MAR would have received greater support had missionary women known this fact. See *Vestlandsposten* February 9, 1907. Lars Dahle replied in *Vestlandsposten* February 16, 1907. Both articles are found in Michelet's papers, Ms 40 1835, packet XXI. See also Gina Krog, '*Missionens kvindeforeninger og kvindernes nationalraad*', Michelet's papers, Ms 40 1835.

27 *Aarsberetning* (1909-1910, 5). The LMF was founded in 1902, and from 1905 was led by Henny Dons. Dons became leader of MAR in 1909. In 1910 the LMF leadership suggested that its journal *Missionshilsen* become the joint journal of LMF and MAR. See *Tillæg til Missionshilsen nr.* 2 March-April 1910.

28 *Aarsberetning for Missionsarbeidernes Ring: Fra 1. April 1910-1. April 1911*. Michelet's papers, Ms 40 1835 II, packet XVI.

29 See also *Husmoderen* (1907: 210, 224) for the two camps of NNCW women.

30 See the letter '*Til formanden*', May 1907, signed by Anna Hvoslef, Michelet's papers, Ms 40 1835.
31 See letter '*Fra N.K.N's styre*', June 4, 1907, Michelet's papers, Ms 40 1835.
32 See letter '*Til formanden*', May 1907.
33 See also *Nylænde* July 15, 1907, 213, and letter by Bolette Gjør, 'Aabent brev...', *Husmoderen* (1907, 262-263).
34 See letter from Gina Krog 'To NKN's [NNCW's] members', 1908, in Michelet's papers, Ms 40 1835, packet XXI. See also Krog (1907).
35 The letter became a news item in *Morgenbladet*, September 17, 1907. See *Damekomiteens protokoll*, no.2.
36 For the continued debate about MAR and NNCW, see A. D. Bassøe, 'Missionskvindeforeningerne og missionsringen', published in two issues of *Kristeligt Ugeblad* (Michelet's papers, Ms 40 1835, packet XXI) and the letter 'Missionskvindernes ring', in *Buskerud Blad* January 31, 1908 (Michelet's papers, Ms 40 1835, packet XXI); see also *Damekomiteens protokoll* no.2; *Nylænde* 1907b: 371-375; *Husmoderen* 1907: 210, 240-241, 250-251, 262-263, 294-295.
37 Original letter in English from Bolette Gjør to Marie Michelet, Kristiania, 22 August 1908, Michelet's papers, Ms 40 1835, packet XXI.
38 In 1907 Gina Krog had declared her willingness to accept a representative organization of missionary women as member of NNCW (See Krog 1907: 371-374).

References

Agerholt, A. C. (1980) [1937]. *Den norske kvinnebevegelsens historie* (*The History of the Norwegian Women's Movement*), Oslo: Gyldendal Norsk Forlag.
Burton, A. (1992) 'The white woman's burden: British feminists and the Indian women', in N. Chauduri and M. Strobel (eds.), *Western Women and Imperialism: Complicity and Resistance*, Bloomington: University of Indiana Press. 137-157.
Dahle, Lars. (1923) *Tilbakeblik paa mit liv og særlig paa mit missionsliv. Anden Del* (*A Look Back on My Life, and Especially My Mission Life*), Stavanger: Det norske misjonsselskaps trykkeri.
Dahle, L. (1904) *Norsk Missionstidende*, 15, 350.
Dahle, L. (1906) '*Norsk Missionstidende*, 24, 570.
Dahle, L. (1907) 16 February. *Vestlandsposten*.
Damekomiteens protokoll no. 2 (1906-1920) Mission School for Women's Archive 1901-1978, NMS Archive, Stavanger, Norway.
Dons, H. (1907) 'Lærerindernes Missionsforening ('LMF') og 'Missionsforeningernes ring', *Husmoderen*, 58-59.
Gjør, B. (1909) *Missionslæsning for Kvindeforeninger*, 8.
Gjør, B. (1907) *Urd*, 11, 14,
Hagemann, G. (1999) 'De stummes leir? 1800-1900 (The camp of the silent? 1800-1900)', in I. Blom and S. Sogner (eds.), *Med kjønnsperspektiv på norsk historie. Fra vikingtid til 2000-årsskiftet* (*A Gender Perspective on Norwegian History From the Time of the Vikings Until the Turn of the Year 2000*). Oslo: Cappelen Akademisk Forlag, 135-226.
Hammar, I. (1999) *Emancipation och religion: Den svenska kvinnorörelsens pionjärer i debatt om kvinnans kallelse ca. 1860-1900* (*Emancipation and Religion: The Pioneers of the Swedish Feminist Movement and the Debate on Women's Calling, 1860-1900*). Stockholm: Carlssons Bokförlag.
Høgh, M. and F. Mørck (eds.) (1914) *Norske kvinder. En oversigt over deres stilling og*

livsvilkaar i hundredeaaret 1814-1914 (*Norwegian Women. An Overview of Their Position and Condition in the Hundred years 1814-1914*), Vol. 2., Kristiania: Berg og Høgh's Forlag.

Husmoderen (1907) No. 28.

Krog, G. (1914). 'Organisation (organization)', in M. Høgh and F. Mørck (eds.), *Norske kvinder: En oversigt over deres stilling og livsvilkaar i hundredeaaret 1814-1914*, Kristiania: Berg og Høgh's Forlag, 61-89.

Krog, G. (1907) 'Missionsarbeidernes ring og N.K.N', *Nylænde*, 24, December 15: 373.

Lein, B. N. 1981. *Kirken i felttog mot kvinnefrigjøring* (*The Church's Campaign Against the Emancipation of Women*), Oslo: Universitetsforlaget.

McFadden, M. H. (1999) *Golden Cables of Sympathy. The Transatlantic Course of Nineteenth-Century Feminism*, Lexington: The University of Kentucky Press.

Melby, K. (1999) 'Husmorens epoke, 1900-1950 (The epoch of the housewife, 1900-1950)', in I. Blom and S. Sogner (eds.), *Med kjønnsperspektiv på norsk historie. Fra vikingtid til 2000-årsskiftet* (*A Gender Perspective on Norwegian History From the Time of the Vikings Until the Turn of the Year 2000*), Oslo: Cappelen Akademisk Forlag. 227-297.

Michelet, M. (1946) *Minner og tidsbilleder* (*Memories and Period Pictures*), Oslo: Dreyers Forlag.

'Missionsarbeidernes Ring: Aarsberetning 1911-1912' (1912) *Missionshilsen*, Ekstra-nr., 7 April.

Norsk Kirkeblad (1907a) March 23. 4, 12-13.

Norsk Kirkeblad (1907b) May 11. 4, 19.

Norsk Missionstidende (NMT) (*Norwegian Missionary Tidings*) (1907) 2, Stavanger: Det norske misjonsselskap.

Nylænde (1907a) July 14: 214

Nylænde (1907b) December 15: 372-373.

Nyhagen Predelli, L. (2000) 'Processes of gender democratization in evangelical missions: the case of the Norwegian Missionary Society', *Nordic Journal of Women's Studies (NORA)*, 8, 1, 33-46.

Offen, K. (1988) 'Defining feminism: a comparative historical approach', *Signs,* 14, 1, 119-157.

Oftestad, B., T. Rasmussen and J. Schumacher. (1993) *Norsk kirkehistorie* (*Norwegian Church History*), Oslo: Universitetsforlaget.

Olstad, H. (1907) 'Kirken og vor tids kvindebevægelse', *Urd,* 11, 7, 76-77.

Rømer Christensen, H. (1995) *Mellem backfische og pæne piger* (*Between Backfish and Pretty Girls*), Københavns Universitet: Museum Tusculanums Forlag.

Tjelle, K. F. (1990) *Kvinder hjelper kvinder: misjonskvinneforenings-bevegelsen i Norge 1860-1910* (*Women Help Women: The Movement of Women's Missionary Associations in Norway, 1860-1910*), Unpublished Master's Thesis, Department of History, University of Oslo.

Tokheim, M. (1975) 'Norske Kvinners Nasjonalråd 1904-1916 (Norwegian Council of Women, 1904-1916)', unpublished Master's thesis, University of Bergen.

IV.
FEMINIST CHALLENGES IN PRACTICE
AND VISION

,

THE INDIGENOUS ROOTS

OF UNITED STATES FEMINISM

SALLY ROESCH WAGNER

In the territory of the Haudenosaunee, the six nations of the Iroquois Confederacy, the woman's rights movement was born in 1848. Was there a connection between the authority and responsibilities held by Haudenosaunee women and the vision of the woman's rights movement? Were the suffrage leaders influenced by native women?

The idea never entered my mind. If a student had suggested such a connection in the first women's studies class I taught in 1970 (California State University, Sacramento), I would have demanded strong documentation, highly skeptical of such a notion. I never would have stumbled across this connection if I had not been looking for an answer.

I was puzzled by a question to the past, a mystery of feminist history. *How did the early radical suffragists come to their vision, a vision not of band-aid reform but of a reconstituted world completely transformed?* I wondered.

For twenty years I had immersed myself in the writings of the two major theoreticians and writers of the National Woman Suffrage Association—Matilda Joslyn Gage (1826-1898) and Elizabeth Cady Stanton (1815-1902). Yet, I could not figure out where they received the courage and vision to dream their revolutionary dream. Living under the ideological hegemony of nineteenth-century United States, they had no say in government, religion, economics and social life: 'the fourfold bondage' of women's lives upon which 'society is based', Gage and Stanton called it in the Preface to Volume 3 of their *History of Woman Suffrage*, 'making liberty and equality for her antagonistic to every organized institution' (Stanton, Anthony and Gage 1881: vi). Whatever made them think that, far beyond equal rights for women, a different paradigm, an egalitarian one of human harmony, was achievable? Surely these two white women, living under conditions they likened to slavery, did not receive their vision in a vacuum. How

were they able to see from point A, where women stood—corsetted and ornamental non-persons in the eyes of church and law—to point C, the 'regenerated' world
Gage (1895) predicted in her feminist classic, *Woman, Church and State*, in which
all repressive institutions would be destroyed? What was point B in their lives, the
visible alternative that drove their feminist spirit—not a utopian pipedream but
a living example of society transformed? They had to have seen something that told
them such a vision was possible.

It was several months into work on a National Endowment for the Humanities
fellowship, dedicated to answering this question, when I found the answer in Paula
Gunn Allen's (1986) important work, *The Sacred Hoop: Recovering the Feminine
in American Indian Traditions.* Describing the Iroquois Confederation, Allen
posited:

> Beliefs, attitudes and laws such as these became part of the vision of American
> feminists and of other human liberation movements around the world. Yet
> feminists too often believe that no one has ever experienced the kind of society
> that empowered women and made that empowerment the basis of its rules
> and civilization. The price the feminist community must pay because it is not
> aware of the recent presence of gynarchical societies on this continent is
> unnecessary confusion, division, and much lost time.... The root of oppres-
> sion is the loss of memory.
>
> ... As I write this, I am aware of how far removed my version of the roots
> of American feminism must seem to those steeped in either mainstream or
> radical versions of feminism's history.... I am intensely conscious of popular
> notions of Indian women as beasts of burden, squaws, traitors, or, at best,
> vanished denizens of a long-lost wilderness. How odd, then, must my
> contention seem that the gynocratic tribes of the American continent
> provided the basis for all the dreams of liberation that characterize the modern
> world. (1986: 213-214)

Reading these words, I felt an instantaneous click. I had been skimming over the
source of the suffragists' vision without even noticing it. My academic blinders,
fueled by a deep-seated and unexamined presumption of white supremacy (just as
Allen wrote, I had assumed that native women were silent beasts of burden,
walking five steps behind their dominant husbands) had kept me from registering
what these prototypical feminists kept insisting in their writings. They believed
women's liberation was possible because they knew women who possessed a
position of respect and authority in their own egalitarian society—Haudenosaunee
women.

Key to recognizing this connection was understanding Matilda Joslyn Gage's
formative role in developing feminist theory. Along with Elizabeth Cady Stanton
she authored most of the important documents of the National Woman Suffrage
Association (NWSA), including their Centennial protest 'The Declaration of
Rights of Women' (1876) and the first three volumes of the *History of Woman*

Suffrage (Stanton, Anthony and Gage 1881, 1882, 1886). Gage joined the movement in 1852, along with Susan B. Anthony, at the third national woman's rights convention held in Syracuse and by the 1870s the three—Stanton, Anthony and Gage—were recognized as the leadership 'triumvirate' of the NWSA. Today, for a variety of reasons explained elsewhere (Wagner 2003), Gage is less well known. Stanton and Gage were the primary writers and thinkers of the NWSA; Anthony was the organizer.

Gage wrote about the Iroquois, especially the position of women in what she termed their 'matriarchate' or system of 'mother-rule', and her correspondence indicates she was working on a book about the Haudenosaunee when she died in 1898. While serving as president of the NWSA in 1875, she penned a series of admiring articles about the Haudenosaunee for the New York *Evening Post* in which she wrote that the 'division of power between the sexes in this Indian republic was nearly equal.' (1875b), while the Iroquois family structure 'demonstrated woman's superiority in power' (Gage 1895: 5). The *Evening Post* editor said that Gage expressed

an exhibition of ardent devotion to the cause of women's rights which is very proper in the president of the.... Suffrage Association and gives prominence to the fact that in the old days when the glory of the famous confederation ... was at its height, the power and importance of women were recognized by the allied tribes. ('The Onondaga Indians' 1875: 2)

For over twenty years, in her newspaper and journal articles, the newspaper she edited, *The National Citizen and Ballot Box* (1878-1881), and her magnum opus, *Woman, Church and State* (originally published in 1893), Gage taught her readers about the six nations of the Iroquois confederacy. She explained the form of government of the Mohawk, Oneida, Onondaga, Cayuga, Seneca and Tuscarora and their confederacy of peace. She understood the issue of sovereignty for Indian nations and described Haudenosaunee social, political and economic life. Most importantly, she acknowledged the position of authority held by Haudenosaunee women. She wrote:

The famous Iroquois Indians, or Six Nations, which at the discovery of America held sway from the Great Lakes to the Tombigbe river, from the Hudson to the Ohio ... showed alike in form of government, and in social life, reminiscences of the Matriarchate. (1895: 5)

The European invasion of America resulted in genocide. That is the most important story of contact. But it is not the only one, I learned. While the United States and its citizens concentrated on 'christianizing and civilizing', relocating and slaughtering Indians, the story is more complex. At their best, they also signed treaties, coexisted with and learned from native people. Regular trade, cultural sharing, and, surprisingly, even friendship between Native Americans and

Euroamericans transformed the immigrants. Perhaps nowhere was this social interaction more evident than in the towns and villages in upstate New York where Matilda Joslyn Gage and Elizabeth Cady Stanton grew up, and Gage spent her entire life.

While the separate nations—native and non-native—lived in very different cultural worlds during the early 1800s, Euroamerican settlers in central/western New York were, at most, one person away from direct familiarity with Iroquois people. The Haudenosaunee continued their ancient practice of adopting individuals of other nations, and many white residents of New York (including Matilda Joslyn Gage) carried adoptive Indian names. Friendships and visiting were common between natives and non-natives. Newspapers routinely printed news from Iroquois country. Each local history book began with a lengthy account of the first inhabitants of the land.

Stanton sometimes sat across the dinner table from Oneida women during frequent visits to her cousin, the radical social activist Gerrit Smith, in Peterboro, New York. Smith's daughter, also named Elizabeth, was among the first to shed the twenty pounds of clothing that fashion dictated should hang from a fashionable woman's waist, dangerously deformed from corseting. The reform costume Elizabeth Smith adopted (named the 'Bloomer' after the newspaper editor who popularized it) bore a resemblance to the loose-fitting tunic and leggings worn by the two Elizabeths' Native American acquaintances.

Elizabeth Cady Stanton's cousin, Peter Skenandoah Smith, was named for an Oneida friend of the family, Chief Skenandoah. In addition, her nearest Seneca Falls neighbour, Oren Tyler, came from Onondaga, where he 'had friendly dealings' with the people there and was adopted by them. He spoke their language fluently, and parties of Onondagans passing through Seneca Falls to sell their bead work and baskets 'sought out their "brother"', as they called Capt. Tyler, 'who always befriended them', according to accounts in the Seneca Falls Historical Society (1906).

Matilda Joslyn Gage's ties to the Haudenosaunee were even stronger. She attended ceremonies at the Onondaga nation, entertained friends from Onondaga, and was eventually adopted into the Wolf Clan of the Mohawk Nation. 'I received the name of Ka-ron-ien-ha-wi, or "Sky Carrier", or *She who holds the sky*. It is a clan name of the wolves', she wrote to her daughter in 1893.

Stanton and Gage were not the only suffragists who had contact with citizens of the six nations of the Iroquois Confederacy. Lucretia Mott and her husband James were members of the Indian Committee of the New York and Philadelphia Friends (Quaker) Yearly Meetings, which had for years provided schooling and support for the Seneca at Cattaraugus. The Motts visited the Cattaraugus community in June 1848, where they observed the Seneca women plan the strawberry ceremony and take part in the deliberations over a possible change in the Seneca form of governance (Bacon 1980; Hallowell 1884).

The following month, Lucretia Mott joined Elizabeth Cady Stanton and three of their Quaker friends in planning the first woman's rights convention held in nearby Seneca Falls. Could Mott have been imbued with the sense of women's potential after seeing it in action? Did that add fuel to the fire of indignation that flared into the woman's rights movement?

Personal knowledge of their Haudenosaunee friends and neighbours was reinforced by the daily news. These suffragists regularly read newspaper accounts of everyday Iroquois activities— the sports scores when the Onondaga faced the Mohawks at Lacrosse, a Quaker council called to ask Seneca women to leave their fields and work in the home (as the Friends said God commanded) and a condolence ceremony to mourn a chief's death and to set in place a new one (Iroquois Newspaper Clipping Collection).[1] It took several months of study before I could understand the newspaper accounts of condolence ceremonies; the average nineteenth-century reader was assumed to possess a knowledge of Iroquois history and government held, among Euroamericans, only by scholars today.

New York newspaper readers learned from interviews with white teachers at various Indian nations about the wonderful sense of freedom and safety they felt, since rape was virtually nonexistent on the reservations. These front-page stories admonished big-city 'dandies' to learn a thing or two from Native men's example, so that white women too could walk the streets without fear. An 1883 description of life on the Onondaga nation for a white women was published in the *Skaneateles Democrat*, a paper to which Gage was a sometime contributor:

> It shows the remarkable security of living on an Indian Reservation, that a solitary woman can walk about for miles, at any hour of the day or night, in perfect safety. Miss Remington often starts off, between eight and nine in the evening, lantern in one hand and alpenstock in the other, and a parcel of supplies strung from her shoulder, to walk for a mile or more up the hillsides. (Beauchamp 1893)

Miss Remington 'had long been in charge of the mission house at Onondaga'. Adopted into the snipe clan of the Onondaga nation, she was given the name 'Ki-a-was-say', or A New Word (Beauchamp 1893).

Just as feminists a hundred years later learned from Margaret Mead's research among the Arapesh that rape is not universal, so did the suffragists learn from their research, newspapers and neighbours that not all men in all societies rape women. They understood that rape is socially-structured behaviour. Gage cites another example, that of ancient Egypt, to prove the point: 'Crimes against women were rare in Egypt and when occurring were most severely punished.[2] Rameses III caused this inscription to be engraved upon his monuments: 'To unprotected woman there is freedom to wander through the whole country wheresoever she list without apprehending danger' (1895: 17).

A Tuscarora chief, Elias Johnson, wrote about the absence of rape by Haudenosaunee men in his popular 1881 book, *Legends, Traditions and Laws, of the Iroquois, or Six Nations*. As far as he knew, among white men, it was only the Germans who held the same respect for woman, Johnson wryly added, 'until they became civilized'. Maintaining that sexual violation of women was generally unknown among Indian men, Johnson celebrated the 'marvelous' fact 'that whole nations, consisting of millions, should have been so trained, religiously or domestically, that [nothing] should have tempted them from the strictest honour and the most delicate kindness' (Johnson 1881: 22-23).

What a contrast the suffragists saw in the 1892 scandal that hit the pages of the *New York World* on April 9:

> The Cattaraugus Indian reservation at Versailles is torn up over the recent charges in the Thomas Asylum for Orphan and Destitute Indian Children, the story read. The Superintendent of the Asylum had been accused of sexually abusing the girls under his care. ('Writings of H. M. Converse and miscellaneous scrapbook of Ely S. Parker' 1892: 22-23)

The underpinnings of western women's oppression were to be found in the Bible, Stanton and Gage believed. Woman became subordinate to man because of the sin of Eve, Genesis 3:16 explained. 'Unto the woman he said, I will greatly multiply thy sorrow and thy conception; in sorrow thou shalt bring forth children; and thy desire *shall be* to thy husband, and he shall rule over thee [emphasis mine]'.

These were also the roots of childbirth practices in the West. Giving birth must hurt; it is the eternal punishment for original sin. While Euroamerican women birthed in pain, suffering and possible death, after a lengthy period of confinement, Stanton wrote by contrast, 'We know that among Indians the squaws do not suffer in childbirth. They will step aside from the ranks, even on the march, and return in a short time bearing with them the newborn child' (1927: 365).

Stanton advocated natural childbirth, as did feminist Dr. Alice Stockham, who summarized in her 1886 book on painless birth, *Tokology*:

> The usual testimony of missionaries and travelers is that the squaws of our own Indian tribes experience almost no suffering in childbirth, and the function scarcely interferes with the habits, pleasures or duties of life. I have myself seen a squaw of the Ottawa tribe carrying her papoose upon her back, strapped to a board, when it was only twenty-four hours old. (17)

Dr. Stockham questioned:

> If this pain and travail is a natural accompaniment of physiological functions—if it is a *curse* upon women, then why are the rich, the enlightened and more favored daughters of earth greater sufferers than the peasantry, the savage, the barbarian, and those whom we call heathen? (18)

Did Christian women suffer more because of God's mandate? Stanton (1891) would entertain no such nonsense, proclaiming: 'What an absurdity, then, to suppose that only enlightened Christian women are cursed'! She believed, 'If you suffer, it is not because you are cursed of God, but because you violate His laws. What an incubus it would take from woman could she be educated to know that the pains of maternity are no curse upon her kind! ' (1927: 365).

She practiced a natural, native-directed form of birthing, as her daughter Margaret Lawrence documented:

> My mother was never abed an extra hour, either before or after my birth. Before eleven o'clock she had written several letters announcing the arrival of her first daughter. She had dinner with her boys, took a nap in the glorious October sunshine, walked out to an arbor in the yard and gathered some grapes. The next day she drove three miles to Waterloo to call on a friend and bring her down to see her daughter.

This Waterloo friend was astounded at the speed of Mrs Stanton's recovery, as was Lucretia Mott, who in October 1852 wrote:

> We who live after the older school methods cannot tell what the hardy reformers can bear. I rode out in less than a week after the birth of one of my children and was classed among the Indians for so rash an act. I was persuaded then that the close month's confinement was an injury to mothers and I have encouraged my children to be moderately venturesome. (qtd. in Lutz 1967: 82)

Stanton, whose major edited work, *The Woman's Bible* (published in two parts in 1895 and 1898), (Gage was a contributor) interpreted the story of Eve and its effect on women:

> The Bible teaches that woman brought sin and death into the world, that she precipitated the fall of the race, that she was arraigned before the judgment seat of Heaven, tried, condemned and sentenced. Marriage for her was to be a condition of bondage, maternity a period of suffering and anguish, and in silence and subjection, she was to play the role of a dependent on man's bounty ... so long as woman accepts the position that they assign her, her emancipation is impossible. (7)

Gage (1895) agreed with Stanton about the primary importance of the story of Eve as the source of Eurochristian women's oppression, having written two years before in her *Woman, Church and State* about the nine million women she estimated had been killed by the church—and later, the state—as witches:

> The extreme wickedness of woman, taught as a cardinal doctrine of the church, created the belief that she was desirous of destroying all religion, witchcraft being regarded as her strongest weapon. Therefore no punishment for it was thought too severe. The teaching of the church as to the creation of

women and the origin of evil embodied the ordinary belief of the Christian peoples. And that woman, rather than man, practiced this sin, was attributed by the church to her original sinful nature which led her to disobey God's first command in Eden. (1895: 123)

The Eve legacy continued, even into nineteenth-century law. The legal reality for United States women went far beyond simple lack of rights; once they married they had no legal existence. The two shall become one and the one is the man, taught Christianity. Church law became the foundation for common law, Gage documented in her chapter on Canon Law in *Woman, Church and State* (1895: 59-79), and the married couple legally consisted of only the husband, while married women were considered dead in the law. Considered legal nonentities, married women could not have custody of their children or rights to their own property or earnings. They could not sign contracts, sue or be sued, or vote. Considered non-persons, they had no rights to their bodies. Matilda Joslyn Gage's friend Moses Harmon went to prison under the Comstock Acts for speaking out against the rape of wives by their husbands, which was sanctioned by law (Wagner 1987). Lacking legal rights, or even existence, the wife and mother was the virtual slave of her husband. Not all men were tyrants; but the law, as Lucretia Mott said, gave all men the right of tyranny.

Men 'cling to the idea of the family unit', Stanton (1891) maintained, 'because on that is based the absolute power of the father over the property, children, and the civil and political rights of wives'. A married woman was 'nameless, purseless and childless', Stanton summed up, though she be 'a woman, heiress and mother'. Until the early feminists slowly changed the laws, state by state, throughout the nineteenth century, any money a wife earned or inherited belonged outright to her husband. Calling for an end to all this injustice, the suffragists were labelled hopeless dreamers for imagining a world so clearly against nature, and worse, they were stung with the label 'heretics' for daring to question God's divine plan of female subordination.

Haudenosaunee women, men and children all had control of their own personal property, Stanton and Gage knew. They were not the only American Indian nations in which women had property rights, the suffragists learned. Alice Fletcher (1888), an early ethnographer and suffragist spoke about her concerns working as an agent of the government in its program to 'christianize and civilize' Native Americans. At the 1888 International Council of Women she related this story to an audience that included Stanton and Gage along with the leading suffrage workers from around the western world:

When I was living with the [Omaha], my hostess … one day gave away a very fine horse. I was surprised, for I knew there had been no family talk on the subject, so I asked: 'Will your husband like to have you give the horse away?' Her eyes danced, and, breaking into a peal of laughter, she hastened to tell the story to the other women gathered in the tent, and I became the target of many merry eyes. I tried to explain how a white woman would act, but laughter and contempt met my explanation of the white man's hold upon his wife's property.

As I have tried to explain our statutes to Indian women, I have met with but one response. They have said: 'As an Indian woman I was free. I owned my home, my person, the work of my own hands, and my children could never forget me. I was better as an Indian woman than under white law'. (Fletcher 1888: 240)

Native women were losing their rights as they were forced into a legal system that treated them like Eurochristian women. They were also losing protection. Patricia Monture-Angus writes that, among the Haudenosaunee, 'there were strong cultural taboos' against violence against women 'which were enforced by the women's family members' (1995: 237). The laws (or absence of them) in the United States that allowed wife battering and marital rape also denied native women this protection against violence provided by their families. Fletcher explained to the Council attendees:

Not only does the woman under our laws lose her independent hold on her property and herself, but there are offenses and injuries which can befall a woman which would be avenged and punished by the relatives under tribal law, but which have no penalty or recognition under our laws. If the Indian brother should, as of old, defend his sister, he would himself become liable to the law and suffer for his championship.... She has fallen under the edge of our laws. (1888: 240-241)

Indian men, Fletcher said, had told her: 'Your laws show how little your men care for their women. The wife is nothing of herself' (1888: 240).

In the United States, until women's rights advocates began the painstaking task of changing state laws, a husband had the legal right to batter his wife within limits—as long as he did not inflict permanent harm or use excessive violence, a North Carolina court ruled in 1864—preferring to 'leave the parties to themselves as the best mode of inducing them to make the matter up and live together as a man and wife should' (Dobash and Dobash 1977-78: 430-431).

Suffragists knew that wife battering was not universal, living as neighbours to men of other nations whose religious, legal, social and economic concept of women made such behaviour unacceptable.

Haudenosaunee spiritual practices, encompassed in the Code of Handsome Lake, told this cautionary tale (as reported by a white woman who was a contemporary of Stanton and Gage) of what would befall batterers in the afterlife:

[A man,] who was in the habit of beating his wife, was led to the red-hot statue of a female, and requested to treat it as he had done his wife. He commenced beating it, and the sparks flew out and were continually burning him. Thus would it be done to all who beat their wives. (Myrtle 1855: 138)

Until women's rights advocates began to change divorce laws in the last half of the nineteenth century, women found themselves trapped in marriages, unable to leave. A wife fleeing from a violent husband could be returned to him by the police, as runaway slaves were returned to their masters. Elizabeth Cady Stanton was called a heretic for advocating divorce laws that would allow women to leave violent and loveless marriages. 'What God hath joined together let no man put asunder', traditional Christianity preached. Marriage was a covenant with God, not a social contract, and therefore could not be broken.

Disagreeing, Stanton found a model in the Haudenosaunee, she informed the National Council of Women in an 1891 speech describing divorce, Iroquois-style:

No matter how many children, or whatever goods he might have in the house, he might at any time be ordered to pick up his blanket and budge; and after such an order it would not be healthful for him to attempt to disobey. The house would be too hot for him; and unless saved by the intercession of some aunt or grandmother he must retreat to his own clan, or go and start a new matrimonial alliance in some other. (1891: 223)

These white women lived in a world where wife battering was a Euroamerican tradition and marital rape was commonplace and forbidden by neither church nor state (although the Comstock Laws of the 1870s—pushed through by religious conservatives—outlawed discussion of it). Indian women's violence-free and egalitarian home life could only have given suffragists a vision of how women should be treated, along with the sure knowledge that they, too, could create a social structure of equality.

All things are in balance at the heart of Haudenosaunee spiritual belief. Even the earth is gender-balanced. Sky Woman and her daughter began creation with the earth and out of woman's body came corn, beans and squash and everything that grows *in* the earth. Flint and Sapling, Sky woman's grandsons, completed creation with things *on* it: mountains, rivers, etc. Men and women maintained that balance by carrying out their respective and mutual responsibilities. Women's responsibility rested with everything *in* the earth; men held responsibility for everything *on* the earth. Men's area of responsibility was the forest; women's was the field. Men hunted; women farmed.

As hard as it was for Euroamericans to see this sphere for women, so unlike the one assigned to them, Gage described it: 'Agriculture was in the hands of the men who were too old to fight, the boys who were too young for warriors, and the women—the women being the chief agriculturalists'. She explained the balance inherent in the system with a quote: 'Catlin says that this work was voluntarily taken upon themselves as no more than a just equivalent for the fatiguing labours of the men in war and in the chase' (1875a: 1).

Agriculture retained its ancient spiritual connection to fertility, growth and revival among the Haudenosaunee. Gage believed that this recognition of the spiritual, life-giving wonder of woman's creation of food represented a higher form of civilization than her own:

> To themselves the Five Nations were known as the Ongwe Honwe, that is, a people surpassing all others. In Christian Europe during the Middle Ages, the agriculturalist was despised; the warrior was the aristocrat of civilization. In publicly honouring agriculture as did the Ongwe Honwe three times a year, they surpassed in wisdom the men of Europe. (1875a: 1)

Stanton recognized the indigenous truth that agriculture grew naturally out of woman's ability to birth. In her 1891 speech to the National Council of Women she taught:

> Careful historians now show that the greatest civilizing power ... has been found in ... motherhood ... woman made the first home ... she made the first attempts at agriculture ... all that was known of the medical art was in her hands. She ... cultivated the arts of peace. (1891: 221)

The Haudenosaunee worldview is based on keeping everything in balance. Women and men each have responsibilities that they must carry out to maintain this balance. The clan mother heads the entire extended family that makes up a clan. Since the founding of the League of the Haudenosaunee over 500 years ago, each clan mother has had the responsibility for carrying out the process by which the women of her clan select a male chief. The clan mother also has the duty of deposing the chief if he fails to perform his official duties. The man cannot become a chief or remain a chief if he commits rape or any other major crime. 'Although the principal chief of the confederacy was a man, descent ran through the female line, the sister of the chief possessing the power of nominating his successor', Gage explained:

> Balance also requires that everyone in the nation have a voice, and decision-making is made by consensus in public councils. All questions, including the making of treaties and deciding on issues of war and peace, have always required the approval of both women and men. This democratic government, established before Columbus, continues to this day, with clan mothers still nominating the chiefs and the entire clan (women with full equality) making the final decision. (1875a: 1)

Denied a political role in their own nation, the two major theorists in the woman's right movement, Stanton and Gage, knew and wrote about the decision-making responsibilities of women in the Six Nations. Stanton talked about how the clan mother held the authority for putting and keeping in place the chief that represented her clan:

> The women were the great power among the clan, as everywhere else. They did not hesitate, when occasion required, 'to knock off the horns', as it was technically called, from the head of a chief and send him back to the ranks of the warriors. The original nomination of the chiefs also always rested with the women. (1891: 223)

The authority of women went further, according to Gage: 'The common interests of the confederacy were arranged in councils, each sex holding one of its own, although the women took the initiative in suggestion, orators of their own sex presenting their views to the council of men' (1875b: 1).

Haudenosaunee women also had responsibility for deciding if the nation would go to war: 'Its women exercised controlling power in peace and war, forbidding at will its young braves to enter battle, and often determining its terms of peace' (Gage 1875b: 1).

Finally, the women held political, as well as spiritual and industrial responsibility for the land, Gage explained: 'No sale of lands was valid without consent of the [women] and among the State Archives at Albany, New York, treaties are preserved signed by the"Sachems and Principal Women of the Six Nations"' (1895: 5).

Matilda Joslyn Gage, shortly after being found guilty of the 'crime' of voting for School Commissioner, was adopted into the Wolf clan of the Mohawk nation. Gage's adoption, according to her new Mohawk sister 'would admit me to the *Council of Matrons*, where a vote would be taken, as to my having a voice in the chieftainship', Gage (1893) wrote her daughter.

Essentially arrested for voting in her own nation, Gage faced the possibility of receiving a political voice—voting rights—in a foreign nation that had adopted her. What must it have meant to Gage to experience such real-life political authority?

Far from possessing political rights, Euroamerican women came from a tradition of political slavery, as Stanton accused in 'The Declaration of Sentiments', written for the 1848 Seneca Falls convention and modelled on the language of the Declaration of Independence:

> The history of mankind is a history of repeated injuries and usurpations on the part of man toward woman, having in direct object the establishment of an absolute tyranny over her. He has never permitted her to exercise her inalienable right to the elective franchise.... Having deprived her of this first right of a citizen ... he has oppressed her on all sides. (Stanton, Anthony and Gage 1881: 70)

Among the resolutions passed at the 1848 Seneca Falls convention had been this one: 'Resolved, That it is the duty of the women of this country to secure to themselves their sacred right to the elective franchise' (Stanton, Anthony and Gage 1881: 70).

Religious conservatives, Stanton and Gage charged, were responsible for the laws in each state that made it a crime for women to vote. Traditional ministers preached against woman suffrage, claiming it would force women out of their divinely-decreed role of subordination. Suffragists disagreed, waging a campaign of civil disobedience in which they broke the law (by voting) refused to pay their taxes (no taxation without representation) and accused the government of failing to live up to its founding principle—a government based on the consent of the governed.

Ridiculed, labelled heretics and arrested for the crime of voting, these courageous women continued to believe in the rightness of their cause. It was neither natural nor religiously mandated for women to be denied a voice in decisions affecting their lives and the lives of their children, they believed. They knew women could be decision-makers. They had seen such women in real life.

Haudenosaunee men acknowledged the lack of political freedom suffered by United States women and the injustice of it. Dr Peter Wilson, a Cayuga chief, addressed the New York Historical Society in 1866, encouraging United States men to give everyone the vote, 'even the women, as in his nation', according to a newspaper report read by Gage (*Syracuse Journal* 1866).

While Iroquois men recognized the great injustice being done to United States women by their government, Gage acknowledged a similar United States injustice toward Native Americans. When New York state considered legislation which would force citizenship on Indian men, she supported the decision of the Council of Chiefs to oppose it. In an editorial in her suffrage newspaper, *The National Citizen and Ballot Box*, Gage (1878a) wrote:

That the Indians have been oppressed—are now, is true, but the United States has treaties with them, recognizing them as distinct political communities, and duty towards them demands not an enforced citizenship but a faithful living up to its obligations on the part of the Government.

In this editorial, Gage (1878a) pointed out the hypocrisy of the United States government trying to force citizenship on Indians—who didn't want it—while denying the right to tax-paying women of the United States:

This council of Indians at Onondaga Castle, in the center of the great Empire State, and the convention of the women of the country at Washington in January, the one protesting against citizenship about to be forced upon them, because with it would come further deprivation of their rights— the other demanding citizenship denied them, in order to protect their rights, are two forcible commentaries upon our so-called republican form of government.

She clearly understood the issue of native sovereignty, writing: 'Our Indians are in reality foreign powers, though living among us…. Compelling them to become citizens would be like the forcible annexation of Cuba, Mexico, or Canada to our government, and as unjust'. (Gage 1878a)

Suffragists should take political direction from native activists in their struggle for recognition by the United States government, Gage (1878a) suggested:

A delegation of Indians called at the White House on New Year's Day. As a sarcasm of justice, on their 'Happy New Year' cards were inscribed extracts from various treaties made with them, and disregarded rights guaranteed them in treaty by the Government. The women of the nation might take hint from the Indians and on July 4th, send to the legislative, judicial and executive bodies, cards inscribed with such sentiments as 'Governments derive their *just* powers from the *consent* of the governed'. 'Taxation without representation is tyranny', and others of like character.

Gage (1878b) once again drew on the parallel struggles for political self-determination between Native nations and United States women in a resolution adopted by the NWSA at their convention the following year:

Resolved. That the policy of this government in appointing agents to educate and civilize the Indians, to obtain calico dresses for [Indian women] and aprons for papooses and a comfortable salary for their own pockets out of money justly due the Indian tribes, is in harmony with man's treatment of woman in appropriating her property, talents, time and labours, and using the proceeds as he pleases in the name of protection.

The foundation of United States government—each citizen having a voice— was solid. The goal was making the government live up to its founding principle. That too, Gage wrote, had been a gift of the Haudenosaunee:

But the most notable fact connected with woman's participation in govern-mental affairs among the Iroquois is the statement of Hon. George Bancroft that the form of government of the United States was borrowed from that of the Six Nations. Thus to the Matriarchate or Mother-rule is the modern world indebted for its first conception of inherent rights, natural equality of condition, and the establishment of a civilized government upon this basis. (1895: 6)

'Under their women', she wrote, 'the science of government reached the highest form known to the world' (1895: 6).

Common knowledge held that Christianity and civilization meant progress for women, but Stanton and Gage disagreed. After many years of unsuccessful campaigns to get the male United States government to recognize the right women clearly had to the vote, Elizabeth Cady Stanton was growing frustrated:

> For twelve years in succession I have travelled from Maine to Texas trying by public lectures and private conversations 'to teach women to think'. The chief obstacle in the way of success has everywhere been their false theology, their religious superstitions (qtd. in Banner 1980: 158).

She wrote to a friend, '... as I have passed from the political to the religious phase of this question, I now see more clearly than ever, that the arch enemy to woman's freedom skulks behind the altar' (Stanton 18[86-89]).

From the beginning of the movement, Stanton and Gage were agreed, their chief opponent had been the church. The argument put forth was this: God has decreed that woman shall be subordinate to man. If you place woman as man's equal at the ballot box, you are challenging God's wisdom and His divine plan. You are opposing nature as well, for woman, physically and mentally weaker, needs man to cling to for support.

There was nothing natural or God-ordained about their oppression, Gage and Stanton agreed. Their proof? 'In the councils of the Iroquois gens every adult male or female had a voice upon all questions brought before it', Stanton wrote (1891: 227). One example, that's all it took, of a government that functioned with women having an equal voice, to put the lie to the 'natural' argument against woman suffrage. There were more examples, like this news article from the *Woman's Tribune*, published by their friend Clara Colby:

> It is stated that an Indian Pueblo about fifty miles from the City of Mexico, is governed by a council of twelve, half of whom are elderly women who must have raised large families and proved devoted mothers and kind neighbours. 'The venerable mothers', is the title by which they are known, which is certainly an improvement on the 'old grannies' which we so often hear. (1887: 1)

When religious fundamentalists tried to destroy religious freedom by placing God in the Constitution and prayer in public schools and by pushing a conservative political agenda in the 1890s, Gage and Stanton determined it was finally time to challenge the church. Their theory, which each developed in their later writing, held that indigenous women in early history—the Haudenosaunee were a continuing example—had respect and authority in egalitarian and woman-centered societies that often worshipped a female deity, sometimes in combination with a male consort. This matriarchal system was overthrown, Stanton contended, when 'Christianity putting the religious weapon into man's hand made his conquest complete' (1891: 227).

A few years ago I was invited to lecture at the annual Elizabeth Cady Stanton birthday tea in Seneca Falls with Audrey Shenandoah, the Onondaga nation Eel clan mother. A crowd of my feminist contemporaries packed the elegant, century-old hotel and I spoke about the rights of Haudenosaunee women. Then Audrey talked matter-of-factly about the responsibilities of clan mothers, who continue today to nominate, counsel and keep in office their clan's chief, as they always have. In the six nations of the Iroquois confederacy, she explained, Haudenosaunee women have worked with the men to successfully guard their sovereign political status against persistent attempts to turn them into United States citizens. In Audrey's direct and simple telling, the social and political authority of the Haudenosaunee women seemed almost unremarkable. 'We have always had these responsibilities', she said.

My feminist terminology, I realized, had revealed my cultural bias. Out of habit I had referred to women's empowerment as women's 'rights'. But for Haudenosaunee women who have maintained many of their traditional ways despite two centuries of United States attempts to 'civilize and Christianize' them, the concept of women's 'rights' actually has little meaning. To the Haudenosaunee, it is simply their way of life. Their egalitarian relationships and their political authority are a reality of which—like my foresisters—I still but dream.

Sisters in Spirit with Haudenosaunee women, Euroamerican suffragists looked forward to a future inspired by the knowledge that woman's rights was a lived reality, not just a longing. It would take 72 years of continuous hard work before the women of the United States achieved the political position Haudenosaunee women held long before Europeans landed on these shores. By the time the suffrage amendment passed in 1920, both Gage and Stanton were dead. We are far from achieving the egalitarian society in balance that gave these early feminists their vision.

But they left us an empowering hope that comes with the knowledge that the people of the world have not always created social, economic and religious systems of unequal power. Knowing that peace and harmony are achievable because others have achieved them, we can continue the work to make them a reality in our country. And, as the suffragists understood clearly, this transformation cannot take place without the major participation of women. As Stanton said in her 1891 speech on the Matriarchate:

> Every woman present must have a new sense of dignity and self-respect, feeling that our mothers, during some periods in the long past, have been the ruling power, and that they used that power for the best interests of humanity. As history is said to repeat itself, we have every reason to believe that our turn will come again. (1891: 227)

Sally Roesch Wagner is the executive director of the Matilda Joslyn Gage Foundation in Fayetteville, New York. She is one of the first women to receive a doctorate for work in women's studies in the United States (University of California Santa Cruz) and a founder of one of the country's first women's studies programs at California State University, Sacramento.

Notes

1   The extensive Iroquois newspaper clipping file in the Onondaga Historical Association, Syracuse, New York, covering almost 150 years from the 1840s to present time, is a rich source of Onondaga County and New York City newspaper coverage of Iroquois news and public interest stories.

2   Gage (1895) relates in footnote 37: 'In relation to women the laws were very severe, for one that committed a rape upon a free woman was condemned to have his privy member cut off; for they judged that the three most heinous offenses were included in that one vile act, that is wrong, defilement and bastardy' (17).

References

Allen, P. G. (1986) *The Sacred Hoop: Recovering the Feminine in American Indian Traditions,* Boston: Beacon Press.

Bacon, M. H. (1980) *Valiant Friend: The Life of Lucretia Mott,* New York: Walker and Company.

Banner, L. W. (1980) *Elizabeth Cady Stanton,* Boston: Little, Brown and Company.

Beauchamp, M. E. (1893) 'Letter', *Skaneateles Democrat,* Fall.

Dobash, R. Emerson and R. P. Dobash (1977-78) 'Wives: the 'appropriate' victims of marital violence', *Victimology: An International Journal,* 2, 430-431.

Fletcher, A. (1888) 'The Legal Conditions of Indian Women,' *Proceedings of the International Council of Women,* 238-240.

Gage, M. J. (1895) *Woman, Church and State: A Historical Account of the States of Woman Through the Christian Ages with Reminiscences of the Matriarchate,* S. R. Wagner (ed.), Aberdeen, SD: Sky Carrier Press, 1998.

Gage, M. J. (1893) 'My dear Helen', Letter, 11 Dec., Gage Collection, Schlesinger Library.

Gage, M. J. (1878a) 'Indian citizenship', Editorial, *National Citizen and Ballot Box,* May.

Gage, M. J. (1878b) 'Resolution adopted by the National Woman Suffrage Association Convention, January 1878', *National Citizen and Ballot Box,* August.

Gage, M. J. (1875a) 'The Onondaga Indians', *New York Evening Post,* 3 November, 1.

Gage, M. J. (1875b) 'The remnant of the five nations', *New York Evening Post,* 24 September, 1.

Hallowell, A. D. (1884) *James and Lucretia Mott: Life and Letters,* Boston: Houghton, Mifflin and Company.

Iroquois Newspaper Clipping Collection, Onondaga Historical Association, Syracuse, New York.

Johnson, E. (1881) *Legends, Traditions and Laws, of the Iroquois, or Six Nations, and History of the Tuscarora Indians.* Lockport, NY: Union Printing and Publishing Co.

Lawrence, M. S. (n.d.) *Notes from a Sketch of Elizabeth Cady Stanton's Life by her Eldest Daughter, Margaret Stanton Lawrence,* Unpublished MS, Stanton Collection, Vassar College Library, Poughkeepsie, NY.

Lutz, A. (1967 [1940]) *Created Equal: A Biography of Elizabeth Cady Stanton,* New York: The John Day Company.

Monture-Angus, P. (1995) *Thunder in My Soul: A Mohawk Woman Speaks,* Halifax: Fernwood Publishing.

Myrtle, M. (1855) *The Iroquois: Or, The Bright Side of Indian Character,* New York: D. Appleton and Company.

'The Onondaga Indians' Editorial (1875) *New York Evening Post,* 24 September, 2.

Seneca Falls Historical Society (1906) 'Capt. Oren Tyler,' Seneca Falls Historical Society File, Seneca Falls, New York, 59.

Stanton, E. C. (1927) 'If you would be vigorous and healthy', in M. L. Hobrook, 'Parturition without pain', appendix to George H. Napheys, *The Physical Life of Woman: Advice to the Maiden, Wife and Mother,* New York: M. A. Donohue and Company, 365-366.

Stanton, E. C. (18[86-89]) Letter to Sara Underwood, 19 October, Stanton Papers, Vassar College Library, Poughkeepsie, NY.

Stanton, E. C. (1891) 'The matriarchate or mother-age', in R. F. Avery (ed.), *Transactions of the National Council Women of the United States, Assembled in Washington, D.C. February 22 to 25, 1891,* Philadelphia: N.P., 218-227.

Stanton, E. C., 1974 [1895, 1898] *The Woman's Bible,* Seattle: Coalition Task Force on Women and Religion.

Stanton, E. C., S. B. Anthony and M. J. Gage (eds.) 1985 [1881] *History of Woman Suffrage,* Vol. 1, Salem: Ayer Company.

Stanton, E. C., S. B. Anthony and M. J. Gage (eds.) 1985 [1882] *History of Woman Suffrage,* Vol. 2, Salem: Ayer Company.

Stanton, E. C., S. B. Anthony and M. J. Gage (eds.) 1985 [1886] *History of Woman Suffrage,* Vol. 3, Salem: Ayer Company.

Stockham, A. B. (1886) *Tokology: A Book for Every Woman,* Chicago: Sanitary Publishing Company.

Syracuse Journal (1866) 10 January: 1.

Wagner, S. R. (2003) *Matilda Joslyn Gage: She Who Holds the Sky,* Fayetteville, NY: Sky Carrier Press.

Wagner, S. R. (1987) 'Moses Harman: Champion of reproductive rights', *Changing Men,* 18, (Summer/Fall), 29-30.

Woman's Tribune (1887) November: 1 [Beatrice, NE].

'Writings of H. M. Converse and miscellaneous scrapbook of Ely S. Parker' (1892) *New York World,* 9 April: 33. Converse Collection, New York State Archives, Albany.

WOMEN'S HUMAN RIGHTS ACTIVISTS AS POLITICAL THEORISTS

BROOKE A. ACKERLY

Women's human rights activism demonstrates that the challenges of gaining recognition of women's human rights are as much the challenges of changing local social contexts as they are the challenges of promoting transnational norms of human rights. Given that the universality of human rights, particularly women's human rights, remains contested both in theoretical discourse and in international political fora, promoting human rights through changing local social mores and practices is an essential strategy for realizing women's human rights. However, local activists need the support of international human rights norms, especially when rights (particularly social and economic rights) are subject to local interpretation. Consequently, international human rights norms were operationalized in many United Nations (UN) Conference agreements of the 1990s with 'specific targets and indicators that can be used to define and monitor progress and compliance' (UNIFEM 2000: 38).[1]

Despite the value of legitimate universals for activism, women's human rights activists and their scholar co-travelers argue for modifications in international human rights norms that would yield greater recognition of women's human rights (Bunch 1990, 1995; Burrows 1986; Charlesworth 1994; Gallagher 1997). The current human rights standards do not protect those humans whose rights violations do not take the paradigmatic form of discrimination. Existing institutions are inadequate for attributing responsibility for human rights violations by state and non-state actors.[2] Transnationally, we need to support the conditions of human rights and not just to rely on international punitive measures to address national failures (UNDP 2000).[3]

Women's human rights activists thus collectively occupy the seemingly incoherent theoretical position that *human rights are local and universal and contested*. In this article, I argue that activists resolve the oxymoron by offering a model for 1) recognizing and using the contingent common ground in which the parallel efforts of human rights activists around the world can be acknowledged; 2) appreciating that though sometimes networked and integrated with those parallel efforts, activism for social change is *local* and needs locally appropriate ways to promote women's human rights; 3) accepting that the current articulation of universal human rights in international law is insufficient for supporting the realization of the human rights of all of humanity; and yet 4) employing that international law as a contingent universal when advocating for local change. While practical in orientation, I argue, their effort has import for political theory.

I extend the reference to women's experience in feminist human rights theorizing beyond its use as a basis for posing theoretical challenges to the human rights paradigm to its respect as a resource for theoretical insight and theory building. First, drawing on the activism of two online working groups, I identify six forms of women's activism that illustrate the general problems of, and common strategies for, promoting universal human rights across various local contexts. Second, I outline the activists' assumptions, theoretical framework, and method of using practice to inform theory. Third, I develop the implications of the activists' model for the scholar-activist.

Before getting to the substance of their work, let me first give some theoretical context to the activists' ontological perspective. Some contemporary political theorists have developed their theoretical projects in such a way that, although commonly associated with liberal, communitarian, critical and post-modern perspectives individually, they can be appreciated as exploring the similar terrain of weak ontology (White 2000).[4] A weak ontology is valuable for considering questions of human rights (and justice and globalization among others) because it presumably allows us to hold fast to universals when some human beings are being harmed by their violation, and to revise the universals when some human beings' harms are being ignored by their (limited) scope (see, for e.g., O'Neill 1993).

Yet we can quickly see a problem with a weak ontology for human rights by looking at rights violations that are perpetuated in practices around the world. In an attempt to redress them, do we respect the rights of parents to educate their children (UDHR 1948: Article 26, 3), or do we respect the children's right to freedom of consciousness (UDHR 1948: Article 18) that will certainly be compromised by some parents' educational practices? Do we respect the right of a wife not to experience inhuman or degrading treatment (UDHR 1948: Article 5) when her abuse takes place in private and thus is not visible to us or do we respect an abusive husband's right to privacy (UDHR 1948: Article 12)? How do we adjudicate between seemingly competing liberal rights? The issue is further complicated when we are asked to weigh individual rights against community rights. Or, to take the questioning in a slightly different direction, can we hold states accountable for human rights violations that take place in the home or in autonomous communities?[5] These are practical and theoretical questions. Can a weak ontological framework be decisive and specific enough to address them?

Women's human rights activists have tried to resolve these theoretical questions with specificity. They have sought further specification of international and national legal instruments.[6] And they have sought locally specific remedies for universal human rights violations at home. In this way, the practice of women's human rights advocacy yields an important insight into the possibility for using contingent universals as guidelines for ethical and political decision-making.

Although political theorists traditionally build their arguments from the wealth of theoretical knowledge shared through theoretical texts, activist discourse is an important source for building theory about human rights. Most political theorists who have explored weak ontological grounds have done so to move away from the inadequacy of the strong ontological views that have been providing justification for moral and political reasoning.[7] I want to suggest that, rather than turning away from certain intellectual traditions, these theorists should turn toward another tradition, the tradition of activism. With its employ of practical reasoning and of praxis, the tradition of activism already has much in common with certain strands of political theory, principally Marxist critical theory and pragmatism. But activists' intellectual debt to these western traditions is remote at best and coloured with a racist, sexist and colonial past at worst such that it would be fraudulent to portray their ideas and practice as derivative of these traditions.[8]

According to my interpretation, feminist practice around women's human rights has drafted the significant pieces of a model of cross-cultural human rights theory that can be used to reinforce norms of international customary human rights law and to assess critically claims of culturally legitimate deviance from those norms while respecting value plurality across *and* within cultures. Though this may not be the explicit project of many feminist theorists, activists and practitioners, I interpret it as one collective result of their work. This is an important theoretical methodological move on my part. J. Oloka-Onyango and Sylvia Tamale (1995) argue that feminist human rights discourse incorporates southern women as sources of illustration but not as authors in the theory-building project. For the cross-cultural model in this article, I explicitly turn to activists around the world for participation in the theory-building project. While working for women's human rights, activists have articulated a cross-cultural theory of human rights which respects variety and differences within cultures and nations, does not have a static view of culture, and does not rely on state actors to participate in drafting international customary law on human rights.

The women's human rights activists' basis for human rights criticism and activism is contestable. From their collective perspective the rights-bearing individual is situated in community and is a product of social mores, but not a product without her own agency. And she may use that agency to try to change her community's, another community's, or international norms. Respect for human rights needs to be cultivated but at the same time, critics can turn our attention to the particular articulations of human rights that are our local and international political and cultural heritages.[9]

Within a weak ontological framework, the cross-cultural account of universal human rights is provisional. First, there are logistical reasons for its provisional quality. The activists cited are not all of the participants in the working groups. The working groups did not enable participation by all of those around the world whose views would have been relevant. And, as discussed in the next section, the dialogue among non-governmental organization (NGO) activists and others was mediated by Education Development Centre Inc. (EDC) as moderators for UNIFEM, an international NGO. Second, my account of it is provisional because I am but one interpreter of the activists' work at theory building. Perhaps some of those whom I consider activists would disagree with the account I offer as being too accepting of mainstreaming strategies or too exposed to relativistic interpretation and abuse. Others might find the conflicting strategies and philosophies of women's human rights advocates as prohibitive of any cohesion among theorists. The provisional character of the model is intended to deal with concerns about mainstreaming (or other efforts to universalize), and the use of the provisional universal for criticism is intended to deal with concerns of relativism without abandoning the effort for theoretical coherence. Third, this account is provisional as a function of its collective authorship and the on-going dialogue about women's human rights. In sum, the imperfection of the account presented here rests on both the limited input by activists and on the always ongoing nature of the project of feminist praxis. This and any account of universal human rights can be only provisional.

Working Within Local and International Norms

In what women's human rights activists have to say about their work, they offer not only the basis for criticizing the international human rights paradigm and not only advice that may be effective in other locations. Through their work, in the strategic use of international norms and in the thoughtful revisions to those norms, activists offer also a basis for a cross-cultural theory of human rights.

Although generally I work with a more specific definition of activism (Ackerly 2001a), for the purposes of this article, I consider all those who participate in dialogue about the meaning of women's human rights and those who articulate their view of the meaning of women's human rights through their actions to be 'activists'. The activists cited in this article participated in two particular online dialogues about their work. They defined themselves a scholars, activists and policy-makers. Although the main focus of the online working groups was to identify practices that work,[10] I argue that they also identified a theoretical perspective on human rights that provides an ontological basis for promoting women's human rights across cultural, regional and national contexts.

The descriptions of women's activism below are from research with two online working groups—End-of-Violence and CEDAW-in-Action—sponsored by UNIFEM and managed by Education Development Center Inc. in Cambridge, Massachusetts.[11] From October 1998 through January 2000 and from February through September 1999 respectively, these working groups invited participants from around the world to share their knowledge and program experience working against violence against women and for the Convention on the Elimination of All Forms of Discrimination Against Women (CEDAW). Membership was open to all and there was overlap between the groups. The content was moderated by EDC. The few citations included here come from members who are policy-makers, practitioners, activists and scholars, but they do not adequately convey the range of contexts in which participants work.[12]

The role of the moderators was significant in making the online working groups useful and inclusive. In order for the group not to degenerate, the moderators served an important gate-keeping function of keeping the postings relevant to the purpose of the group. Thus in order for the group to be successful, the moderators exercised discretionary exclusions. In the first couple of months of the End-of-Violence list, 75 per cent of the messages received were not posted. Rather than merely not posting those messages, the moderators responded to the individual authors and worked with them to improve the substance and language in their posting. Such active moderation was particularly necessary with participants from Eastern Europe and parts of Asia due to the lack of proficiency in English (Brodman 1998). Through their behind the scenes editing, the moderators actively included those participants whose ideas would have been marginalized without active moderation.[13] The moderators were important activists because they enabled the lists to be inclusive. In order to be confident that the practice of moderation was inclusive despite its power to be exclusive, the rules and the practices of moderation need to be closely examined.

The necessity of such active moderation also illustrates an important theoretical point. Although it may be attractive to theorize about international or transnational communities that enable cross-cultural dialogue among equal participants as a resource for thinking about universal human rights (or other universals), in practice such communities cannot exist.[14] The more appropriate theoretical approach is to learn from actual practices that approximate the results to which the theorist of international or transnational dialogue aspires.

The midterm review of the End-of-Violence working group chronicles the EDC's efforts to extend the circle of participants (Brodman 1998). While the resources of UNIFEM enabled the scope and length of the working groups, we have no account of who was excluded by the structure of the dialogue or by its taking place under the aegis of UNIFEM. By citing from the End-of-Violence working group, I do not mean to present the group as definitively inclusive or even as representative of all women's human rights activism. However, I recognize it as an *interesting* source of information about many activists' practical and theoretical ideas.

Despite working in a broad range of contexts, there are remarkable parallels in the ways in which women's human rights activists conduct their work as indicated by their contributions to the online groups. From my observation I have identified six ways of promoting women's human rights. These methods complement each other and many activists are involved in more than one approach. In parentheses I have labeled these categories to make it easier to refer to them in the text and discussion. Activists seek to: 1) make legal changes such that domestic or international laws better conform with the CEDAW and other international agreements which recognize women's human rights (*legal change*); 2) reinvent local legal practices (for example by training judges and police officers, establishing ombuds-women for survivors of violence, or establishing women's police stations) (*training*); 3) support survivors of violence (*support*); 4) educate society broadly (for example in schools, through the media and through gender training programs) (*education*); 5) network and promote alliances among organizations working to end violence against women; share methods, resources and information with other organizations; promote activism (such as letter writing campaigns, marches and boycotts), or offer funding for any of the above activities (*networking*); and 6) integrate women's human rights efforts with other initiatives for social, economic, and political change (including but not limited to economic development, health and environmental initiatives) (*integration*).[15]

Within a given context, these are six ways of mainstreaming women's human rights. Gender mainstreaming is the multi-faceted project of using gender analysis in addressing the mainstream agenda and of getting gender-related issues onto the mainstream agenda. Although some may view gender mainstreaming as accepting certain aspects of international political economy (such as consumerism and global capitalism), in my view, gender mainstreaming strategies may accept certain norms and institutions provisionally but challenge them at an appropriate time. Thus, gender mainstreaming, though incremental, does not preclude revolution.[16]

In mainstreaming women's human rights, activists have used gender analysis to rethink human rights norms such that women's human rights are protected as human rights and they have shown that addressing women's human rights means addressing the political, economic and social contexts of human life. Women's human rights activists work internationally and transnationally to promote a gender-sensitive understanding of human rights and their violations and intra-culturally to change local views such that women can realize their human rights.

Legal Change

The first way draws primarily on legal resources and promotes legal changes that are endorsed by precedents and conventions in international law. For example, the Women's Caucus for Gender Justice in the International Criminal Court (ICC) worked to promote a Statute of the International Criminal Court that reflected a respectful gender perspective. The ICC is the institution negotiated in July 1998 as the forum for individuals to be tried for genocide, war crimes, and crimes against humanity, when national level authorities fail to prosecute. The Women's Caucus sought to make this institution—an important institution for addressing human rights violations—gender sensitive from its foundation. A member of the Caucus writes,

> The Women's Caucus presciently laid the groundwork for the incorporation of a gender perspective early, during the Preparatory Committee's drafting process beginning in February 1997. The caucus also brought a critical mass of women from all regions of the world to lobby the delegations in Rome. This ultimately helped counter the small but vociferous minority's tireless attack on the gender-sensitive provisions ... written into the Rome draft text. (Martinez 1998) [17]

Thus, women's human rights activists promoted a gendered international understanding of human rights.

Other examples include domestic efforts to bring national law in line with the CEDAW. Even when well-intentioned, these efforts require the guidance of feminist activists, in order that legal changes be actionable and in practice do not result in unintended consequences that undermine their effectiveness. For example in India and Turkey, governments have proposed increasing the punishment for rape and domestic violence. Activists in India argue that the certainty of punishment, not the extent of the punishment, is a more successful deterrent. Activists in Turkey argue that for survivors of domestic violence a cessation of violence without cessation of financial support is the greatest need of victims. In both instances, activists seek to reorient government thinking from a criminal-orientated perspective to a survivor-oriented perspective.

Training

In a second way, activists interested in promoting women's human rights work to change domestic law. They educate lawmakers, reorient their thinking, and propose laws that are more usable by survivors. As Women for Women's Human Rights (WWHR) (1998) an autonomous NGO in Turkey explains,

> In the case of domestic violence, an amendment of the criminal code to increase the punishment for the perpetrator of violence did not provide women with the most effective legal mechanism.... We argued that a much better strategy would be not to increase the punishment but rather to introduce other laws, such as the protection order, which would provide women with other means of ending the violence to which they are subjected. The protection order, which would be under the civil code, would involve less complicated and much quicker legal proceedings resulting in the enforced separation of the perpetrator of violence from the family home for a certain period of time. In other words, it would facilitate what women who are subjected to domestic violence need the most: A cessation of the violence without them having to leave home. A protection order also allows for the enforcement of the spouse to continue to provide for his family during the time he is separated from the family home.[18]

By contrast, in Sweden activists endorsed an enhancement provision that under certain conditions would increase the punishment for domestic violence related crimes (Pietilä 1999, 2001). In addition to working with lawmakers, activists work to reeducate the executive and judiciary including training judges and police.[19]

Taken together, these activists illustrate an important theoretical consideration. Intra-national dialogue about the best way to realize universal norms in the local context is based on the theoretical common ground that domestic violence is wrong according to both international and local norms, and on the need for variety in its antidotes.

Support

The third form of women's activism compensates for shortcomings in the legal system by providing women with shelters, education and other self-development tools. Due to shortcomings in the legal system, while working to change laws and practices, activists also provide support to women as they navigate the deficiencies of the legal system in pursuit of their own security and interests. For example, an English as a Second Language instructor at York University in Canada suggests incorporating information about domestic violence and women's legal rights into ESL curriculum (Fong 1999). Due to political reasons (such as anti-immigrant attitudes in some places), it may be difficult for such information to be incorporated formally into curricula. Giving effective support may require coordinating with efforts around change and training.

In some cases activists combine efforts to change police and legal mores and practices with efforts to support women survivors. For example, in Augusta, Georgia, SAFE Homes of Augusta, Inc. has partnered with local law enforcement for offering crisis support services. In one county,

> A member of our staff serves as a team member of [the police] domestic violence unit.... Each victim identified in the police reports is contacted as quickly as possible and arrangements made to visit with her either in her home, at her place of employment, the sheriff's office or another neutral location depending on what best meets the need [of] the victim. At those interviews, an assessment is done to determine what might best help the victim and includes information and referral, domestic violence education, legal assistance and support in obtaining whatever criminal or civil remedies the victim may choose to avail herself of and a safety plan prepared.... Follow-up visits continue as long as necessary to empower her to become independent and self-sufficient. The program has been very successful and has enabled the Agency to take a more proactive approach to aiding victims—unlike our earlier approach of merely hoping the victim found her way to making contact with us on her own. (Nelson 1999)

The liaison person is part of a larger set of resources SAFE provides to educate the Sheriff's offices about domestic violence. Thus, while supporting the women survivors of domestic violence, SAFE also promotes changes in the legal officers' mores, practices, and beliefs around women, gender and violence against women.

Because changes to the legal system are slow and uneven, activism that changes women's interface with the legal system is necessary. Thus, even when laws do not change, social mores and practices that affect women's experience of negotiating the legal system can be changed through activism. The forms these changes take vary around the world from an ombudsperson for victims of domestic violence in Arizona, USA to legal advice to the women's police station in Lima, Peru. Such changes, and the variety of perspectives across and within cultures about women's human rights that they illustrate, have theoretical import.

Education

Quite commonly, work in the first three areas of women's human rights leads activists to recognize the need to educate the community in order to gain broad support for and understanding of their initiatives. One scholar participant from India argues for the need for community education directed at the social attitudes of women and men. Mahila Police Thanas (women's police districts) have been established in which female police officers are responsible for dealing with crimes against women. Women can thus report a crime without in the process violating social norms. However, this local observer of the women officers notes that merely using women to make the criminal investigations does not guarantee that there will be a sufficient challenge to social mores and practices such that women's human rights will actually be affected.

> [T]hese police officers recognize violence only in its gross forms, [like domestic] beating, rape, dowry death, etc. They refuse to believe that violence can also be structural, that is in a very subdued and subtle form, within the family structure, in power relations [within] the family and in your just being a woman. When a case was brought where there was a misunderstanding between a man and woman the police official kept asking the women why she did not perform her functions as a wife. The women in question had on one particular occasion refused to wash the clothes of the mother-in-law. The female police official kept harping on the duties of the women, stating all the kinds of works which she also as a married women had to do in spite of having a job, and [in] this women had no choice. (Pande 1999)

From the perspective of the reporting researcher, the support offered by the Mahila Police does not adequately challenge social mores and practices,[20] but instead uses the mechanism of law enforcement to reinforce unexamined social norms.

To achieve responsiveness in the community (from women and men) to *change, training* and *support* initiatives, activists work in a fourth way: they foster changes in the community's mores and practices through education using both traditional educational institutions and the media. For example, in Kenya, the Coalition On Violence Against Women has an active Outreach Committee which goes to schools and educates young boys and girls about the proper respect due one another as human beings and the inappropriateness of violence in their relationships with one another (Sitati 1999).

Agenda, a journal devoted to gender equity issues in South Africa, illustrates another form of community education. *Agenda* promotes mainstream media attention to reported increases in violence against women, crime patterns and priorities, and the treatment of victims by the police and the judicial system. In addition, *Agenda* encourages the use of the media to change attitudes about women, virility and the causes of rape (Marrian 1998). Soul City Multi-Media Health Promotion Project, another South African NGO, uses the media by creating radio and television dramas into which they integrate 'issues to inform the public and stimulate debate'. Discussions of these primetime dramas are supplemented by booklets of information reproduced in serial in local newspapers. Further they 'adapt the mass media material into youth life skills material' incorporated into secondary school curricula (Usdin 1998).

In appreciating the educative function of activists, we should not underestimate the potential for differences among activists and for class or other biases to manifest themselves in the effort to change local norms. For instance, in the example above the Mahila police officer and the researcher differ in their understandings of how international human rights law should be realized locally. The tone of the researcher is exclusive. Promoting her own understanding of structural violence, the researcher here seeks to exclude the police women's interpretation of violence. The example illustrates the need for further intra-cultural and intra-national dialogue in India about women's human rights. More generally, cross-cultural human rights theory requires attention to intra-cultural heterogeneity.

Networking

Activism of the third and fourth kinds tends to be done by local NGOs, which may or may not be linked with efforts to effect legal change or to train law enforcement and judicial personnel. Because NGOs are at the forefront of support for women survivors and community education most of this activism is done drawing on scant resources. The fifth mode of activism leverages these scant resources and supports other activism through research, networking and discussions. Those using this fifth method promote the sharing of materials and knowledge transnationally and locally. They foster reporting, linkages, support and partnerships among organizations, dissemination of training materials, exchange of research tools and findings, identification of best practices, grassroots-academic links, cross-cultural research, databases, teleconferencing, intergovernmental support and global activism (Gauthier 1999; Riangkruar 1999).[21] Such networking functions to leverage the strategic skills and tactical information developed in one setting for successful activism in other contexts.[22] Local activists leverage off the successes of international activism when they promote local change in conformity with CEDAW, the Beijing *Platform for Action*, and regional conventions. Transnational activists leverage off local successes to increase pressure internationally and across nations.[23] Further, networking addresses the isolation and frustration that many local activists feel at times of setback.

Integration

Finally, in order for women's human rights to be addressed, it is not enough merely to get them recognized as important. Given the economic and infrastructural demands on governments, there are always many needs that go unfunded and unaddressed. Frequently, women's rights are a lower priority politically than other needs. Although, using the CEDAW, the *Platform for Action*, and related regional treaties, activists have been able to raise women's human rights on the list of local priorities (True and Mintrom 2001), their long term success will be a function of integrating attempts to address women's human rights with attempts to address other needs.

Thus, strategically, activists incorporate women's human rights into their activism around economic development, health, and environmentalism where funding is more certain and where attention to women's human rights has payoffs in terms of the increased success of those development, health, and environmental initiatives. For example, CARE in Zambia integrates violence against women programming with institution building, micro-finance, and gender support groups (Malasha 1998).[24] Efforts to change the social practices that affect women's human rights may be part of other efforts at social, political and economic change and these efforts can be designed to incorporate fundamental change in gender norms.

In sum, these ways of activism—of working within the existing paradigm to change it by changing the social context of rights—reveal the theoretical insights of these activists. According to women's human rights activists, human rights are a function of universal individual rights and social context, and therefore recognition of human rights requires a conscious process of social change. That process is respectful of cultural diversity but not limited by a view of any culture (or any culture's feminism) as static or homogeneous. Their model of social change is incremental in that it draws on existing laws and practices while working to change their meaning and function.

The changes appropriate to each cultural and sociopolitical context vary such that across cultures activists may question one another's specific goals, but the specification of targets and indicators in official international documents are intended to prevent the misappropriation or misinterpretation of universal human rights language (UNIFEM 2000: 38). Across cultures women's human rights activists seek a voice for women in the process of determining their societies' values, practices, norms and mores and of shaping international human rights law. By example, they illustrate a method for theorizing about universal human rights that reflects their collective learning. In the next section I elaborate on these theoretical insights.

The Activists' Cross-Cultural Theory of Universal Human Rights

In this section, I show that the practical examples described above offer the basis of a cross-cultural theory of universal human rights that employs contingent universals and locally articulated norms for promoting women's human rights without sacrificing respect for value pluralism within and across cultures. Universal human rights are valuable criteria for guiding local social change and yet, the exact set of rights that are treated as universal is contingent and subject to reinterpretation.

The model of universal human rights theory that emerges from the feminist activist discourse about human rights is one consistent with certain aspects of International Relations and political theory arguments about universal human rights made by academics. Yet, fashioned from the bottom up, the theory has unique qualities that render it more resilient to criticism than other forms of universal human rights theory and render its policy implications demonstrably plausible.[25]

Assumptions

Though some activists are more inclined to celebrate similarities across contexts and others are more inclined to celebrate differences across cultures, their experientially-based, collective dialogue about similarities and differences yield a common set of assumptions that are the basis for further theoretical argument. These assumptions are: cross-cultural diversity, the possibility (and history) of cultural change and internal cultural diversity. They share certain of these assumptions with many theorists, but the full set of assumptions informs the human rights theory of only a few academics.

Even where common ground is recognized, the activists appreciate the fact of cross-cultural pluralism. Universal human rights scholars as different from one another as An-Na'im (1992a, 1992b), Bell (1999), de Bary (1998), Donnelly (1985), Falk (1992, 2000), Rawls (1999), Suu Kyi (1988), Taylor (1999) and Yasuaki (1999) share this view. In fact, for most contemporary human rights scholars the challenge is to justify universal norms despite value pluralism across cultures.[26]

Consistent with some human rights theorists, the activists recognize that cultures are not static (An-Na'im 1992b; Chan 1997).[27] But unlike these theorists, the activists have a more expansive understanding of the diverse sources of knowledge and legitimacy within cultures.[28] As the examples from the preceding section show, women's human rights activists have employed strategies that include allowing multiple voices to speak and exploring internal sources of legitimacy. These voices and sources of legitimacy do not necessarily conform with the norms of discourse followed by political and intellectual elites. Such a practice is essential for recognizing the value of a universal human rights theory in the service of social change.

The activists' strategy is similar to Abdullahi Ahmed An-Na'im's (1992b) strategy of drawing on reinterpretation of legitimate texts as a basis for fostering social change. An-Na'im claims the right to interpret Islamic texts and uses respected forms of discourse about those texts to criticize existing Muslim practices and law. However, unlike An-Na'im, women's human rights activists look to non-elite sources of knowledge (such as storytelling and personal narrative) and strengthen the social currency of these sources in order to legitimatize changes in social practices, mores and norms that are necessary to foster women's human rights in practice.[29] Thus the activists are able to recognize greater intra-cultural plurality within their model.

Theory

By virtue of their participation in the imperfect speech community of the working groups, the activists may seem to be offering a modified form of Habermasian discourse theory (Habermas 1980, 1987, 1989; see, for e.g., Linklater 1998; Falk 1992, 2000; Cox 1999). However, the activists' model is significantly different in its construction. The online working groups are not a rough approximation of an ideal speech community. The necessity and imperfection of the moderation rules and of active moderation as well as the technological limitations on participation mean that the online public sphere is not an ideal, but rather a situated best practice. And as activists know, best practices are subject to improvement. In this sense, the theory requires an appreciation that both our universal human rights and our tools for talking about them with one another are always imperfect.

The activists' model of universal human rights allows for the tentative embrace of international norms of universal human rights when promoting change in local practice, and the revision of those norms to be better informed by women's experience of rights violations. Recognition of different norms can be necessary to realizing women's human rights (Burrows 1986), and yet where different harmful norms are legitimatized on cultural grounds, they may be an obstacle to recognizing women's human rights (Okin 1999). Some policy makers who publicly endorse women's human rights also maintain that what it means to be a human differs for women and men and thus the human rights of women are not the same as those of men.[30] The difference in human experience for men and women is a function of the norms that a culture attributes to the biological differences between men and women (see also Ackerly 2000b, 2001a). Through practices these cultural norms may limit the extent to which universal individual rights are *in fact* secured for women.

Activists work toward recognizing universal rights in their home societies by changing the formal and informal practices of those societies. Moreover, they recognize that international rights norms are also a function of international norms, principally in the form of international common law. Thus, even while some are working to change local practices to enable the realization of women's human rights in specific contexts, activists are also engaged in trying to change international legal norms such that they better recognize women's human rights.

The multiplicity and networking of public and counterpublic spheres of activism demonstrated by activists has theoretical implications for universal human rights theory. As feminist scholars have noted in their critiques of Habermas, in nonpublic 'counterpublics', the marginalized can regroup and strategize for social and political change (Fraser 1992, also 1989, 1995; Benhabib 1988, 1989, 1991). Because of their concern with the realization of human rights norms under diverse sets of social values, practices and norms, in designing their political strategies activists group, regroup, and network locally and transnationally. Their strategies require a judicious use of transnational and local sources for appropriate audiences. Activists risk being perceived as foreign-influenced if their arguments do not have local cultural legitimacy (O'Brien, Goetz, Scholte, and Williams 2000: 62-63).

Despite the contingent quality of universal human rights, because of the emancipatory agenda of women's human rights activists, according to the theory they inspire, the process of reinterpretation cannot be simple, conservative or regressive. It must be an on-going and collective process. The reevaluation of universal human rights cannot limit the scope of humans protected by human rights and cannot lead to the codification within universal human rights norms of the human rights of some at the expense of the human rights of others.

Praxis: Theory of Practice, Theory in Practice, the Practice of Theory

Given its contingencies—the qualified embrace of international human rights norms and the imperfect ways we talk about them—an account of *how* to think theoretically about human rights practice and about how to use practice to think theoretically is an essential aspect of the cross-cultural theory. According to women's human rights activists, the universal theory of human rights needs to include an account of its own *theoretical* methodology and method such that the theorist is able to guide criticism with *contingent* guidelines which at another moment of inquiry she is able to suspend and submit to examination.

When the Turkish women question whether the proposed law regarding domestic violence is one they should endorse, they are suspending the guidelines that the government used in arriving at the law. They examine those guidelines against the knowledge of women's experience of domestic violence and deploy revised guidelines for justifying their proposed law.

Women's human rights activists show us that we need not only criteria like human rights and specified targets to guide our human rights thinking, but also criteria for subjecting those guidelines to scrutiny. Thus, the activists tell us that a universal human rights theory needs a *theoretical* methodology that requires critical attention to exclusion, exploitable hierarchies, coercion, and difference within and across cultures (see Ackerly 2000a; Alker 1996; Harding 1987). A theoretical methodology guides the creation and revision of a theoretical argument and is applied to theoretical and empirical research in the formation of the research agenda, in the choice of theoretical and empirical methods, and in the analysis of the findings for their theoretical import.

The cross-cultural universal human rights theory needs a theoretical *method* also. Just as, from within a fixed theoretical framework, an empirical method guides the choice of data, its collection, coding and analysis, so too a theoretical method guides the selection of texts and other legitimate sources of information, and determines the interpretive processes by which the information and insights from those texts and sources will be understood as contributing to the theoretical project. In this case, this method must include ways of drawing theoretical knowledge from the experience of women and other marginalized constituents of humanity and from non-elite forms of knowledge.[31] However, while empirical methods are replicable by different theorists, theoretical methods likely yield different results in the employ of different theorists. The multiplicity of results from the use of the feminist theoretical method is itself an important implication of the method.

Violations of women's human rights occur within societies without recognition by the community that they constitute rights violations. This theoretical method *requires* theorists to engage with the real life experience of human rights violations of all whose rights are violated. According to the women's human rights activists' theoretical method, experience provides important information for theory. Experience from multiple subjects provides greater sources of insights.

Women's human rights activists promote equality by challenging exploitable hierarchies, they undermine discrimination by transforming social values, and they promote freedom by fostering norms of inclusive participation. Collectively, their activism is multi-leveled. Through their activism they demonstrate a theory of human rights that is imperfectly collective, inclusive, noncoercive. Collectively, activists accept incremental change without abandoning aspirations for greater recognition of women's human rights.

Internationally (as well as nationally), the political context of human rights discourse is constrained by social mores and practices, specifically, the norms of international law, lobbying and even global feminist activism. As a result feminist criticism is rightly directed not only at human rights norms but also at the norms of critical thinking and discourse about human rights norms. Beyond contributing to the broader discussion of culture and human rights, activists' thinking about women's human rights violations in practice also directs theoretical attention to *how* we think about human rights.

Cross-Cultural Theoretical Practice of Universal Human Rights

The activists' cross-cultural theory of universal human rights is a workable guide for women's human rights activism. It also offers scholars a theoretical context in which to engage with activists and other scholars concerned about the cross-cultural legitimacy of human rights discourse (Bell 1999; Oloka-Onyango and Tamale 1995). Further, it offers a theoretical framework for activists and scholars to engage with one another on matters of public policy. In this section, as a scholar of human rights who engages the activists' model of cross-cultural universal human rights theory, I reflect on what embracing this theory requires of the scholar.[32]

Theorizing

Without explicitly articulating their own theory of universal human rights, the women's human rights activists have provided the outline of one. Their theoretical model is consistent with international human rights law, women's experience of rights violations, and activists' experience with trying to realize international and local law despite the obstacles conditioned in social contexts. Although I have noted its similarities with other theoretical perspectives on universal human rights that also appreciate cross-cultural variety and yet the need for common ground, the activists' theoretical model of universal human rights is distinct from these other theoretical models in that it requires a theoretical (or critical) method for its own re-evaluation.

Whether activists or scholars, social critics employ the method in the on-going critique of exploitable hierarchies and inequalities in two interrelated ways. First, cross-cultural theoretical method uses transnational dialogue to challenge exploitable hierarchies and inequalities. Second, the method enables the theorist to challenge hierarchies and inequalities in order to improve the quality of the on-going dialogue about the foundations of universal human rights. Scholar-activists develop the practice of cross-cultural theory by enhancing intra-cultural discourse. New data on the experience of marginalized people, public discussion of particular cases (like *Magaya v. Magaya* Zimbabwe 1999, see note 41), and public discussion of issues (like legal reform around domestic violence in Turkey) are all bases for expanding discourse intra-culturally. Such expanded local dialogue has implications for transcultural discourse as well.

Finally, this approach to universal human rights furthers the on-going cross-cultural theoretical project through dialogue among participants from a wide range of perspectives. These participants include those whose voices and experiences are not easily heard or observed.[33] Therefore, in practicing the theory, those scholar-activists who are heard must be assertive and ambitious in seeking an audience for those who are not and in seeking alternative venues and accurate linguistic and cultural translation for those who are marginalized.

Politicizing

While this activism has theoretical import, it also has urgency. Feminists wrestle with the struggles and wishes of the age as Karl Marx (1843) said critics should and they have a sense of urgency that requires working within existing practices and institutions while working towards better ones.[34]

In its sense of urgency and grounding in experience, cross-cultural human rights theory is more like the Preamble of the Universal Declaration than it is like any other theory of human rights. Both cross-cultural human rights theory and the Universal Declaration are explicitly political in their formation and use.

The Preamble provides a universal justification for universal human rights—

one based on values and on experience—that can be used to guide internal and cross-cultural discussions. According to the Universal Declaration, universal human rights have their basis both in universally recognized generalities such as the 'recognition of the inherent dignity and of the equal and inalienable rights of all members of the human family' and the values of 'freedom, justice and peace in the world' *and* in the historical facts of 'barbarous acts which have outraged the conscience of mankind' (UDHR 1948; Lindholm 1992: 399).

Actual cases of alleged 'barbarous acts' and of failures to protect human rights 'outraged the conscience of mankind' and push forward local and transnational dialogue. The circumstances of actual claimants may raise questions about the scope and meaning of universal human rights. These considerations may lead to revising our list of specific universal human rights or to revising our understanding of what constitutes its violation. Theorists or activists then use that broader theoretical understanding to guide decision-making about individual cases. In addition, cases such as the Bosnian War Crimes can force us to rethink the paradigm of nondiscrimination (MacKinnon 1993) and issues associated with globalization can force us to rethink the meaning of state responsibilities for human rights violations that take place within and beyond their borders.[35] With each decision, we contribute to intra-cultural and cross-cultural dialogue and we should be able to justify our decision as being consistent with universal human rights. Each particular decision should be a move toward fostering universal human rights, here[36] and everywhere.

Universal human rights are no less universal as a result of our paying attention to political contexts. Neither cross-cultural human rights theory nor the Universal Declaration suggests that we should bracket political issues while considering questions of human rights. In many instances of activism or individual cases, there are larger national and international relations issues at stake. The fact that political expedience (not theoretical coherence) may require a particular action at a particular time should not prevent us from using a particular issue or case to think about the broader implications for the substantive universal meaning of human rights it raises. Regardless of the political ramifications, each case or issue is an opportunity to ask 'from a universal human rights perspective, what is the right thing to do?' Case by case, collectively, we refine and expand customary universal human rights and local customary practices.

From this theoretical perspective, rights as formal and legal merge with social practice. We recognize that a notion of rights is contingent, a customary understanding put awkwardly and imperfectly into legal practice through legislation, execution and judicial practice. Likewise rights are imperfectly theorized through contingent and inadequately informed arguments.

In *practice* we must treat one another as human beings. In *practice* we must adjudicate between competing claims without denying either claim. In *practice* we can attribute responsibility even where formal institutions and organizational charts cannot. In *practice* we reconcile universal human rights with cultural difference without abandoning the inviolability of some rights and the problematic nature of some social practices. In *theory* we can do likewise (imperfectly).

Conclusion: Universality Without Universals

While theorists may discuss the universality of human rights, as the struggles of activists demonstrate, the reality of human rights are not universally realized. Consequently, discussions about the possible universality of a particular account of human rights, while interesting and useful for transnational discussions, will not yield universal recognition of human rights in real life. Such realization is a function of social mores and practices and thus subject to the processes of social change within particular contexts. Realizing human rights requires a local practice of social change that is inclusive and noncoercive.

Within a weak ontological framework, cross-cultural human rights theory provides an account of intra-national and transnational dialogue. Such dialogue can guide revision of the human rights theoretical and legal paradigm while using those rights enumerated within that paradigm to revise practices that violate human rights.[37] Universal human rights are an important tool of social criticism but their exact articulation today is contingent on the state of current cross-cultural and intra-cultural dialogues. As these dialogues continue, the substantive meaning of human rights will change. Women's human rights activists and their scholar co-travelers want to continue to influence the change.

The theoretical contribution of the women's human rights activists helps mute the debates about whether human rights—the general concept[38] or the specific list[39]—are the product of particularly-western cultural history.[40] These activists reveal that human rights are not merely a matter of realizing a universal list whose historical authors are western, liberal, and democratic, or the nations of the UN in 1948. Rather the list has meaning only contextually; that is, the social and historical context of particular mores and practices give meaning to and constrain the use of any universal rights as a tool for social criticism.[41]

Despite the importance it gives to contextualization, in order to avoid the paralyzing effects of relativism on activism cross-cultural human rights theorizing must not be understood as a tool for the justification of existing practices. The account of cross-cultural universal human rights theory presented here emerged from the observation of activists. For women's human rights activists, the cross-cultural theory is a means for *challenging* the power of mores and practices. Women's human rights activists seek inclusion in political processes, end to coercion in political, social and economic practices, and end to exploitation of inequalities and hierarchies. They promote a process of social criticism that is respectful of diversity and yet has critical teeth. Recognizing the local diversity in the realization of, and activism for, human rights does not mean embracing the status quo anywhere. Everywhere social critics work locally in appropriate ways (though others may work in locally inappropriate ways) to change their social contexts. Cross-cultural human rights theory is not a basis from which to argue for a relativistic or uncritical stance toward any practice which *might* be understood by some as threatening human rights.

Rather, women's human rights activists strengthen individual rights where they are weak, challenge customary law where it threatens the individual rights of the marginalized, strengthen social practices conducive to human rights, and criticize those that undermine human rights. Their scholar-activist allies create means for the marginalized to have their views contribute to universalist discourse and foster respect for non-elite forms of discourse.

I have described here one model of cross-cultural human rights theory that can be used to wrestle with human rights questions in the ever-constant conditions of cross-cultural and intra-cultural value pluralism. The process of reflecting critically on local variety may enable us to identify an overlapping consensus on human rights according to which a universal set of individual rights are respected in contexts that vary according to social practices—as long as those practices are revised through local processes of social change such that individual rights are not substantively vacuous. Thus the universality of human rights may be substantively meaningful even while the realization of human rights is not uniform.

The Center for International Studies at the University of California generously supported this research in the academic year 2000-2001.

Reprinted with permission from Taylor and Francis Ltd. and the International Feminist Journal of Politics *3 (3) (2001): 311-346. Available online: www.tandf. co.uk/journals.*

Brooke A. Ackerly (Ph.D. Stanford University) is Assistant Professor, Department of Political Science, Vanderbilt University. Her research interests include democratic theory, cross-cultural human rights theory, feminist theory, social criticism and feminist methodologies and methods. She integrates into her theoretical work empirical research on democratization, human rights, credit programs and women's activism. Her publications include Political Theory and Feminist Social Criticism *(Cambridge University Press, 2000). She teaches courses in political theory.*

Notes

[1] For a brief summary of women's activism at UN conferences through the women's caucus see UNIFEM (2000: 48). For greater detail and analysis see Friedman (2000). The 1990s UN Conferences were World Conference on Education for All (Jamtien 1990), UN Conference on Environment and Development (Rio de Janeiro 1992), World Conference on Human Rights (Vienna 1993), Global Conference on the Sustainable Development of Small Island Developing States (Barbados 1994), International Conference on Population and Development (Cairo 1994), World Summit on Social Development (Copenhagen 1995), Fourth World Conference on Women (Beijing 1995), Second UN Conference on Human Settlements (Istanbul 1996), and World Food Summit (Rome 1997).

2   For a more developed discussion of these problems within the current and historical international human rights paradigm see Ackerly (2001a), Charlesworth et al. (1991), and Cook (1989). See also Stamatopoulou (1995); Gallagher (1997); Burrows (1986).

3   Throughout the text, I use the first person plural to refer to activists and scholars interested in promoting the human rights of all of humanity.

4   For an explication of the use of weak ontology in contemporary theory see White (2000).

5   Communities with some autonomy include some indigenous communities and for example Muslim communities within India which have autonomy over family law.

6   For example, significant progress has been made in breaking down the barriers to attributing responsibility for rights violations by state and non-state actors, first in the Convention of the Rights of the Child (1989), then with the Declaration on the Elimination of Violence Against Women (DEVAW) (1994). Regionally, the Inter-American Convention on the Prevention, Punishment and Eradication of Violence Against Women addresses violence against women in the private sphere (1994).

7   Consider the work of O'Neill (1993, 1999) and White (2000).

8   However, we might appreciate many activists' tools and strategies as being arrived at in response to these legacies. See Scott (1985, 1990).

9   These qualities are consistent with White's characterization of a weak ontology (2000: chapter 1).

10 For documentation of the group by UNIFEM, see UNIFEM 1999a and 1999b.

11 CEDAW-in-Action was co-sponsored by UNIFEM (1998) and International Women's Rights Action Watch. The entire texts from which the following excerpts were drawn have been publicly available at http://www.globalknowledge.org/english/archives/mailarchives/endviolence/home.html. The text of the CEDAW working group is available at http://www.sdnp.undp.org/ww/lists/cedaw/threads.html#00128. For reports on these working groups see http://www.undp.org/unifem/w@work/, http://www.undp.org/unifem/campaign/violence/unfpatxt.htm, http://www.un.org/womenwatch/forums/beijing5/ (the report on violence). CEDAW-in-Action continued to operate as a listserv after the end of the working group. A comparison between the moderated and unmoderated period of the CEDAW working group is one demonstration of the value of the moderated format for inclusive discussions where speakers and audiences remain engaged in dialogue.

12 As of December 1998 the End-of-Violence list had 1019 participants from 80 countries. As of August 1999, there were approximately 1600 End-of-Violence members and 600 CEDAW-in-Action members (Brodman 1999).

   Although the emphasis within the group is on certain forms of violence against women and neglects others, particularly some of the more social and economic forms of violence against women, the need for cultural approaches to these latter forms of women's human rights violations is similar, though social changes needs to be even more comprehensive. In 1999 the UN Special Rapporteur on Violence Against Women made '[e]conomic and social policies of the state that cause, contribute to, or constitute violence against women' one of its three main foci of research (Kois and Saunders 1999).

13 In addition, the moderators provided weekly summaries in English, Spanish and French thereby enabling those with limited time and those who read Spanish and French to be able to follow the dialogues.

14 Theorists including Andrew Linklater (1998), Richard Falk (1992, 2000) and Robert

Cox (1999) have described international publics spheres which are defined along the lines of Habermasian discourse theory (1980, 1987, 1989). In these international public spheres, citizens of a world community seek common ground despite cross-cultural differences.

[15] This is my categorization based on working group contributions and the categories are somewhat fluid as I discuss in the text. By categorizing their actions for the purposes of discussion I do not mean to limit anyone's ability to imagine other forms of activism.

After the end of the CEDAW-in-Action working group, as part of fulfilling my perceived obligation to the groups incurred by learning from them, and in order to practice networking and integration, I shared these categories with the End-of-Violence working group and received some commentary which led to my specifying some forms of integration. I shared the entire paper with those interested. Two wrote me to tell me they were incorporating the categories in their training materials. For more on the bases for a constructive working relationship between scholars and activists see 'Learnings from Scholar-Activists Dialogue' (Ackerly 2001b).

[16] For a critical view of gender mainstreaming see Beijing Declaration of Indigenous Women (1995).

[17] Note that participation in this level of lobbying can be exclusionary of certain voices even while participants seek to include others' voices (Busia 1996). See also the Rome Statute of the ICC.

[18] This message and a solicitation by the moderators spawned a discussion about legal reform and other measures. The 17 November 1998 response from Francesca Pesce describes the work of Associazione Differenza Donna in Rome, Italy. While explicitly interested in similar legal reforms, she also discusses the many other ways in which Associazione Differenza Donna has worked, including training, support, education, networking and integration.

[19] For examples see Niemann (1999) and Schmidt (1999)

[20] This example also demonstrates the need for uncoerced discussion about social mores and practices as the wife and the researcher who is recounting the incident differ with the police woman in their understandings of what constitutes a woman's duty.

[21] Publishing feminist scholarship is also a form of networking and in this respect, I understand my own project as one of activism.

[22] For discussions of these, see Ackerly and Okin (1999) and Keck and Sikkink (1998).

[23] For example, the network Women Living Under Muslim Laws brings strategies and arguments successful in promoting certain laws in one Muslim country to others (Shaheed 1994).

[24] See also Hina Jalani's (1993) account of the Pakistan women's human rights movement and the alliances with movements around democracy, development, and human rights. See also Raka Ray (1999).

[25] For a more thorough treatment of the theorists referred to in this article see Ackerly 2000b and 2001a.

[26] For an alternative approach see Michael Perry (1998).

[27] Note that Donnelly (1985), Howard Hassmann (1992), Rawls (1999), and Taylor (1999) all treat cultures as relatively static when discussing human rights.

[28] Much feminist scholarship likewise appreciates internal cultural diversity (Ackerly 2000a).

[29] Some Muslim feminist scholars have likewise relied on elite texts (Ahmed 1982; Hassan 1991; Shaheed 1994; Zein Ed-Din 1982; see also Majid 1998). What

constitutes elite sources of knowledge in terms of legitimate texts (for example religious texts, historical accounts, constitutions, law and legal precedents) and legitimate actors (for example male theologians, historians and judges) varies within and across cultures. Non-elite sources of knowledge are generally accompanied by claims to legitimacy that seem unnecessary to authors who use elite forms of knowledge or who themselves have legitimacy.

30   For examples of these see individual countries' reasons given for reservations to the CEDAW website http://untreaty.un.org/ENGLISH/bible/englishinternetbible/partI/chapterIV/treaty9.asp and related text http://www.un.org/womenwatch/daw/cedaw/reservations.htm.

31   Practiced properly such a theoretical method requires the examination of all forms of exclusion.

32   For the method, qualifications and roles of social critics whether scholars or activists see Ackerly 2000a.

33   See for example research on home-based workers, domestic workers, sex workers and transnational women's movements by Prügl (1999), Chin (1998), Moon (1997) and Stienstra (1994) respectively. Perhaps ironically, the cross-cultural project must also reflect the views of those whose political strategy has been one of segregation and therefore poses real logistical and theoretical challenges.

34   Karl Marx defines the role of criticism as promoting the 'self-understanding of the age concerning its struggles and wishes. This is the task for the world and for us' (1843: 215). As John Maynard Keynes said, the '*long run* is a misleading guide for current affairs. *In the long run* we are all dead. Economists set themselves too easy, too useless a task if in tempestuous seasons they can only tell us that when the storm is long past the ocean is flat again' (1923: 65).

35   In *Basic Rights* Henry Shue (1996) helps us think about a state's responsibilities for human rights violations beyond its borders. See also O'Neill (1999).

36   Wherever here happens to be for a given case or issue.

37   In the 1990s Charlotte Bunch's 'Women's Rights as Human Rights' functioned in this way for many women's human rights activists. See also Bunch (1995).

38   Donnelly argues that the general concept of human rights is western and relevant to societies facing the 'threat to personal autonomy and equality presented by a modern state' (1989: 72) and that it is the growing standard of 'civilization' internationally. Adamantia Pollis and Peter Schwab argue that the general concept is western and not applicable to Third World nations or to certain parts of the West (1979: 13).

39   Chan argues that a specific list does have universal applicability (1997) whereas Kausikan argues that local interpretations of a universal list will vary importantly (1993).

40   Individual rights may be more western than universal, as Donnelly (1989) argues, but their extension to all humans is not a western idea. Recognizing universal human rights requires recognizing universal humanity. The western tradition has not been one of extending individual rights to all humans, though in the past two centuries it has increasingly done so. Women's human rights activism promotes mores and practices that not only are necessary to respect women's human rights but also embody universal humanity and equal human worth.

41   Even international legal norms are subject to their practice. Diane Bell (1992) questions the fact that law has come to dominate human rights discourse. She argues that the legal framework of rights discourse is flawed because the law cannot resolve political questions. As Nariman (1993) describes, the Indian courts failed to recognize

universal human rights when they failed to condemn the suspension of Article 21 of the Indian Constitution—'No person shall be deprived of his life or personal liberty except according to procedure established by law'—by Mrs. Indira Gandhi which she used to detain her political opposition during 1975 through 1977. In the international arena, the International Court of Justice failed to condemn the clearly discriminatory practice of apartheid when suit was brought by Ethiopia and Liberia in 1966. These courts determined that law allowed detention and discrimination that violates the Universal Declaration. On February 16, 1999, the Supreme Court of Zimbabwe ruled against Venia Magaya citing Shona Customary Law, according to which 'males are preferred to females as heirs' (*Magaya v. Magaya* 1999). Evidently, as these examples from India, South Africa and Zimbabwe show, rights claimed against the state or society are questions of politics and power and thus can be inadequately addressed through legal means which are also influenced by politics and power.

References

Ackerly, B. (2001a) 'Human rights practice and grassroots theory: towards a cross-cultural theory of universal human rights', paper presented to the *Annual Meeting of the International Studies Association*, February 23.

Ackerly, B. (2001b) 'Learnings from scholar-activists dialogue', paper presented to the *Annual Meeting of the International Studies Association*, 24 February 24.

Ackerly, B. (2000a) *Political Theory and Feminist Social Criticism,* Cambridge: Cambridge University Press.

Ackerly, B. (2000b) 'Women's rights are human rites: women's human rights activists as cross-cultural theorists', working paper, Center for International Studies, University of Southern California.

Ackerly, B. and Okin, S. M. (1999) 'Feminist social criticism and the international movement for women's rights as human rights', in I. Shapiro and C. Hacker-Cordòn (eds.), *Democracy's Edges*, Cambridge: Cambridge University Press, 134-162.

Ahmed, L. (1982) 'Feminism and feminist movements in the Middle East, a preliminary exploration: Turkey, Egypt, Algeria, People's Democratic Republic of Yemen, *Women's Studies International Forum*, 5, 2, 153-168.

Alker, H. (1996) *Rediscoveries and Reformulations: Humanistic Methodologies for International Studies*, New York: Cambridge University Press.

An-Na'im, A. A. (1992a) 'Introduction', in A. A. An-Na'im (ed.), *Human Rights in Cross-Cultural Perspectives: A Quest for Consensus*, Philadelphia: University of Pennsylvania Press, 1-15.

An-Na'im, A. A. (1992b) 'Toward a cross-cultural approach', in A. A. An-Na'im (ed.), *Human Rights in Cross-Cultural Perspectives: A Quest for Consensus*, Philadelphia: University of Pennsylvania Press, 19-43.

Beijing Declaration of Indigenous Women (1995) Online: http://www.ipcb.org/resolutions/beijingdec.html.

Bell, D. (1999) 'Which rights are universal', *Political Theory*, 27, 6, 849-56.

Bell, D. (1992) 'Considering gender: are human rights for women, too? an Australian case', in A. A. An-Na'im (ed.), *Human Rights in Cross-Cultural Perspectives: A Quest for Consensus*, Philadelphia: University of Pennsylvania Press, 339-62.

Benhabib, S. (1991) 'Models of public space: Hannah Arendt, the liberal tradition, and Jürgen Habermas', in C. Calhoun (ed.), *Habermas and the Public Sphere*, Cambridge: MIT Press, 73-98.

Benhabib, S. (1989) 'Liberal dialogue versus a critical theory of discursive legitimation', In *Liberalism and the Moral Life*. Cambridge, MA: Harvard University Press.

Benhabib, S. (1988) 'The generalized and the concrete other: the kohlberg-gilligan controversy and feminist theory', in S. Benhabib and D. Cornell (eds.), *Feminism as Critique: On the Politics of Gender*, Minneapolis: University of Minnesota Press, 77-95.

Brodman, J. (2001) Education Development Centre (EDC), personal communication, 30 April.

Brodman, J. (1999) personal communication, 4 August.

Brodman, J. (1998) 'Building online communities: UNIFEM's Global Working Group To End Violence Against Women', On file with the author.

Bunch, C. (1995) 'Transforming human rights from a feminist perspective', in J. Peters and A. Wolper (eds), *Women's Rights, Human Rights: International Feminist Perspectives*, New York: Routledge, 11-17.

Bunch, C. (1990) 'Women's rights as human rights: toward a re-vision of human rights', *Gender Violence: A Development and Human Rights Issue*, 3-18.

Burrows, N. (1986) 'International law and human rights: the case of women's rights', in T. Campbell, D. Goldberg, S. McLean, and T. Mullen (eds.), *Human Rights: From Rhetoric to Reality*, New York: Basil Blackwell, 80-98.

Busia, A. P. A. (1996) 'On cultures of communication: reflections from Beijing', *Signs: Journal of Women in Culture and Society*, 22, 1, 204-210.

Chan, J. (1997) 'An alternative view', *Journal of Democracy* 8, 2, 35-48.

Charlesworth, H. (1994) 'What are "women's international human rights"'? in Rebecca J. Cook (ed), *Human Rights of Women: National and International Perspectives*, Philadelphia: University of Pennsylvania Press, 58-84.

Charlesworth, H. C. Chinkin and S. Wright (1991) 'Feminist approaches to international law', *American Journal of International Law*, 85, 613-45.

Charney, E. (1999) 'Cultural interpretation and universal human rights', *Political Theory* 27, 6, 840-848.

Chin, C. B. N. (1998) *In Service and Servitude: Foreign Female Domestic Workers and the Malaysian 'Modernity' Project*, New York: Columbia University Press.

Convention on the Elimination of All Forms of Discrimination Against Women (CEDAW) (1979) G.A. Res. 34/180, U.N. Doc. A/Res/34/180. Adopted 18 December 1979.

Cook, R. J. (1989) 'The international right to nondiscrimination on the basis of sex', *Yale Journal of International Law* 14, 161-81.

Cox, R. W. (1999) 'Thinking about civilizations', lecture to the *Annual Meeting of the British International Studies Association*, December.

Cox, R. W. (1997) 'Civilisations, encounters and transformations', *Studies in Political Economy*, 47, 7-32.

de Bary, W. T. (1998) *Asian Values and Human Rights: A Confucian Communitarian Perspective*, Cambridge: Harvard University Press.

Declaration on the Elimination of Violence Against Women (1994) G.A. Res. 48/104, U.N. GAOR, 48th Session, Agenda Item 111, U.N. Doc A/Res/48/104. Adopted 23 February 1994.

Donnelly, J. (ed.) (1989) *Universal Human Rights in Theory and Practice*, Ithaca: Cornell University Press.

Donnelly, J. (1985) *The Concept of Human Rights*, New York: St. Martin's Press.

Falk, R. (1992) 'Cultural foundations for the international protection of human rights', in A. A. An-Na'im (ed.), *Human Rights in Cross-Cultural Perspectives: A Quest for Consensus*, Philadelphia: University of Pennsylvania Press, 44-64.

Falk, R. (2000) *Human Rights Horizons*, New York: Routledge.

Fong, J. (1999) Freelance researcher and a teaching assistant in York University, End-of-Violence Working Group, personal correspondence, 9 October.

Fraser, N. (1995) 'Politics, culture and the public sphere: toward a postmodern conception' in L. Nicholson and S. Seidman (eds.), *Social Postmodernism: Beyond Identity Politics*, Cambridge: Cambridge University Press, 287-312.

Fraser, N. (1992) 'Rethinking the public sphere: a contribution to the critique of actually existing democracy', in C. Calhoun (ed.), *Habermas and the Public Sphere*, Cambridge: MIT Press, 109-42.

Fraser, N. (1989) 'What's critical about critical theory? The case of Habermas and gender', in M. L. Shanley and C. Pateman (eds.), *Feminist Interpretations and Political Theory*, University Park, PA: The Pennsylvania State University Press, 253-76.

Friedman, E. J. (2000) 'Getting gender on the agenda: women's transnational organizing at the UN conferences of the 1990s', paper presented at the *International Studies Association* Meeting, Los Angeles, CA., March 14-17.

Gallagher, A. (1997) 'Ending the marginalization: strategies for incorporating women into the United Nations human rights system', *Human Rights Quarterly* 19, 2, 283-333.

Gauthier, L. (1999) International Centre for the Prevention of Crime, End-of-Violence Working Group posting, 8 June. Online: http://www.globalknowledge.org/english/archives/mailarchives/endviolence/endviolence-jun99/0006.html.

Habermas, J. (1989) 'Justice and solidarity: on the discussion concerning "Stage 6"', *Philosophical Forum* 21, 1-2, 32-52.

Habermas, J. (1987) *The Philosophical Discourse of Modernity*, trans. F. G. Lawrence. Cambridge: MIT Press.

Habermas, J. (1980) 'Discourse ethics: notes on philosophical justification', *Moral Consciousness and Communicative Action*, trans. C. Lenhart and S. Weber Nicholson, Cambridge: MIT Press.

Harding, S. (1987) 'Introduction', in S. Harding (ed.), *Feminism and Methodology: Social Science Issues*, Bloomington: Indiana University Press, 1-14.

Hassan, R. (1991) 'The issue of woman-man equality in the Islamic tradition', in L. Grob, R. Hassan, and H. Gordon (eds.), *Women's and Men's Liberation: Testimonies of Spirit*, New York: Greenwood Press, 65-82.

Howard Hassman, R. (1992) 'Dignity, community and human rights', in A. A. Na'im (ed.), *Human Rights in Cross-Cultural Perspectives: A Quest for Consensus*, Philadelphia: University of Pennsylvania Press, 81-102.

Inter-American Convention on the Prevention, Punishment, and Eradication of Violence Against Women (1994) Online: http://www.oas.org/juridico/english/Treaties/a-61.htm.

International Covenant on Civil and Political Rights (1966) G.A. Res. 2200(XXI), 21 U.N. GAOR, Supp. (No. 16) at 52, U.N. Doc. A/6316. Adopted December 16, 1966.

Jalani, H. (1993) 'Diversity in character and role of human rights NGOs', in M. Schuler (ed.), *Claiming Our Place: Working the Human Rights System to Women's Advantage*, Washington: Institute for Women, Law and Development, 107-114.

Kausikan, B. (1993) 'Asia's different standard', *Foreign Policy*, 92, 24-41.

Keck, M. and K. Sikkink (1998) *Activists Beyond Borders: Advocacy Networks in International Politics*, Ithaca: Cornell University Press.

Keynes, J. M. (1923) [1971] *A Tract on Monetary Reform*, in *The Collected Writings of John Maynard Keynes* Vol. IV. London: Macmillan St. Martin's Press for the Royal Economic Society.

Kois, L. and C. Saunders (1999) Human Rights Officers, Office of the High Commissioner for Human Rights (OHCHR), Colombo, Sri Lanka and Geneva, Switzerland, End-of-Violence Working Group posting, 20 July. Online: http://www.globalknowledge.org/english/archives/mailarchives/endviolence/endviolence-jul99/0018.html.

Lindholm, T. (1992) 'Prospects for research on the cultural legitimacy of human rights: the cases of liberalism and marxism', in A. A. An-Na'im (ed.), *Human Rights in Cross-Cultural Perspectives: A Quest for Consensus*, Philadelphia: University of Pennsylvania Press, 387-426.

Linklater, A. (1998) *The Transformation of Political Community*, Columbia: University of South Carolina Press.

MacKinnon, C. (1993) 'Crimes of war, crimes of peace', in S. Shute and S.Hurley (eds.), *On Human Rights: the Oxford Amnesty Lectures 1993*, New York: Basic Books, 83-109.

Majid, A. (1998) 'The politics of feminism in Islam', *Signs: Journal of Women in Culture and Society* 23, 2, 321-61.

Malasha, P. (1998) Gender Coordinator, CARE International Program of Support for Poverty Elimination and Community Transformation (PROSPECT), Lusaka, Zambia, End-of-Violence Working Group posting, 19 November. Online: http://www.globalknowledge.org/english/archives/mailarchives/endviolence/endviolence-nov98/0045.html.

Marrian, A. (1998) Director, Agenda, Durban, KwaZulu Natal Rep. of South Africa, End-of-Violence Working Group posting, 11 November. Online: http://www.globalknowledge.org/english/archives/mailarchives/endviolence/endviolence-nov98/0023.html.

Martinez, K. H. (1998) Staff Attorney, International Program, Center for Reproductive Law and Policy End-of-Violence, New York, NY, End-of-Violence Working Group posting, 26 November. Online: http://www.globalknowledge.org/english/archives/mailarchives/endviolence/endviolence-nov98/0057.html.

Marx, K. (1843) [1967] 'Letter to A. Ruge, September 1843' in L. D. Easton and K. H. Guddat (eds. & trans.), *Writings of the Young Marx on Philosophy and Society*, Garden City, NY: Anchor Books, 211-25.

Moon, K. (1997) *Sex Among Allies*, Princeton: Princeton University Press.

Nariman, F. (1993) 'The universality of human rights', *The Review of the International Commission of Jurists*, 50, 8-22.

Niemann, M. (1999) Victims Outreach, Dallas, TX, 29 January. Online: http://www.globalknowledge.org/english/archives/mailarchives/endviolence/endviolence-jan99/0045.html.

Nelson, N. C. (1999) SAFE Homes of Augusta, Inc., Augusta, GA USA, End-of-Violence Working Group posting, 25 June. Online: http://www.globalknowledge.org/english/archives/mailarchives/endviolence/endviolence-jun99/0033.html.

O'Brien, R., A. M. Goetz, J. A. Scholte, and M. Williams (2000) *Contesting Global Governance: Multilateral Economic Institutions and Global Social Movements*. Cambridge: Cambridge University Press.

O'Neill, O. (1999) [2000] 'Women's rights: whose obligations?' *Bounds of Justice*, Cambridge: Cambridge University Press, 97-111.

O'Neill, O. (1993) 'Justice, gender and international boundaries', in M. C. Nussbaum and A. Sen (eds.), *The Quality of Life*, Oxford: Clarendon Press, 303-23.

Okin, S. (1999) 'Is multiculturalism bad for women,' in J. Cohen, M. Howard, and M. C. Nussbaum (eds.), *Is Multiculturalism Bad for Women*, Princeton: Princeton University Press, 9-24.

Oloka-Onyango, J. and S. Tamale (1995) '"The personal is political", or why women's rights are indeed human rights: an African perspective on international feminism', *Human Rights Quarterly* 17, 4, 691-731.

Optional Protocol, Revised. (1999) UN ESCOR Commission on the Status of Women, 43rd Sess., Agenda Item 6, UN Doc E/CN.6/1999/WG/L.2. Adopted 12 March. Online: http://www.un.org/womenwatch/daw/cedaw/protocol/protocol.htm.

Pande, R. (1999) University of Hyderabad, India, End-of-Violence Working Group posting, 13 January. Online: http://www.globalknowledge.org/english/archives/mail archives/endviolence/endviolence-jan99/0022.html.

Perry, M. (1998) *The Idea of Human Rights: Four Inquiries*, Oxford: Oxford University Press.

Pesce, F. (1998) Italy, End-of-Violence Working Group posting, 17 November. Online: http://www.globalknowledge.org/english/archives/mailarchives/endviolence/endviolence-nov98/0039.html.

Pietilä, H. (1999) Finland, End-of-Violence Working Group posting, 17 September. Online: http://www.globalknowledge.org/english/archives/mailarchives/endviolence/endviolence-sep99/0012.html.

Pietilä, H. (2001) Personal correspondence, 28 and 29 April.

Pollis, A. and P. Schwab (1979) 'Humna rights: a western construct with limited applicability', in A. Pollis and P. Schwab (eds.), *Human Rights: Cultural and Ideological Perspectives*, New York: Praeger Publishers, 1-18.

Prügl, E. (1999) *The Global Construction of Gender: Home-Based Work in the Political Economy of the Twentieth Century*, New York: Columbia University Press.

Rawls, J. (1999) *The Law of Peoples*, Cambridge: Harvard University Press.

Ray R. (1999) *Fields of Protest: Women's Movements in India*, Minneapolis: University of Minnesota Press.

Riangkruar, P. (1999) Chief Provincial State Attorney, Chief Coordinator, CWRP, Child and Woman Rights Protection Network, Bangkok, Thailand, 15 June. Online: http://www.globalknowledge.org/english/archives/mailarchives/endviolence/endviolence-jun99/0023.html.

Rome Statute of the International Criminal Court (ICC) (1998) Online: http://www.igc.org/icc/html>./icc19990712.html.

Schmidt, B. (1999) Advocacy Officer, WOMANKIND Worldwide, UK, End-of-Violence Working Group posting, 8 January. Online: http://www.globalknowledge.org/english/archives/mailarchives/endviolence/endviolence-jan99/0013.html.

Scott, J. C. (1990) *Domination and the Arts of Resistance: Hidden Transcripts*, New Haven: Yale University Press.

Scott, J. C. (1985) *Weapons of the Weak*, New Haven: Yale University Press.

Shaheed, F. (1994) 'Controlled or autonomous: identity and the experience of the network, Women Living under Muslim Laws', *Signs: Journal of Women in Culture and Society* 19, 4, 997-1019.

Shue, H. (1980) [1996] *Basic Rights: Subsistence, Affluence, and US Foreign Policy*, Princeton: Princeton University Press.

Sitati, M. (1999) The Coalition On Violence Against Women (COVAW)—Kenya, End-of-Violence Working Group posting, 27 January. Online: http://www.globalknowledge.org/english/archives/mailarchives/endviolence/endviolence-jan99/0039.html.

Stamatopoulou, E. (1995) 'Women's rights and the United Nations' in J. Peters and A. Wolper (eds.), *Women's Rights, Human Rights: International Feminist Perspectives*, New York: Routledge, 36-48.

Stienstra, D. (1994) *Women's Movements and International Organizations*, London: Macmillan.

Suu Kyi, A. S. (1988) [1995] 'Freedom from fear', in M. Aris (ed.), *Freedom from Fear*. London: Penguin Books, 180-5.

Taylor, C. (1999) 'Conditions of an unforced concsensus on human rights' in J. R. Bauer and D. Bell (eds.), *The East Asian Challenge for Human Rights*, Cambridge: Cambridge University Press, 124-144.

True, J. and M. Mintrom (2001) 'Transnational networks and policy diffusion: the case of gender mainstreaming', *International Studies Quarterly* 45, 1, 27-57.

United Nations Convention on the Rights of the Child (1989) Annex GA Res. 44/25 Doc. A/Res/4425. Adopted 20 November. Online: http://www.unhchr.ch/html/menu3/b/k2crc.htm.

United Nations Development Fund for Women (UNIFEM) (2000) *Progress of the World's Women 2000: A New Biennial Report*, Online: http://www.undp.org/unifem/progressww/2000/index.html.

United Nations Development Fund for Women (UNIFEM) (1999a). 'Women @ work to end violence: voices in cyberspace', Online: http://www.undp.org/unifem/w@work.

United Nations Development Fund for Women (UNIFEM) (1999b) 'Effective strategies to end violence against women (as identified by the Virtual Working Group to end violence against women)', Online: http://www.undp.org/unifem/campaign/violence/unfpatxt.htm.

United Nations Development Fund for Women (UNIFEM) (1998) 'Bringing equality home: implementing the Convention on the Elimination of All Forms of Discrimination Against Women (CEDAW)', Online: http//www.undp.org/unifem/cedaw/indexen.htm.

Universal Declaration of Human Rights (UDHR) (1948) G.A. Res. 217A(III), U.N. Doc. A/810, adopted 10 December. Online: http://www.un.org/Overview/rights.html.

United Nations Development Programme (UNDP) (2000) *Human Development Report 2000*, Oxford: Oxford University Press. Online: http://www.undp.org/hdr2000/english/HDR2000.html.

Usdin, S. (1998) Soul City Multi-Media Health Promotion Project, Johannesburg, South Africa, End-of-Violence Working Group posting, 16 November. Online: http://www.globalknowledge.org/english/archives/mailarchives/endviolence/endviolence-nov98/0036.html.

White, S. K. (2000) *Sustaining Affirmation: The Strengths of Weak Ontology in Political Theory*, Princeton, NJ: Princeton University Press.

Women for Women's Human Rights (WWHR) (1998) Istanbul, Turkey, End-of-Violence Working Group posting, 10 November. Online: http://www.globalknowledge.org/english/archives/mailarchives/endviolence/endviolence-nov98/0021.html.

Yasuaki, O. (1999) 'Toward an intercivilizational approach to human rights', in J. R. Bauer and D. Bell (eds.), *The East Asian Challenge for Human Rights*, Cambridge: Cambridge University Press, 103-23.

Zein Ed-Din, N. (1982) [1928] 'Removing the veil and veiling', *Women's Studies International Forum*, 5, 2, 221-226.

ALTERNATIVE LEADERSHIP IN AFRICA

SOME CRITICAL FEMINIST REFLECTIONS

SYLVIA TAMALE

We stand at the threshold of self-government and do not waver. The paths have been tortuous, and fraught with peril, but the positive and tactical action we have adopted is leading us to the new Jerusalem, the golden city of our hearts' desire! ...What our ancestors achieved in the context of their contemporary society gives us confidence that we can create, out of the past, a glorious future, not in terms of war and military pomp, but in terms of social progress and peace.

—Kwame Nkrumah (1953)[1]

Africa is in a mess.

—Mwalimu Julius Nyerere (1999)[2]

I believe that women and men working in equal partnerships in politics and public life would lead to a quantum shift in the way different countries and different ethnic groups relate to each other.

—Lesley Abdela (2000: 16)

Africa needs to forge alternative leadership styles if the continent is to liberate her peoples—economically, politically and socially. The quotations above reflect the trajectory that African political leadership has followed from flag independence to date: from euphoria to disillusionment to hope. There is an urgent need to build a trusted, democratic, transparent, progressive and patriotic leadership, particularly in the wake of the phenomenon of globalization. Fortunately, it is not too late for Africa to do so.

Like elsewhere in the world, political leadership in Africa has largely been for men and by men. Despite their numerical dominance, African women have been consistently excluded from the "public" political realm of formal decision-making (Tripp 2003; Geisler 1995; Parpart and Staudt 1989) However, it is important to note that although systems of patriarchy were already entrenched in most pre-colonial African societies, women in fact participated (directly and indirectly) in traditional African politics and in anti-colonial and national struggles (Agorsah 1990; Mba 1982; Smock 1977; Okonjo 1976). Colonial intrusion introduced both structures and policies that eroded women's political power while solidifying male authority and excluding women from the redefined political order (Stobel 1982; Sacks 1982). This state of affairs has persisted to date, but women all over the continent are increasingly demanding for an alternative and transformational model of governance (Longwe 2000; Tamale 1999; Tsikata 1997).

In Africa, a change of government has become synonymous with a change of guard with leadership styles that are predictably similar. Some common features that run through many of the post-independence leadership models include: patriarchy, elitism, patrimony, autocracy, corruption, nepotism, bureaucracy, mismanagement, arrogance, militarism and top-heavy policies. In short, what we have in Africa is a democratic façade at best and at worst, despotic, kleptocratic and personalized leadership (see Mwakikagile 2001). We recognize that leadership is not the sole explanation for the 'mess' that Africa is currently steeped in. Unequal global economic forces, cultural problems and some natural disasters all contribute to the 'messy' situation. However, I submit that leadership remains *the* major obstacle responsible for Africa's crisis and I believe that with effective leadership, the continent would be in a position to take most of its problems within stride.

This article addresses two simple issues that relate to formal political leadership: What is wrong with the quality of present leadership in Africa? In answering this complex question, I will, first, justify the need for an alternative leadership arrangement and second, present what I consider to be the main tenets of an alternative leadership paradigm that can promote pro-people governance on the continent.

Colonial Legacies

A strong link has been drawn between Africa's colonial history and the current leadership mess on the continent (see, for example, Mafeje 1971; Davidson 1992; Young 1994; Ake 1996; Mamdani 1996; Monga 1996). The lingering effects of colonialism (and its antecedents in the slave trade) that have adversely influenced political leadership structures on the continent are many. The British policy of 'divide-and-rule' was, for example, largely responsible for ethnic fissures, polari-zation and uneven regional development. Such policies left deep-seated and destabilizing effects in the region, ones that remain significant to political leadership styles to date. It is crucial for us to confront these legacies if we are to develop alternative and more effective leadership models.

Moreover, when African states gained formal independence, they all inherited democratic structures based on liberal democratic theory. Its central premise is that the fundamental prerequisite of democracy lies in the existence of a polity or 'political society'. Electoral systems and institutions are its *raison d'etre*. Such a narrow definition of democracy excluded the majority of people and the 'political society' consisted mostly of the educated male elite within our societies.[3] Thus, right from independence, the greater number of Africans knew only the form but not the substance of democracy. Similarly, citizenship was merely a notional concept for marginal groups such as women, peasants and the poor.

Furthermore, the underpinning material base of African colonial economies consisted of activities controlled by the state and dependent on the imperial metropolis. This affected African linkages (both internal and external, horizontal and vertical). To date, colonial experiences continue to dictate multi-regional cooperation (Anglophone, Francophone, Lusophone, communist, capitalist, etc.) The economies were sustained through a systematic exploitation of women and the rural masses. Since the early 1980s, the latest form of imperialism (i.e., globalization), has unleashed an unjust international economic system, exacerbating the leadership problem on the continent. Attempts at restructuring Africa's economies with International Monetary Fund and World Bank-prescribed antidotes has only succeeded in pushing our countries further and further to the periphery in the backyard of the so-called global village.

Patriarchal Norms and Structures

All the leadership models that are currently functioning on the continent do so within a framework of patriarchy, patrimony and a 'boys club' network. Women's voices are generally absent from the corridors and halls of power where important decisions that affect their lives are taken—be it in national assemblies or within the African Union. This is so despite the fact that women constitute over half of the total population in Africa.

There is an invisible but real line in our societies that carves life into the private (domestic) and the public (political) spheres. Under the aegis of patriarchal gender ideology, women learn that their space is the private domain while men are taught to take their place in the public realm (through cultural instructions, socialization, religion, law, policy, etc.). The distinction between the 'private' and 'public' spheres has not always been that obvious. In Africa, the divorce between these two spaces was consolidated and emphasized during the era of colonialism when colonial powers introduced structures (e.g., voting rights) and policies (e.g., educational and tax policies) focused on delineating a clear distinction guided by an ideology that perceived men as public actors and women as private performers (see Mama 1996). As a consequence of these gendered spaces, women are largely excluded from politics, which is perceived as the preserve of men. However, it should be noted that while women are the 'lynchpins' of the private/domestic sphere, it is men who are the bosses as 'heads of the household/family'. In Africa, concepts such as 'material altruism' and wifely duties, reinforced by men's right to women's service and nurturance, all work to emphasize women's 'rightful' place in society (Mama 1996). These structures, norms and traditions of both the family and public institutions have historically influenced political leadership in Africa.

The Institution of the Family

The leadership problem starts in the basic unit of society, i.e., the family. It is important to link gender oppression within the family (particularly domestic violence) to the deficient leadership styles at the local, national, regional and even international levels. Patriarchal societies' construction of the family, both as the basic unit and as an institution, generally privileges male power. As 'head of the family', the husband exercises power over his wife and the rest of the family, including through the mechanism of domestic violence. Indeed, there exists a pattern of physical violence for conflict resolution from the smallest unit of society (the patriarchal family) through the national, regional and international levels. As Joe Oloka-Onyango observes: 'The state is simply the family writ large. If there are problems of human rights violations at this microscopic level, how can we avoid them at the level of the state, which itself is simply a collectivity of several families?' (2000: 4).

Resorting to violence as a way of conflict resolution and management is the norm for many men in the domestic arena. The patriarchal leader is apt to carry these violent tendencies of conflict resolution to his leadership style outside the home. In the May 2001 Ugandan presidential elections, each of the two main contenders spent a lot of campaign time trying to out-compete the other in convincing the electorate that they had control of the army. Politicizing the army and flexing military might is part and parcel of masculine leadership styles. In May 2002, the Ugandan minister of Defence, Amama Mbabazi stressed, 'You need war to bring about development'.[4] The continent has witnessed non-peaceful ways of conflict resolution through wars, coups d'états, stockpiling of defence equipment and other forms of militarism.

Patriarchal politics and the law dictate a policy of non-interference with the private/domestic sphere. Issues of the home and family are considered personal and are to be dealt with privately. Most traditional wisdom in Africa teaches that home affairs are not to be talked about in the public square.[5] Thus the concept of a single, all-powerful leader begins at the most basic unit of society, legitimated by society at large and sanctioned by the law. As Frederick Engels (1972 [1884]) noted over 120 years ago, the roots of patriarchal domination grow out of the paternal authority men hold over their families/households (see also Weber 1968 [1922]: 1007). It is hardly surprising therefore that the notion of leadership in Africa evokes particular (male) individuals in high political office (Gonzalez 2000).

The lives of African women are defined by the ideology of domesticity. Domesticity as an ideology is historically and culturally constructed and is closely linked to patriarchy, gender/power relations and the artificial private/public distinction (Hansen 1992). The way patriarchy defines women is such that their full self-realization depends on getting married, producing children and caring for their family.[6] Girl children are raised and socialized into this ideology and few ever question or challenge its basic tenets. Single, childless women carry a permanent stigma like a lodestone about their necks. They are viewed as half-baked, even half-human. Thus, the domestic roles of mother, wife and homemaker become the key constructions of women's identity in Africa.

Patriarchy uses several tools including culture, the law, religion and the media to safeguard the public sphere as a domain of male hegemony; it will resist any attempts by women who try to make the transition to the public sphere. The media in Africa, one of the strong pillars of patriarchy, is especially ruthless in its perpetuation of the status quo. A misogynist article that appeared in one of the local Ugandan newspapers under the title, 'Kick women out of politics', argued:

> The biggest threat facing the stability of elite families today is the desire for women to join high-level politics. There are shortcomings to this, most important being the lack of 'quality time' and parental love to their children.... Women should be limited to ten percent political representation and should be stopped from voting for presidents and MPs at least for 200 years. (2002: iv)

Domesticity is thus deployed in the African context to systematically disenfranchise women from participating in political leadership. In effect, African women are relegated to second-class citizenship. Domesticating women subordinates their citizenship and, as such, they are less likely to participate in those activities that are associated with citizenship (e.g., participating in legislation decision-making, voting, paying taxes, etc.). Society—which perceives them as wives and mothers—persistently refuses to register them in a non-domestic space.

During the past four decades of post-colonial politics and public life in Africa, a small but significant percentage of women have, however, managed to break through the glass ceiling that separates the private and public spheres. This has been possible partly because of women's own struggles against all odds and partly because of some deliberate policies (e.g., affirmative action) on the part of some 'benevolent dictators' to increase women's representation in the public sector.

There has been a dramatic increase in female representation in the national assemblies of several African countries in the last decade. For example, in South Africa female representation shifted from three per cent in 1991 to 30 per cent in 1999, in Mozambique it increased from sixteen per cent in 1991 to 30 per cent in 1999 and in Namibia from seven per cent in 1994 to 26 per cent in 1999 (Tripp 2003). Aili Tripp (2003) observes that 'Africa, which had the lowest rates of female participation in politics in the 1960s has since then seen the fastest rates of growth in female representation of any world region.'

Indeed, by the close of the twentieth century, a breeze of invigorating air had swept the continent with women seriously organizing to claim their rightful place in the various processes of local and national decision-making which had been unoccupied for too long. The refreshing waft could be felt in the form of new political parties led by women such as Inonge Mbikusita-Lewanika's National Party in Zambia, Margaret Dongo's Zimbabwe Union of Democrats and Limakatso Ntakatsane's Kopanang Basotho party in Lesotho. It could be felt in women giving men a run for their money in races for presidency such as Eileen Sirleaf-Johnson of Liberia, Charity Ngilu of Kenya, Ruh Rolland-Jeanne-Marie of the Central African Republic and Amália de Vitorai Perira of Angola (Tripp 2003). These positive developments are largely a result of the persistent struggles of the women's movements at the local, national, regional and international levels.

However, such women represent only a small drop in the calabash and have yet to make a significant impact on the existing status quo of African societies (Goetz and Hassim 2000). Moreover, numerous studies have shown that the bureaucratic 'add-women-and stir' approaches witnessed in most affirmative action experiments, have limited impact on leadership models if the patriarchal political structures and institutions are left intact (see, for example, Tamale 1999). In short, it is not enough to increase women's participation in politics without democratizing the 'public' spaces where such politics are 'done'.

Structures and Norms of the Public Sphere

The fact that men predominate in the public/political sphere in Africa means that its organization and structures are heavily influenced by male values. The dominant political culture is androcentric by nature and good leadership is synonymous with masculine leadership. Setting male values and interests as the norm in the public sphere easily achieves the purpose of excluding women from politics. Hence any woman who wishes to transcend this sphere is forced to meet the male/masculine standards required in the public world (e.g., by employers, voters, etc.). Masculine standards operate as a delicate 'glass ceiling' that stops many women from entering the public world. In that world, the female leader becomes the 'other' who has to contend with male power structures and is forced to 'act like men' in order to meet the desired standards.

Despite the guarantees of formal equality that appear in most African constitutions, social, economic, cultural and political structures continue to reproduce unequal social patterns for men and women (plus other marginalized groups). The educational structure, for instance, has enormous influence on the type of leadership that we have in Africa. At the Beijing+5 mid-term review of the implementation of the Beijing Platform for Action in 2000, it was pointed out that many obstacles continue to stand in the way of progress in the educational sector, including: persistent cultural sexist norms and social practices that keep girls from attending school; formal educational systems that have not changed curricula; teachers who have not been trained with a gender perspective; lack of resources; lack of political will to improve infrastructure; unfriendly learning environments, including sexual harassment; discriminatory learning materials; and the effects of poverty, unemployment, crime or depression (United Nations 2000).

African states and their political structures are facing a serious threat in the new international economic order. The contradictions between sovereignty/national-ism and globalization are quite obvious. In the face of a recoiling state apparatus and powerful forces engulfing the world within the loop of globalization, the odds are against marginalized social groups such as women. Even if the patriarchal states are genuinely committed to implementing their various gender policies (which they are not), their weakened position does not leave much room for realizing such programs.

What options do African women have to improve leadership within such a state apparatus? Is the solution to get rid of the nation state? I think not. As Amina Mama (1999) underscores, 'Women cannot afford to ditch the state', for it is the best apparatus at our disposal for protecting and promoting the interests of marginalized groups. If international market forces (whose driving force is by no means pro-people) completely take over from the shrinking state, our project for alternative leadership will be thrown out of the window. In short, the rolling back of the state goes hand-in-glove with the rolling back of social services such as healthcare, education and employment.

These are areas in which the interests of women are critical. Against this background, does the New Partnership for Africa's Development (NEPAD)[7] hold any promise for us? With its neo-liberal underpinnings, propped by the same old patriarchal pillars, it does not. What we need is to reconceptualize and reconstruct the state and its leadership as a way of saving our continent from its current socio-political quagmire.

Reconceptualizing Equality in Africa

Most constitutions in Africa provide for formal gender equity, requiring that women and men be treated equally. In Uganda, the principle of gender equity is found in Article 21 of the constitution. It is the most important legal tool that guarantees the ideal of the 'the rule of law' in our country.[8] It clearly states that under the law everyone is entitled to the same consideration as everyone else, to be treated without personal favour or prejudice. The concept of equality under the law as we know it today can be traced back to ancient Greece, in particular as it is espoused in Aristotle's (1946 [c320BC]) renowned book, *The Politics*. He wrote: 'Equality consists in the same treatment of similar persons'. Greek society at the time was extremely hierarchical—e.g., non-males, non-Greeks and slaves were treated differently.

The Aristotelian approach to equality has influenced mainstream thinking about equality under the law (MacKinnon 2001). Equality has come to mean treating likes alike and un-likes differently: if one is the same, one is to be treated the same; if one is different, one is to be treated differently.[9] Using this conception of equality, one can easily justify genocide, slavery, etc. It is this equality principle that was exported to Africa during colonialism.

There are two main problems embedded in the mainstream notion of equality. First, it is an abstract, universalistic notion that places blinders on status distinctions. In other words, it treats inequalities as differences and measures similarities by dominant standards.

Secondly, it does not understand groups as it only recognizes the right of individuals rather than groups of people. Individuals have to be similar empirically in order to make a claim for normative equality. It ignores the fact that people are subordinated because of being members of groups (for example, women). The Aristotelian notion of equality does not understand that in between universality and individuality, we are all members of groups, e.g., women, ethnic, religious, etc. It is only through groups that people can begin to assert their equality rights (MacKinnon 2001).

Thus, a leadership model that hinges on such a conceptualization of equality is extremely harmful to the majority of citizens. Reconceptualizing formal equality as substantive equality makes it possible to envision an alternative model of leadership in Africa.

Building New Scenarios: An Alternative Leadership Paradigm

My experience as an African lecturer, researcher, daughter, wife and mother has given me some insights into the popular model of leadership shaped by patriarchal values and norms. This model consists of a single leader who is strong, aggressive, charismatic and unemotional. His (for he is usually male) style of leadership is technocratic, rationalistic and linear. This concept of leadership is accepted as a given and is rarely challenged (Ospina and Schall 2000).

Progress for Africa is not possible if we continue with 'business as usual' leadership. Implicit in an effective alternative style of leadership is the concept of *transformation*. Not only are we looking to transformational styles of leadership, but leadership that also has economic, political and social transformation as its goal (see Antrobus 2000). I cannot propose any specific model of leadership, as no particular arrangement would work perfectly for the heterogeneous nation states of Africa. Instead, I will examine the overarching principles that would create an enabling environment for alternative and effective leadership models and styles on the continent. In so doing, I propose a general framework for conceptualizing alternative leadership.

Major Elements of the Alternative Leadership Paradigm

In the late 1990s, scholars of leadership studies began to explore alternative approaches to leadership. From the scholarship, most of which is western-based, two general models of alternative leadership have emerged. First, those that build on the single-individual leader and second, those based on social leadership (see, for example, Heifitz 1994; Drath and Palus 1994; Northouse 1997). Most of the scholarship takes the former approach and builds on existing contemporary models, which focus on creative leadership in the private entrepreneurial sector, seeking ways of contending with new trends in globalization, consumerism and the 'dot.com' world. The underlying influence behind this leadership model—largely developed in the applied psychology and management disciplines—is to create a type of leadership that will balance efficiency with effectiveness within the cutthroat competition and profit-driven capitalist enterprise. Such leadership models include: trait theory (the idea that effective leaders possess certain characteristics that differentiate them from followers); styles theory (focuses not on personalities but on effective leadership styles); and contingency theory (links effective leadership models to changing contexts) (Gardner 1989; Blake and Mouton 1978; Fiedler 1997).

The second approach, which views leadership as a collective enterprise, is the one I find most exciting because of its transformational promise in the public/political sector. The field of scholarship that has made considerable strides in theorizing around the issue of transformational leadership is feminist scholarship. Central to feminist scholarship on alternative leadership is the analysis of gender relations. By 'gender relations' I refer to the interaction that occurs between men and women as they carry out their different roles in society. Such relations are a reflection of the roles/activities that males and females perform in society *and* the relative value/meaning attached to those roles by wider society (Brydon and Chant 1989). In particular, the power imbalances between social groups based on gender, race, class, ethnicity, religion, age, etc. are emphasized. Addressing and challenging these imbalances becomes the focal point in the construction of an alternative leadership paradigm.

Thus, the paradigm of transformational feminist leadership[10] can promote models of 'alternative leadership' that would engender a fundamental change on our continent. The United Nations recognized this fact in 1995 when it stated: 'Without the active participation of women and the incorporation of women's perspective at all levels of decision-making, the goals of equality, development and peace cannot be achieved' (Beijing Declaration and Platform for Action 1995).

Central to the values that define feminist sensibility are issues such as participation and collaboration, diversity and pluralism, critical dialogue, substantive justice, qualitative language and methodologies, inclusiveness, common good, and a consensus-oriented policy-making process (Rost 1993).

The proposed paradigm of alternative leadership views leadership as a process and not a tenured position. It poses an alternative model based on the rationalization that effective leadership—leadership that serves both women and men, poor and rich, and the powerless and powerful—is inclusive, participatory and horizontal. In sum, the following would be the requisite elements of a transformative feminist alternative leadership model:

- It uses power to nurture people and to build communities;
- It is non-hierarchical and participatory in its structures and processes;
- It is transparent and accountable in its decision-making processes;
- It accords priority to the disadvantaged sectors such as rural, grassroots and peasant women;

•It seeks economic, social and political equity between genders and among sectors; and

•It promotes a way of life that is sustainable.[11]

The importance of creating an 'enabling' environment cannot be overstressed in facilitating alternative leadership. There are certain legal and institutional changes that must take place in the private (family) and public (government, educational, religious, media, etc.) institutions in order to actualize our goals. Such institutional changes would entail the following:

•Reconceptualizing the family by stripping it of its patriarchal garb which privileges men and promoting the rights and dignity of women as equal partners with men.

•Transforming the institution of the family so that it is not at odds with women's equality and their participation in formal politics (for example, through shared parenting between fathers and mothers, state-supported childcare and maternity rights).

•Scrapping and/or amending laws and policies that perpetuate the subordination of women and marginalized social groups. Enacting laws that promote women's rights, including but not limited to laws on citizenship, marriage, divorce, custody, property rights and electoral systems.

•Broadening the conventional concepts of leadership and power at the micro (private) and macro (public) political levels, by recognizing that 'the personal is political'.

•Institutionalizing gender into public institutions such as parliament, the judiciary, cabinet, the civil service, education and so forth.

•Strengthening the social (grassroots) base through lobbying, advocacy and mobilization with the aim of enhancing the institutional capacity of communities to implement and manage their development programmes.

•Building on local government structures to make them more inclusive and democratic.

•Raising public gender-awareness through formal and informal education. Marginalized groups, especially, must reach within themselves, break through their established identities, alter their consciousness and confront all their mental and physical inhibitions.

•Promoting citizens' literacy and formal higher education.

•Integrating conflict management skills (for example, dialogue, consensus-building, mediation, etc.) into the formal educational curricula to teach youth that there are options other than violence for settling disputes.

Collective leadership and shared decision-making must be kept at the forefront of the political alternative leadership models. Such models of leadership would begin in the home and thus extend to the village, municipal, national and international levels. They are the key to gender equality, as well as tolerance for a diversity of perspectives, culture and tradition; a first step in moving away from the all-knowing arrogant patriarchal leader with all the attendant problems such as empire-building, gate-keeping, patrimonialism and failure to sustain programs when the leader is gone.

In the alternative models of leadership, for example, the top executive government position (e.g., presidency or prime minister) must never fall on the shoulders of one individual. Because of our culturally generated and nourished mindset, most people find it difficult to imagine leadership in pluralist terms, believing there must be that one top leader responsible for making tough decisions whether in the family or in national government. In such a mindset, collective leadership holds no substance at all. But when constructing alternative leadership models, it is crucial that we emancipate ourselves from such mental slavery.

Alternative leadership is synonymous to creative leadership. It is the duty of the present African generation to develop alternative models of leadership that will emancipate our continent from its present status and help it adapt to the realities of globalization. Why, for example, should we continue to insist on a male head of the family, even in light of the changing family structures (e.g., women-headed households)? Because of its tendency to perpetuate patriarchy, some jurisdictions have moved away from the concept of 'head of the family' (e.g., France). Instead, they talk about 'parental authority', which is collective and shared equally between the mother and father.

Similarly, at the national level, several heads can be better than one. A group of elected representatives has the power to shape the future of a country in ways that were previously unimaginable with a single leader. Collective leadership would oppose 'big-man' politics, leadership of closed-circles and government by intrigue. In this era of globalization, the stakes are high and Africa's life is on the line. We have no choice but to invest in collective, inclusive and democratic leadership. It is not as if collective leadership is completely new to Africa; during the pre-colonial times the continent enjoyed a long tradition of consultative decision-making, albeit against a backdrop of patriarchy.

The biggest challenge to collective leadership models is determining where authority and responsibility lie. However, such details and modalities would have to be worked out on a country-by-country basis, taking into account each country's unique circumstances. Care must be taken in striking a balance between democratic consultation and an unwieldy consultation process. The need to strengthen leadership capacity for all citizens is crucial for this type of leadership. All major interest groups in the country, women, peasants, people with disabilities, workers, youth, elders, business people, etc., would have to be represented in the joint leadership.

How Do We Get There?

It is one thing to propose transformational feminist leadership and quite another to actualize the process. It is important to keep our feet on the ground by recognizing that social change tends to occur slowly. An alternative leadership paradigm is a long-term goal that entails transforming institutions, structures, traditions and norms. We need to adopt multiple strategies in order to achieve our goals. The strategies and methods should be diverse, varying from reformist to radical. The process will be gradual and incremental.

The reformist strategy, for example, would entail working our way into existing power structures and effecting change from within. Working inside existing bureaucracies will facilitate changes in leadership systems and structures and the building of alternative leadership models. The advantage of this methodology is that people with scarce resources (such as women) can exploit the institutional environment to achieve their goals (Martin 1990). In short, despite the structural limitations involved, accessing pre-existing political infrastructures to achieve the target of alternative leadership can be viewed as 'co-opting' government and not vice-versa.

Another strategy, which could be used concurrently with the moderate/reformist one, would take a more radical approach by directly challenging patriarchal privileges and undemocratic leadership styles. Although the reformist strategy also involves some degree of taking bold risks, radical strategies require sticking one's neck out, especially in the disabling context of our repressive political regimes.

Feminists cannot achieve their goals on their own. In our work of constructing alternative models of leadership we must forge alliances and build coalitions with other marginalized groups of society; for example, poor peasant women and men, people with disabilities, minority ethnic groups, environmental activists, anti-corporate activists and so forth. We must also create strategic links and networks with sympathetic elements within parliament, academia, the media, grassroots organizations, as well as regional and international women's movements.

Conclusion

A case has been made for a more inclusive, ethical, egalitarian and gender-sensitive leadership style in Africa. Confronted by weakening state structures, increasingly more despotic regimes and the globalization 'face-off' (led by the US), the implications for African women's attempts to create spaces for alternative models are brought into sharp relief.

What is clear is that nothing is going to change without radical transformation. This transformation must entail the complete overhaul of the institutions and power structures inherited at independence. And, to reflect African realities and aspirations, it must take place across the entire spectrum of economic and political as well as social contexts. A clear conceptual understanding and agreement on some basic principles is vital in guiding the process of instituting alternative leadership models. Alternative leadership will not be achieved by pouring old wine in new wineskins, nor by pouring new wine in old wineskins; what Africa needs is new wine in new wineskins. It can be done; the ball is in our court!

Originally presented at the East African Meeting on Alternative Leadership under the auspices of the Forum for Women in Democracy (FOWODE), Entebbe, May 23-26, 2002.

Sylvia Tamale is a Ugandan feminist activist. She holds a Bachelor of Laws from Makerere University, a Masters in Law from Harvard Law School and a Ph.D. in Sociology and Feminist Studies from the University of Minnesota. She is currently the dean at Makerere University's Faculty of Law where she teaches, among others, a course on Gender and the Law. Her research interests include gender and politics, gender and sexuality, Third World women and the law, feminist legal theory and method, and the ideology of race and class. She has published widely on a variety of topics, including her groundbreaking book, When Hens Begin to Crow: Gender and Parliamentary Politics in Uganda *(Westview Press, 1999).*

Notes

1   This is an excerpt from Kwame Nkrumah's famous speech delivered to the Gold Coast Legislative Assembly. He was moving a motion on Constitutional Reform on July 10, 1953 (four years before Ghana attained its independence). See Bankole (1963: 137, 139).

2   The respected former president of Tanzania made this remark shortly before he died in 1999.

3   Elsewhere, I discuss how the colonial vestiges present in the operation and workings of the national assembly in one former colony (Uganda) adversely impinge on leadership and democracy. Preservation of both symbolic and real vestiges of colonialism (e.g., insistence on the exclusive use of English or French in parliament) serves to perpetuate the patriarchal structure and to alienate the greater majority of the population. See Tamale (1999).

4   This comment was made in an interview with Robin White, British Broadcasting Corporation, World Service (Network Africa Programme, 22 May 2002). The Ugandan government has been waging a war against the insurgent group, Lord's Resistance Army, led by Joseph Kony since 1988. This means that for fourteen years out of the sixteen that the National Resistance Movement (NRM) government has been in power, thousands of civilians in northern Uganda and southern Sudan have lost their lives, been displaced, suffered abductions, rapes and all manner of violence. It defies logic for anyone to argue that continued war is the solution to resolving the conflict and the path to development.

5   A defining moment in the struggle against domestic violence in Uganda was March 2002 when Vice-President Specioza Kazibwe 'broke the silence' by publicly announcing that domestic violence was the main reason for her separation from her husband. Since then, domestic violence has ceased to be a closeted topic and there has been a lot of public awareness.

6   In Luganda we have several proverbs that mirror domesticity. For example: '*Ekitiibwa ky'omukyala ekisoka, bufumbo*' (woman's principal dignity is derived from marriage) and '*Bulikugwa, obukyala si bumbejja*' (woman loses her dignity when her husband dies or when she falls out of his favour).

7   NEPAD is a 'home-grown' continental initiative that is supposed to guide and shape the new beginning for a transformed Africa. It is the programme that the African Union adopted in 2001 as a blueprint to implement the spirit of an 'African Renaissance'.

8   Other legal tools available to us include international instruments such as the Convention on the Elimination of All Forms of Discrimination Against Women (CEDAW) and statutory provision in specific legislations.

9   For more details on this argument and a comprehensive analysis of law and sex equality see MacKinnon (2001).

10   Care must be taken not to confuse 'transformational feminist leadership' with 'women's leadership'. Womanhood is not synonymous with feminist; indeed, some female leaders have done more to consolidate sexist undemocratic leaderships than certain men.

11   Adopted from the Centre for Asia-Pacific Women in Politics' (CAPWIP) plan for action for achieving the vision of transformative politics, see http://www.capwip.org/aboutcapwip/planofaction.html.

References

Abdela, L. (2000) 'From palm tree to parliament: training women for political leadership and public life', in C. Sweetman (ed.), *Women and Leadership*, Oxford: Oxfam, 16-23.

Agorsah, K. (1990) 'Women in African traditional politics,' *Journal of Legal Pluralism and Unofficial Law*, 30, 77-86.

Ake, C. (1996) *Democracy and Development in Africa*, Washington: Brookings Institution.

Antrobus, P. (2000) 'Transformational leadership: Advancing the agenda for gender justice', in C. Sweetman (ed.), *Women and Leadership*, Oxford: Oxfam, 50-56.

Aristotle (1946) [c320BC] *The Politics of Aristotle* (translated by Ernest Barker), Oxford: Oxford University Press.

Bankole, T. (1963) *Kwame Nkrumah: His Rise to Power*, second edition, London: George Allen and Unwin Ltd.

Beijing Declaration and Platform for Action (1995) United Nations Fourth World Conference on Women, A/CONF.177/20 and A/CONF.177/20/Add.1 Online: http://www.un.org/womenwatch/daw/beijing/platform/plat1.htm

Blake, R. and J. Mouton (1978) *The New Managerial Grid*, Houston, TX: Gulf.

Brydon, L. and S. Chant (1989) *Women in the Third World: Gender Issues in Rural and Urban Areas*, New Brunswick, NJ: Rutgers University Press.

Davidson, B. (1992) *The Black Man's Burden*, Nairobi: East African Educational Publishers.

Drath, W. and C. Palus (1994) *Making Common Sense: Leadership as Meaning Making in a Community of Practice*, Greensboro, NC: Center for Creative Leadership.

Engels, F. (1972) [1884] *Origin of the Family, Private Property and the State*, New York: Penguin Books.

Fiedler, F. (1997) 'Situational control and a dynamic theory of leadership' in K. Grint (ed.), *Leadership: Classical, Contemporary and Critical Approaches*, Oxford: Oxford University Press, 126-154.

Gardner, J. (1989) *On Leadership*, New York: Free Press.

Geisler, G. (1995). 'Troubled sisterhood: women and politics in Southern Africa,' *African Affairs*, 94, 545-578.

Goetz, A. and S. Hassim (2000) *In and Against the Party: Women's Representation and*

Constituency-Building in Uganda and South Africa, Geneva: United Nations Rearch Institute for Social Development (UNRISD).

Gonzalez, D. (2000) 'Who leads to where? African leadership into the 21st century', in H. Othman (ed.), *Reflections on Leadership in Africa: Forty Years After Independence,* Brussels: VUB University Press.

Hansen, K. T. (ed.) (1992) *African Encounters with Domesticity,* New Brunswick, NJ: Rutgers University Press.

Heifitz, R. (1994) *Leadership Without Easy Answers,* Cambridge, MA: Harvard University, 'Kick women out of politics,' (2002) *The Monitor,* 17 May: iv.

Longwe, S. (2000) 'Towards realistic strategies for women's political empowerment in Africa,' *Gender and Development,* 8, 3, 24-30.

MacKinnon, C. A. (2001) *Sex Equality,* New York: Foundation Press.

Mafeje, A. (1971) 'The ideology of "tribalism"', *The Journal of Modern African Studies,* 9, 2, 253-261.

Mama, A. (1999) 'Preliminary thoughts on gender, politics and power in African contexts', in *Cracks in the Edifice: Critical African Feminist Perspectives on Women and Governance: Dawn Political Restructuring and Social Transformation (PRST) Africa Report,* Online: http://www.dawn.org.fj/publications/docs/cracksintheedifice/eng3.pdf.

Mama, A. (1996) *Women's Studies and Studies of Women in Africa During the 1990s,* CODESRIA Working Paper Series, No. 5, Dakar: CODESRIA.

Mamdani, M. (1996) *Citizen and Subject: Contemporary Africa and the Legacy of Late Colonialism,* Princeton, NJ: Princeton University Press.

Martin, P. (1990) 'Rethinking feminist organizations', *Gender and Society* 4, 2, 182-206.

Mba, N. (1982) *Nigerian Women Mobilized: Women's Political Activity in Southern Nigerian, 1990-1965,* Berkeley: University of California Press.

Monga, C. (1996) *The Anthropology of Anger: Civil Society and Democracy in Africa,* Boulder: Lynne Rienner.

Mwakikagile, G. (2001) *The Modern African State: Quest for Transformation,* Huntington, NY: Nova Science Publishers.

Northouse, P. G. (1997) *Leadership: Theory and Practice,* Thousand Oaks, CA: Sage Publications.

Okonjo, K. (1976), 'The dual sex political system in operation: Igbo women and community politics in Midwestern Nigeria,' in N. Hafkin and E. Bay (eds.), *Women in Africa: Studies in Social and Economic Change,* Stanford, CA: Stanford University Press. 45-58.

Oloka-Onyango, J. (2000) 'Gender and conflict in contemporary Africa: Engendering the mechanisms for promotion of human rights and conflict prevention', *The Review of African Commission on Human and Peoples' Rights,* 9, 1, 1-19.

Ospina, S. and E. Schall (2000) *Perspectives on Leadership: Our Approach to Research and Documentation for the Leadership for a Changing World Program,* 22 December (updated 2001). Online: http://leadershipforchange.org/research/papers/perspectives.php3

Parpart, J. and K. Staudt (eds.) (1989) *Women and the State in Africa,* London: Lynne Rienner.

Rost, J. (1993) *Leadership for the Twenty-first Century,* Westport: Praeger.

Sacks, K. (1982), 'An overview of women and power in Africa,' in J. O'Barr (ed.), *Perspectives on Power: Women in Africa, Asia and Latin America,* Durha, NC: Duke University Centre for International Studies, 1-10.

Smock, A. (1977) 'Ghana: from autonomy to subordination,' in J. Giele and A. Smock (eds.), *Women: Roles and Status in Eight Countries,* New York: John Wiley and Sons.

Stobel, M. (1982), 'African women: review essay,' *Signs: Journal of Women in Culture and Society,* 8, 1, 109-131.

Tamale, S. (1999) *When Hens Begin to Crow: Gender and Parliamentary Politics in Uganda,* Denver, CO: Westview Press.

Tripp, A. (2003) 'New trends in women's political participation in Africa' in *Gender and Governance Resource Database Asian Women's Resource Exchange, The Centre for Legislative Development,* Phillipines. Online: http://www.cld.org/wip.

Tsikata, D. (1997) *The State and National Machinery for Women in Africa,* National Machinery Series, No.11, Accra: Third World Network-Africa.

United Nations (UN). (2000) United Nations General Assembly Special Session, 'Women 2000: Gender Equality, Development and Peace for the Twenty-first Century', New York 5-9 June. Online: http://www.un.org/womenwatch/daw/followup/session/presskit/brochure.htm

Weber, M. (1968) [1922] *Economy and Society,* New York: Bedminster Press.

Young, C. (1994) *The African Colonial State in Comparative Perspective,* New Haven: Yale University Press.

TESTING THE LIMITS OF EUROPEAN CITIZENSHIP

ETHNIC HATRED AND MALE VIOLENCE

R. AMY ELMAN

In 1992, the architects of European integration unfurled the banner of European citizenship. Faced with growing economic uncertainty, Europe's current leaders have relied increasingly on varied strategies to grant greater legitimacy to the new, liberal economic order. 'Economic integration bore the burden of building a polity' (Laffan 1996: 92). Historically, the definitive attributes of any polity are three-fold: territory, sovereignty, and citizenship. In the context of the European Union (EU), much attention has been focused on sovereignty (e.g., subsidiarity) and the expansion of territory (through extended membership); by comparison, EU citizenship is a relatively recent concern, its formal establishment dating only from the Treaty on European Union (i.e., Maastricht Treaty).[1]

Most analyses of EU citizenship are constructed far from the conditions that pose crucial obstacles to women's participation in, and benefit from, the project of EU integration. These include, but are not limited to, xenophobia, poverty and male violence. This article explores briefly the meaning of EU citizenship for those who have historically been excluded from state construction and transnational bargaining, principally the women of Europe. The central argument is that the status of this citizenship is decidedly ambiguous and its application inspires ambivalence, particularly for feminists. We shall consider the reasons why this is the case by focusing on those women residing on the periphery of integration— third-country nationals and battered wives.[2] This focus provides an unusual opportunity to test the potential for, and limits of, European citizenship.

The growing disparities of wealth within and between states are gendered and many of the most seriously disadvantaged are 'women who are racialised, migrantised and/or without access to formal citizenship' (Pettman 1999: 209). Women of colour are especially vulnerable because, until the Treaty of Amsterdam (see Duff 1997) the EU took no legislative action to specifically counter race discrimination.

Mari Matsuda observes that 'the places where law does not go to redress harm have tended to be the places where women, children, people of colour, and poor people live'. She insists that the absence of legal redress 'is itself another story with a message, perhaps unintended, about the relative value of different human lives' (1993: 18). Women's worth is also evidenced in the paltry remuneration, if any, that they receive for their work.

Despite their increased presence within the labour market, women's pay remains significantly lower than that of men and their rate of unemployment is generally much higher. In a labour market in which gender segregation is the norm and women comprise 77 per cent of Europe's 'low wage workers' and over half of the total unemployed in almost every EU Member State, women are often reluctant to initiate grievances against their co-workers and employers for fear of retribution.

Though scholars have begun to appreciate that 'powerful market forces' can deny women the full impact of existing equality legislation (i.e., Beveridge, Nott and Stephen 1996: 398), many still ignore the power of abusive conditions women face at home. Given that male violence against women is pervasive, this is a glaring oversight. The EU estimates that throughout the Member States, one woman in five is assaulted by her male partner at least once in her life (European Commission 2000). There are, however, additional reasons why addressing the issue of male violence is important. First, throughout Europe, the suffering produced by such violence gave rise to feminist movements that mobilized to end it. In selecting to ignore nearly three decades of such activism, one fails to grasp the success that feminists have had in politicizing what was previously 'private'. Second, developing an understanding of male violence is central to considerations of women and labour markets if only because such abuse sabotages women's success at waged work. Moreover, just as male violence is an obstacle to women's work, without access to stable, well-paid and supportive work environments, women are especially vulnerable to the men who abuse them (Brush 2000). In a 1999 survey of abused women in Swedish refuges, over one-third of these respondents cited economic hardship as an obstacle toward leaving (Elman 2001). Nearly a decade earlier, the same survey found that only fifteen per cent of women respondents had remarked that economics was a factor in their decision to stay. That anxiety over finances became more prominent in 1999 may be explained, in part, by the slight increase in the percentage of women respondents who are immigrants as well as the deteriorating socio-economic position of women in Sweden and throughout Europe (Mazey 1998).

Considering women's pervasive ethnic, economic and physically brutal subordination, it is extraordinary that the EU is still considered a peaceful and affluent region, one whose stability has been attributed in no small measure to European integration. However, as Eliane Vogel-Polsky (2000) perceptively remarks, women's subordination 'is perceived neither as a central element of crisis affecting our democracies nor as an unacceptable failing of democracy' (70). However, an additional explanation may be especially relevant to the EU. Because the project of European integration is in constant flux, one is better able to retain a persistent confidence in the institution's potential for remedy.

Many political analysts are optimistic that the EU 'offers a wide range of potential venue opportunities for strategically motivated actors at various levels of governance: local, national and European' (Wendon 1998: 342; see also Pollack 1997), a position that often overlooks the power differentials between claimants. Others have sagely observed that 'the effects of the EU have been highly variable', depending on the actors, issues and movements under consideration (Marks and McAdam 1996: 119). Analysts of the anti-nuclear movement, for example, observe that the refusal of Member States to transfer any real policy authority to the EU has effectively circumscribed the mobilization of this movement to the national level (Marks and McAdam 1996). By contrast, focusing on Britain's gay rights movement, Carl Stychin (1998) concludes: 'in the U.K. [United Kingdom], where rights discourse is comparatively underdeveloped (for better or worse), Europe provides a new arena for social and legal struggle' (136).

Most scholarship on women's rights has been confined to work-related issues that, when assessed, generally credits the EU (and, in particular, the European Commission) with the cultivation of 'close relations with the relevant policy community in an attempt to create "constituency" support for EC intervention in a particular policy sector' (Mazey 1998: 138). Sonia Mazey's astute recognition of the Commission's favoured ties to *femocrats* and ostensible non-governmental actors like the European Women's Lobby (EWL) does not, however, necessarily mean that the Commission and/or other European institutions are permeable to, and successful in, addressing those demands originating from grassroots feminist organizations. Indeed, the EWL is funded by the Commission on whose behalf it labours to portray the community as 'woman-friendly' to an estimated 2,700 affiliates that range from the Vatican to pro-abortion, feminist groups.[3] A direct assessment of the Commission's own record, and that of other EU institutions, in forcefully mitigating male violence and xenophobia may alter the perception of the EU as a crucial venue for promoting progressive social change.

Women's conspicuous exclusion from the first three decades of Europe's construction, and now their conditional access to its most powerful institutions, suggest that, as relative newcomers, their knowledge of and influence within the EU is likely to be limited when compared to men. Despite considerable variation across Member States, these two factors, among many, place the women of Europe at a particular disadvantage with regard to citizenship and the politics of integration (Elman 1996a).

Historical Precedents

Citizenship has always entailed both privilege and exclusion, affording benefits to those who possess it and legitimizing discrimination (and even destruction) against those who lack it. In *The Origins of Totalitarianism*, Hannah Arendt (1979) reminds us that, as stateless persons, Europe's Jews were among the first in the twentieth century to experience unrestricted police domination. For Arendt, 'only nationals could be citizens, only people of the same national origin could enjoy the full protection of legal institutions' (275).

While Arendt attributes (Jewish) genocide to statelessness, anarchists argue that states provide a nationalistic impetus to celebrate crimes against humanity as heroic deeds. For Emma Goldman (1969) 'the State is itself the greatest criminal' (59). From this vantage point, one cannot transcend the crimes of states by either creating new states or conferring their particularized privileges. Like Arendt, Virginia Woolf (1966 [1938]) witnessed some of the horrors associated with the rise of fascism. However, she seems to part company with her contemporary by sharing the state scepticism of her anarchist predecessor, Goldman. Reflecting on Britain's patriotic appeals to defeat fascism, Woolf (1966) renounces (her) national identity. She refuses to regard British patriarchy as a bastion against fascism and insists she has no country because, like so many others, she has been excluded from its construction. More importantly, she insists, 'As a woman *I want no country*. As a woman my country is the whole world' (109 [emphasis added]). Ironically, the appeal of a united Europe appears, in part, predicated upon partial sympathy for this rather radical sentiment. Although the architects of Europe were loath to abandon their states—they wished to establish a slightly larger and inclusive identity—their ambition was regional. Woolf, by contrast, identified herself as a citizen of the world until, through suicide, she chose to leave it.

For many who survived the Second World War, a united Europe promised the transcendence of those national rivalries and parochial loyalties that helped make the horrors of that period possible. Indeed, the Preamble to the Treaty of Paris explicitly calls upon its members 'to substitute for age-old rivalries the merging of their essential interests' and 'create, by establishing an economic community, the basis for a broader and deeper community among peoples long divided by bloody conflicts' (qtd. in Nelsen and Stubb 1998: 16). It was assumed that the eventual prosperity, prompted by a cohesive economic community, would diminish dissension. This presumption proved false for a number of reasons, not the least of which concerns chronic unemployment, the collapse of communism in Eastern Europe, and the renewed assertion of national identities throughout (and beyond) the continent.

With diminished influence and affluence, Europe's political actors came to appreciate that 'An emphasis only on the material benefits of integration [would] not guarantee continued commitment to the process' (Laffan 1996: 95). They, thus, set anchor in the sentiments of prestige and solidarity. European emblems (e.g., European flags, anthems and feasts), democratic rhetoric and European citizenship were designed to inspire such commitment. EU citizenship emerged as one of the most recent and arguably ambiguous of these devices, distinctive for the limited legal rights it has conferred.

Unlike conventional citizenship, defined as 'a status bestowed on those who are full members of a community', which includes civil, political and social rights and obligations (Marshall 1950: 14), the political status of the EU citizen is presently circumscribed. 'It is a citizenship whose legal and normative bases are located in the wider community, and whose actual implementation is assigned to the Member States' (Soysal 1994: 148). 'Every person holding the nationality of a Member State shall be a citizen of the Union', a status that entitles one to free movement within all Member States (Art. 8[1] EC qtd. in O'Leary 1996, ii). Union citizenship is thus extended to member state nationals, not European nationals. The absence of a European 'people' is the most remarkable aspect of EU citizenship as well as perhaps its chief limitation (O'Leary 1996; Weiler, Halpern and Mayer 1995; Weiler 1997; Wiener 1997).

EU citizenship is, at present, neither social nor participatory. According to the European Commission (1995a), the 'purpose' of European citizenship is 'to deepen European citizens' sense of belonging to the European Union and make that sense more tangible by conferring on them the rights associated with it' (21). However, the most novel application of this 'right' is the ability of any (member state) citizen to vote and stand for office outside of one's own member state in local and European Parliamentary elections.[4] The fact that policy outcomes appear minimally influenced by these civic acts helps explain the low voter turnout in European elections as well as its steady decline, from 63 per cent in 1979 to 56 per cent in 1994. Voter turnout increased in 1999 to 64 per cent only after an Ecu24 million (30.4USD) public relations campaign (begun in 1997) to promote EU citizenship. Given the expense of this Citizen's First initiative, a single percentage point increase over that of two decades earlier seems unimpressive. Nonetheless, EU officials persist in attributing voter apathy to an ignorant electorate and not to a well-informed citizenry cognizant of and perhaps frustrated by its limited ability to influence matters of integration.

Engendering Citizenship

Apart from the opportunity to vote (exercised every five years) and a Social Action Program (1991-1995) designed to encourage women's entrance into politics and civil dialogue, the EU has emphasized women's and men's market-oriented participation. Remarking on the escalating importance of economics more generally, Dominique Schnapper (1997) notes that, 'True membership in the community is no longer defined by political participation but by economic activity' (204). Indeed, Patrick R. Ireland (1995) explains, 'Geographical mobility accrued to nationals of the Member States not on the basis of their citizenship status but when they traveled as workers, for economic reasons' (237). European citizenship is grounded in free market ideology with its related rights often predicated on calculations of the bottom line and not on the intrinsic value of persons and/or sexual equality. This condition influences the form that rights claims take. For example, Carl F. Stychin (1998) observes that various gay rights lobbyists (e.g., Britain's Stonewall) now insist that Europe's failure to mitigate heterosexism hampers a 'wealth maximizing citizenry' (124; see also Stychin

2000).[5] In short, Europeans have long been engaged as consumers and workers, not as citizens (Laffan 1996).

Efforts to improve and enhance a sense of democratic accountability within the EU were considered, often behind closed doors, at the 1996 Intergovernmental Conference (IGC). At that time, fewer than fifteen per cent of member state nationals even knew about such discussions specifically because their access to them was restricted. Still, the Commission (1996a) declared that 'ordinary people must *feel* actively involved [emphasis added]' (9). Several commentators remarked that the incessant rhetoric of 'giving people a voice' failed to mask the Commission's insincerity (e.g., Meulenaere 1996).

A draft agenda for the IGC, which was composed exclusively by men, suggests 'the Treaty should clearly proclaim such European values as equality between men and women, non-discrimination on grounds of race, religion, sexual orientation, age or disability and that it should include an express condemnation of racism and xenophobia' (European Commission 1995b: 4).

In Amsterdam, the EU incorporated the principles of non-discrimination in Article 13. The article empowers but does not oblige the European Commission to combat discrimination. It reads:

> Without prejudice to the other provisions of this Treaty and within the limits of powers conferred by it upon the Community, the Council, acting unanimously on a proposal from the Commission and after consulting the European Parliament may take appropriate action to combat discrimination based on sex, racial or ethnic origin, religion or belief, disability, age or sexual orientation. (qtd. in Duff 1997: 6)

The Amsterdam Treaty's requirement that the Council must reach a unanimous vote on a Commission proposal before it 'may take appropriate action' tempers the reach of the clause. In consequence, Member States did not establish a directly effective provision but, instead, left it to the EC institutions to adopt 'appropriate' measures. In turn, the Commission (1999a) proposed legislation and a Community Action Programme to Combat Discrimination (2001-2006), both specifically designed to implement Article 13.

Since adopting Article 13, the Commission (1999b) reasons that the 'Community is already active in the fight against discrimination' and insists that the 'responsibility for implementing the fight against discrimination rests principally with the Member States' (3). These states were expected to adopt the laws, regulations, and administrative procedures necessary to comply with the new law by 31 December 2002. Through the adoption of the Directive and Action Program, the EU is itself able to evade direct action while appearing to provide redress. Member States may take a similar position of circumvention by emphasizing the EU's power to intervene through Article 13.

Feminists (and other activists) are currently caught between Member States and the larger European Community as both systems of governance seek credit for providing redress and avoid responsibility for its enforcement. In short, activists must determine the emphasis they should extend to each venue so that they may effectively meet their goals. This is an arduous determination, especially when one considers the history and current character of both the Member States and the EU. Each, in its own way, has subverted citizenship's promise of uniform access to social rights.

While women were conspicuously absent from Europe's key deliberative body, the Commission, during the first 30 years of its operation, Member States have shared a similar, if not more oppressive, history of sexual exclusion. Europe was man-made, a fact often politely overlooked. Those burdened by this past are quick to list the numerous advances that women have since made. These include, but are not limited to, an increased participation in the wage labour market and greater presence within various political institutions. At present, five of the twenty European commissioners are women. Women similarly increased their percentage in the European Parliament, from 19 per cent in 1989 to over 25 per cent in 1994 and 31 per cent since 1999 (a percentage higher than nearly all the national legislatures throughout the EU). While such achievements are not insignificant, assessing gender (in)equality through women's numerical presence within established political institutions, as opposed to the substance of the policies and material conditions they promote, is as problematic as it is naïve (Rossilli 2000; Vogel-Polsky 2000; Weldon 2002).

Emphasizing the formal rights of EU citizenship that women are now assumed to possess obscures the numerous obstacles to their effective use. There are several reasons for caution. First, unlike the call for gender equality and the resultant Directives, the request for European citizenship resulted not from a call from Europe's masses but, instead, from the elites who governed them. To note that 'ordinary' Europeans approve of it is not the same as being able to demonstrate that they demanded it. Second, considering that leaders have long conferred citizenship on those whom they sought to rule legitimately, the establishment of citizenship need not be extreme or innovative. As noted earlier, European citizenship confers few new rights on current citizens of Member States. Thus, its extension was hardly popular.

For both women and men, European citizenship has sparked confusion and, at times, a powerful reaction against it. For example, in 1992, those opposed to the Maastricht Treaty's citizenship provision included many (e.g., French and Danes) who equated the Treaty with the destruction of the nation-state (Laffan 1996). Still others 'felt that the citizenship proposals were not far-reaching enough' (Meehan 1993: 184, n28). The enduring concern among Danes over citizenship's possible usurpation of their sovereignty (Petersen 1993) was most recently manifest in Denmark's rejection of the euro.

Despite the European Commission's assurances that European citizenship does not conflict with national citizenship, 51 per cent of Europeans state that they have never even felt European (Reif qtd. in Laffan 1996: 99). This figure has some wondering if European identity is merely a 'preserve of Europe's elites'

(Laffan 1996: 99), a suspicion buttressed by the relative absence of enthusiasm for unification among Europe's less privileged. Brigid Laffan (1996) reminds us that the voting patterns in three national referenda on the Maastricht Treaty suggest that socio-economic status played a significant role in determining attitudes concerning integration. She concludes, 'workers and poorer sections of society see little benefit and many dangers in the 'Europeanization' of the contemporary state' (89).

Women's displeasure with European integration could increase as reforms (e.g., equality legislation) previously enacted on their behalf are increasingly portrayed as 'unwarranted and unworkable infringement[s] on freedom in market transactions' (Conaghan qtd. in Beveridge, Nott, and Stephen 2000: 388). Nonetheless, there are many EU scholars and others who acknowledge the substantial social costs of closer economic integration but still insist that suffering is best alleviated by more, not less, integration (e.g., Simpson and Walker 1993). Competing assessments aside, the pursuit of a single currency (with its Treaty requirement that Member States have deficits below three per cent of GDP [gross domestic product] and outstanding public debts below 60 per cent of the GDP before joining it) has, in part, legitimized the chorus of post-Keynesian calls for cuts in social welfare programs (Ostner 2000; Rossilli 2000). Such austerity measures have, in turn, led to large protests throughout the EU, most notably in France and Germany.[6]

Considering that women constitute over half of the total unemployed in almost every member state and are a significant majority of Europe's service sector employees, it is not surprising that women have been less favourably disposed to integration than have men. For example, a Eurobarometer poll in 2000 revealed that 55 per cent of men surveyed favour their country's membership in the EU versus 47 per cent of women surveyed (2000: 34). In addition, women are less willing to vote in European elections (Eurobarometer 2000: 89), a point that should not be interpreted to mean that they are apathetic. After all, women have been prominent in political campaigns to counter unification (Hoskyns 1996).

Third-Country Nationals and Battered Women

Although European citizenship implies a more integrated continent, recent efforts to limit immigration have resulted in increasingly obdurate definitions of conventional (i.e., national) citizenship throughout the Member States. For example, children once born in France to non-French parents acquired French citizenship automatically at eighteen, provided they had been a resident in the country for the previous five years. Since 1993, such children have had to apply for citizenship between the age of sixteen and twenty-one, with the possibility that their application could be refused (*Loi no. 93-933*).[7] Germany also changed its course in 1993. That year the Federal Parliament (*Bundestag*) retreated from its liberal asylum policy by amending its Basic Law (Art. 16A) and began closing its borders to many, including those fleeing war-torn countries consumed by nationalism.

With an emergency influx of refugees, many Member States had an incentive to closely coordinate their policies on refugees and asylum-seekers. The Amsterdam Treaty gave shape to this desire when it gave the European Court of Justice jurisdiction over asylum and immigration policies. Before this time, the Court's role was negligible; now it can hope to ensure a uniform interpretation on such matters (Duff 1997). Whether the enhanced cohesion bodes well for refugees, asylum-seekers and immigrants remains contested, particularly within a polity whose character remains so unsettled.

Xenophobia has increased throughout Europe as right wing politicians and press reports often portray immigrants as a key destabilizing force. Indeed, this tactic proved especially effective for Austria's far right Freedom Party, which garnered nearly one-third of the vote in the national election of 1999. The alleged inextricability of escalating unemployment and immigration has also been made abundantly clear in a notorious poster of France's far right party, the National Front (FN). It exclaims: 'Three million unemployed, that's three million too many immigrants'.[8] Deportation is one proposed solution; French women figure prominently in the second (see Kofman 1998). Interestingly, while mothers who are not French are depicted as bearers of an onerous immigrant population, French women are encouraged to reproduce for 'the homeland'. Austria's Freedom Party adopted a similar position to that of the FN when, during the 1999 election, Mr Haider (the party's leader) promised $400 a month to Austrian mothers as an incentive for them to stay at home to raise their children. Martin Schain (2000) suggests that the issue of immigration in national politics has been redefined 'from a labour market problem, to an integration/incorporation problem, to a problem that touches on national identity' and 'to problems of citizenship requirements' (20).

Afraid to alienate a potential voter base, politicians in France, Austria and throughout Europe have been reluctant to challenge the far right. Even Sweden's Social Democratic party challenged neither the racist rhetoric nor the agenda of a newly established (New Democracy) party which, among other things, called for additional restrictions in refugee policies in the 1991 election. Bengt Westerberg, of the Swedish Liberal party, was the only party leader to publicly criticize the increasing xenophobia of Swedes. He demanded that other parties also address the problem; his request was met with silence, an increasingly common response. Schain (2000) observes that many conventional parties throughout Europe have reacted to the far right by co-opting some aspects of their program in an effort to undermine their appeal, a tactic that has been ineffective. Most recently, the fragility of the European left has been expressed, in part, through its lukewarm opposition to the racism of the Austrian right.

While the EU's condemnation of Austria's Freedom Party implied that a shift towards decisive action is possible, a more considered examination suggests that this is unlikely. In the spring of 2000, the EU suspended normal links with Austria through limiting ambassadorial contact and withdrawing its support of Austrian candidates to international posts. Yet, because Austria did not break any specific rules and unprecedented sanctions were imposed with limited discussion, the censure lasted only seven months. The opaque and feeble foundation of the EU's response has not gone unnoticed (see Judt 2000).

Just prior to the Austrian debacle, the EU endeavoured to take action through a range of reports, resolutions, and declarations that condemns racism and xenophobia. In addition, the Commission (1998a) proclaimed 1997 the European Year against Racism and agreed, in Amsterdam, to establish the European Monitoring Centre on Racism and Xenophobia in Vienna. Rhetorical pronouncements and monitoring aside, the EU concedes that it will not 'take specific measures to combat racism and xenophobia' nor will it 'modify the system for protecting human rights in the Community or … make any major change to the institutional system in the Community or any of its Member States' (European Commission 1996b: 3). *Subsidiarity* may pose a further constraint on effective action.[9] Moreover, Member States have yet to fully honour their promise (made several years ago) that they would relinquish their internal borders (Duff 1997: 20).

While EU citizenship may augment Europe's accessibility for many member state nationals, it may also more firmly etch a boundary 'around a culturalist and physical Europe so to ensure the exclusion of non-European foreigners' as well as Europeans of colour (Feldblum 1996: 11; see also Hervey 1995). In 1997, Eurobarometer data revealed that of the 16,241 people questioned across the Member States, 33 per cent openly described themselves as 'quite racist' or 'very racist'. No similar study has since been conducted. Thus, the success of recent EU measures to counter xenophobia cannot be effectively measured.

At the closing conference on the 1997 European Year against Racism, then Commission President Jacques Santer acknowledged that the 1997 survey revealed a 'worrying and unacceptable banalisation of the expression of racist sentiments' (qtd. in European Commission 1998a: 5). Writing from Britain, John Clarke and Mary Langan remark: 'perhaps more powerfully than before, 'race' came to be seen as the single most visible demonstration of 'citizenship' combining the implicit racial 'test' as the basis of detecting suspected non-citizens among citizen residents' (1993, 73). Writing from France, Pierre Bourdieu asks: 'What does it mean to be a citizen if at any moment proof of citizenship has to be provided?' Like Clarke and Langan, he objects to the ways in which numerous civil servants are authorized 'to cast doubt on the citizenship of a citizen at the mere sight of her face or the sound of her name' (1998, 79). The fact that Article 13 of the Amsterdam Treaty may provide redress is encouraging, though, again, the EU is under no obligation to secure relief for the victims of such (race) discrimination.

The price of exclusion is borne increasingly among women throughout Europe, particularly third-country nationals (EWL 1995; Hervey 1995; Kofman and Sales 1992; Lutz 1997). Over the past decade, the number of asylum seekers has dramatically increased and it is believed that two-thirds of the world's estimated 17.5 million refugees are female (Bhabha and Shutter 1994). More recently, a majority of the survivors of Serbia's war against Bosnia-Herzegovina and Croatia are Muslim women seeking refuge. This is, perhaps, the most significant case in point. The fact that this genocide happened in non-Member States within Europe makes it no less compelling to consider.[10] In fact, a decade ago, the EC expressly declared its commitment to the protection and promotion of democracy and human rights not only within its Community but also in non-Member States (Preamble to the *Single European Act* cited in Nelsen and Stubb 1998: 45-7). In its Statement on Human Rights, the Community declared that, 'The Twelve seek universal observance of human rights' and insisted that such rights are 'an important element in relations between third countries and the Europe of Twelve' (European Commission 1986). Less than a decade would pass before the reality fell far short of the rhetoric (see Nenadic 1996). Member States responded to the genocidal war through 'concerted efforts to stop refugees from leaving' and sought 'to keep these refugees "as close to their home areas as possible", and within the confines of the former Yugoslavia' (Sassen 1999: 125). Although the EU has long been interested in the affairs of third countries, the essentially economic character of the EU has undoubtedly dulled its interest in fundamental human rights issues. Moreover, the absence of any specific and detailed articles concerning human rights has made it easier for the EU to evade action in this and other important areas, impressive statements notwithstanding.

Within seemingly peaceful Europe, male violence against women at home is as pervasive as it is perilous. As noted earlier, the European Commission (2000) estimates that 20 per cent of all women within the EU have been assaulted by their husband or partner. Moreover, it notes that 25 per cent of all violent crimes reported to police involve such male violence. Alarming as these statistics are, authorities often concede that under-reporting remains a serious analytic problem. Women do not report the men that beat them for fear of retribution.[11] The above statistics, therefore, are probably low. Not only do estimations of the problem remain conservative; they fail to capture the horror of the abuse itself. Indeed, the violence is often so severe that the strongest reason for a woman staying with her assailant is, paradoxically, the fear of what the batterer will do if she attempts to leave. In Sweden, approximately 60 per cent of all homicides involve men who murder the women in their lives (Elman 1996b) while in Britain authorities estimate the percentage at 50 (Kotatakos 1999).

Given the grave danger in which batterers place their victims, it is not surprising that throughout Europe, most efforts on behalf of battered women have centered on establishing and maintaining shelters; a safe place to stay is always the most immediate and pressing need of battered women. Indeed, while women constitute, on average, between one-fifth and one-third of the homeless throughout Europe, a significant percentage of these are believed to be those fleeing male violence at home (Harvey 1999, 60; see also Malos and Hague 1997).

One of the major issues confronting women's refuges throughout Europe is how best to meet the needs of newly arrived immigrant women married to batterers (Nordic Council of Ministers 1998). To escape their abusers, many women are forced from their homes and, in consequence, risk statelessness. Immigrant women, for whom it is difficult to return to their homelands, face a situation in which they are unable to stay in Member States unless they remain married for a specified number of years. In the Netherlands, for example, a woman must reside with her partner for at least five years and in Sweden, she must remain with him for two years. In Britain, women are required to stay with their husbands for at least one year or return to their country of origin. Women are, thus, sometimes expected to endure abuse for the privilege of (legal) residence.

Should a third-country national woman leave her EU citizen husband, she must leave 'his' country. The European Court of Justice reinforced this position in *Diatta v Berlin Land* (Case 267/83 [1985] ECR 567). The case concerned a Member State husband separated (though not formally divorced) from his third-country national wife. The Court ruled that the woman was entitled to the protections of Community law only until the marriage was formally annulled. Tamara K. Hervey (1995) explains, 'The effect of the ruling ... was to give the EUN [European Union National] husband control over expulsion of his wife: on divorce she would cease to be a member of the family for purposes of Community law' (106). In 1997, a High Level Panel found such situations 'hard to accept' and recommended that Community provisions be amended so as 'to recognize a right of residence for the divorced spouse who is a third country national' (60-61). As well, it invited national authorities to consider the difficulties these women face when subjected to the threat of divorce.

Several Member States have sought to mitigate the hardships of such a stateless existence by decreasing residence requirements specifically for abused women. Given the absence of any explicit legal basis in the Treaty, the EU had been hesitant to promote a uniform approach to this particular issue (Gradin 1999). Thus, it has only just begun to acknowledge violence against women as political in nature and economic in consequence (Elman 1996a).

In 1997, the European Commission released a report acknowledging that while male violence is the most endemic form of violence within all Member States, the elderly, poor and migrant women may be especially vulnerable. The following year, the European Parliament designated 1999 as the 'European Year against Violence against Women'. The Commission concomitantly proposed funding for investigations into the problem as well as an information campaign, called Daphne, to promote the notion of zero tolerance for violence against women throughout Member States. Daphne has since been renewed as a Community action program (2000-2004) and is funded as a public health initiative (European Commission 1998b). Similar efforts are being undertaken to combat (sexual) trafficking in women under a separate program called STOP (European Commission 1998b).

This increased interest among Europe's policy-makers corresponds to escalating public concern throughout the Member States (Duffin 1999; Simpson 1999), a concern that results in no small measure from the efforts of feminists who have struggled to politicize male violence and sexual abuse (Hanmer 1996). In the last Eurobarometer (1999) data on violence against women reveal that over two-thirds (67 per cent) of Member State nationals polled believed that the EU should 'definitely' be involved in countering violence against women and only five per cent suggested a non-inteventionalist approach as appropriate (103). For those image entrepreneurs whose job it is to sell Europe, the above-mentioned efforts may facilitate support for Europe's political institutions without necessarily requiring innovative policies and effective implementation. According to Bryan Wendon (1998), the Commission has realized that its position is 'strengthened by being less responsible for policy formulation' and by 'enabling others to deal with the detail'. He concludes: 'In a difficult period in EU social policy DGV [the Directorate-General for Employment, Industrial Relations and Social Affairs] has found new roles in helping, funding, researching and nurturing—while staying well out of the firing line' (350).

Conclusion

The practice of citizenship has characteristically involved the assertion of claims directed toward the state that, in turn, authoritatively develops policy for the members of its shared national community (Wiener 1997). Citizenship inspires ambivalence among feminists and others seeking social justice not merely because it entails exclusion for those who do not possess it but because it legitimizes the very polities able to confer it. As J. H. H. Weiler (1997) has argued: 'The importance of European citizenship is much more than a device for placating an alienated populace. It goes to the very foundations of political legitimacy' (502). Having established EU citizenship, the architects of Europe may suggest that those who fail to fully avail themselves of their rights are somehow complicit in the persistence of their own subordination. After all, the novelty of this citizenship is that 'it equips individuals with rights enforceable outside the borders of the Nation State' (Everson 1996: 206).

Throughout much of Europe, the current struggles for rights (e.g., for third-country nationals and battered women) are remarkable, less for their claims, than for the political context within which their movements must now mobilize. 'The Union is neither a centrally organized state nor does it follow state-centric types of policy making' (Wiener 1997: 548). In consequence, the practice of EU citizenship necessitates that demands be made both toward the Member States and to the EU, a point clearly evidenced by the response of each to issues involving racism and xenophobia. Both arenas of governance insisted that remedy remained a responsibility of the other.

While EU citizenship can occasionally provide an additional venue for movements to make claims, the ability of autonomous actors to move freely between alternate avenues (e.g., state and transnational levels) may be limited. Efforts to locate the arena most permeable to one's position(s) necessitate vast resources with which activists may make smart determinations. It also requires political experience and a deep knowledge of the intricacies of policy making—whether in Brussels or elsewhere. Lastly, knowledge is necessary but insufficient in countering powerful myths that suggest that rights can be uniformly accessed when, until now, they have not. Women's citizenship is inextricably bound by socio-economic constraints that the mechanism of citizenship is not empowered to undo, appearances to the contrary notwithstanding.

The EU is much less likely to dismiss the significance of xenophobia and male violence against women, though it does make clear that the responsibility to mitigate these harms ultimately resides with states. The EU's reluctance to redress women's subordination may send a powerful message, however unintended, about the relative worth of women's lives within this European polity. European citizenship has not altered the value of women's lives, though it may have increased the expectation that it would.

The author her extends gratitude to the Title VI Center for West European Studies at Kalamazoo College for its partial support of this research.

Reprinted with permission from the National Women's Studies Association Journal *(NWSA) 13 (3) (2001): 49-69.*

R. Amy Elman's Sexual Subordination and State Intervention: Comparing Sweden and the United States *(1996) is a comparative study of state policies designed to mitigate violence against women in both countries. She also edited* Sexual Politics and the European Union: The New Feminist Challenge *(1996). She has published widely on matters pertaining to male violence and has been active in efforts to end it. Send correspondence to Department of Political Science, 1200 Academy St., Kalamazoo College, Kalamazoo, MI 49006; elman@kzoo.edu.*

Notes

1   Although the practice of citizenship remained largely invisible before the Maastricht Treaty, the roots of citizenship policy and its actual practice can be traced to the early 1970s when the term 'Citizens' Europe' was first introduced (Durand 1979; Evans 1984; Lyons 1996; Wiener 1997).

2   The term 'third-country national' typically refers to all those persons who are not citizens within any one of the fifteen Member States.

3   Given its funding source and disparate constituency, the European Women's Lobby's primary allegiance extends to the European Commission and not its numerous affiliates as its name implies.

4   This privilege was first proposed nearly two decades before it was established throughout the EU. With an eye toward its first election by direct suffrage (in 1979), the European Parliament issued a report in 1975 that called for the extension of political rights to migrants from Member States. Five years later (in 1980), the Commission insisted that local voting rights be extended to immigrants meeting certain residence requirements. Several states (e.g., Denmark, the Netherlands and Ireland) needed little coaxing as they had granted similar rights already.

5   For a further consideration of the social, economic and political exclusion premised in sexuality, see Elman 2000.

6   French dissatisfaction erupted in a series of winter strikes (1996-1997) that led
      President Chirac to reverse some of his deficit reducing measures. This situation also
      weakened his government in the parliamentary elections that followed. On 15 June
      1996, 350,000 people turned out in Bonn, Germany to express their dissatisfaction.
      Later, in October of 1999, tens of thousands of teachers, police officers, and other civil
      servants closed down the centre of Berlin after Chancellor Gerhard Shroeder's
      announcement to further trim Germany's 'nanny state'. The same month, Ireland
      witnessed the largest work stoppage in the nation's history as 27,500 nurses went on
      strike for nine days over paltry wages. Women were clearly key players in these, and
      other, demonstrations.

7   Five years later, the government essentially reverted the law to its pre-1993 status (*Loi
      no. 98-170*). Article 21-7, effective in 1998, reads: 'Any child born in France to foreign
      parents acquires French nationality when he is 18 if, at this date, he is residing in
      France and if he has habitually done so for five years since the age of 11' (author's
      translation; the original French text can be found at http://www.legifrance.gouv.fr/
      html/frame_codes_lois_reglt.htm). For a thorough analysis of French immigration
      law and the politics of French citizenship (and European citizenship more generally),
      see Feldblum 1999.

8   In Germany, in 1931, the Nazi party produced a similar poster which read: 'Five
      hundred thousand unemployed, four hundred thousand Jews, the solution is simple'.
      Today, it would be foolish to underestimate the support enjoyed by the National
      Front. While French opinion polls indicate that most French regard the party as racist,
      30 per cent admit to having, at one time, voted for it. In 1995, Jean LePen (the party's
      leader) garnered fifteen per cent of the presidential ballot. In 1997, his party enjoyed
      the same percentage of support in the first round of parliamentary elections (Gourevitch
      1997). In 2000, LePen came in second on the Presidential ballot, achieving victory
      over the Socialist candidate, Jospin. For an analysis of the National Front's influence
      on the politics and policies of France's established parties, see Schain 1999.

9   The principle of *subsidiarity* was articulated in Article 3b of Maastricht: 'In areas which
      do not fall within its exclusive competence, the Community shall take action, in
      accordance with the principle of subsidiarity, only if and in so far as the objectives of
      the proposed action cannot be sufficiently achieved by the Member States and can
      therefore, by reason of scale or effects of the proposed action, be better achieved by the
      Community'. Interestingly, subsidiarity cannot be extended to matters where the
      Community holds 'exclusive competence'. Moreover, there are no certainties about
      whether an action is best achieved by the Member States or the larger Community.
      Such uncertainties are an inextricable dimension of European integration.

10   Croatia is currently negotiating its membership within the EU through a Stabilization
      and Association Agreement.

11   As earlier mentioned, women are similarly fearful of the retribution that male
      employers and co-workers can exact should women report them for sex discrimina-
      tion.

References

Arendt, H. (1979) *The Origins of Totalitarianism*, New York: Harvest/HBJ Book.

Beveridge, F., S. Nott and K. Stephen (2000) 'Mainstreaming and the engendering of
   policy: a means to an end?' *Journal of European Public Policy*, 7, 3, 385-405.

Beveridge, F., S. Nott and K. Stephen (1996) 'Gender auditing: Making the community work for women', In T. Hervey and D. O'Keefe (eds.), *Sex Equality in the European Union*, New York: Wiley and Sons, 383-98.

Bhabha, J. and S. Shutter (1994) *Women's Movement: Women under Immigration, Nationality and Refugee Law*, Staffordshire, UK: Trentham Books.

Bourdieu, P. (1998) *Acts of Resistance: Against the Tyranny of the Market*, New York: The New Press.

Brush, L. (2000) 'Battering, traumatic stress, and welfare-to-work transition', *Violence Against Women*, 6, 10, 1039-65.

Clarke, J. and M. Langan. (1993) 'Restructuring welfare: the British welfare regime in the 1980s', in A. Cochrane and J. Clarke (eds.), *Comparing Welfare States: Britain in International Context*, London: Sage Publications, 49-76.

Duff, A. (1997) *The Treaty of Amsterdam: Text and Commentary*, London: Federal Trust.

Duffin, S. (1999) Audiotaped interview with author, Brussels, Belgium, 28, July.

Durand, A. (1979) 'European citizenship', *European Law Review*, 4, 3-14.

Elman, R. A. (2001) 'Unprotected by the Swedish welfare state revisited: assessing a decade of reforms for battered women', *Women's Studies International Forum*, 24, 1, 39-52.

Elman, R. A. (2000) 'The limits of citizenship: migration, sex discrimination and same-sex partners in EU law', *Journal of Common Market Studies*, 38, 5, 729-49.

Elman, R. A. (ed.) (1996a) *Sexual Politics and the European Union: The New Feminist Challenge*, Oxford, UK: Berghahn Books.

Elman, R. A. (1996b) *Sexual Subordination and State Intervention: Comparing Sweden and the United States*, Oxford, UK: Berghahn Books.

Eurobarometer (2000) *Eurobarometer Report Number 52*, Brussels, Belgium. Retrieved 18 August 2000. Online: http://europa.eu.int/comm/dg10/epo/eb/surveys.html.

Eurobarometer (1999) *Europeans and Their Views on Domestic Violence against Women*, Brussels, Belguim: DGX.

European Commission (2000) *European Campaign against Domestic Violence: Rationale*, Retrieved 29 July 2000. Online: http://europa.eu.int/comm/dg10/women/violence/index3_en.html.

European Commission (1999a) *Proposal for a Council Directive Establishing a General Framework for Equal Treatment in Employment and Occupation*, COM (99) 565 Final.

European Commission (1999b) *Proposal for a Council Decision Establishing a Community Action Programme to Combat Discrimination 2001-2006*, COM (99) 567 Final.

European Commission (1998a) *1997 European Year Against Racism: Closing Conference Report*, Luxembourg: OOPEC.

European Commission (1998b) *Proposal for a Council Decision on a Medium-Term Community Action Program on Measures Providing a Community-Wide Support to Member States Action Relating to Violence Against Children, Young Persons, and Women (The DAPHNE Programme)*, COM (98) 335 Final.

European Commission (1997) *Report from the Commission on the State of Women's Health in the European Community, 22. 05. 97,* COM (97) 224 Final.

European Commission (1996a) *Intergovernmental Conference 1996: Commission Opinion— Reinforcing Political Union and Preparing for Enlargement.* Luxembourg: OOPEC.

European Commission (1996b) *Draft Regulation Establishing a European Centre for Racism and Xenophobia*, COM (96) 615, Fifteenth Report.

European Commission (1995a) *Intergovernmental Conference 1996: Commission Report for the Reflection Group*, Luxembourg: OOPEC.

European Commission (1995b) 'Reflection group's report' SN520/95 (Reflex), Luxembourg: OOPEC.

European Commission (1986) 'Statement on human rights'. Bulletin of the European Communties, No. 7/8.

European Women's Lobby (EWL). (1995) *Confronting the Fortress–Black and Migrant Women in the European Community*, Luxembourg: European Parliament.

Evans, A. C. (1984) 'European citizenship: a novel concept in EEC law', *American Journal of Comparative Law*, 32, 679-715.

Everson, M. (1996) 'Women and citizenship of the European Union', in T. Hervey and D. O'Keeffe (eds.), *Sex Equality Law in the European Union*, New York: John Wiley and Sons, 203-19.

Feldblum, M. (1999) *Reconstructing Citizenship: The Politics of Nationality Reform and Immigration in Contemporary France*, Albany: State University of New York Press.

Feldblum, M. (1996) 'Reconstructing citizenship in Europe: changing trends and strategies', paper presented at the American Political Science Association Annual Meeting, San Francisco, CA., 29 August-1 September.

Goldman, E. (1969) *Anarchism and Other Essays*, New York: Dover Publications.

Gourevitch, P. (1997) 'The unthinkable: how dangerous is LePen's National Front?' *The New Yorker*, 28 April-5 May, 110-49.

Gradin, A. (1999) Phone interview with author, London-Brussels, 19 July.

Hanmer, J. (1996) 'The common market of violence', in R. Amy Elman (ed.), *Sexual Politics and the European Union: The New Feminist Challenge*, Oxford, England: Berghahn Books,. 131-45.

Harvey, B. (1999) 'The problem of homelessness: a European perspective', in S. Hutson and D. Clapham (eds.), *Homelessness: Public Policies and Private Troubles*, London: Cassell, 58-73.

Hervey, T. (1995) 'Migrant workers and their families in the European Union: the pervasive market ideology of community law', in J. Shaw and G. More (eds.), *New Legal Dynamics of European Union*, Oxford: Oxford University Press, 91-110.

High Level Panel. (1997) *Report of High Panel on Free Movement of Persons*. Retrieved 16 June 2000. Online: http://europa.eu.int/comm/internal_market/en/people/hlp/hlphtml.htm.

Hoskyns, C. (1996) 'The European Union and the women within: an overview of women's rights policy', in R. A. Elman (ed.), *Sexual Politics and the European Union: The New Feminist Challenge*, Oxford, England: Berghahn Books, 13-22.

Ireland, P. (1995) 'Migration, free movement, and immigration in the EU: a bifurcated policy response', in S. Leibfried and P. Pierson (eds.), *European Social Policy: Between Fragmentation and Integration*, Washington, DC: The Brookings Institution, 231-66.

Judt, T. (2000) 'Tale from the Vienna woods', *The New York Review of Books*, 23 March, 8-9.

Kofman, E. (1998) 'When society was simple: gender and ethnic divisions of the far and new right in France', in N. Charles and H. Hintjens (eds.), *Gender, Ethnicity and Political Ideologies*, London: Routledge Press, 91-106.

Kofman, E., and R. Sales (1992) 'Toward fortress Europe?' *Women's Studies international Forum* 15(1, 29-39.

Kotatakos, C. (1999) *Europeans and Their Opinion about Domestic Violence Against Women. Executive Summary*. Brussels, Belguim: European Commission Women's information Sector.

Laffan, B. (1996) 'The politics of identity and political order in Europe'. *Journal of Common Market Studies* 34, 1, 81-102.

Loi no. 93-933 (1993) Published in *Journal Officiel*, 23 July, 10342-10348.

Loi no. 98-170 Articles 19-1; 21-7; 21-11. Online: http://www.legifrance.gouv.fr/html/ frame_codes_lois_reglt.htm [Retrieved 14 July 1998].

Lutz, H. (1997) 'The limits of European-ness: immigrant women in fortress Europe', *Feminist Review*, 57, 93-111.

Lyons, Carole. (1996) 'Citizenship in the constitution of the European Union: Rhetoric or reality', in R. Bellamy (ed.), *Constitutionalism, Democracy and Sovereignty: American and European Perspectives*, Aldershot, UK: Avebury, 96-110.

Malos, E. and G. Hague (1997) 'Women, housing, homelessness and domestic violence', *Women's Studies International Forum*, 20, 3, 397-409.

Marks, G. and D. McAdam (1996) 'Social movements and the changing structure of political opportunity in the European Union', in G. Marks, F. W. Scharpf, P. Schmitter and W. Streeck (eds.), *Governance in the European Union*, London: Sage Publications, 95-120.

Marshall, T. H. (1950) *Citizenship and Social Class*, Cambridge, UK: Cambridge University Press.

Matsuda, M. J. (1993) 'Public response to racist speech: considering the victim's story', in M. J. Matsuda, C. R. Lawrence III, R. Delgado and K. Williams Crenshaw. (eds.), *Words That Wound*, Boulder, CO: Westview Press, 17-51.

Mazey, S. P. (1998) 'The European Union and women's rights: from the Europeanization of national agendas to the nationalization of a European Agenda?' *Journal of European Public Policy*, 5, 1, 131-52.

Meehan, E. (1993) 'Citizenship and the European Community', *The Political Quarterly*, 64, 2, 172-86.

Meulenaere, M. (1996) 'Citizenship: will a conference suffice?', *Women of Europe Newsletter*, 60, 2.

Nelsen, B. F. and A. C. G Stubb (eds.) (1998) *The European Union: Readings on the Theory and Practice of European Integration*, Boulder, CO: Lynne Rienner.

Nenadic, N. (1996) 'Femicide: a framework for understanding genocide', in D. Bell and R.Klein (eds.), *Radically Speaking: Feminism Reclaimed*, North Melbourne, Australia: Spinifex Press, 456-64.

Nordic Council of Ministers (1998) *Shelters for Battered Women and the Needs of Immigrant Women*, Copenhagen, Denmark: Nordic Council of Ministers.

O'Leary, S. (1996) *European Union Citizenship: Options for Reform*, London: Institute for Public Policy Research.

Ostner, I. (2000) 'From equal pay to equal employability: four decades of European gender policies', in M. Rossilli (ed.), *Gender Policies in the European Union*, New York: Peter Lang, 25-42.

Petersen, N. (1993) *Game, Set, Match: Denmark and the European Union after Edinburgh*, Århus: University of Århus.

Pettman, J. J. (1999) 'Globalisation and the gendered politics of citizenship', in N. Yuval Davis and P. Webner (eds.), *Women, Citizenship and Difference*, London: Zed Books, 207-20.

Pollack, M. A. (1997) 'Representing diffuse interests in EU policy-making', *Journal of European Public Policy*, 4, 4, 572-90.

Rossilli, M. (2000) 'Introduction: the European Union's gender policies', in M. Rossilli ed.), *Gender Policies in the European Union*, New York: Peter Lang, 1-23.

Sassen, S. (1999) *Guests and Aliens*, New York: The New Press.

Schain, M. A. (2000) 'The impact of the extreme right on immigration policy', paper presented at the International conference on Explaining Changes in Migration Policies:

Debates from Different Perspectives, Geneva, Switzerland, 20-21.

Schain, M. A. (1999) 'The National Front and the French party system', *French Politics and Society,* 17, 1, 1-14.

Schnapper, D. (1997) 'The European debate on citizenship', *Daedalus,* 126, 3, 199-222.

Simpson, A. (1999) Audiotaped interview with author, Brussels, Belguim, 28 July.

Simpson, R. and R. Walker (eds.) (1993) *Europe: For Richer or Poorer,* London: CPAG.

Soysal, Y. N. (1994) *Limits of Citizenship: Migrants and Postnational Membership in Europe,* Chicago, IL: University of Chicago.

Stychin, C. F. (2000) 'Granting rights: the politics of rights, sexuality and European Union', *Northern Ireland Legal Quarterly,* 51, 2, 281-302.

Stychin, C. F. (1998) *A Nation by Rights: National Cultures, Sexual Identity Politics, and the Discourse of Rights,* Philadelphia: Temple University Press.

Vogel-Polsky, E. (2000) 'Parity democracy: law and Europe', in M. Rossilli (ed.), *Gender Policies in the European Union,* New York: Peter Lang, 61-85.

Weiler, J. H. H. (1997) 'To be a European citizen: eros and civilization'. *Journal of European Public Policy,* 4, 4, 495-519.

Weiler, J. H. H., U. R. Halpern and F. C. Mayer (1995) 'European democracy and its critique', *West European Politics,* 18, 3, 4-39.

Weldon, S. L. (2002) *From Protest to Public Policy: Democratic Political Institutions and Violence Against Women in Democratic Policy Making,* Pittsburgh, PA: Pittsburgh University Press.

Wendon, B. (1998) 'The Commission as image venue entrepreneur in EU social policy', *Journal of European Public Policy,* 5, 2, 339-53.

Wiener, A. (1997) 'Making sense of the new geography of citizenship: fragmented citizenship in the European Union', *Theory and Society,* 26, 529-60.

Woolf, V. (1966) [1938] *Three Guineas,* New York: Harvest/HJB Book.

FEMINIST INTERVENTION IN THE RISE
OF 'ASIAN' DISCOURSE

CHO HAEJOANG

I presented this paper at a conference titled, 'The Rise of Feminist Consciousness Against Asian Patriarchy' which was held on May 10, 1996 at Ewha Women's University. I was opposed to the title of the conference, and especially to the words 'Asian Patriarchy'. This paper thus begins by focusing on the theme originally given to me by the conference organizers, 'Overcoming Asian Patriarchy and the Prospects for the Future' and by explaining at some length why I was opposed to the conference title.

Some years ago Malaysia and Thailand jumped into capitalist development, and more recently, China started wriggling along. Now even those countries that were socialist, such as Vietnam and Cambodia, have joined in and all of Asia seems to be involved in the strong wave of capitalist development. In the midst of this changing situation, views such as 'Asia will soon be the centre of the world', or 'Confucian tradition is highly compatible with capitalism', are gaining currency in South Korea and its neighbouring countries. Mass media have begun to emphasize the importance of cooperation among Asian countries as well as the revival of traditional cultures. It does not take long, however, for one who travels across Asia to note that Asia cannot be categorized into a single homogeneous group. It is especially difficult for South Koreans to understand multi-racial countries such as Malaysia or Indonesia, because racial and cultural homogeneity have been central to their nationalism. Furthermore, it is not easy for South Koreans to understand the long colonial history of other Asian countries. Nonetheless, there is a fairly strong movement for binding Asia into one, and there are forces that have 'found Asia' and want to determinedly hold it together as a single massive entity. The pertinent question here is: do we, feminists, belong to those forces?

There are two major groups who emphasize Asian unity: one group consists of anti-western nationalists who basically want to overcome their dependence on the western world, and the other one includes the capitalists who think that endorsing Asian solidarity will help open up new markets. Feminists cannot help but feel uncomfortable with both of these groups.

Feminists of the Third World have realized that in nationalism, men have tried to give concrete entity to the nation, often by portraying women as the personification of national traditions.[1] Even now, many men who are considered to be 'progressive intellectuals' disapprove of 'modern' women, accusing them of being westernized. They have not been cooperative when women tried to develop in their own arenas. Now that men are trying to recover their damaged egos as patriarchs, it is natural for them to wish that women remain nationalistic beings. This phenomenon is particularly relevant given the fact that modernization has occurred in the midst of a hostile relationship between nationalism and modernism, and one which has not been the fruit of a healthy union between the two.[2]

Women who have started making new demands are a nuisance not only for nationalists but also for capitalists or developmentalists whose ultimate goal is economic growth. Capitalists would like women to remain members of an industrial reserve force who will either serve as shields in the economic war or as faithful slaves who take care of invisible chores silently. The 'Confucian Culture Theory' that Asian elders, including Lee Kwan-Yew, the prime minister of Singapore, try to propagate allegedly respects women by emphasizing the harmony of *yin* and *yang*. The truth is that in practice it does not. Instead, in their discourse, patriarchal authoritarianism is glorified as the driving force of Asian capitalism, in conjunction with a revival of neo-conservatism and justification of gender discrimination.

On this matter, however, the differences within Asia should not be overlooked. A recent study by Mary Brinton (1993, 1995) about labour force participation of Taiwanese and South Korean married women highlights this point very well.[3] The pattern of labour force participation of South Korean married women has a very typical M-curve (married women quit their jobs to raise children and return to work when their children are older), whereas Taiwanese women tend to continue working outside home regardless of how long they are married. Also, the increasing number of women who have access to higher education has not resulted in increased labour force participation of women in South Korea, whereas these two factors are significantly correlated in Taiwan. Even though South Korea and Taiwan show a marked similarity in that both went through compressed industrialization and moved from peripheral countries into central countries through an export-centred industry, the two are quite different in the pattern of women's labour force participation. Brinton (1995) suggests that the difference is due to differential industrial structures established by the two countries since the 1970s. While South Korea experienced capital-intensive and conglomerate-centred industrialization, Taiwan had labour-intensive and minor enterprises-centred industrialization. In Taiwan, women entered the labour market on a large scale as the demand for labour increased significantly in the 1970s, and in this process, traditional cultural factors that discouraged women's working outside home were modified considerably (Brinton 1995).

In contrast to Taiwan, South Korea had an industrial structure in which a man's income could support the entire family, and the gender dichotomy that women stay home and men work outside remained intact. In this sense, South Korea and Japan are similar. In both countries, economic activities in the public sector are monopolized by men. Even now, South Korean employers prefer to automate work processes or increase working hours to make up for the shortage in the labour force, rather than employ women. If we follow Brinton's (1993, 1995) logic, Japanese and South Korean women have missed an opportunity to enter the labour force on a large scale. This implies that the dichotomy of public versus private spheres was reinforced instead of being abolished during the period of rapid economic growth.

In the 1970s, many South Korean men left home to earn money in other cities or countries for an extended period. During this time, as women's responsibilities increased, families were restructured with women at the centre. Since then, however, there has not been an opportunity to re-restructure the family unit. While the number of college students increased dramatically in the early 1980s (Brinton 1995) it did not have a significant impact on women's employment outside the home. Economic growth created a new labour market for college graduates, but the positions went to the newly-generated pool of male college graduates.

Once again, South Korean women missed what should have been a great opportunity to form a critical mass as workers. As a result, South Korean women still have to fight for basic rights to participate in the labour force and their situation is much harder than that of Taiwanese women. Although South Korean men endure long work hours, they want women to stay home.

When men hire women, they expect them to be merely ornamental in the office or to serve as men's assistants. Hiring announcements for female office workers sent to girls' commercial high schools often demand that the prospective employee should be at least 160 centimeters tall and good-looking. Sometimes a personnel manager visits schools to 'pick pretty girls just as they pick apples', said a high school teacher. There has been little sanction against this kind of blatant sexism, which may be part of a backlash against feminism and the revival of neo-conservatism. In a recent lawsuit over a sexual harassment case filed by a female graduate student against a university professor, the High Court of Justice decided that the defendant was not guilty, overturning the decision of a district court. The final ruling read

... the judgment should be made from the perspective of an average person with common sense who regards the relationship between men and women as a cooperative and harmonious one. The feminist perspective, which regards the relationship only as an antagonistic and combative one, should be rejected'.[4]

Many men viewed this as a victory for the men's side.

We know all too well that the 'discourse of Confucian culture' or Asianism tends to silence powerless groups, especially women and minors. We also know that it is imperialistic (Choi 1996). There have been some discussions that the forces that emphasize Asianism or the Asian-Pacific area the most are Australia, the United States and Japan (Dirlik 1995).

Thus my opposition to the title of the conference. If I had been asked to give a title to the conference, I would probably have called it 'Asian Feminist Alliance/ Network against Global Capitalistic Patriarchy'. Perhaps the conference organizers chose the title they did as a strategy. They must have thought that using the word 'Asian' would improve their chances of receiving financial support and media attention. It would also allow them to develop in this conference a counter-narrative, thereby putting a damper on the movement that seeks to glorify 'Asian traditions'. They may also have considered that by emphasizing 'Asia' they could avoid making western experience central to the discussions.

Linguistic Hurdles

Despite my initial hesitation when I was asked to write a paper on the theme of 'Overcoming Asian Patriarchy and Prospects for the Future'. I eventually decided to come to the conference because I was persuaded that I could simply talk about what I have been doing, and also because I wanted to meet feminists from other societies. However, I agreed to come on one condition: that I would write in Korean. So far, I have written papers in English whenever I have attended international conferences. But I have since decided not to write in English any more. While on sabbatical in America last year, I came to realize how writing in English, which is not my first language, restrained my thinking. My decision not to do so any more has two implications: either I will no longer go to international conferences, or I will get my papers translated.

I used to go to international conferences on women's issues frequently during the early 1980s. However, I subsequently found myself going abroad less and less often. The most important reason for this was that these conferences tended to centre around the western world. This was not solely because the West has more power than the East, but also because western feminists inevitably lead the conferences. When I spoke at international conferences I felt like a squealer, telling my sisters who live in powerful and so-called rational countries about my country's irrational patriarchal men, or about the hostility of nationalists who blame the powerful imperialistic whites as being the source of all problems. Even when we did not end up with such situations, participants found their experiences far too different from one another to provide or receive help in solving their particular problems. Thus I came to believe that going to international conferences was a waste of time and that investing my time in local meetings and sharing our wisdom for addressing local issues is more meaningful.

The other reason I do not feel comfortable at international conferences is because of language. I do not like the subtle power relations formed around fluent English-speakers. Those who do not have any problems with language, i.e., those who are from English-speaking countries or from former colonies of Britain, usually lead the conferences. One of my father's favorite jokes regarding international conferences is that the best moderator of an international conference is one who makes the Indians speak less and lets the Japanese speak out. Do Indians speak 'too much' because they love conferences? I do not think so. This is partly so because they have a huge pool of intellectuals trained in the western way and they have been exposed to such conferences ever since the colonial era. However, I think the most important reason for their fluency in English is that they learn it in childhood. I have also studied in the United States for my graduate degree, but it still takes a lot of energy for me to write in English because it is not my mother tongue. I therefore feel it is extremely difficult to hold a fruitful international conference unless the differences in linguistic ability are taken into full consideration.

For all the reasons I have outlined above, I wrote this paper in Korean. I would like to go to conferences where high-quality translation and interpretation systems are available so that all participants can speak their minds freely. I am not suggesting that I do not want to exchange information with scholars in foreign countries. In fact, translation and information systems have advanced greatly and I can readily access the work of my foreign sisters through books and the internet.

Taking Positions

Recently I spent a sabbatical year at Stanford University in the United States. While I was there, I attended a feminist conference on 'Women, Culture and Differences'. The participants' sensitivity about white hegemony was very acute and made this conference rather different from other international conferences. White people tended to take the position of observers and spoke very carefully when discussing Third World problems, while non-westerners got involved in heated arguments among themselves, revealing considerable differences in their perspectives. I presented a paper on 'Colonial Modernization and Formation of South Korean Women's Subjectivities'. Many white feminists listened to my presentation with interest, seemingly reminded of their own past feminist struggles, but they did not voice their opinions because the unspoken rule was that no one dared to challenge 'the native feminist'.

Instead, I was criticized by a Japan-born feminist who had gone to college in Japan, received a doctoral degree in the States and was working as an assistant professor at a US university at the time. She was quite indignant at my choice of words, such as, 'we' or 'you, American feminists', and said, 'There are no such things as 'American feminists' here. What gives you the right to lump us together in a single category? I am neither Japanese nor American'. I understood that she meant to criticize my tendency to generalize and I could only respond as follows: 'You may not be Japanese, nor American, but it remains a fact that you make a living out of teaching American students at an American university and you may have the alternative of going back to Japan if you do not like your life here. There certainly is a position you take and there still are countries called Japan and the United States'. She rejected me readily as someone taking a middle-class, elitist, heterosexual, nationalist position and I felt sorry that we feminists had to waste our energy on this kind of confrontation. Nonetheless, it provided me a good opportunity to observe feminist society within American academia caught up in identity politics.

As a feminist who completely practices localism, living in Seoul, South Korea, and teaching at a university in the Shinchon area, where there are five universities, I would like to talk about what kind of relationship I would like to have with sisters from other countries, and on what occasions I have felt that we needed these relationships in order to conceptualize 'Asian feminist solidarity'.

Themes for Asian Solidarity

I have been involved in a feminist group, 'Alternative Culture', since 1983. Women's studies courses emerged among the most popular classes at universities during the 1980s. This is an ongoing trend and we are experiencing difficulty in accommodating all the students wanting to attend women's studies classes. This group led an awareness-raising campaign that emphasized women's autonomy and sisterhood. Our message was: 'Women also have rights. Women should work outside the home. Do not submit yourself to injustice, because when you do, you fail and our society fails with you'. The media responded to this feminist movement enthusiastically and, therefore, feminism and the 'women's rights movement' became widely popular.

During the 1980s, the nationalist movement geared itself for reunification of South and North Korea and while men focused on overcoming monopolistic capitalism, women were actively demanding human rights for themselves and trying to find their own voice. The '80s were indeed the period when discourse on 'social justice' was forcefully launched in South Korea.

This enthusiasm cooled down quickly, however, in the early '90s. Labourers and the 'people' who are the subjects and the object of any movement began to suddenly disappear, including the women. Activists were lost. This may have happened because we overlooked the possibility of resistance generated in the process of developing women's autonomy. I realized that it was wrong to believe that the citizens of erstwhile colonial countries were lucky to get a supposedly ideal constitution as a 'gift', thereby skipping an important stage in the women's movement where western sisters fought for women's suffrage. The women's movement is a process of forming new subjectivity and nurturing its strength; thus no stage of the process can be skipped.

I could not help but ponder the weak foundation of the women's movement in some non-western and formerly colonial societies which had never struggled to achieve suffrage and therefore lost an opportunity to learn how to organize women for institutional transformation. The feminist movement that we led delivered the message of self-actualization to women, but failed to get them ready for the difficulties of the on-going struggle to achieve that goal. Women who had just graduated from college, and marched into society fearlessly, soon ran into the huge wall of gender discrimination and collapsed. Also, as competition in the work place became more and more intense, 'smart' women decided to stay home full-time even earlier. Having witnessed feminists struggling so hard, women increasingly wanted to distance themselves from feminism.

Forming Female Subjectivity: Diversity and Division

I will dwell briefly on the process of the formation of women's subjectivity in a society rapidly swept into the vortex of western-centred global capitalism. Focusing on South Korean society, I will try to show how men and women relate to each other and how they form modern subjectivity while experiencing forced, compressed and unequal development.

For a long time I have struggled with the issue of mother power in the South Korean patriarchal family. When I went to the United States to study right after graduating from college in 1971, I was surprised to see many American women paying so much attention to men. They were so dependent on men while all the Korean women I knew at home were self-confident and did not expend so much energy in attracting men's attention. I began to think that South Korean women were much more self-reliant than American women. In a recent paper, architect Kim Jin-ae (1995) pointed out that the physical space of contemporary South Korean housing is 'over-dominated' by women, and there is little room left for men. Women attend schools separated by gender from childhood up to the college years, and even after getting married. Women confide in one another, hang out together, and share information regarding financial management. Gender-segregated educational settings have also produced some elite women who have taken the plunge into men's world fearlessly and committed themselves to a professional career. Married women stay in a domestic world as household managers and mothers and wield tremendous power because the family has always been the most important unit in South Korean society. It was only natural for me to feel sorry for the American women who seemed to be preoccupied with men because I grew up among women who were powerful mothers and who had a strong female subculture.

Initially, I thought a women's movement could be very successful in South Korea if mother power and female subculture were activated in the movement. However, it did not take me very long to realize that motherhood for South Korean women is excessively instrumental, and that many mothers are far too faithful to patriarchy to change. These women were committed to keeping their families intact during the stormy and chaotic era of colonial modernization that lasted a few centuries. They were especially invested in their sons and loyal to the patrilineal tradition. Women who had sons were opposed to affirmative action for women and fiercely protected marriage-related institutions. In the short term, they knew well how to make the system work for their own interests.

The powerful identity of the mother formed during the turbulent years of change was further reinforced during the time of rapid economic growth. At the same time issues became diversified by class and generation. Mothers who had struggled for the survival of their families started putting all their energy into improving their families' social status in the 1970s. They would do anything to move up into the middle class. When they were successful, women's status was also advanced and these women were called *samonim* (madam) distinguishing themselves from lower-class married women (*ajumma*). *Samonims* spent huge amounts of money on their children's private education, which eventually created an enormous private education market. They invented complicated and expensive wedding rituals. There are still many women, who along with their husbands, live in relative deprivation because of the expenses incurred by them for their children's private education and marriages. A lot of the energy of able women thus went into the enhancement of their social status. The newly developed culture of the middle class that emerged during this period was therefore very materialistic and modernization in South Korea did not result in a new civil society. By the same token, it failed to create a narrative of gender justice. Women who lived through the era of rapid economic development became extremely powerful mothers within their own families. However, they remained vulnerable and powerless in society. Their accomplishment as mothers and household managers was tremendous, but their energy did not go into forming an identity as autonomous citizens.

The younger generation rejects the women of their mothers' generation. Young people have not experienced poverty, and they despise these un-stylish mothers (*ajummas*) with their permed hair, who are often shamelessly aggressive, self-confident but tremendously adaptable. In contrast, they tend to find the gentle, lovable, dependent women from the Hollywood movies attractive. In South Korea, there used to be images of dignified women with strong personalities that we as feminists would find desirable. Today, most young women want to be 'feminine', want to marry able men and live their lives as consumers. They belong to the generation of consumption, advertisement and mass media. They perceive themselves as sexual subjects, and invest tremendous amounts of time and energy into polishing their appearance and dating. This is the emerging crowd of so-called 'missy'[5] housewives who want to look like unmarried college students and fashion models (Cho 1995). These middle-class women of the new generation are busy keeping themselves young and attractive, whereas their mothers had struggled hard to move up into the middle class. Class inequality among women is growing deeper and conflicts between mothers and daughters are becoming increasingly serious. Further, the culture of young middle-class couples is conspicuously centred around heterosexual relationships.

Feminists who have been busy raising awareness of the 'attractive life of independent women' are dismayed by this situation. Young women who once explored feminism, looking for a new lifestyle and swearing to never be like their mothers, are now 'buying' into consumer capitalism. That choice seems more attractive, newer and easier. Feminists now must fight against not only feudal patriarchy and patriarchs created by the process of colonial modernization, but also those created by modern/postmodern patriarchy. The independent women who once had time for the feminist movement are far too busy surviving on their own in a competitive late-industrial society where problems are accumulating, but the activists are disappearing.

Through the process of modernization, female subjectivity has been diversified, but is still confined within a larger frame. The family in South Korea remains a sacred unit and women develop their subjectivity primarily as mothers within their families. Women are not ready to build solidarity among themselves because they are committed to the tasks of upward mobility and enhancing the status of the family as a unit, all in the name of the 'family' and the 'nation'. Family is women's priority. Mothers identify with their children and refuse to stand up as individuals. In contrast, daughters reject their mother's world and are rapidly becoming postmodern subjects. Many visitors to Seoul say that all South Korean women look like fashion models. Indeed, their faces are made up with thick white foundation and with the same colour of lipstick. Recently, an expert who creates new lipstick colors was interviewed by a newspaper and mentioned how well her new colour, called 'Sexy Number One', sold.[6] A friend of mine who is a journalist at a daily newspaper confided to me recently that since 1994 her editor has been telling her not to write articles on gender equality or feminism, but to fill the women's section with food, clothes and make-up.

I call this situation 'Colonial-Postmodern'. People are becoming busier and at the same time, are getting mixed up. They are realizing that history does not always imply progress and economic growth does not guarantee a happy life. While earlier it was a time of want generated by hunger, this is an era of greed generated by advertisements. People are busy gratifying private desires they have suddenly discovered. Young people want to look conspicuously different from others, but they are neither interested in living differently nor in building a secondary group of their own generation. They want to play within their own group at an exclusive café that discriminates against people by age and appearance. What they hate the most are meddlesome adults and their moralizing and scolding. They are overwhelmed by the power of money.

This is a bewildering situation, overtaking people as they enter the consumer society without resolving contradictions created in earlier stages of colonial capitalist development. At this point, sharing our experiences with feminists from Asian societies that have experienced colonial capitalism becomes necessary. I think the characteristics of colonial modernization are the outcome of unequal development, in which the family is held in pledge, while individuals display superficial transformation as though they are responding to general social change.

We might start with deconstructing motherhood, which is controlling and instrumental in a way that sustains the institution of the patriarchal family. Thus, in order to discuss Asian solidarity, we need to begin to dismantle motherhood as an institution and start building a new family based on 'motherhood as experience' (Rich 1976). Can these two projects happen at the same time? Currently the story, 'Wet Fallen Leaf', is popular in South Korea as it once was in Japan. The wet fallen leaf refers to a man of retirement age who has come home from work. He clings to his wife desperately and is hard to get rid of. The divorce rate of couples in their 50s and 60s is increasing in South Korea as more and more women are leaving their husbands after their children marry. They seemingly decide that they no longer have to put up with an unsatisfactory marriage once their children are gone. A currently popular joke is about 'the bold man in his 50s'. A bold man is one who talks back to his wife, who comes home late and asks his wife to serve dinner, who wants to accompany his wife when she goes out, who questions his wife on what she has bought when she returns from shopping, or who asks his wife who is calling when a man telephones her. Another joke begins by stating that in earlier years, a wife took care of everything when the family moved to a new home, and all a man had to do was to find the new home with the address after the moving was done. The punchline: now a man in his 50s hops into the moving truck hurriedly, because otherwise his wife would gladly leave him behind!

These women in their 50s have enormous power and a stable financial status. Could they become the subjects of a women's movement in South Korea? The hitch is that their identity is confined within a strict dichotomy of private (family) versus public. Middle-class women are especially obsessed with their socio-economic status, and they invest much of their energy, time and money in showing off this status. How can these women be changed? Are they too old to learn to 'love' and identify themselves with women and be willing to share their resources with other women? We need to find ways to build solidarity with women in their 50s and 60s. The women's movement must be diversified to respond to the different needs of women divided by generation and class.

In order to make change in the women's movement possible, we need to consider another characteristic of the Third World, i.e., the superficiality of cultural change. During the 1980s, the whole country seemed to be swept by the waves of new women's consciousness through the fruit of an active feminist movement. At that time, the ruling class and conservative people decided to support the women's movement because it was much less threatening compared to the growing radical anti-government movement. Now that the feminist movement has gained some power and women have started to voice their opinions in and outside their homes, we are experiencing a strong backlash. This backlash is very powerful; consider the example of the sexual harassment suit I mentioned briefly earlier.

The curriculum at women's professional schools in the 1980s dealt with the labour movement, the women's movement and the popular art activities related to those movements. But young female labourers of the 1990s seem more interested in make-up and dating. Universities, factories and department stores are full of women of the new generation who wear heavy make-up, show off their exaggerated femininity, claim without scruples that they have never been discriminated against because of their gender, or want to live their lives according to their individual desires, separating themselves from anything collective. Feminism in South Korea today is a commodity out of fashion. How can feminism avoid being reduced to a superficial fad but remain a durable commodity that serves women's daily lives? Feminists need to learn strategies for survival in the market.

Regretfully, feminists have not tried hard enough to learn the mechanics of the power structure. Feminist psychoanalyst Jean Shinoda Bolen (1984) discussed different types of women in her book, *Goddesses in Every Woman*. She pointed out that there are women who know what power is and know how to play games with men, whereas there are autonomous women who would rather work alone, and yet other women for whom sisterhood is primarily important. Women who can survive in a political world or any other established institution are likely to be the ones who know what power is, but tend to lack sisterhood. This is a dilemma we must deal with.[7] Male-centred organizations do not nurture women and do not even try to do so. Even at Yonsei University, a forerunner of co-education in South Korea which just celebrated its fiftieth anniversary, there are professors who comment publicly, 'Yonsei will soon perish because there are too many female students'.

The world is governed by violence on a daily level, as well as by less-obvious institutionalized violence, and women live their lives repressed and hemmed in by it. For example, in South Korean banks, when a female worker carries a cash box, a male worker must accompany her. Divorced or single women are still exposed to various kinds of rough treatment from other people all the time. Men must have a lot to gain for many men by maintaining this society as violent and dangerous and by emphasizing the gender differences in aggression and productivity. This must be the reason many men do not want changes to the status quo.

Nevertheless, we will find a solution in the long run. We may need to see that 'the glass is half-full, rather than half-empty'. We may need to pat ourselves on the back for what we have accomplished to date and recharge our batteries while continuing to poke holes in the wall of reality. We need to return to the issues of marriage and family and the absence of civil society. It is time to realign our movement and challenge the institutions, starting with the legal system.

Working in Solidarity and Traveling Together

Many feminists currently living in Seoul believe that it is indeed time for a radical reorientation to take place. At a feminist camp organized by Alternative Culture in the spring of 1996, we discussed new orientations and strategies for our feminist movement in relation to the Alternative Culture activities. The following is a summary:[8]

1) We will launch a narrative on subjectivity formation through modernization. We will start a comprehensive discussion beyond the dimensions of narrow rationalism and individualism presumed by western modernity. There will be a

special focus on subjectivity formation in the historical context of colonial-capitalistic development. The purpose is to move beyond the limitations of institutional politics and open up a new dimension of politics of ordinary life. It is necessary to create a new language for the movement that includes body and mind, reason and emotion, verbal and nonverbal language, and thus move beyond each dichotomy. Thereby a counter-narrative to instrumental rationalism and militarism will be launched.

2) We will discard universal assumptions, and try to understand subjectivity formation. We will acknowledge the substantial gap between women's and men's experience of life, and develop a politics that does not intend to abolish the difference but starts from the difference. Also, we will acknowledge the gap between generations and classes among women, and develop a 'politics of difference'.

3) We will intervene in the processes of social life both as consumers and producers. We will not complacently remain 'amateurs', but nurture professional activists out of our group. We will not perceive women as mere 'victims' but will focus on empowering women, both economically and politically. We will endorse 'media activism', and utilize mass media actively.

4) Specific programs under diverse themes will be developed, as also face-to-face and local small group activities such as after-school programs and the sponsoring of a feminist café. We will encourage women to use electronic mail systems more actively in order to overcome geographical limitations. Further, we will enter the politics of the information era through cyber-space. We will not separate play from work, but try to play and lead the movement at the same time. We do not want to be workaholic feminists. We want to be feminists who know how to enjoy life. We will often find time to feast together.

5) We will support co-education in order to challenge the ideology of gender separation, and try to designate 'take-your-daughter-to-work day' and 'teach-your-son-housework day' in order to abrogate gender stereotypes. We will utilize those characteristics of Korean culture that emphasize family. We will support the building of women's clinics that respect women's dignity, especially maternity clinics where baby girls are welcomed wholeheartedly. We will also start a movement to change the current men-only compulsory military service system into a voluntary service system for both men and women.

My current task is to find feminist ways of living decently without throwing ourselves into the sea of greed that is continuously being created by male-centred commercialism and the global waves of capitalism. I am especially hoping to see many women crossing the boundaries of family (domestic) and society (public), and blurring the boundaries. Today academic discussions are largely pointless. What we need the most right now is to build mutually helpful relationships among us. We need feminists who will analyze their own local condition in terms of 'compressed and colonial' modernization and who can do joint work on this theme. However, patriarchal oppression is very complex, and we cannot see our enemies until we actually start shaking the system.

I suggest that we start shaking things up. The South Korean patriarchs who gained self-confidence through economic development have ambitions of making their nation powerful. However, we feminists should ignore this obsession. Instead, it is better to put our energy into creating new lifestyles and new networks. Small groups should be activated in local communities to solve specific daily problems. Feminist cafés and bookstores should be established to provide 'real' space to the small groups. 'Virtual' space, through computer networks, needs to be created for wider groups and in due course, many creative planners will gather together.

A firm and fruitful solidarity beyond local communities will be made possible by 'traveling together'. Local feminist festivals should be held, welcoming feminists from other places. On these occasions, we can advertise and distribute films that celebrate sisterhood. These kinds of movies are not generally well-received by male-centred movie critics. We should show that women's judgment is powerful, not only as consumers but also as cultural critics. By this I mean, feminists should intervene actively in the industry of culture. We should make movies that we want to go and see, or create places which we want to visit, and where we disseminate information. Feminists should not play only on university campuses but start filling the streets.

Internet would be an effective means to make an intervention in cultural life as well. In South Korea, internet is booming currently, and many people think that English is the only language on internet. I would like to point out the danger of this thinking. In order to use the internet as a communication system to activate the feminist movement, the first thing to do is to develop a program for women to learn to access it easily. Also, they should be able to use their own language on internet. Each group should be able to make a home page in their own language. Then, professional translators should be employed to do the translation jobs. Learning English should not be another burden to women in non-English speaking societies. Communication through computer networks will be especially powerful for women who are not free to move around and away from home. Therefore, feminist cafés should be cyber cafes where women can learn about computer communications and the internet.

As I have repeatedly pointed out in this article, the current situation of South Korea is not great. Many women are too busy or too burnt out, a result of rapid economic growth. This is one more reason why I think feminism should be a festival, and a life-preserving, revitalizing movement. Alternative Culture has recently set up 'A Room of Her Own' (see Woolf 1929) to provide women a place where they can work alone on writing. The room can also be used for an all-night discussion of a small group. A feminist café is expected to open soon in the basement of the same building. Small groups for travel just started going for a trip once a month. I expect that these small steps will bear fruit in a few years. There is no such thing as 'Asian patriarchy', but I do believe that when these kinds of small activities dance across the boundaries of nations like small waves, the oppressive clouds in our lives will eventually disappear.

I am waiting for a travel-maniac feminist to establish a successful travel agency. Travel is a great opportunity to recreate oneself. Feminist historical travel programs that are meaningful and pleasant would produce an exodus of women moving freely beyond national boundaries. When it is actualized, women's sensitivity, repressed 'in the name of father' and 'in the name of nation', will be liberated and then there will be a stream that no one can block. By that time 'bad things' or 'improper things' that the patriarchs hate to see will happen everywhere and at anytime.

What I have said so far does not represent a typical South Korean feminist discourse by any means. I have never been a representative South Korean feminist, and I have never intended to be one. I am just a realistic dreamer, who has hardly gone out of the Shinchon area, working on several projects in building sisterhood. It is my belief that the personal cannot but be political, and ordinary cannot but be political in the feminist movement, and therefore a feminist movement rooted in my own personal life is likely to be most helpful to other people also. Of course, we need extensive training to see the politics within us. Moreover, we need to learn how to maintain integrity and vitality by moving lightly and happily.

This article was translated from Korean into English by Um Young-rae.

A version of this article was originally presented at the conference, 'The Rise of Feminist Consciousness Against the Asian Patriarchy' organized by the Asian Centre for Women's Studies, Ewha Women's University in May 1996.

Reprinted with permission from the Asian Journal of Women's Studies *3 (3) 1997: 127-156*

Cho (Han) Haejoang, a practicing cultural anthropologist and feminist, is a professor at Yonsei University, Seoul. Her early research focused on gender studies in Korean modern history. Her current research interests lie in the area of youth culture and modernity in the global/local and post-colonial context of modern-day Korea. She is the author of Women and Men in South Korea *(1988),* Reading Texts, Reading Lives in the Postcolonial Era *(three volumes 1992, 1994),* Children Refusing School, Society Refusing Children *(1996),* Reflexive Modernity and Feminism *(1998), and* Children Searching School, Society Searching Children *(2000) (all in Korean). In 2004, a series of dialogues she had with Ueno Chizuko, a feminist sociologist at Tokyo University on issues of globalization, localization, youth, aging, learning and the future of feminism (under the title 'Talking at the Edge: Letters Exchanged by Two Feminists') were published in Japanese,* Can the Words Reach? *(Iwanami Publishing) and in Korean,* Talking at the Edge *(Saeg-gak ui Namu Publishing). She is the director of the Center for Youth and Cultural Studies of Yonsei University as well as the founding director of Haja Center (Seoul Youth Factory for Alternative Culture), a project of action research focused on youth and the culture industry.*

Notes

1.   The desire to portray women as personifications of the nation is to be found in various forums, ranging from academic discussions to less professional debates. This comes through vividly in a 1994 hit movie, *Sopyonje*. An unpublished criticism of the movie by Park Heh-rahn (1994) discussed this, highlighting the praise and wistful desire for 'meek' North Korean women by Korean-American men who traveled to North Korea.

2.   For a broader discussion on the relationship between nationalism and patriarchy, see Kim Eun-shil 1994 and Em Henry 1995. The related issue of Comfort Women during World War II has recently received international attention.

3.   Mary Brinton conducted a statistical study on South Korean and Taiwanese women's employment. A seminar was held on April 24, 1996 entitled, 'Industrialization and Married Women's Employment in East Asia', and there was much discussion on married women's labour force participation in the two countries.

4.   Judicial decision by Judge Park Yong-sang of the High Court of Justice on July 25, 1995 with regard to the sexual harassment case involving Professor Shin Chung-hyu and his research assistant, Woo.

5.   The image of 'missy' was created by a department store advertisement to encourage young and middle-aged women to not only buy their clothes, cosmetics and other products, but to cultivate the image of an eternally young and glamorous superwoman.

6.   This was a newspaper interview with the creator of the new lipstick colour called 'Sexy Number One', of which 500,000 lipsticks were sold in a forty-five day period (*Chosun Ilbo* 1995: 20).

7.   In contrast, women in the Alternative Culture group, to which I belong, tend to abhor power. They detest power games because they find them distasteful. Therefore this group tends to be isolated from the 'power structure' and it cannot grow out of its marginal status. Fortunately a small academic group has just formed within the larger group to study 'power' and a new academic journal will soon be published by it.

8.   I have mainly discussed the activities of the Alternative Culture group in creating feminist language. Actually my feminist friends in Alternative Culture have been involved in other projects including preparations for reunification of North and South Korea. Sending baby food and medical supplies to North Korea is one of the specific projects proposed by the group. There is a group of divorced women who discuss the issue of child rearing together and yet another group for a child care cooperative is currently working on establishment and amendment of related laws. Some women directly participate in existing political circles to seek improvements in the legal sphere.

References

Bolen, J. S. (1984) *Goddesses in Every Woman*, San Francisco: Harper and Row.

Brinton, M. (1993) *Women and the Economic Miracle: Gender and Work in Postwar Japan*, Berkeley: University of California Press.

Brinton, M. (1995) 'Married women's employment in rapidly industrializing societies: Examples from East Asia', *American Journal of Sociology*, 100, 5, 1099-1130.

Cho, H. (1995) 'Living with conflicting subjectivities of mother, motherly wife and sexy woman: a transition from colonial-modern to post-modern', paper presented at the Workshop on Gender and Social Change in Late Twentieth Century Korea, Columbia

University, 10-11 March.

Choi, W. (1996) 'Experiences of non-western colonies and the ghost of Asianism', paper presented at the International Conference, Toward a New Global Civilization—The Role of Activists of People's Movement, Nationalist Movement, and Local Activism, Seoul, South Korea, 24-26 April.

Chosun Ilbo (1995) 25 March: 20.

Dirlik, A. (1995), 'The concept of Asian-Pacific Area', in M. Chung et al. (eds.), *Tong Asia, munche wa sikak (East Asia: The Problems and Perspectives)*, Seoul: Munhak kwa Chisng.

Em, H. (1995) *Wings as Colonial Allegory: An Anti-colonialist Interpretation of Yi Sang's Most Widely Read Work, MUAE 1*, New York: Kaya Production.

Kim, E. (1994) 'Korean nationalism, discourse and feminism', *Korean Women's Studies*, 10: 18-52.

Kim, J. (1995) 'Which gender is this house? Gender discrimination, gender separation, and gender crossing', paper presented at South Korean and Japanese Women Architects Symposium, New Housing Culture in the 21st Century: Women are Leaders, Seoul, 30 September.

Park H. (1994), 'Gender critique of *Sopyonje*: on national sentiment, modernity, and tradition', unpublished manuscript.

Rich, A. (1976) *Of Woman Born: Motherhood as Experience and Institution*, New York: Norton.

Woolf, V. (1929) *A Room of One's Own*, New York: Harcourt Brace Jovanovich.

BACK TO WOMANHOOD

FEMINISM IN GLOBALIZED ISRAEL

ERELLA SHADMI

About a year ago, in an Edinburgh airport store, I found a book entitled *The End of Everything: Postmodernism and the Vanishing of the Human* (Appignanesi 2003). The book talks about techno-science, artificial intelligence, virtual reality, genetically engineered products, and argues that the human is vanishing. I was outraged. The humans I know are not only alive but also in danger because of the inhuman acts done in the name of progress, development and science. It is not the end of the human but the end of the humane. In this age of depression, occupation and war, exactly when strong economic forces, legitimized by postmodern thinking, are working to put an end to history and the human subject, it is essential to trace the feminist path of the struggle for the humane.

As a feminist who became involved in feminist politics and theory in the 1970s and 1980s, I come from a radical/cultural feminist standpoint. The feminist struggles I know have evolved from women's shared oppression and life experience of reproduction, motherhood, the sexual division of labour and the control of women's sexed body—what Angela Miles (1996) calls 'women's specificities'. Our different experience of the world generates a feminist politics that both undermines oppressive social institutions and crosses social borders. It is concurrently oriented against male domination and for justice, care and solidarity among women across differences such as class, nationality, sexuality and religion.

Indeed, these politics have been marginalized mainly by liberal and postmodernist feminisms. For quite a long time we abandoned women's standpoints and politics and adopted men's approaches, images and aspirations. Perhaps we did not have another choice if we wished to achieve political and sexual freedom in a male-dominated society. But we paid a high price for this move. Exactly when individualistic male power is re-crowned, women's ethics based on a combination of care and justice and particularly on the commitment to protecting and empowering women in other race and class positions may offer the basis for anti-globalization politics.

In what follows I will attempt to show how and why Israeli feminism has lost its woman-centered grounding and consequently much of its significance, and how a return to womanhood may put it in the forefront of anti-globalization and peace-directed politics. I will do so by focusing in this article on the peace and lesbian movements.

Israeli Feminism

After years of a 400 per cent inflation rate, the Israeli government adopted in 1985 the Price Stabilization Plan and globalization was formally introduced into Israeli society. As part of it, the doctrines of 'small government', free market and free trade zones, multinationals, manpower companies, oversight by the World Bank and the International Monetary Fund and, above all, the sway of capital owners became the new rules of the game. Israel, once a labour-controlled and welfare-oriented state, became second only to the US in its widening social conflicts and economic gaps, growing numbers of homeless, impoverished and unemployed people, notoriously increasing rates of violence, organized crime, corruption and prostituted women, and, of course, stronger military and police forces.

Whereas both men and women suffer from globalization, women pay the higher price: women constitute 70 per cent of manpower companies' workers, with no decent working conditions and earning less than minimum wage; 60 per cent of the unemployed and most of the lower ranks of the public sector are women; single mothers and elder women have lost much of their social security allowances.

In the twilight of the welfare state era, two women's initiatives had been launched by veterans of the radical feminist left: the peace movement, Women in Black, and the Lesbian Feminist Community known as Claf. Both stemmed from women's experience of oppression, silencing and exploitation in the male-dominated, heterosexist, Zionist Jewish State. And this women's grounding was well reflected in their politics.

Women in Black was a network of all-woman weekly vigils wearing black and protesting silently the Israeli occupation of Palestinian territories. It was organized three weeks after the first Intifada broke out in 1987. They stood once a week for an hour in central locations all over Israel.

Women in Black was unique among women's peace initiatives since it used three novel means: first, the silent bodyspeak, that is, exposing their body in the public sphere to communicate the anti-occupation message, thus constructing the connection between the occupation of Palestinian land and people and the occupation of woman's body; second, the colour black arousing not only the memory of mourning Middle East women but also rejecting the virginal and puristic symbolic often attached to women; and, finally, the constant and stubborn presence in the public sphere in spite of hostile, sexist and violent responses from passers by and ignorance from the mass media and traditional politics.

The choice of these three novel means stems from the disadvantaged position of women in a society dominated by Zionist colonialism, male militarism and Jewish tradition. Being politically silenced, their bodies occupied and used for nationalistic and religious missions and their roles confined to the domestic, these women gave 'voice' to their distinct worldview through these three alternative channels. Their activism was transformative, first, because it positioned women in the public sphere, a location not many women had occupied until then; second, it put women into the heart of the men-controlled masculinist, militaristic security discourse; and third and most importantly, because the women stood there not as mothers, not as wives, not as males' helpmates, but as citizens in their own right. No wonder that this innovative strategy was adopted by many women in different places all over the world.

Like Women in Black, the Lesbian Feminist Community grew out of the male-centered heterosexist patriarchy in which men are centre-stage, women are confined to their heterosexual roles and women's passion for women is denied. It was established in 1986 to represent lesbian interests, to provide lesbians with a sense of community and—to what perhaps was most important for the founding mothers—to transform the heterosexist Israeli society. It was organized and led by radical-feminist lesbians who emphasized the transformative potential of lesbian existence and believed that only the shattering of the male-dominated compulsory heterosexuality could liberate lesbians.

It did not take long before both Women in Black and the Lesbian Feminist Community lost their transformative significance. Claf replaced its feminist transformative aspirations in favour of, first, civil rights for lesbian couples and mothers, and, then, of gay men's culture, adopting male images and patterns of behaviour. Using the first approach, indeed the liberal feminist approach, lesbians, especially middle-class Ashkenazi lesbians, expressed their desire to be integrated into the middle class heterosexual culture. In the second approach, the queer alternative, lesbians allied with gay men in a struggle for civil rights, yet gave clear priority to gay men's culture, including its emphasis on performance rather than experience, sex rather than woman's full existence, and men's phallocentric images and power rather than women's concepts. Lesbians indeed gained more visibility and social legitimization, but lesbians disconnected themselves from their bodies; lesbianism was silenced and became a non-issue.

Women in Black was dismantled in 1996 and most of the women's peace initiatives that followed lost their feminist aspirations. The Four Mothers, for example, protesting the Israel occupation of Lebanon, legitimized their appearance in the public sphere in their mothers' role, in their care for the safety of their children, leaving behind feminist aspirations for social change. The Coalition of Women for Just Peace, a coalition of ten women's peace movements of which Women in Black is the largest and oldest, began demonstrating shortly after the beginning of the Al-Aksa Intifada (2000). It fearlessly and courageously voices a different position opposing social consensus and protesting the cruel and inhuman acts perpetrated by Israeli government and the military. However, besides being a woman-only movement, it hardly reflects any woman-specific perspective, analysis or strategy. On the contrary, the Coalition adopted with almost no reservations men's peace initiatives like the Geneva Agreements and did not come up with its own feminist understanding of peace. In spite of the pressing economic problems encountered by most men and women in Israel and in spite of the absence of most Israelis from the peace camp, these women remained an almost exclusively white middle class organization. They hardly ever attempted to understand, let alone take into account, for example, the split Mizrahi people feel, as result of Ashkenazi Zionism, between their Arabic and Israeli identities. Women's peace movements, like the peace camp in general, are in the main blind to the class, ethnic and racialized structure of society and, especially, to the relevance of this structure to issues of war and peace. This blindness restricts the women's peace movement to an elitist membership, disassociated from most people of Israel and failing to challenge the power structure of Israeli society. Thus, women's peace activism not only lost its transformative potential but also disassociated itself from women's alternative politics that stress care for all and the interconnection among different forms of oppression.

In fact, both Claf and the women's peace movement lost their radical transformative potential exactly because they abandoned women's specificities as a point of departure and women's culture as an alternative for male-dominated culture. I would suggest that this loss is a result of, first and foremost, the overriding impact of globalization. Globalization, under which the labour market is shrinking, working conditions are worsening, social gaps are widening and competition is growing, incites women one against the other, especially middle-class white women, as most feminist activists are, and working class women. The 'small government' policy, one of the aftermaths of neo-liberalism, shifts many responsibilities from the public sector to NGOs. The burden on feminist organizations has increased dramatically and they have turned into service- rather than politics-oriented organizations. Feminist activism has thus been de-politicized and de-radicalized. These developments have been fortified by postmodernism's emphasis on the concept of identity, constituted in the existing social order and overlooking power relations, hollowing out the concept 'woman' and thus denying the possibility for political action and sisterhood, and on discourse, representation and performance, abandoning women's experience as the main focus and leaving the political field to the sway of the economic forces of the capital enforced by globalization. Both make coalition politics, let alone alliances among women, almost impossible.

In Israel these social forces are reflected in what I call Neo-Zionism, that is, a return to old Zionist ideas, albeit in a new version. Neo-Zionism brings back to Israeli society, after opening up to winds of feminism and multi-culturalism, a machoistic, militaristic, patriarchal, white Ashkenazi Jewish middle-class hegemony and conservative and neo-liberal economy.

In the face of globalization, post-modernism and Neo-Zionism many of the feminist achievements have been lost. The situation of many women has quickly been deteriorating, anti-feminist backlashes began to be visible and women's culture has been repressed once again.

The problematic of Israeli feminism was clearly revealed in the summer of 2003. On July 1st, harsh government measures taken as part of the new economic plan went into effect at the expense of the poor, the homeless and the unemployed. Among those most drastically hit were 150,000 single mothers (Swirsky 2003). One of them, Vicki Knafo, a part-time working mother from Mitzpeh Ramon, a poor southern development town, decided to march to Jerusalem in a week-long protest. Hundreds of single mothers and their supporters hit the roads in solidarity with her, ending up encamped outside government offices in Jerusalem. Many feminists rushed to give a hand: we cooked, washed laundry, provided counselling and support, laughed and wept with the mothers. In spite of our enormous help, we, the feminists, failed to stimulate a wider resistance movement, to mobilize women to the cause. We provided services; we failed to build a movement. Israeli feminism, de-radicalized by globalization, isolated from most Israeli women, and detached from its woman-grounding, lost its power. Our work at the campsite had indeed been characterized by solidarity and caring, but it remained no more than charity exactly because it did not connect the protest to the institutional structure. We failed, therefore, to translate the solidarity into a political movement.

The single mothers' protest was, in a way, an awakening point for quite a few feminists. It made clear that new directions are urgently needed. Feminists began to come up with new initiatives that once again are founded on women's experiences and standpoints (Shadmi 2004a, 2004b).

This had begun even before the single mothers' protest in what was called the 'Conference of Connection'. In this conference some peace activists strongly advocated the need both theoretically and strategically to connect issues of war and social injustice and to build new alliances across differences (Shadmi 2002). Such an alliance began to be forged in the single mothers' protest and it has the potential to effect real change in Israeli society. This would bring together people from poor development towns and kibbutzim and workers from urban neighbourhoods, Ashkenazi radicals and underprivileged Mizrahi women, religious and secular, old timers and new immigrants from Russia and Ethiopia along with Palestinians. This alliance goes beyond the (indeed still relevant) distinctions along class, race, ethnicity, political orientation and religious belief, and brings to life the old socialist solidarity, albeit in a new form. It draws the contour lines of the new left in the era of late capitalism and globalization. It is a left that is consciously feminist and anti-racist, built on experience gained by feminism and post-colonialism of the last 30 years or so. It embraces all the relevant groups involved, and recognizes the interconnection among all forms of oppression. It is aware of the role of religion in global politics and does not reject it in the name of science and reason and, finally, it enables people, regardless of their class, ethnicity, race, sexuality or gender, to unite around concepts of social justice in as much as it is anti-domination and anti-late capitalism. Moreover, it supplements the important but insufficient work of human and civil rights groups, which have not paid adequate attention to the material conditions and rights of the disenfranchised. In the same vein, it discards the over-emphasis put by postmodernists and some academic feminists on discourse, myths and history.

This politics of connection—among allies, agendas and perspectives—is also revealed in a new feminist understanding of peace that is beginning to emerge lately in Israel. This women's approach to peace crosses borders between nations and sectors. Women's peace cannot be owned by one group as it is in Israel—the Ashkenazi/white middle class. It must address Mizrahi, Russian and working-class interests and connect peace with issues of social and ethnic justice. Fadua Tukan, the famous Palestinian poet, taught us that national liberation depends on social and gender justice (Tzoreff 2000). So does peace. Peace agreement needs the approval of all peoples, not only elites. If it is no more than a treaty between elites—as Oslo Accords were—its failure is guaranteed.

Such new understanding of peace stands also behind a new initiative—the Middle East parliament. This parliament is not meant to be an elected institution but rather a forum that will move from one location to another to discuss issues that are on the public agenda from women's perspectives. Such a forum will cooperate across borders in a struggle for human dignity, will infuse the feminist discourse into the political discourse and will construct a Semitic space that Israel will be part of. This Semitic space is different from Shimon Peres's concept of a New Middle East that was no more than a means to replace military power by economic domination for purposes of western colonialization.

Women have the ability to be leaders on such a different path to peace because of our historical experience in taking responsibility for our community and its future, because of our moral commitment to social solidarity and because of our ability for long-term and multifaceted activism: in short, because of our specificities.

In the same way, lesbians begin to reject false homosexuality and the covert heterosexual norms that characterized the Lesbian Feminist Community for quite a long time. Lesbians now suggest celebrating women's bodies and identity and constructing women's space outside of both heterosexuality and gay homosexuality.

All these new initiatives are founded once again on women's specificities: they are holistic, integrative, border crossing, multi-cultural, non-power oriented. The analysis presented here shows the forces that inhibit such direction. It also shows that the return to womanhood gives Israeli feminism a new hope in this age of globalization exactly since such a move attempts to shatter male-dominated institutions and to promote solidarity among women across differences.

One last comment: the return to womanhood as a source of power and politics may also provide women with a feminist meaning. The depression that comes with globalization and war drives women to find comfort in religion, New Age beliefs or traditional women's roles. These routes provide women with an easy escape from the hardships of this dark age as they give meaning to their lives and experiences. Women-centered resistance and culture as advocated here may give women an alternative source for identification in this age of meaningless consumerism, exploitation and cruelty.

This paper was presented to the UK Women's Studies Conference on 'Feminism Contesting Globalization', University College, Dublin, July 8-10, 2004.

Erella Shadmi, a feminist, lesbian and peace activist, and a former Lieutenant-Colonel in the Israeli police, is the head of Women's and Gender Studies at Beit Berl College in Israel. She also teaches sociology of police. She has written books and articles on Ashkenazi/white identity feminism, lesbianism, pedagogy and policing.

References

Appignanesi R. (ed.) (2003) *The End of Everything: Postmodernism and the Vanishing of the Human.* Cambridge, UK: Icon Books.

Miles, A. (1996) *Integrative Feminisms: Building Global Visions, 1960s-1990s.* New York: Routledge.

Shadmi, E. (2004a) 'Feminism–to where? From the quarter's system to a new vision', paper presented at the Israeli Feminist Conference, Givat Haviva, 3-5 May.

Shadmi, E. (2004b) 'From peace treaty to peoples's peace', paper presented at the Middle East Women's Conference, Istanbul, 25-28 March.

Shadmi, E. (2002) 'The paradoxes of whiteness: the contemporary Israeli women's peace movement', paper presented at the XV World Congress of Sociology, Brisbane, Australia, 7-13 July.

Swirsky, B. (2003) *A Year of Economic Harms to Women,* Tel Aviv: Adva.

Tzoreff, M. (2000) 'Fauda Tukan's autobiography: restructuring a personal history into the Palestinian national narrative', in B. Shoshan (ed.), *Gender/Gendered Discourse in the Middle East,* Westport, Conn.: Praeger Publishers, 57-78.

V.

CONCLUSION

THE EMPIRE STRIKES BACK BUT FINDS FEMINISM INVINCIBLE

ALDA FACIO

This article is set in the future, and is given from the perspective of a history professor lecturing on patriarchy in the twentieth and twenty-first centuries.

In the beginning of the so-called twenty-first century, on one of the least civilized planets of the universe, the economic, political, symbolic, social and military power was in the hands of a few sick men who suffered from such a severe misogyny that they had come to despise life itself. The illness had appeared some five or six thousand years earlier, when the male humans discovered that they had something to do with the reproduction of their species. Instead of jumping for joy at such a discovery, some became extremely resentful, hating all the years lost in veneration of the creative powers of the female. Their disease advanced to such an extent that they hated and proceeded to declare war on anything and everything related to the feminine. This led them to invent a science of destruction and a necrophilic technology that, nevertheless, permitted them to accumulate a great deal of power.

So great was their power, that by the twenty-first century, a single Empire existed, formed by the group of States that previously were known as the developed countries, with a decentralized regulation apparatus, that progressively and openly incorporated global reality, expanding borders way beyond what their colonialist forefathers had imagined.

In order for some men to have the power to create and control such an enormous Empire, a system of domination accepted by most of the earthlings who inhabited that planet had to be in place. This universal system of domination was named Patriarchy by those women who saw it and understood it for the first time. At first, this form of domination was based on a family system in which fathers had absolute power over mothers and children of any sex. With time, the system became more subtle and intricate. By the eighteenth century, the mere fact of being defined as female or male at birth determined what would be the economic, social, ideological, symbolic or cultural value attributed to each new human and what roles he or she would be able to perform. The astonishing part was that the system was so sophisticated that for many centuries, the majority of earthlings believed that this was the natural order of things handed down by God himself.

But by the twenty-first century the system was not so easily identifiable. The discourse was now that women and men were equal even though hardly anything had really changed. Women continued to do most of the unpaid labour, continued to be victimized by violence and were still excluded from all but one per cent of the wealth. But all women were not allotted the same value, nor was it prohibited for all women to perform certain functions. In fact, some women were powerful indeed.

Such was the sophistication of Patriarchy that extreme violence against women came to be understood, both by men and women, as eroticism. The colonizing of all women, known by certain scientists as 'socialization,' made women 'voluntarily' submit to the most painful and humiliating tortures: in some nations, the mothers broke the feet of their small daughters so that they would become objects of sexual pleasure for their future husbands—men who were not able to have erotic feelings towards women who were able to walk without pain.

In other nations, the colonization of the female humans had become so perfected that it was the women themselves who would place special instruments of torture on their own feet while insisting that it did not hurt them. These instruments, called 'high-heeled shoes,' in time would deform their feet, their spine and their reproductive organs, but their 'socialization' was so complete that even knowing the consequences to their health and their lives, the women of these nations continued using them because they knew that women who could walk with their feet well on the ground were not 'feminine'.

In fact, such was the absurdity of many of these earthly traditions that in order for females to be feminine, they had to be molded into shapes thought up by the more powerful males of each culture. Thus in some cultures women were stripped of their sexual organs, while in others their breasts, hips, lips, eyes, legs or any other part of their bodies were enlarged or otherwise modified to fit the standards of beauty set by the patriarchs. Still in other traditions, women had to hide all but their eyes because their patriarchs had decided their physical self was disturbing to the men of their cultures. So it came to be that in all earthly cultures women's physical appearance and well-being was decided by the patriarchs of religion, tradition or fashion.

But the misogyny and violence went further. In all the cultures and in all the States, many women were raped by their own fathers, brothers, companions and friends. In all nations they were mutilated, beaten, trafficked, forced into pregnancy and all kinds of sexual and domestic exploitation and in all nations it was believed that this was their fault and that they deserved or liked it. And even when some male earthlings accepted that violence against women was a human rights violation, the majority of humans continued to believe that this was a minor problem compared to the many other cruelties humans committed against each other. Or worse still, that due to the need to respect cultural diversity, this violence was not real violence, even though it was the product of the broader misogynist culture at the base of all earthly societies or communities.

The hatred and the violence against the mothers, the daughters, the sisters, the friends and colleagues of the men was so extended, and the complicity of many men with this system was such, that it was hard to see that this also affected the majority of men. Humans did not understand that a system that degrades precisely those who have the sacred power of giving life, was a system based on contempt for the process of creation and life itself. A system so hostile to its female population could only degenerate into a system at war with nature. Thus, by the twenty-first century, humans had depleted the ozone, polluted their water and contaminated their crops with pesticides.

And yet, most humans did not see that such a system would inevitably become a system of exploitation of the many by a few, as it actually occurred: the Empire took advantage of a system already international, Patriarchy, in order to globalize its faith in the God of Free Market and declare war on all those who did not submit to it. Thus, the Empire had its roots firmly anchored in Patriarchy and would never be defeated without uprooting it.

As in all wars, there were forces that opposed this Empire. Among the opponents were some as misogynist as the Empire itself. Their objective was to destroy it in order to create states as cruel and dehumanizing as the Empire. Their energy also sprang from their hatred of women and everything associated with the feminine. But there were other, less misogynist groups that longed to recuperate and maintain their cultural and ethnic identity; or who were opposed to racism, homophobia, ageism, ableism, or any form of exploitation, slavery, genocide and torture; groups that fought for a healthy environment, for the respect of other beings and groups that prayed and marched for peace on earth.

Many of these groups used special tools that the earthlings called international treaties of human rights. On that planet, these Human Rights Instruments had been founded on the knowledge that in spite of their incredibly rich diversity, human beings shared a kindred spirit which made them realize that beneath the skin, they were all equal in dignity and worth. This drove them to maintain that human beings had rights and responsibilities towards each other based on the simple fact of being born human. It was further understood that this principle of universality meant that all human beings should be free from exploitation and injustice and it was the responsibility of each State and of the community of States to guarantee this.

In time, many human rights advocates came to understand that the welfare of the individual human was coterminous with the whole of society, and that the welfare of both the individual human and society depended on the welfare of the planet, including its rivers, mountains, cities and non-human dwellers. That is why by the twenty-first century human rights were used to defend more than the individual. Collective rights and the rights of first nations as well as the rights of animals and of Mother Earth herself came into the picture. The Empire did not like this expansion of a theory it was using for its own purposes and therefore misinformed the many about its transformative potential.

Illogical and contradictory as it might seem to us, many humans of all genders, colours and classes, even those who were human rights advocates, did not think that eliminating discrimination against women, and thus transforming the very basic structures on which the Empire based its power, was part of their battle against the Empire. They did not understand that their own sexism blinded them from seeing beyond the androcentric construction of their discourse and practice. And so, human rights theory became useless to more than half of the planet's humans.

In fact, many of the earthlings who took part in an anti-globalization movement which was formed in the late twentieth century were as sexist as the patriarchs of the Empire themselves. Certainly they did not advocate women's inferiority, but they made no effort to understand the connections between Patriarchy and the Empire's globalization. This had been so ever since the birth of this movement, which sprang from other movements that had been created centuries before, when the absolute power of the Empire had not yet been established, when the powerful countries that formed the Empire were still in their imperialistic phase. These movements against dictatorial, colonial, authoritarian and racist regimes had all emerged as sexist. And, although these movements were victorious in some parts of the world and were able to establish socialist or nationalist governments, they were not able to establish real democracies since they did not have the courage to eliminate their own male privileges. Thus, by not uprooting the most basic system of domination, they left a fertile ground in which other systems of exploitation of the many by the few would soon arise.

That is why a feminist reinterpretation of human rights theory became so crucial if the Empire was to be defeated. By the end of the eighth decade of the twentieth century, a powerful international feminist human rights movement had been born which was successful in demonstrating that because sex discrimination affected half of the population of this planet, since earthlings conceived of only two sexes, eliminating it was indeed necessary if the principle of universality was to be upheld.

Taking advantage of the Empire's need to be seen as democratic, respectful of human rights and in favour of equality between the sexes, feminists were able to enter such sacredly male institutions as the military and the church. True, this later proved not to be such a great tactic, as women could be as misogynist as the patriarchs; but it did demonstrate that women and men were not so different after all.

But feminist human rights theory was not constructed or accepted from day one. Many centuries of wars, deaths, genocides and destruction of the planet were suffered by earthlings before feminist principles became part of the collective imagination. Many men and women had to fight and die for their ideals of equality, liberty and fraternity. Later, when women realized that these principles did not apply to them, they had to struggle so that human rights would also include female humans. These battles and their triumphs were achieved in several stages as new understandings became available to humans.

The first concept that had to be accepted was that earthlings could have certain rights under international laws that had to be respected by each State. This was achieved when men, with the support of women, were able to establish some international treaties that guaranteed rights vis-à-vis the State. Once this was established, women were able to lobby in favour of other treaties explicitly concerning them. Nevertheless, these first women's treaties were still not considered human rights conventions and did not guarantee women equality, nor were they gender-sensitive, since these concepts would come much later.

Furthermore, the concept of international human rights had to be accepted. The horrors of a war known as the Second World War, and the need to protect individuals from such horrors, led many States to agree on the need for an international system of protection of human rights. Thus, The Charter of the United Nations was created in 1945 and the Universal Declaration of Human Rights in 1948, both establishing that human rights were universal, interdependent and indivisible. These principles meant that all humans without distinctions as to race, sex, nationality, age, etc., had the right to enjoy and exercise all human rights and that each sovereign State had the obligation to respect, protect and fulfill them for all the inhabitants of each State.

Another concept that had to be accepted was women's capacity to have legal rights. This was not easy since the law itself had denied them this right for centuries. Throughout patriarchal history there had been many that had fought against the oppression of women in every culture and region, but it was not until the so-called eighteenth century that a women's rights movement emerged in what was later to become the dominant culture of the Empire. Little by little this movement put the notion of women's legal rights in the minds of the more progressive male humans. Two prominent women among the very many unknown activists were Mary Wollstonecraft, who published her famous *Vindication of the Rights of Women*, in 1779 and, Olympe de Gouges, who wrote, in 1791, The Declaration of Women's Rights, based on the principles found in the French Declaration of the Rights of Man. Some decades later, Elizabeth Cady-Stanton and Lucrecia Mott retook and modified the Declaration of Independence of the country that would later become the most powerful oppressor, and wrote another early proclamation on the rights of women, known as the Declaration of Seneca Falls, written in 1848.[1]

Once the fact that women could have legal rights was established, the idea that men and women could have equal rights had to be accepted. This did not mean that they had to have exactly the same rights, but that women had the same right to have all the rights needed in order to live a dignified life. It was therefore understood that men and women were not identical and that women did not have to be like men to enjoy all human rights. On the contrary, it was understood that human rights had to be fulfilled in such a way that the different needs and experiences of men and women would be considered. It was further understood that women did not have to be identical to each other in order to be equal under human rights law. The most important treaty regarding this concept came into force in the 1980s of the twentieth century, known as the Convention On The Elimination Of All Forms Of Discrimination Against Women or the CEDAW Convention. By the end of that century, this treaty had become the second most ratified international instrument. Hence, women's human rights was truly a planetary concept although, of course, not in the minds of all.

Later, feminism, a theory that explained the power structures that kept women subordinated and oppressed, had to develop methodologies that would place the lives of women at the center of human rights theory and erase the artificial distinction between the private and public spheres. The feminist methodologies and theories developed worldwide during the 1970s and 1980s of the so-called twentieth century proved that gender not only referred to the ways in which roles, attitudes, values and relations with regard to children, women and men were constructed in earthling societies; but that gender also structured social institutions, such as the law, religion, the family, the market, as well as the concept of beauty, kindness, sanity, etc. Through these methodologies, it became evident that gender created distinct social positions for an uneven assignment of rights and responsibilities between the sexes. The development of feminist perspectives helped to make visible the power relations among women and men and, therefore, the incredible discrimination and violence suffered by women in all spheres throughout the entire world.

Finally, the androcentric bias in the theory and practice of international human rights had to be unveiled. This did not happen until the 1980s of the twentieth century, when a few feminist thinkers began their critique of the human rights paradigm, demonstrating that the 'human' in human rights theory was not representative of all humans. He was a heterosexual, middle- to upper-class white male, a father, a property owner, with no visible disabilities, and most probably a Christian or, if not, of the dominant Muslim, Hindu or any other of the main Earth religions. These women proposed a more inclusive gender-sensitive formula that would include women and men of all colours, ages, sexualities, abilities, regions, spiritualities and cultures.

However, by the end of the first year of the twenty-first century, feminists were losing their faith and their strength. The Empire had penetrated the feminist discourse to such an extent, that it had lost its identity. It became impossible to know when a feminist or an agent of the Empire was speaking. Both feminists and non-feminists spoke of the need to have more women in decision-making political positions, of penalizing domestic violence and 'putting an end to impunity' and even, of the innumerable improvements in the life of women achieved because of globalization. In their eagerness to speak the language accepted in the age of globalization, feminist discourse and practice had lost a great deal of its transformational potential. In fact, many feminists had forgotten that the whole idea of feminism was not to have a bigger slice of the pie, but to change the recipe.

It must be recognized that the Empire was very sophisticated in its strategies to maintain itself in power and even to increase it. One strategy was the very old but always successful one of 'divide and conquer.' For example, the Empire encouraged large world conferences where participation by all the representatives of the distinct forms of exploitation and discrimination was welcomed but that ended in a wearisome battle for meager bits of power. Boycotting the union of all the oppressed people against it, the Empire was able to replace the language of unity with a discourse on diversity that hid the common causes of their oppression. Though feminists had insisted that women's sense of themselves could only be built on the recognition of their diversity, this particular tactic of the Empire undermined women's potential for female solidarity through women identifying as women because it fell on ears that were trained to fear and distrust women. Even in the gender studies programs that were instituted all over the world by the twenty-first century, many feminist scholars maintained that there were no commonalities among women. Some went as far as to say that the very notion of 'woman' was obsolete.

But the most efficient strategy used by the Empire during these times was to use the power of naming so as to confuse its enemies. In this way, it called 'globalization' not only the greedy advance of the most fierce form of capitalism, but also the free exchange of ideas, cultures and strategies of the exploited and discriminated. Thus, even in the minds of the many who were suffering its policies, globalization came to be understood as something good that should be welcomed by all.

The Empire was also successful in making those who dared to question the goodness of globalization appear as 'uncool' reactionaries whose clocks had stopped. In the new millennium, its very good publicity said, globalization is the answer to poverty and underdevelopment. Especially after the defeat of the USSR—an imperialist centre that was opposed to the proto Empire regarding its economic tactics, but shared its contempt of the feminine—and since 1994, the year in which the powerful of the world economy gathered in Bretton Woods in order to set the new rules of the who-can-get-richer game, an army of businessmen repeated insistently the wonders of living in a world regulated by the omniscient wisdom of the Free Market.

Nevertheless, just a few years after the new world order was established with the tools of globalization, the economy of the Empire began to break down. In the United States, the most powerful locus of the Empire, one fourth of the children lived in poverty; in Europe, another important locus of the Empire, fifteen million persons were unemployed. By the beginning of the twenty-first century, stock markets plunged further and further down, causing numerous and abundant losses, affecting, at first, only small investors who had fallen into debt in order to acquire stock. Later on, the plunge affected more and more large trans or multinationals that began to carryout massive layoffs. In other words, things were not so rosy in the Empire.

As history has shown, just when empires begin to feel omnipotent, large protests of people opposing them rise up everywhere. So it was in the Empire. In spite of its complete control of the mass media, many earthlings began to see the difference between neo-liberal globalization and a global movement to improve the lives of the inhabitants of that planet. This became a great danger for the Empire. If people became aware of its strategy, it could lose its power. And the Empire began to worry.

But, on September 11th of the year 2001, some men, obedient to the same misogynist forces of the Empire, but with different strategies and objectives, offered the Empire the perfect excuse to legitimize its intention of imposing its economical, political, cultural and social power, not only through its strategy of neo-liberal globalization, but with the use of its military might.

In spite of the fact that he and his predecessors had always used the same tactics, the supreme ruler of the Empire labeled as 'terrorists' not only the murderous actions of 'fanatic groups,' but also the innocent inhabitants of all nations whose leaders provided shelter to an alleged terrorist. Following this logic, the Congress of the United States passed a law that would punish any State that declared itself neutral towards its new Holy War. The Empire decided that the time of pretending to be democratic and respectful of human rights was over. It argued that faced with the threat of terrorism, every restriction of rights and liberties to the inhabitants of the periphery was justified.

In a position questioned by many of its own, it went as far as deciding that even a restriction to some rights of the citizens of the Empire was also justified. And, in order to gain support from the female half of this Great Nation, the Empire gave one of its wars against a famine-struck nation, a touch of indignation at the treatment that the leaders gave to their women.

So it came to pass that feminists after September 11th were faced with a new and old situation at the same time. Old because patriarchs had always used women to justify their wars. Old because in spite of some progress for some women, the gender structures that maintained women's oppression had been kept almost intact. New, because September 11th marked in the history of this planet, the unequivocal militarization of the process of globalization of extreme capitalism.

With regards to the old problems, feminists continued to follow a strategy of dialogue with each State, to get them to fulfill their human rights. But given the escalation of the Empire's war against humanity, feminists realized that this was not effective. Most States no longer had much power, nor were capable of solving any problem. So, feminists continued to work within the State whenever this was worthwhile, but channeled most of their energies into creating a strong movement. With an Empire willing to remove its democratic mask and impose its power with the use of military force, feminists could only stop the negative impact of globalization with the creation of a counterculture and a new reality that would bring hope to humanity.

To create this new reality, feminists had to stop believing that if they wanted to have any influence on the power structures of the Empire and its transnational corporations, women needed to be pragmatic, realistic and tailor their discourse to what the political leaders and CEOs could or would accept. Feminists needed to see that by speaking the language accepted by the Empire, they were not able to give voice to women's needs or interests. They remembered what they had discovered many times, that feminism was not about getting for women what men already had. That it was not about making proposals that could fit neatly into the patriarchal mode. Neither was it about prestige and fame for feminist scholars, or intellectual property or who is the most discriminated against, or the most brilliant or even about who has the truth. Feminism was about women valuing and seeking the power that lies in friendship and solidarity in an environment that encouraged women to distrust or even hate each other. Feminism was about women joining together to continue the struggle against imperialism by opposing globalization.

If feminists could succeed at consolidating a strong international feminist movement, firmly rooted at the local level, women were in the best position to unite all the groups against globalization and ultimately defeat the Empire. After all, women belonged to all walks of life, sectors of society, all races, classes, ages, abilities, sexualities, etc. and if they could unite, they would be invincible.

To create this new way of being in reality, feminists had to convince all those opposing the Empire's strategy of globalization, that the caring and nurturing of human beings had to be at the center of all utopias. Feminists had to be able to get everyone to understand that globalization was a phenomenon that replaced an economy based on production of goods, for one based on speculation—and that this had been possible thanks to an earlier system that valued production of goods over the reproduction of people. In other words, feminists had to make the other groups that fought against the Empire see that contempt for life was the energy that fueled the process of globalization. Feminists needed to convince everyone that the only way to counter imperial capitalism's over-valuation of virtual goods was for everyone to incorporate into their discourse and their utopias, the complete range of issues relating to the caring and nurturing of life, including eroticism and pleasure. Without this, they were doomed.

Feminists, conscious of the fact that structural adjustment policies imposed through the Empire's strategy of globalization, had brought a greater impoverishment of women, were in an ideal position to understand that in the globalized world, women and men were living in societies that despised the daily acts of caring and nurturing and had no respect for those who produced food, clothing, housing, etc. Incredible as it may seem, most did not see that a system which devalued the activities around the preparing of food, could easily degenerate into a system that devalued its production. Most did not understand that a system that devalues those who do the cleaning and keeping of the homes could very well degenerate into a system that devalued those who did the constructing and fixing of them. Thus it came to pass that in the Empire, not only what was considered women's work was undervalued but also that of carpenters, farmers, builders and all craftspeople. In the Empire, only the accumulation of money and power was considered successful. And still, most earthlings believed that those who had enormous wealth were not the real thieves, because they did the thieving through Trade Agreements signed by the leaders who had not been chosen to lead. And it came to pass that by the early twenty-first century, the wealth of a few very powerful men, meant the poverty of billions, 70 per cent of whom were females.

Globalization, by overvaluing the intangible and the virtual, had managed to replace action with discourse. This complicated things because the majority of women were not feminist nor did they see through the Empire's tactics. Many women were convinced that mainstreaming gender into the institutions of the Empire would bring about 'equity'. Even the major architects of the Empire's globalization tactics, such as the World Bank or the International Monetary Fund, were able to implement their structural adjustment plans without much opposition from the women in power because, 'they were doing it with a gender perspective'. In an evaluation made five years after one of the largest world conferences, known as the Beijing Conference, the women of the world were found to be poorer, suffer more violence and be more marginalized from the real power centres than ever. And yet, at that same evaluation meeting, many insisted that women had advanced because they were present in the discourse of the powerful and a gender perspective had been incorporated in most policies and projects.

Globalization was destroying hope, because by trapping millions in poverty, recourse to violence became a means of survival to many. Most people could no longer expect the situation to improve, thus, their only exit was to steal, to traffic, to kill. And as the most marginalized had no access to the rich, they stole, trafficked and killed their sisters and brothers, companions and neighbours. A central issue of feminism had been the right to live without violence, but without hope it became nearly impossible to ask anybody to believe in non-violence, because the silencing of hope itself is violence. That is why feminists were in an ideal position to call upon all the groups to make out of non-violence, a right to hope.

Globalization, with its tactics of neo-liberal adjustment, privatizations and labour flexibilization, was eliminating both urban and rural small and medium-sized productive units, creating more and more countries stripped of their sovereignty for lack of their own development projects. Feminists had long known that equality between men and women, difficult to achieve even in the Empire, was absolutely impossible in an unjust and impoverished economy. But they also knew that nations that kept their women poor and illiterate were also doomed. That is why feminists were able to make the links between the commercial inequalities between poor and rich countries and the social inequalities between men and women. They knew that in order to eliminate the former, the latter had also to be eradicated.

Redefining democracy, fundamental liberties and human rights in general, had been a good strategy of feminism in the decades before September 11th. However, the militarization of globalization had poisoned these concepts, which capitalism itself valued, to such an extent that this redefinition seemed meaningless to many. Democracy had become a system where people could elect among two or three corrupt or incompetent candidates and this only if they pleased the Empire. Equality had come to be understood as sameness with the dominant males of the

Empire and so the choice for everyone was between being an oppressor or being oppressed. Again feminists had a strategy which proved that these were not real choices, nor the only ones. For centuries many feminists had insisted that equality was not about sameness or democracy about elections, and they were able to help others see through the Empire's strategy of maligning human rights by imposing a very limited understanding of them. Feminists knew that equality for women was about recognizing differences while upholding the possibility of solidarity among all women. Feminists, even while struggling for the right to vote, had insisted that Democracy was a political system based on respect for the totality of human rights for everyone, not on mere formalities or ritual elections. Because of their long history of struggling for these rights, feminists had given richer meanings to them.

Before the consolidation of the Empire, many feminists had supported the unrestricted freedom of expression, thinking that thus they would be able to express their own ideas and images. But the Empire was clever. It transformed freedom of expression, into freedom of trade for enormous corporations that were able to alter the truth to serve their own interests. Still worse, these globalized businesses became experts in presenting the ways citizens of the Empire lived, looked and felt as the aspiration of all humanity. All the inhabitants of the planet wanted to dress, eat, dance, sing and feel as did the inhabitants of the Empire's TV Land. And again, feminists had already discovered that the media's treatment of truth fell on the fertile grounds of patriarchal misogyny. They saw the connection between the contempt for real women in the fabricated images of the female in the media and the contempt for nature as a whole because neither could be packaged and sold. And selling, not informing, was their business.

Globalization had permitted the country with the largest market of intangible products and a military system to support it, to be seen as the leader in questions that had nothing to do with military and economic power. Thus, the educational, legal, and political system of the Empire were models to emulate, in spite of the fact that in the most powerful country of the Empire, the last president had not been chosen by the majority of the voters, prisons were full of ethnic minorities, most women did not enjoy basic human rights, and generally, higher education was not producing greater thinkers, but better technocrats. In a world less and less critical of what emanated from that centre of arrogance and despotism, few questioned why the Empire's science, medicine, technology had not brought even the inhabitants of the Empire, more leisure, liberty or health.

So it came to pass that feminists began to lose their fear of being labeled essentialists or inefficient idealists. They allowed themselves once more to be rebels, transgressors and subversives. More importantly, they became dreamers and builders of other realities. They began to create other ways of feeling in their bodies, other forms of relating to divinity, other aesthetics and other ethics. At the same time they joined others in a more egalitarian future, carrying their own luggage and enriching the ideas and practices of the indigenous, youth, farmers', workers', consumers', landless, homeless, people with disabilities, and gay and lesbian movements. They joined the struggle against racial, ethnic and class discrimination and exploitation. They learned to listen to the wisdom of many non-dominant cultures and they began to listen to themselves with love and compassion never forgetting that it was in the Empire's interest that women compete and destroy each other. They stopped believing that just because the experience of implementing communism had proved so despotic and dehuman-izing, capitalism was the only viable model, or that the Empire was invincible. They saw the need to feminize all progressive ideologies with their dreams and ideals. Otherwise these would fail again and things would get much harder for women.

Obviously, for the consolidation of an alliance, feminists had to make a great effort to forgive their progressive brothers for their historically repeated betrayal of women. Using their raised consciousness to go inward, feminists were able to deal with the possibility of future betrayals by making contact with their own spirituality instead of feeding their pain. On this journey inward they awoke to the fear the betrayal had provoked in them and acknowledged it with a newfound respect. In doing so, feminists were able to see how the anger that sprang from this betrayal impeded most women from enjoying the road towards equality and justice. Thus they came to understand that their love for life and all its creatures urged them to forgive while staying in touch with their anger and pain. They decided to heal the injury by dropping guilt and manipulation. In their stead, they awoke to the fierceness of the wild mother, the boldness of the young enchantress, the wisdom of the old crone and the tantric power of the three combined. This is how they rediscovered that there was more happiness in forgiving, more energy in love, more possibilities of success in tenderness.

This new way of seeing and understanding feminists' relationships with progressive men did not stop them from knowing that a new betrayal was possible. After so many revolutions in which they had fought shoulder to shoulder with them, the 'new men' had proven to be quite old: they wanted power only for themselves, decorated themselves with elegant, slender, young women and decided not to be dirtied with domestic work. So, a new strategy had to be found. And it was. Feminists decided to use the human rights instruments, especially the CEDAW convention, this time to raise the consciousness of their progressive brothers.

And thus, with the maternal patience they had used in training and convincing the officials of the State, corporations and other international institutions on the importance of the incorporation of a feminist human rights framework, they began channeling their energy towards their progressive brothers. It was time to convince them that without feminist analysis and strategies, there was no possibil-ity of sustained triumph over this or any other Empire. It was important that these men understand the subtleties of the patriarchal system of domination and how it was the basis of the one imposed by the Empire. Men and women needed to see that globalization, being the model of capitalist domination on an international scale that the Empire had imposed, could only be defeated by a planetary movement with feminist ideals.

That is why feminists spoke of the need for all groups to embrace a feminist worldview based on compassion and love for all things living instead of the Empire's fascination with death and destruction. If the Empire was to be defeated, the widespread distrust and hatred of the feminine needed to be flushed out of the hearts and minds of earthlings. This implied interpretations of reality different to the globalized one, which at its core, was Patriarchal. It implied the re-elaboration of values, reformulations in language and symbols, science, art, in the movies and music and literature, in sports as in every other activity based on feminist principles. It required a re-discovering of humanity and a reinventing of the self in the midst of a war the Empire called pre-emptive. The Empire was striking back, said its propaganda, but everyone knew it was striking out.

And that was how the adventures of the new feminists began. Women and men willing to stop the Empire, not with its necrophilic arms of death and destruction, but with the instruments arising out of the ability to take pleasure in and revere life; the critical analysis of reality; a willingness to embrace a spirituality based on love; a commitment to abandon the fear-based worldview that purported to have answers to everything; and a profound desire to enjoy another possible world. Those who have read about these adventures know that the first steps were taken when most feminists began to laugh at their own mistakes and imperfections and did it so often and so hard that the Empire trembled.

This article is the Seventh Annual Dame Nita Barrow Lecture ponsored by the Centre for Women's Studies in Eduation in, association with AWID, at the Ontario Institute for Studies in Education at the University of Toronto in November 2003. Online: http://www1.oise.utoronto.ca/cwse/lectext.htm.

Alda Facio is a jurist, writer and international expert on women's human rights, violence against women and feminist analysis of the law. In September 1996, she was awarded the first Women's Human Rights Award from International Women, Law and Development in Washington D.C. As one of the founders of the Women's Caucus for Gender Justice in the International Criminal Court (ICC), she was its first Director from July 1997 to September 1999. Since 1990, she has been the Director of the Women, Gender and Justice Program at the United Nations Latin American Institute for Crime Prevention (ILANUD) based in Costa Rica. The Program focuses its work around the elimination of gender inequality and violence against women from a criminal and human rights perspective. Facio has written widely on these issues and was one of the first women in Latin America to denounce the androcentric bias in human rights law and practices.

Notes

[1] Of course, many women who lived before Mary and Olympe spoke out and fought against the subordination and exploitation of women, but what they spoke out about and what they fought for specifically on women 'rights' is not known.

INDEX